THE THEATRE OF REGRET

LITERATURE, ART, AND THE POLITICS OF RECONCILIATION IN CANADA

David Gaertner

UBCPress · Vancouver · Toronto

Excerpts from the following books of poetry were reprinted with permission: Louise Bernice Halfe's *Bear Bones & Feathers*, 1995, and *Blue Marrow*, 2004 (Regina: Coteau Books); Billy-Ray Belcourt, *This Wound is a World* (Frontenac House, 2017); and Joshua Whitehead, *Full-Metal Indigiqueer* (Talon Books, 2017).

29 28 27 26 25 24 23 22 21 20 5 4 3 2 1

Printed in Canada on FSC-certified ancient-forest-free paper (100% post-consumer recycled) that is processed chlorine- and acid-free.

Library and Archives Canada Cataloguing in Publication

Title: The theatre of regret : literature, art, and the politics of reconciliation in Canada / David Gaertner.
Names: Gaertner, David, 1979– author.
Description: Includes bibliographical references and index.
Identifiers: Canadiana (print) 20200306502 | Canadiana (ebook) 20200306804 | ISBN 9780774865357 (hardcover) | ISBN 9780774865364 (softcover) | ISBN 9780774865371 (PDF) | ISBN 9780774865388 (EPUB) | ISBN 9780774865395 (Kindle)
Subjects: LCSH: Truth and Reconciliation Commission of Canada. | LCSH: Truth commissions—Canada. | LCSH: Reconciliation—Political aspects—Canada. | LCSH: Reconciliation in literature. | LCSH: Canada—Race relations. | CSH: Indigenous peoples—Canada—Residential schools. | LCSH: Indigenous art—Canada. | CSH: Canadian literature—Indigenous authors—History and criticism.
Classification: LCC E78.C2 G34 2020 | DDC 971.004/97—dc23

Canada

UBC Press gratefully acknowledges the financial support for our publishing program of the Government of Canada (through the Canada Book Fund), the Canada Council for the Arts, and the British Columbia Arts Council.

This book has been published with the help of a grant from the Canadian Federation for the Humanities and Social Sciences, through the Awards to Scholarly Publications Program, using funds provided by the Social Sciences and Humanities Research Council of Canada.

Printed and bound in Canada by Friesens
Set in Segoe and Warnock by Apex CoVantage, LLC
Copy editor: Audrey McClellan
Proofreader: Caitlin Gordon-Walker
Indexer: Adi Burton
Cover designer: Will Brown

UBC Press
The University of British Columbia
2029 West Mall
Vancouver, BC V6T 1Z2
www.ubcpress.ca

This book is gratefully dedicated to my parents, Ron and Pam Gaertner, who gifted me a love for reading, and the strength to turn that love into a career.

Contents

Acknowledgments

The University of British Columbia, the place where I both live and work and where the majority of this book was written, sits on traditional, ancestral, and unceded territories of the hən̓q̓əmin̓əm̓-speaking Musqueam (xʷməθkʷəy̓əm) people. xʷməθkʷəy̓əm is an inspiring place to research, teach, write, and raise my children, and I owe an ongoing debt of gratitude to the xʷməθkʷəy̓əm people for the opportunity to consider and engage with the concept of reconciliation on this land.

Much of this book is about listening and unlearning. The xʷməθkʷəy̓əm community has helped me productively readdress the way I view my accountability and relationships as a researcher and teacher. This would be a much different book without the conversations I have had and friendships I have developed with xʷməθkʷəy̓əm teachers, artists, and community members. xʷməθkʷəy̓əm – or what is now known as Greater Vancouver – is where the majority of this work was written and revised and, as such, it has been greatly influenced by the land and the people in this community. My deepest thanks to Elder Larry Grant, who has so graciously shared his knowledge with me and with my students during my time on xʷməθkʷəy̓əm. The stories and knowledge Elder Grant shared with me about the history of witnessing on this territory played a formative role in how my ideas and methodology came to fruition. Many humble thanks as well to Jill Campbell, who has patiently guided me through the meaning and pronunciation of several hən̓q̓əmin̓əm̓ words and phrases and always asks after my children and family. Thank you also to the xʷməθkʷəy̓əm community and the organizers of Musqueam 101, particularly Leona Sparrow and Sue Rowley, for the many inspiring nights of learning. hay ce:p q̓ə.

I am exceptionally fortunate to work in a program surrounded by thoughtful, compassionate, and brilliant scholars who have all gone out of their way to share their experiences and research with me in various capacities. Sarah Hunt's leadership and intellectual rigour has been hugely inspiring as I set to work framing the argument here, and her friendship made the tough writing days in the office manageable. My deepest gratitude also goes to Daniel Justice, who has been a friend and mentor since I first stumbled, awkward, ambitious, and largely oblivious, out of grad school. Daniel has offered so much invaluable feedback on my writing and teaching over the years, and he has done so much for the field of critical Indigenous studies that I hardly know where to begin with my thanks, but please know they are heartfelt and profound. Daniel has taught me so much about what it means to be a good scholar and a good relation. Much of the energy I needed to complete this book came from feedback I received at a panel that Sheryl Lightfoot organized for the 2016 Native American and Indigenous Studies Association (NAISA) conference in Honolulu. Thanks also to the friends, teachers, and colleagues I have shared office spaces, conference lecterns, and Google docs with over the years, including Jeffrey Ansloos, Warren Cariou, Glen Coulthard, Mique'l Dangeli, Margery Fee, Dallas Hunt, Lindsay Lachance, Sheryl Lightfoot, Dory Nason, Karyn Recollet, Dylan Robinson, Daisy Rosenblum, June Scudeler, Coll Thrush, Mark Turin, Daniel Voth, Matt Wildcat, and Kelsey Wrightson. I must also mention my students in the Institute for Critical Indigenous Studies who have shared so much of themselves, including their experiences of reconciliation. You have all, at one point or another, been a real or imagined audience for this work.

This book has been a long time in the making and many people have played instrumental roles in its development. Without Sophie McCall's careful reading and sound advice, the ideas you see here would never have made it onto the page and eventually into a book. Thanks also Peter Dickinson, Christine Kim, Kirsten McAllister, and Pauline Wakeham, all of whom provided instrumental feedback during early stages and encouraged me in my writing and research along the way. When speaking of my colleagues at Simon Fraser University, thanks must also go to Deanna Reder, who often knows the advice I need before I need to ask for it. Laura Moss and reviewers for *Canadian Literature* also provided feedback on an early draft of the conclusion to this book and pressed me to think more deeply about *The*

Marrow Thieves. I also owe a deep debt of gratitude to my research assistant extraordinaire, Adi Burton, who kept me organized and on track during the final stages of this manuscript. Her keen eye for detail and her remarkable research skills have made this a stronger and more focused text.

I am a settler scholar of German heritage and I come to this research as a teacher and researcher specializing in Indigenous literatures and new media. I grew up in what is now known as Surrey, British Columbia, on Semyome (Semiahmoo) traditional territory. My great-grandparents, on both my mother's and my father's sides, were German immigrants. My mom was raised on an army base in Tsawwassen, British Columbia, and my dad was born into a farming community in Tisdale, Saskatchewan. When positioning myself in classrooms or at conferences, I sometimes tell people that my own story comes from the two great pillars of settler colonialism: war and agriculture. This is the history I write from and against, toward addressing, if not undoing, my inherited colonial legacies.

My immediate and extended family has tirelessly supported my work, even when I did not have the energy to support it myself. My parents, Pam and Ron Gaertner, instilled in me a love for reading, knowledge, and social justice, and held me up through the anxiety, self-doubt, and the loneliness of academia. My mother-in-law, Susan Deering, has always shown interest in my research and asked genuine and thought-provoking questions while also caring for my children while I wrote. Aaron Mauro, Byron Slack, Adam Slack, and Jason Starnes have shared so many enriching, intellectual conversations with me on culture and critical theory, and they continue to inspire me to be creative in my thinking, writing, and experience of the arts.

Thanks most of all, however, to Kathleen Deering, who has always been my best editor and most incisive critic. Her support and understanding allowed me to find a place where even the idea of writing a book was possible. Thank you for continuing to inspire me. And last, thank you to our children, Oliver, Eloise, and Alistair, who have only ever known me as working on this project. Writing can be cranky work, but you make it worthwhile. I hope, at some point, this book helps you to better understand your position on the land you grew up on and inspires you to be compassionate and informed relations.

THE THEATRE OF REGRET

Introduction

Bearing Witness to the TRC

> The Oxford Dictionary has three definitions for conciliate. The first is to "make calm and amenable." The second definition is to "pacify," and the third is to "gain the good will of." I may be misunderstanding the full meaning of the intent for reconciliation between Aboriginal people and Canadian society, but these definitions communicate a process of manipulation and potential exploitation.
>
> – STAN MCKAY (FISHER RIVER CREE FIRST NATION)[1]

> No one would decently dare to object to the imperative of reconciliation.
>
> – JACQUES DERRIDA[2]

Reconciliation is a structure, not an event.[3] On September 6, 2013, the Belkin Art Gallery at the University of British Columbia launched *Witnesses: Bringing Residential Schools into the Present,* a collection of contemporary Indigenous art contending with Canada's history of Indian Residential Schools. *Witnesses* was timed to open just before the Truth and Reconciliation Commission (TRC) arrived in Vancouver for the sixth of seven national events aimed at educating the public and holding up those impacted by residential schools. As such, it served both as a preparative encounter with residential school history as well as a point of critique for the politics and aesthetics of political reconciliation. Twenty-two Indigenous artists contributed to the exhibition, including Rebecca Belmore, Skeena Reece, Jamasie Pitseolak, Henry Speck, Carl Beam, Adrian Stimson, and Lisa Jackson, among others. *Witnesses* was the best-attended exhibition ever mounted at the Belkin Gallery (which, at the time, had been open for eighteen years), demonstrating the deep resonances (and, more cynically, the commercial viability) of residential school issues for the university and the gallery-going publics.[4] In its ability to represent at least some of the pain and horror of residential schools, *Witnesses* spoke to a desire – in both Indigenous and settler communities – to contend with this dark chapter of Canadian history more openly and to push the conversation of colonial violence beyond the event of the TRC and the exhibition itself.[5]

At the time *Witnesses* opened, I was a postdoctoral fellow in First Nations and Indigenous Studies at the University of British Columbia. A year before taking up this position, I had written and defended a dissertation on discourses of reconciliation in Canadian and Indigenous literatures, which would go on to form the skeleton for the book you now hold in your hands. By design, my work on reconciliation ran adjacent to the Truth and Reconciliation Commission of Canada and traced its development (and sometimes collapse) as it established itself as a Canadian political movement. I began my research in 2006, just as the Indian Residential Schools Settlement Agreement (IRSSA) was ratified, and I defended my dissertation in 2012, at the time the Commission's interim report was released, and two years before the closing ceremonies in Ottawa.[6]

As the scope of the TRC changed and expanded, so did my own thinking on reconciliation, moving from a generalized account of the international TRC model as it had developed out of Chile and South Africa to a more focused analysis of the thoughts and provocations on reconciliation initiated by Indigenous artists, novelists, theorists, poets, and playwrights. As the TRC became more specific, engaging in more detailed ways with the lives and experiences of individuals, so too did my work, moving from sweeping historical conceptions of reconciliation and redress to close reading of a few lines of poetry, and then back again. As I worked, I began to identify some of the primary tenets of both the general and specific discourses and, with the assistance of Indigenous literature, to develop arguments arising from those tenets. I have structured this book around these ideas, which are acknowledgment, apology, redress, and forgiveness. *The Theatre of Regret* is an interdisciplinary engagement with the discourses of reconciliation as they unfolded – and continue to unfold – out of the first ten years of the TRC, during which I attempted to collect and trace paths through the constellations of voices that have spoken to, against, and just to the side of the reconciliation debates.

I don't pretend to provide a solution to reconciliation in this book, in part because I believe that the insistence on "solution" in the discourse of reconciliation is part of the problem. The chapters in this book raise far more questions than they solve. In bringing many of these voices together for the first time, however, I hope to provide a more rigorous, informed structure in which to think about reconciliation, its consequences, and its possibilities, in a way that decentres and destabilizes the European and Christian thinking that sits at its core. I unsettle and trouble reconciliation by reading it in relation to critical Indigenous studies, Canadian studies, and Canadian and Indigenous literatures.

More specifically, I aim to illustrate why reconciliation, as it has been defined in international politics, is a troubling approach to historical injustice and Indigenous-settler relations in Canada. The emphasis on *reconciliation,* as opposed to Truth and Reconciliation Commissions, is at the core of what I see as my intervention into the literature. The majority of book-length studies that address this topic approach truth and reconciliation concurrently, illustrating how these concepts work together toward (a) transitional justice or (b) nation-state redress for historical injustice.[7] Working in reciprocity with Indigenous scholars and activists, such as Patricia M. Barkaskas and Sarah Hunt, who call for an emphasis on truth in the TRC of Canada, this work aims to illustrate, via a genealogical account of "reconciliation," the ways in which the second half of the TRC formulation has been recaptured by settler colonialism.[8] I argue that, within the Canadian context, truth is obscured in the TRC formulation because settler emphasis on reconciliation obstructs intellectual access to the ongoing histories of settler violence that sit at the core of Indigenous-settler relations. In my emphasis on "reconciliation" in this text, I stand in solidarity with the residential school survivors – who originally called for a TRC in Canada – by illustrating how the logics of settler colonialism work to twist and distort the terms of the conversation by privileging reconciliation over truth.

We are at a point now, in the wake of the TRC of Canada, at which critiques of reconciliation are easy to find, and many of those critiques are pointed and impactful. However, as I tell my students, critics of reconciliation should not overlook the labour – taken up by survivors – that made the TRC of Canada possible. As such, I delineate the TRC that occurred in Canada as the "Truth and Reconciliation Commission of Canada," rather than "Canada's Truth and Reconciliation Commission," to subvert the possession implied by the latter phrasing. I argue throughout this book that if reconciliation is possible with Indigenous peoples living in a colonial state, it cannot be the possession of that state or a register of the dominant discourse. While it may often appear differently, "reconciliation" is not a state good – by which I mean it is not a product that the settler colonial government should be able to manufacture, trade, and profit from. Nor is it a Canadian act of goodwill that can be manipulated to act as a demonstration of Canada's moral superiority in the international state order. Reconciliation in what is now known as Canada was established by Indigenous peoples and survivors of residential schools and, as such, is subject to the sovereignty and self-determination of those communities. Building from this important point, *The Theatre of Regret* contributes to the growing discourse of critique around reconciliation by interrogating settler perspectives on acknowledgment, apology, forgiveness, and redress as a means to hold space for Indigenous authors and thinkers working with – and against – the possibility of reconciliation. More specifically, I aim to illustrate why reconciliation, as it has been defined in international politics, is a troubling concept in a settler colonial state.

Bearing Witness

Like the Belkin exhibit I began with, the methodology of this book is also rooted in the land from which I write and the notion of "bearing witness," with which I attempt to act in reciprocity. I attempt to do so by holding up the voices that have done, and are doing, the hard work of critiquing reconciliation. Working with these voices, I hope to illustrate, primarily to non-Indigenous audiences, the ideology that confounds reconciliation as it is absorbed into settler colonialism.

In a Western framework, witnessing is rooted in legal contexts and the "juridical imperative of the witness's oath,"[9] but in Coast Salish traditions, to witness means to give oneself over to a story and to be accountable to that narrative, its history, its teller(s), and the way it was experienced when told. Witnesses are keepers of this knowledge and may be called back to speak to it at future events.[10]

For instance, in a traditional Stó:lō gathering, such as a potlatch or naming ceremony, one of the first tasks of the speaker named by the host family is to call witnesses.[11] The speaker moves counter-clockwise through the Longhouse and, one by one, identifies certain respected guests, calling out to them in halq'eméylem: "Xó:lhmet te syóysthet tset, há:kweles chap itló slát," which in English translates to, "Please witness, respectfully watch, and carefully remember the events you are going to see and hear this evening."[12] It is a great honour to be called to witness in this tradition. After the named individual accepts, a member of the host family clasps their hands and leaves a few coins with them: "Witnesses fully understand," M. Teresa Carlson, Keith Thor Carlson, Brian Thom, and Albert "Sonny" McHalsie write, "that if in the future any question arises as to what occurred during the ceremony ... they can be called upon to recall what they had seen and heard in an accurate and truthful manner."[13] After all the witnesses have been called, the ceremony begins. Following the ceremony, witnesses are given the floor and the right to speak: "Each witness comments on the work which has been done, and usually reminds those gathered to keep Stó:lō oral traditions strong."[14] Following the ceremony, at future points down the road, if an account or history of the event is needed, those witnesses may be called upon to share their experiences.

xʷməθkʷəy̓əm Elder Larry Grant, who first pointed me toward the Stó:lō text I reference here, and who has taught me much about the ways in which the act of witnessing functions on his territory, further articulates the importance of the witnessing ceremony in xʷməθkʷəy̓əm, Stó:lō, and Tsleil-Waututh cultures, particularly in reference to his own community:

> We call witnesses to be the keepers of our history when an event of historic significance occurs in the Coast Salish world. We do this in part because our traditions are oral, but also in recognition of the importance of conducting business, and building and maintaining relationships, in person and face to face ... We call upon all of the members of the audience to record this event in their minds and their hearts and to share the story of what happened here today.[15]

Grant connects witnessing to a long-standing tradition on the northwest coast and emphasizes how bearing witness is both a commemorative and a responsive act. Witnesses are asked to carry events within them as a record. They are asked to hold up those voices and those stories should they ever need to do so if those events were to be called into question or if there were to be disagreement over what occurred.

History is at stake in the witnessing ceremony, but never at the expense of community. Jordan Wilson, also a member of the xʷməθkʷəy̓əm community, explains witnessing this way, emphasizing the ways in which witnessing works to form a living, community-based archive of history and events:

> Each witness observes the event from their own perspective. When they recount what they've witnessed to those who hired them, they do so by drawing on their own personal experiences and teachings. The practice of witnessing also serves a role in the biography of individuals, as important events in one's life are recorded in this system. Witnesses must observe and listen closely, as they can be called upon at any point in the future to provide an account of what they observed at a particular gathering. Witnessing is one way of demonstrating how in our community (and in our neighboring communities), knowledge, history, and life narratives are dispersed among many. Thus, gathering together as individuals is akin to bringing together components of a history.[16]

Both Wilson and Grant challenge Western legal definitions of witnessing by putting the responsibility of the act of witnessing on the individual(s) who receive and accept testimony on historical events, as opposed to the individual(s) who directly (and often unwillingly) experienced those events. Witnessing, for Wilson and Grant, is an act rooted in tradition and community, and it demonstrates the collective ways in which history is recorded and disseminated, as well as the ways in which collective memory serves to shape culture and bind community.

This ethic of witnessing, as a means of holding up community voices, is also captured in *Witness Blanket,* a twelve-metre-long art structure assembled by Kwakwa̱ka̱'wakw master carver Carey Newman and funded by the Truth and Reconciliation Commission. The witness blanket is constructed from 887 objects, including pieces of residential schools, government buildings, churches, photographs, shoes, children's letters, and locks of hair.[17] The objects have been gathered from seventy-seven Indigenous communities across Canada as a means to "mak[e] a visual representation of reconciliation."[18] I visited *Witness Blanket* when it was being housed at the Canadian Museum for Human Rights in Winnipeg, Manitoba. Woven together, the individual pieces of the blanket provide powerful and deeply affecting testimony to residential schools. Each piece is replete with the history of the schools, inflecting back at the viewer, in their resonant silence, testament to the lives of children and survivors.

By bringing these various objects together – objects which, on their own, might only whisper of the past – Newman generates a context in which shared experience amplifies and augments stories that may have otherwise gone unheard. Newman himself speaks to the blanket's ability to hold up the truth of residential schools. In an interview with Shari Narine, he states that his "personal view is [that] for us to achieve full reconciliation we need to include all parts of the story ... It's about the actual truth of what happened."[19] In this sense, the witness blanket bears witness with and for survivors by holding space for them and their stories. It also asks audiences to bear witness, to be attentive to the voices that risk being lost in the excitement surrounding reconciliation. Frieda Esau Klippenstein writes that the witness blanket "communicates the illusion of order and beauty, and the need to look closer. It also conveys the startling insight that among the fragmented ruins are people, lives, and communities. The pieces of pain need to be faced."[20]

As the *Witness Blanket* helps to illustrate, witnessing is a vital part of the TRC of Canada. Early in the Commission's life, Commissioner Marie Wilson established that the TRC required "prominent helpers who will not only live out their right to know the truth here, their responsibility to *remember* what they have learned here, but who will also commit to *taking forward and teaching others* and spreading the word" [emphasis added].[21] Paralleling the National Research Centre, which will house the statements, documents, and other materials gathered by the TRC over the course of its mandate, TRC witnesses are instructed to carry with them a living record of residential schools along with the emotional and cognitive impacts of receiving and holding such testimony. While they are never outwardly cited as such, the northwest coast principles of witnessing, as outlined by Grant and Wilson, are implicit here. Honorary witnesses include former prime ministers Paul Martin and Joe Clark, along with former Governor General of Canada Adrienne Clarkson, Grand Chief Ed John, and CBC journalist Shelagh Rogers. Rogers writes about what being an honorary witness means to her:

> My mission is to listen, learn and then transmit, and create understanding. As a Witness, you keep the memory and you take the story further down the road and deliver it to more people ... It is bigger than just telling the story – I want to see policy change, curriculum change, to see concrete fixes in civil society that will enable us to have much better partnerships than we have right now.[22]

In his statement to survivors, Maori anthropologist and historian Sir Sidney Mead held up the strength of Indigenous peoples and guaranteed that strength against the stories that had been told to him: "We acknowledge your bravery. We acknowledge the pain you've been through and also draw attention to what may be a miracle. That, after all of those efforts to knock the Indian out of you, you are still Indian today."[23] Mead's and Rogers' words demonstrate the role of the TRC witness as individuals who hold fast to difficult truths and do not simply advocate for their reconciliation. To bear witness is to be pulled toward truth and to resist the centripetal pull of reconciliation.

Unlike Rogers and Mead, however, I have not been called to witness by the TRC of Canada. Although I live and work on xʷməθkʷəy̓əm territory, I am not from this place and I have no personal connection to the witnessing tradition. While I draw on much of what has been shared with me about witnessing on the northwest coast, how I am using the concept in this work comes more directly from its application in Indigenous studies contexts than from xʷməθkʷəy̓əm protocol. In Indigenous studies, the act of bearing witness is generated in the reciprocal act of listening to and sharing stories and the active deconstruction of settler colonial narratives.[24] Witnessing in this sense is, therefore, about reinterpreting the past relationally, holding up the stories and histories of those who do not have the same platform for voice that I am privileged to have as a white, cis male academic. Métis scholar Judy Iseke refers to this type of witnessing, which aims to unsettle colonial memories of an event, as "pedagogical witnessing."[25] For Iseke, pedagogical witnessing "allows my reading, viewing, or listening to be an event in which I allow the understanding of someone's life to interrupt my own life."[26] Witnessing in this sense is an act of unsettling accomplished in the act of sharing stories.

In its academic formulation, the movement of story between individuals shakes the foundational narratives that shape our worldviews, thus opening the potential, not just for empathy, but – more radically – for structural change. Indeed, for Iseke, much as it does for Rogers, bearing witness means proliferating Indigenous voices and therefore undoing the colonial narratives that dampen and silence those perspectives. In this sense, "witnessing can be a powerful form of recovery from a colonial past."[27] In bearing witness, according to Iseke, we mobilize our privilege as academics to push back against silence. Sarah Hunt builds on this idea. She writes that "Witnessing ... might be understood as a methodology in which we are obligated, through a set of relational responsibilities, to ensure frameworks of representation allow for the lives that we have witnessed to be made visible."[28] In the sense that Hunt develops it, bearing witness is not simply about the one who sees or directly experiences an event. It is also about the one who propagates testimony: who shares and disseminates it.[29] Indeed, as a scholarly methodology, witnessing carries this responsibility: "It is in witnessing the stories," Hunt writes, "[that] I am obligated to ensure they are not denied, ignored or silenced."[30]

Ensuring that stories are not silenced is a particular kind of academic work, which can take on different forms. Settler colonialism works actively to repress and silence Indigenous voices, particularly those who would speak truth to power. Even in the era of reconciliation, perhaps even because of the era of reconciliation, Indigenous voices and stories continue to be unheard. Bearing witness, as a scholar and teacher, is therefore about our responsibility to hold space for the Indigenous thinkers, activists, and community members who are already doing the hard work of speaking truth. But it also means, as Hunt highlights, doing so while being in good relation to those communities and people. It means being accountable to community, even when doing so means being "in tension with the values underlying academic knowledge creation within universities."[31]

Building from Iseke's and Hunt's work on what it means to bear witness as an academic, I attempt to bear witness in this book by writing in reciprocity with some of the many Indigenous voices that have rigorously contributed to the critique of reconciliation and its primary tenets: acknowledgment, apology, redress, and forgiveness. As articulated by the state, "reconciliation" is too often a story of a necessary good. And the primacy of this narrative – and who tells it – has the potential to shut out critique. Jacques Derrida makes this plain when he writes, in one of the passages I use as an epigraph for this introduction, "no one would decently dare to object to the imperative of reconciliation."[32] The threat of silence that reconciliation carries with it, which Derrida points to here, has material effects on the ways in which truth is engaged and proliferated. If "reconciliation" becomes that which is unobjectionable, then to bear witness means to object and to stand in solidarity with those who would dare to do the same.

Many Indigenous authors and activists, some of whom I engage with in this book, have spoken loudly against reconciliation. Those authors and activists do not need me to rescue their words, and I do not mean to frame my use of witnessing as an act of white saviourism. Indigenous peoples dare to speak against reconciliation when doing so represents a threat to their well-being or the security of their family. To dare to speak against reconciliation is a much different thing for me, as a white, cis-gendered, straight man with a tenure-stream position in an R1 university, than it is for an

Indigenous scholar, or for a racialized activist or community member. To speak against reconciliation, for many, is to risk violence. The risk I take on in this book, that I "dare" to take on, is relatively small, and this is precisely part of the problem. That is to say, the question of reconciliation is folded within a much larger system of structural racism and violence that renders the dare a threat operationalized by the settler state. As such, being a witness as a settler scholar means mobilizing my privilege to hold up the voices of Indigenous peoples as a means of chipping away at structural racism and white supremacy. Bearing witness, in this sense, means taking up some of the intense labour necessary to object to reconciliation and to together create a space where that reconciliation can and will be heard as the purview of Indigenous peoples.

As such, I have constructed this book around works by the Indigenous authors, activists, and scholars who have impacted me and who have persuaded me that further critique of reconciliation is necessary. Creative writers such as Sky Dancer Louise Bernice Halfe, Thomas King, Marie Clements, Richard Wagamese, Billy-Ray Belcourt, and Leanne Betasamosake Simpson have been instrumental here, as well as critical thinkers such as Daniel Heath Justice, Glen Coulthard, Sarah Hunt, Val Napoleon, and Heidi Kiiwetinepinesiik Stark. Alongside these perspectives, I have also woven in critiques of reconciliation coming from authors of colour, such as Nalo Hopkinson, Roy Miki, and Joy Kogawa. As I hope to illustrate, those who dare to object to reconciliation and redress are often the most vulnerable, and this book is an attempt to hold up the work of those who took on considerable risk to make critiques of reconciliation, such as mine, possible. Writing by activists and authors such as Miki, Kogawa, and Hopkinson brings valuable critical perspective from those who are also impacted by racism and white supremacy; it also bears witness to the fact that critiques of reconciliation are made possible by people of colour. It is my hope that this book bears witness by working *with* these voices in the fight to address the settler colonial ideology that creeps into reconciliation as it has been taken up by the Canadian state.

Apparition

For me, as an academic author and a settler scholar, bearing witness also means being aware of what can't be said and what one does not have the right to circulate. Thus, while this book discusses the many points at which Indigenous knowledges disrupt reconciliation, it is also attentive to the silences that must be respected. This is a lesson I felt most deeply through Anishinaabe artist Rebecca Belmore's work, particularly her contribution to the *Witnesses* exhibit: *Apparition. Apparition* was a large-scale video installation that featured Belmore posed against an ethereal white background. The video loop, four minutes in length, began by slowly fading in on Belmore, in a white T-shirt and jeans, kneeling in front of the audience, a piece of duct tape covering her mouth. Belmore stared directly into the camera and therefore directly at those watching her in the video, but her gaze, like the background she was set against, was tabula rasa, contributing to the overall sense that this piece was more a space to collect the projections of the viewer than it was a projection of the artist's thoughts on residential schools. Roughly midway through the piece, Belmore moved from the kneeling position – which emulated the position of prayer that residential school students were forced to assume – to a cross-legged sitting position. Still holding the audience's gaze, she then slowly tore the duct tape away from her lips. Once the tape was removed, she broke the gaze for the first time, stood up, and walked out of the frame. The loop then repeated, returning to Belmore kneeling, her mouth covered once again.

Apparition speaks to a number of key issues within the framework of "witnessing" and the conversations I hope to elicit with this book, many of which circulate, paradoxically, around the silence and the cycles of oppression reiterated in reconciliation politics. Key to this in Belmore's work is language. In her artist statement, Belmore acknowledges that *Apparition* "is an artwork that reflects [her] understanding of the loss of our language [Anishinaabemowin]."[33] While the artist grew up around her language, she, like many others from her community, is unable to speak it. Residential schools played a determining role in this loss, interrupting the inheritance of language as it is passed from one generation to the next by punishing students for speaking their mother tongues and generating shame around Indigenous languages and Indigenous epistemologies. Residential schools were built on the idea that "only by removing children from their parents, prohibiting Indigenous languages, and banning cultural practices could students be removed 'from evil surroundings' and be relocated in the 'circle of civilized conditions.'"[34] The tape across Belmore's mouth in *Apparition* is thus indicative of the ways in which Indigenous languages were taken from communities through the residential school system.

Inasmuch as their languages were stolen, there is also a critical epistemological gap in the ways in which survivors can communicate their experiences in these schools – given that English, the language of the perpetrator, becomes the vehicle through which they must bear witness to that violence. Using the *lack* of language as an entry point, Belmore's video installation intervenes into colonial history – and the colonial gaze more specifically – not by breaking silence, but by mobilizing it: while the audience is captivated by Belmore's gaze in *Apparition,* the artist offers no words, either in English or Anishinaabemowin, that might fulfill the consumptive desire of a colonial audience. Indeed, Belmore draws attention to that desire when she removes the duct tape from her mouth but continues without speaking. Removing the tape suggests personal agency – the ways in which the artist has freed herself from settler colonial hegemony and the silence of the subaltern – but her continued refusal to speak – to bear witness to the trauma and violence that inflicted her silence – interrupts the survivor/perpetrator dialectic of testimony/apology and subverts settler expectations, which circulate around knowing and consuming the pain of the other.[35] In walking out of the scene, Belmore completes the gesture of refusal, leaving the audience with only a blank canvas, a radical space of lack that refuses recuperation into a settler colonial narrative of forgiveness, apology, or redress.[36]

It is because it refuses access that *Apparition* compels its audiences to consider the implications of their own desire as it relates to the trauma of residential school survivors. In these moments of reflection, Belmore holds space to attend to the stories of survivors and their families as they resonate around her work. To borrow from bell hooks, *Apparition* is thus concerned with critiquing a model of witnessing and testimony that "only speaks from that space in the margin that is a sign of deprivation, a wound, an unfulfilled longing. Only speaks ... pain."[37] *Apparition* refuses to offer that deprivation up for consumption to settler audiences who Rachel Flowers, drawing from the hul'qumi'num' language, identifies as "hwulunitum," the "hungry people."[38] In the stillness of Belmore's work, then, there is a possibility to hear reconciliation from the perspectives of Indigenous knowledge keepers and community members, which, of course, was the larger principle of the *Witnesses* exhibit. Against her refusal and the tabula rasa of the white backdrop, audiences were compelled to hear the testimony that reverberated in and through the Belkin Gallery, to bear witness to the knowledge that Indigenous artists were bringing to the concept of reconciliation.

In this, *Apparition* calls for us to decentre our gaze and draws our attention to the margins, to the work that is happening even as we try to pry answers out of refusal. But then the loop begins again. The tape is back across the mouth. The story remains untold, making the non-telling, and its repetition, one of the primary takeaways. With *Apparition,* we had, as viewers, in this moment of quiet, a small window through which we might challenge hegemonic state representations of reconciliation. Belmore invited us to use this space to consider Indigenous thinkers, writers, and artists as they spoke to reconciliation. We are now in a different time than when this show first opened, and the window afforded by *Apparition* may have closed. Silence itself may be impossible in the neo-colonial din that has arisen around reconciliation in the years following the Belkin exhibition. But Belmore's silence still resonates as a condemnation of the hwulunitum desire to consume pain.

Apparition also made me think more deeply about what it is that I hoped this book could give back, and to whom. From *Apparition* I realized that I did not want this work to be another piece of academic research caught up in the feedback loop that Belmore identifies: a gaze that looks, a gaze that is sympathetic or even outraged, but ultimately a gaze that contributes to the continuation of the cycle. *The Theatre of Regret* attempts to bear witness not only by hearing the pain caused by residential schools, but also, more specifically, by listening to the ways in which the uncritical, self-involved discourses of reconciliation contribute to and continue that pain. In pulling the lens back to the international TRC model, I hope to provide a macroscopic view of the TRC of Canada, which will give Indigenous and non-Indigenous researchers and activists an even larger tool box from which to unpack, critique, and deconstruct state-centred reconciliation, its mandates, and its goals.

In the chapters that follow, I discuss why settlers are so preoccupied with reconciliation. Why has reconciliation become, in the terms of psychoanalysis, a drive: the compulsion not to achieve a goal but to continually circle around it, thus generating an unending cycle, a feedback loop such as the one Belmore identifies? I consider the ideas, emotions, and history that make the story of reconciliation so powerful and the ways in which its (re)telling can suppress and circumvent certain truths about racism and settler colonialism. I trace reconciliation and the TRC model through its development out of the Nuremberg trials and into national commissions for truth and reconciliation in Uganda, Chile, and South America. I discuss and examine the key terms that supplement and support reconciliation as it develops out of the Second World War and the Cold War – acknowledgment, apology, redress, and forgiveness – and I explore the ideological implications of these terms: the ways in which they enable silence, forgetting, and neo-colonial models of "moving on" and "progress." I unpack settlers' understandings of reconciliation in relation to colonial models of power and settler definitions of race and Indigeneity, and I look at the ways in which the discourse of reconciliation enables resource extraction and protects settler fragility.

But I also look at the ways in which Indigenous authors, intellectuals, and community members push back against the TRC template. I discuss the ways in which Indigenous poets and playwrights, such as Sky Dancer Louise Bernice Halfe, Thomas King, Kevin Loring, Billy-Ray Belcourt, Cherie Dimaline, Leanne Betasamosake Simpson, Eden Robinson, Richard Wagamese, Joshua Whitehead, and Marie Clements, undo the narratives of healing and forgiveness that undergird the TRC and challenge the Christian sanctification of personal suffering as a moral good – indeed, the only good available to Indigenous peoples within colonization. I illustrate how Indigenous peoples refuse and interrupt discourses of apology. And I address the ways in which allied thinkers from racialized settler groups in Canada unpack the narratives of redress that preceded the TRC. Together, Indigenous and allied thinkers and authors disrupt and displace the hegemony of contemporary reconciliation discourse and add new depth and complexity to what I call "the theatre of regret" – that is, the political shift toward performances of morality that we see developing, on an international level, out of the Second World War. Reconciliation is not one-size-fits-all. The voices I engage with here demonstrate that fact carefully and rigorously.

The chapters in this book are organized around four of the key stages on the path to reconciliation: acknowledgment, apology, redress, and forgiveness. As a whole, these four stages represent the multiple levels on which survivors and perpetrators work toward addressing and responding to historical injustice. Read separately, each category represents a provocative and rigorous space in which to engage with and challenge the interpersonal relationships encompassed within the reconciliation framework. The categories I provide are not meant to be exclusive, and they do not represent a "true" path toward coexistence, whatever that might mean. However, given the regularity with which they are evoked in the TRC genre, and hence the weight they hold in that discourse, they provide vital spaces from which to unpack and critique reconciliation at a modular level. I examine acknowledgement, apology, redress, and forgiveness in detail in Chapters 2 to 4, respectively. Around these chapters, I provide additional framework that contextualizes those concepts within the global discourses of reconciliation: Chapter 1 provides background and history on the truth and reconciliation model and theorizes its development in settler states such as Canada and Australia; my Conclusion offers an analysis of reconciliation itself via Cherie Dimaline's *The Marrow Thieves*, and ends with reflections on the TRC of Canada's Calls to Action.

The *Witnesses* exhibit, and in particular Rebecca Belmore's piece, have helped me to ask what reconciliation wants in a settler vernacular. *Apparition* placed the TRC in a larger constellation of relationships between those who bear witness and those who offer testimony on Indian Residential Schools and Canada's long, violent history of colonialism. It reminded us that reconciliation takes place within certain power structures and in relationship to the other. In so many instances, what settlers believe they know about reconciliation does not resonate with the history of colonialism or the stories and practices of Indigenous peoples and this land. It is my hope that this book compels non-Indigenous readers to hear reconciliation otherwise and, through that, operates in reciprocity with the Indigenous voices that continue to bear witness to the TRC and Canada's history of colonialism.

1

The Theatre of Regret

The Politics of Reconciliation after the Second World War

> The word "reconciliation" ... is my daily bread. Compromise, accommodate, provide, make space for. Understand. Tolerate. Empathize. Endure ... Without it, no relationship, no work, no progress, is possible. Yes. Piece by piece we die into reconciliation.
>
> – ANTJIE KROG[1]

> It makes them part of it; they can be part of the solution without doing anything.
>
> – LEANNE BETASAMOSAKE SIMPSON[2]

We live in a new era of state morality. For the first time, Western governments are compelled to confront their histories, not as inheritors of grand narratives of struggle, perseverance, and conquest, but, as Edward Said once put it, as "representatives of a culture and even a race accused of crimes – crimes of violence, crimes of suppression, crimes of conscience."[3] Between the time of the first Truth and Reconciliation Commission (TRC) in Chile in 1991 and the time of this writing, there have been over thirty TRCs implemented across the globe, which is more than one commission per year.[4] On a superficial level, TRCs change the ways in which governments perform their relationship to state history, but these performances of morality do not necessarily amount to material change for the survivors of historical injustice. Detached from its historical, geographical, and cultural contexts, reconciliation is precarious at best and injurious at worst. Kevin Avruch and Beatriz Vejarano argue that "notions such as justice, truth, forgiveness, reconciliation ... are always socially constructed and culturally constituted."[5] Following Avruch and Vejarano, this chapter is about the contexts that made possible the social construction of reconciliation as we know it today – about the history, geography, and legality of reconciliation as it developed out of the Western World and was impinged on Indigenous peoples. It makes plain the conditions that allow for this discourse and interrupts the notion of reconciliation as a floating signifier: a word that points to nothing and has no agreed-upon meaning – a word without history and without relations.[6]

In the autumn of 1945, in the city of Nuremberg, Germany, the ways in which states responded to historical injustice changed forever. In the wake of the moral atrocities committed during the Second World War, the Nuremberg trials (and, to a lesser degree, the Tokyo Trials) drew global attention to the punitive measures that could be levied against state officials who participated in crimes against humanity. Facilitated by media technology (namely, newspapers and radios), the world was made to watch and listen: not only to how perpetrators were held accountable for their actions, but also to the ways in which the rest of the world established itself on the "right" side of history.[7] As I am writing this book, more than seventy years after Nuremberg, states continue to scramble to register their accountability in the theatre of regret established out of Nuremberg, perpetuating not only the necessity of appearing moral in a post–Second World War global economy, but also retroactively determining the founding violence of Nuremberg as a truth of human rights.

The Truth and Reconciliation Commission of Canada is only a small piece of a much larger genealogy of moral politics that developed out of Nuremberg and was consequently naturalized in tribunals, truth commissions, truth and reconciliation commissions, and reconciliation initiatives across the world, most notably in Uganda, Chile, South Africa, and Australia. It is not an accident that in Canada, healing and redress are operationalized out of a TRC model. The truth and reconciliation commission is a very particular genre of redress, and as a genre it carries with it a specific set of codes and procedures that shape the way in which content is processed and imagined. By evoking "reconciliation," settler Canadians enact, or attempt to enact, a specific kind of healing by appealing to the power of that word. Thus, understanding what "reconciliation" means in Canada necessitates that we understand the history of the TRC itself and the ways in which it maps onto – and is incommensurable with – Indigenous experiences and the history of settler colonialism. Contending with the TRC in Canada means first unpacking the genre of reconciliation, its history, and its specific development in the Western imagination. It means coming to terms with the ways in which reconciliation and the TRC are performed. This is where *The Theatre of Regret* begins.

In this chapter, I provide a roadmap for activists and reconciliation scholars beginning enquiries into TRCs today, particularly in settler contexts such as Canada. The roadmap is not intended to be a comprehensive or definitive guide to TRCs. Rather, it is an illustration of major moments of reconciliation in the TRC model, moments that demonstrate most clearly the *how* and the *why* of reconciliation: *how* it was defined and *why* it was defined that way. Some of these moments, such as in South Africa, have already been the subject of vast amounts of scholarship. Others, such as those in Uganda, have been largely abstracted from the TRC genealogy, but, for reasons I will demonstrate, need to be brought back into the conversation. The goal in this chapter is to provide readers with a more nuanced understanding of reconciliation as a political tool developed in response to particular times and places, thus providing a critical space from which to contextualize, interpret, and critique contemporary reconciliation as it exists in Canada and for Indigenous peoples.

Germany, 1945–46: The Nuremberg Trials

In order to begin contextualizing the TRC of Canada, we need to look back to the Second World War and the now pervasive human rights model that developed out of the Nuremberg trials, the first international trial for war crimes and, to quote Robert H. Jackson, Chief US Prosecutor, "one of the most significant tributes that Power has ever paid to reason."[8] Reconciliation is a direct descendent of Nuremberg inasmuch as it was here that the legal foundation for crimes against humanity was established. Without this baseline, TRCs would not have the legal foundation for their interventions nor the external pressure to follow them through.

The Nuremberg trials, during which former Nazi leaders were indicted and tried as war criminals, took place between 1945 and 1946, and were prosecuted by the International Military Tribunal (IMT), a body composed of eight judges, two from each of the war's Allied powers. The authority of the IMT stemmed from the London Agreement of 1945, which gave the tribunal the authority to declare any individual, group, or organization "criminal" under the following charges: (1) conspiracy to wage an aggressive war; (2) waging aggressive war; (3) war crimes; (4) crimes against humanity.[9] On October 1, 1946, following 216 court sessions, twenty-two verdicts were handed down through the IMT. These verdicts sentenced twelve of the defendants to death by hanging and the remainder to various terms of imprisonment. A subsequent series of trials came to an end in the spring of 1949.

In a juridical sense, the effects of Nuremberg run deep. Only weeks after the IMT sentences were carried out, the United Nations General Assembly endorsed the Nuremberg principles under Resolution 95, which established that "crimes against international law are committed by men, not abstract entities, and only by punishing individuals who commit such crimes can the provisions of international law be enforced."[10] In 1948, building on the General Assembly's decision, the nations of the Americas adopted the American Declaration of Rights and Duties of Man (ADRDM), and six months after that the United Nations adopted the Universal Declaration of Human Rights (UDHR).[11] Norbert Ehrenfreund, a former US Superior Court judge and a news correspondent who reported on the Nuremberg trials, argued that whether the Nuremberg prosecutors believed it or not, they "created a new relationship between individuals in oppressed societies and their governments, a new way of perceiving each other."[12] This new relationship, I argue, would go on to form the core of reconciliation in the years to come.

Yet as much as human rights were naturalized and granted "universal" status out of Nuremberg, they were also rooted in a founding instance of illegitimacy and the "victor's justice" of the West.[13] At their base, Nazi war crimes and the international body that sought to prosecute them were without precedent and thus fell under *nullem crimen sine lege:* no crime, no punishment without a previous penal law. In other words, there was no legal basis for prosecution. Thus, in 1946, with the world watching, Chief Justice Robert Jackson, head prosecutor for the Allies during the trials, had to construct a case that demonstrated Nazi defendants as *a priori* guilty of a moral crime. Nazi war criminals had to be established as an evil that necessitated the Allies breaking the law in order to then, in turn, prosecute them with the law. Giorgio Agamben names this paradox the "sovereign exception," the space outside the law, enacted by sovereign power, which defines the validity of the juridico-political order. Agamben writes, "Only the state of exception opens the space in which the determination of a certain juridical order and a particular territory first becomes possible."[14] It is through the sovereign exception that the Allies first generate the possibility for reconciliation, in that their actions in Nuremberg provided the possibility for a new juridical order via an original violence.

Jackson's team enacted the sovereign exception through an elaborate legal event in which Nazis and the rest of humanity were drawn out as distinct – and universal – representations of evil and good, respectively. Most of us are aware of this formulation thanks to the work of Hannah Arendt, who famously noted that the Nuremberg trials were constructed to explicitly interrupt the notion that there is "an 'Eichmann in every one of us,'"[15] thus positioning perpetrators as an exterior threat that required the law be broken in order to hold them at bay. Depicted as a radicalized other (even as a banal radicalized other), human defendants were thus made capable of inhuman acts for which, until 1946, no one could be held to account in either natural or positive law. As such, it was necessary for the Allied prosecutors to draw new boundaries to account for their actions – even if that meant breaking the law to do so.

Indeed, because the language of Nuremberg is often evoked to justify the need for a TRC or an investigation into historical injustice, its particular language of human rights is taken as universal and therefore without specific cultural or historical contexts.[16] However, despite the massive support to prosecute the Nazis, the Allies and their legal teams were not applying a law or enforcing legal consequences for war crimes in these trials; rather, they were staging a new production of the rule of law via the sovereign exception. Indeed, in order to pass its verdicts, the Nuremberg prosecution overruled almost all of the key arguments offered by the defence, including the contention that only a state, and not individuals, could be found guilty of war crimes, and that the trial and adjudication were *ex post facto* (retroactively effective or forceful). Furthermore, regardless of the chief prosecutor's appeal to the Kellogg-Briand Pact as a foundation for the tribunal's charges,[17] in 1947, "crimes against humanity" could not be anchored to any legal or historical reading of international politics. It was therefore a "crime" only insofar as the Allies named it as such. Former US Supreme Court Justice William O. Douglas put it this way:

> But no matter how many books are written or briefs filed, no matter how finely the lawyers analyze it, the crime for which the Nazis were tried had never been formalized as a crime with the definiteness required by our legal standards ... nor outlawed with a death penalty by the international community. By our standards that crime arose under an *ex post facto* law.

> Goering et al. deserved severe punishment. But their guilt did not justify us in substituting *power* for *principle*. [emphasis added][18]

Douglas helps to point out here that the disavowal implicit in the Nuremberg trials is that "crimes against humanity" are founded on what Jacques Derrida names a "simulacra of legalization."[19] That is to say, despite the consensus that the Nazis on trial deserved punishment, there was no legal way to justify that punishment. In fact, punishing the Nazis via the law was – in a strictly juridical, as opposed to moral, sense – more criminal than the crime itself. International law clearly states that "if a person commits an act at a time when there is no law against it, the person should not be held liable."[20] Thus, the Nazis were guilty only via some form of anachronism in which they set a precedent for a law that they retroactively transgressed. Yet, inasmuch as they devised a precedent for prosecuting human rights violations, the Allies initiated a structure of morality out of Nuremberg in which perpetrators of genocide could be legally charged. According to Ehrenfreund, after Nuremberg, "no ruthless dictator of the future could ever again claim that such crimes had no precedent or that they were *ex post facto* law."[21]

As perhaps the first international enactment of the sovereign exception, the Nuremberg trials did not depend on the accurate and rigorous application of established regulation. Rather, the tribunal relied on a spectacle of legality that was founded and preserved itself in the recursive performance spinning out of that event and into future legislation. That is to say, the precedent established by Nuremberg is retroactively justified through future re-enactments of its key principles. The International Criminal Court, for instance, enacted in the former Yugoslavia and Rwanda, built its authority out of the edifice of Nuremberg.[22] Nuremberg was also established as a founding concept for the South African TRC.[23] In Canada, the Nuremberg human rights definitions are at the core of five of the TRC of Canada's ninety-four calls to action.[24] While many scholars are at pains to identify the distinction between Nuremberg and the TRC, no matter how the model has been adapted across time and space, the core of those trials remains a necessary foundation for contemporary reconciliation as well as tribunals and truth commissions.

Relying heavily on Nuremberg and the human rights model that developed out of it, TRCs are justified by their application of Nuremberg principles. But they also justify the force of law ratified in Nuremberg in their re-enactments.[25] In this sense, state morality is a recursive event, characterized by an interpretation that is dependent on routine or repetition. Recursivity, as Nathan Stormer puts it, is "the tireless circulation between past and present."[26] Each successive moment both validates and is validated by its predecessor in ongoing constellations of emergent meaning. Recursivity, in this context, is thus much more than the simple "play" of language. Understanding how and by what authority "morality" functions, theorists and activists have a much better chance of interrupting or intervening in that system, which actively works to elide local contexts and epistemologies. As with any recursive action, Nuremberg law is effective only insofar as it continues to generate a new code of moral conduct out of its inception. Only in its reiteration out of the founding force brought into being by the IMT is the necessity of European law established, and the general public can continue to suspend its disbelief in the validity of *nullem crimen sine lege*.[27] While a recursive action brings into being a new rule or definition, in order for the category to be maintained as a viable ideological order, it must be repeated, or restaged, ad infinitum: "a structure only remains a structure," Judith Butler tells us, "through being reinstated as one."[28] In this sense, "crimes against humanity" is a convention in which each utterance informs, and is informed by, its echoes. To put it differently, it is only in the ongoing application of "crimes against humanity" that the utterance gains its force as a legal and moral category, accumulating, as Butler puts it, "the force of authority through the repetition or citation of a prior and authoritative set of practices."[29] What makes a recursive rule successful is therefore not the aim behind it, but the authority it garners from a tradition of similar actions. It is repetition, not "truth," that makes it viable.

What Nuremberg helps demonstrate, then, is that the authority of reiteration is, temporally speaking, a two-way process. Because the tribunal was not founded in a tradition of human rights, it gains its authority as such after the fact, determining its legitimacy via subsequent commissions – such as tribunals, truth commissions, and TRCs – that demonstrate the validity of the initial break from law. Subsequent iterations are, in a legal, historical, and discursive sense, tied to a very Western framework of restitution, which enables – but also constrains – the (re)animation of moral politics across time and space.

To summarize, in order to maintain the foundation of the edifice, the "structure" of "crimes against humanity" needs to be continually re-enacted on an international stage so as to maintain its force as law. The massive wave of truth commissions, including Canada's own TRC, thus retroactively determine the Allies' transgression, and Western law, as just.

Hence, the Nuremberg legacy is not simply a set of laws and institutions, but, more importantly, the beginning of a set of performances that, as much as we might agree with them, continually revitalize, recode, and galvanize an ideological determination of human rights. Critiquing the ways in which Nuremberg ideology is performed provides a much-needed entree into a discourse that works to deflect criticism in its innate reference to universal moral correctness. In identifying the historical factuality of this universal as sovereign exception, we interrupt the smooth flow of the universal and open space for local knowledges. It is in the sense that performance has informed the translation of the TRC model to Canadian contexts that I named this book "the theatre of regret." I will now turn to some of the key performances in the TRC genealogy as a means to further that critique.

Uganda, 1974: Commission of Inquiry into the Disappearances of People in Uganda

In 1971, under pressure from the international community, the infamous dictator and tyrant Idi Amin hosted the first post-Nuremberg truth commission, known by the rather ungainly name Commission of Inquiry into Disappearances of People in Uganda since the 25th of January, 1971. Amin's commission holds a remarkable position in the TRC genealogy as a founding iteration of Nuremberg principles and the first event in an ongoing series of truth commissions. That being said, Amin's commission has largely been erased from TRC history because of the violence it facilitated. According to Priscilla Hayner, who conducted one of the first comparative analyses of truth commissions in 1994, "The 1974 Ugandan commission has been all but forgotten or discounted in history."[30] I would argue that history has discounted Amin's commission – or, rather, purposefully repressed it – because it radically contradicts the dominant interpretation attached to the TRC model. Amin's commission had little to do with morality and everything to do with protecting power and wealth. Hayner states plainly that "the commission was set up without any political will or commitment to real change in human rights policy or practice."[31] Contrary to the way it has been treated thus far, however, Amin's commission is essential to TRC history not despite the violence it inflicted, but because of it. Indeed, this founding commission is not an exception to the TRC model; it is, in fact, part of its very makeup and of the tradition that carries on today, and exemplifies what we must be ready and willing to address in Canada.

Locating Amin's inaugural commission within the larger TRC genealogy is a crucial step toward untangling reconciliation because it illustrates most concretely the self-interest and economic principles that underpin benevolent action in the wake of Nuremberg. What Amin's commission lays bare, in fact, is that reconciliation can and will be used as yet another means to protect the interests of state authorities while paying lip service to an international moral code. Unlike the *realpolitik* relations of the Cold War period, which emphasized practical over moral decisions, Amin's performance of morality generates a much more insidious inflection of power: one that does not extend authority with explicit displays of force, but rather conceals power beneath a cowl of decency and goodwill.

As scholars move forward in reconciliation studies, the initial Ugandan commission needs to be redrawn into the TRC genealogy, thus highlighting the self-interest and performance that sit at the foundation of moral politics. Indeed, at stake in the Ugandan commission is the theatre of regret out of which reconciliation is enacted. Rather than erasing it from the narrative, we must hold Amin's commission up as an explicit example of the unseemly possibility of reconciliation as a tool of power and oppression. Doing so will provide a more transparent picture of the politics of reconciliation and the violences they are founded on.

The Commission of Inquiry into "Disappearances" (commissioned in 1974) was conceived by Amin as a means to address the political "disappearances" of thousands of Ugandans between 1971 and 1974.[32] Idi Amin was the third president of Uganda and a former major general in the postcolonial Ugandan army. In 1971, he overthrew Milton Obote and appointed himself as Field Marshall while head of the state. Under Amin's regime, somewhere between 100,000 and 500,000 people were murdered or "disappeared."[33] Violence under his rule was egregious. P.G. Okoth writes:

> The tactics Amin used against his adversaries defy description. He did not merely order his henchmen to kill people but also encouraged them to subject their victims to unspeakable atrocities after they were dead. Ugandans regularly discovered the mutilated bodies of their relatives, friends, and acquaintances with "livers, noses, lips, genitals or eyes missing." Amin himself was suspected of cannibalism and practising traditional Kakwa blood rituals on slain enemies.[34]

Under public pressure to respond to the rampant violence occurring under his rule, Amin established a truth commission with the mandate to investigate the disappearances that occurred at the hands of the military during his time in power.[35] Unless requested to be otherwise, hearings during the trials were public, and the commissioners – a Pakistani judge and three Ugandan public servants – heard testimony from 545 witnesses and documented 308 cases of disappearances, a remarkable feat in itself.[36]

The obvious conflict of interest in Amin's commission, however, lay in the fact that while it was mandated to investigate human rights abuses and prepare a report that would outline these mistreatments, the commissioners worked under, and made recommendations to, the same government they were examining. Amin himself received the reports on the crimes he had also committed. Indeed, although most hearings in Uganda were public, a final report was never published. A confidential copy was handed over to Amin, who continued to rule via political repression, ethnic persecution, and extrajudicial killings even as the truth commission was underway. As a result, any conclusions that did not align with Amin's administration were quickly, and violently, quashed.[37] In this sense, it is quite easy to make a case that the Ugandan commission was little more than a performance of human rights. According to Hayner, "The commission report had little impact on the practices of the Amin government."[38] The commissioners themselves were fired from their government positions, and one was even framed for murder, reportedly by the Amin government, and sentenced to death.[39] Amin's violence increased markedly in the years following the commission, eventually earning him the nickname "the butcher of Uganda."

Amin's commission is clearly an example of Nuremberg principles twisted into discourses and practices of power. Hayner writes that it "had no effect on policy or the violence with which Amin ran his government."[40] It was, as I establish above, a performance for the sake of public perception. What Uganda illustrates, then, is that, historically, truth commissions and reconciliation movements are not necessarily founded on moral imperatives. Just because they are taken up or embraced by nation-states does not mean that those nation-states have eschewed their commitment to violence and oppression. Indeed, the Ugandan commission helps to illustrate the performative elements that underlie the optics of human rights on a global stage. Given the demand to *appear* moral so that Uganda could continue to participate in the international commodities market, Amin adopted the Nuremberg model in order to project a particular facade of decency to the world. Yet, beneath that facade, the dictator was able to levy increased violence while advancing his own agenda.

As I note above, Amin has the distinction of deploying the first post-Nuremberg commission in the TRC genealogy, but his commission has been all but erased from history. In 1986, under Yoweri Museveni, Uganda launched its second inquiry into Amin's human rights violations, the Commission of Inquiry into Violations of Human Rights in Uganda. The second commission made no reference to Amin's 1974 endeavour,[41] effectively erasing that portion of history and recovering, if only partially, Uganda's position in what Elazar Barkan calls "the new international morality."[42] By 2009, both Amin's and Museveni's commissions had been written out of the history. That year, in the aftermath of events celebrating the anniversary of Uganda's 1947 independence, the government-owned newspaper, *New Vision,* insisted that, "unlike South Africa, Uganda has never had its truth and reconciliation commission ... Any incident, however insignificant, can destabilize the country and evoke the ghosts of the past because they have never been buried properly."[43]

With the history of Amin's commission stricken from the TRC genealogy, we are at risk of misremembering the ends to which Nuremberg principles have historically been applied. Idi Amin's inaugural truth commission established that while it may indeed be necessary to perform morality to the world after Nuremberg, those performances could easily be empty gestures, devoid of any real change for the citizenry they were composed for. In this very sense, the Commission of Inquiry into Disappearances of People in Uganda is an integral piece of the TRC genealogy because it so clearly illustrates the potential for state-sanctioned violence, which is in fact facilitated beneath the cowl of morality supplied by Nuremberg. While the truth and compassion represented in South Africa, and even in Chile's commission, which I will turn to next, are held up as reasons why a governing body would embrace a TRC, Amin's self-interest needs to be identified as just as viable a motivation for that process.

Chile, 1990–91: Comisión Nacional de Verdad y Reconciliación

For a time, the Cold War stymied the construction of the theatre of regret, putting the truth commission model on hold and compelling politicians and governments to retreat into *realpolitik,* where apology, forgiveness, and redress have no real claim to space. With the exception of Uganda, there were no commissions between the 1950s and the 1980s, simply because the political climate of the time was not conducive to internal state questioning. As the Cold War drew to a close, however, the international community began to once again see the necessity of moral politics and the need to hold governments accountable for human rights abuses, for the most part because a political order driven by pragmatism, as opposed to morality, had left the world on the brink of mutually assured destruction. Barkan explains:

> As the Cold War ended, political language changed from machtpolitik – the politics of power – and began to advocate a shared belief in basic individual and group rights. World public opinion voiced an emerging fundamental agreement that greater prosperity can be achieved not through brute domination but by consent and cooperation. A strong claim for restitution begins from a neo-Enlightenment morality – that is, the recognition of an ensemble of rights, primarily the rights of peoples and nations to decide for themselves and to reject external impositions.[44]

Latin America was instrumental in leading the redevelopment of moral politics, producing four commissions over twelve years and significantly altering the ways in which the South African commission, easily the most identifiable TRC, would address historical injustice in the wake of apartheid. Commissions in Latin America include the Comisión Nacional de Investigación de Desaparecidos (Bolivia, 1982), the Comisión Nacional sobre la Desaparición de Personas (Argentina, 1983), the Comisión Nacional de Verdad y Reconciliación (Chile, 1990), and La Comisión para el Esclarecimiento Histórico (Guatemala, 1994).[45] In 1989, the director of Human Rights Watch, Aryeh Neier, wrote that Argentina was "the most successful effort of the decade anywhere in Latin America, and perhaps worldwide, to hold accountable those who committed gross abuses of human rights."[46] Similarly, Anita Ferrara argues that "the Truth Commissions in Latin America have made a significant contribution to the construction and preservation of historical memory as well as to the determination of institutional, social, and political responsibilities."[47]

Before Chile, reconciliation was not an explicit part of the conversation around truth commissions in South America or elsewhere. While the shift in language is often overlooked in comparative analysis, before 1990 the emphasis in official investigations into historical injustice was solely on truth: making repressed state violence known to history. Power changed all of that, however. The first Truth and Reconciliation Commission took place in Chile under newly elected president Patricio Aylwin, who won power democratically from Augusto Pinochet, against whom the TRC would be levied. Of all the Latin American commissions, Chile's arguably has the greatest impact on the truth commission genealogy, simply because it introduced reconciliation into the conversation and obliged Nuremberg principles to move beyond truth. While he disputes its amnesty process, Desmond Tutu cites Chile's commission as one of the primary influences for the South African TRC,[48] given that it generated a model from which he could build and a set of problems that he could begin to address. Writing in 1994, just as the truth commission model began proliferating outside Latin America, Hayner notes that the Comisión Nacional de Verdad y Reconciliación was "an excellent model for continuing the work of a truth commission and providing a mechanism for implementation of a commission."[49]

When introducing reconciliation, however, Aylwin also announced a new series of political and ideological questions around state morality, and demonstrated the ways in which morality could be recuperated and performed by those in power. In order to understand Canada's relationship to this history, it is necessary to unpack Chile's model of reconciliation as it unfolds out of Pinochet's fall from power and the transitional efforts of Chile's new democratic government.

A provocative place to begin this investigation is the arts, particularly theatre. Ariel Dorfman's renowned play *Death and the Maiden* philosophically and emotionally contends with the Chilean TRC, illustrating the devastating effects Pinochet's rule had on the population and the continued suffering that Aylwin's pursuant TRC enacted.[50] Dorfman himself was born in Argentina, but in 1967 he became a citizen of Chile, where he was a teacher and an active critic of the Pinochet regime, authoring *Exorcising Terror: The Incredible Unending Trial of General Augusto Pinochet. Death and the Maiden,* which has now been staged in more than thirty countries, tells the story of a husband and wife living in the wake of political terror: Paulina is a survivor of a political kidnapping, during which she was tortured and raped; Gerardo is a participant in the nation's burgeoning truth commission. The action of the narrative unfolds when Gerardo brings a man home whom Paulina believes to be one of her kidnappers (she was blindfolded when captured and never saw his face then). She takes the man captive in their home in order to stage her own, homemade truth commission and to extract a confession from him. Throughout, however, Gerardo remains unconvinced of the man's guilt.

Dorfman's play helps to illustrate the intrinsic incompleteness of the TRC model. There is equal tension on both sides of the story, between Paulina's and Gerardo's perspectives of the man in their home, which need to be read contrapuntally: Paulina's desire for revenge on the one hand, and Gerardo's desire for justice on the other. Paulina points out the absurdity of the commission: "The commission can investigate the crimes but nobody is punished for them? There's freedom to say anything you want as long as you don't say everything you want?"[51] Gerardo attempts to illustrate the short-sightedness of revenge: "Imagine what would happen if everyone acted like you did. You satisfy your own personal passion, you punish on your own, while the other people in this country with scores of other problems who finally have a chance to solve some of them, those people can just go screw themselves."[52] The play ends ambiguously, with the audience still unsure of the man's guilt or Paulina's moral correctness in holding him captive. What is left certain, however, is the ongoing suffering inflicted by political terror and the ways in which truth commissions and TRCs continue to be marked with suffering and grief even as they enact justice. James Weaver and Jeanne Colleran write that "Dorfman's play reminds its audience that restorative justice is not installed by political change or political decree and that the legal remedies or public hearings will never be wholly successful."[53] In this sense, Dorfman puts the lie to reconciliation, as a return to harmony, and traces the discord and mistrust that truth commissions can enact in communities and families, justice notwithstanding.

Dorfman's play provides compelling insight into the ways in which truth and reconciliation were being taken up – and rejected – in the private sphere by families driven apart by state violence. In the public sphere, however, Chile's TRC was taken up much more programmatically, toward very specific political ends. Aylwin initiated the Comisión Nacional de Verdad y Reconciliación (also known as the Rettig Report) in 1991 in order to capture as clear a picture as possible of the human rights abuses that had occurred under General Augusto Pinochet for the previous seventeen years. Aylwin, a politician and lawyer, was the first president to be democratically elected following the military dictatorship of Pinochet, who had run the country under a mandate of terror from 1973 to 1990. Under Pinochet, it is estimated that thirty thousand people died, most of them taken away to secret detention centres and camps, where they were tortured and left in unmarked graves.[54] Naomi Roht-Arriaza writes that Pinochet's dictatorship "eventually engulfed the entire Southern Cone of Latin America, as the militarized regimes of Chile, Argentina, Uruguay, Paraguay, Bolivia, and Brazil coordinated their efforts to find and destroy opponents through Operation Condor," a campaign of political repression and interstate terror.[55]

Before Aylwin, the Latin-American model for conflict resolution, constructed and reformulated in Bolivia and Argentina in the 1980s, had been the Truth

Commission (Comisión de la Verdad), which focused specifically on uncovering the truth about disappearances during military rule.[56] Breaking from the precedent set by his neighbours, however, the new Chilean president, who was very much operating in the wake of Pinochet's nearly two decades of power, anticipated the need for a more nuanced approach, which included not only the violent and, as Dorfman illustrates, often volatile incision of truth, but also more moderate possibilities of resolution: hence the Comisión Nacional de Verdad y Reconciliación.[57]

With Aylwin, then, political reconciliation came into favour in the international community as a handmaiden to the implementation of a democratic system. Pinochet's grip on power was simply too tight to levy a truth commission without something in place to cushion his fall. Before leaving government, the military had secured a percentage of foreign exchange from the new government and made Pinochet armed forces chief (until 1997) and a senator for life.[58] The addition of "reconciliation" to the standard truth commission can thus be read in recognition of Pinochet's lingering influence and thus an appeasement to power, which facilitated Aylwin's transition into office and the state's transition to democracy.

Aylwin ran for president on a promise to overturn the military's self-amnesty, but when he came to power, he realized that would be an exceptionally difficult thing to accomplish, particularly because of the many ways in which Pinochet had installed himself and the military in power. Roht-Arriaza writes that "fearing the outcome of a still fragile democracy challenged the military, [Aylwin] decided not to raise the issue directly."[59] Truth – on its own – had the potential to send the country back into military rule. Something else was necessary to mediate between truth and power and provide the space necessary for democracy to develop. Reconciliation provided that mediation. Reconciliation was determined by transitional justice in this context, or, to use stronger language, *defined* by it, insofar as the former was only made possible by the latter.

In order to understand reconciliation in Chile, we must first contend with transitional justice. Transitional justice is its own robust field of study, which developed out of the Cold War in the early 1980s.[60] Predominantly focused on Western legal mechanisms of reconciliation, transitional justice was developed out of interactions between human rights lawyers, activists, and political scientists as a means to understand the ways in which new democracies dealt with the legacies of former regimes. More recent research in transitional justice – in Rwanda and South Africa, particularly – has examined the ways in which emerging democracies strike a balance between the needs and demands of survivors and the reintegration of perpetrators into a post-conflict community.[61] Critics of transitional justice argue that it is specific to the brief period of political transition and, as such, does not address issues such as land reform, which more often than not is excluded from the rubric of prosecution, truth telling, and even reparations. In South Africa, reconciliation and transitional justice were often deployed coterminously, given the emergence of Mandela's democratic party and the TRC's mandate to facilitate improved relations between civilians and the military. However, that slippage must be read out of its specific context. In Canada, and in other settler colonial states, the conflict is eminently present and the democracy that now calls for reconciliation is the same democracy that inflicted (and continues to inflict) the violence that now demands redress.

After the report of the Comisión Nacional de Verdad y Reconciliación was completed, Aylwin announced its main findings on public television and offered a formal apology on behalf of the government for the actions of its agents. He also asked the army to acknowledge its role in the violence, and cleared the space for many of the recommendations in the final report to be implemented.[62] In this initial TRC, then, political transition, reconciliation, and apology were mutually constitutive, each allowing the other to exist and proliferate. By making peaceful relations a necessary complement to truth, Aylwin significantly altered the shape of conflict resolution for all those who would follow. He also instantiated the T*R*C (emphasis on the "R") as a political means to smooth a transition into democracy while acknowledging the past and negotiating the remnants of the power structures left behind by a previous regime. However, by introducing "reconciliation," Aylwin's commission also added a new wrinkle to the ideology of state morality that would carry over into subsequent commissions. As I will address more directly below, this new wrinkle has dangerous connotations when taken out of the contexts of transitional justice. Before moving there, however, it is necessary to first look at the most popular, and influential, TRC, which took place under Archbishop Desmond Tutu in South Africa.

South Africa, 1995–2002: Commission of Truth and Reconciliation

If Patricio Aylwin changed the terms of reference for truth commissions, Desmond Tutu made those terms legible for, and consumable by, an international public. Unlike the commissions that preceded it (including Chile), the South African TRC was designed to be readily engaged by the public, with town halls, public hearings, and radio and television broadcasts. Previous commissions had taken place behind closed doors, with only the final report made publicly available. In South Africa, however, real-time public dissemination was built into the workflow, allowing that commission, as Catherine Cole argues, to "reverberate ... outward to ever-larger circles of witnesses."[63] Thanks in large part to the popularity and charisma of South Africa's newly elected president, Nelson Mandela, and of the man he chose to design and implement the TRC, Archbishop Desmond Tutu, international news bureaus quickly took up the South African TRC and proliferated it west. The commission made headlines the world over as a means to expose the deep violence of apartheid and begin the process of healing.

Mandela and Tutu dramatically changed the face of truth and reconciliation and compelled the world to follow their lead. Audrey R. Chapman and Hugo van der Merwe, editors of *Truth and Reconciliation in South Africa,* write that "South Africa's Truth and Reconciliation quickly became the model for other countries trying to come to terms with a past characterized by pervasive ethnic conflict."[64] Cole, author of *Performing South Africa's Truth Commission,* argues that "South Africa is one of the most significant, most celebrated, and most discussed examples of state transformation in the late twentieth century."[65] For all of its problems – its foundations in Christian ideology, and its dangerous emphasis on radical empathy – *this* is the reconciliation we see resonate most prevalently today in Canada's TRC.

A significant part of the reason why the South African TRC was, and is, such an influential contribution to reconciliation politics is because, building from Chile, it further rebalanced the power dynamics of Nuremberg mediation and deconstructed the once seemingly rigid binaries between perpetrator and survivor. Tutu took up the model devised by Aylwin in the South African commission as a means to facilitate Mandela's own installation into power because it provided new depth to the "victor's justice" model developed out of the Nuremberg trials. The Chilean model also provided a more complex analysis of survivor/perpetrator relations in a state beset by racism and violence. Tutu quotes American judge Marvin Frankel as a means to highlight the necessity for a more nuanced model to address "truth":

> A nation divided during a repressive regime does not emerge suddenly united when the time of repression has passed. The human rights criminals are fellow citizens, living alongside everyone else, and they may be very powerful and dangerous. If the army and police have been agencies of

> terror, the soldiers and cops aren't going to turn overnight into paragons of respect for human rights ... If they are treated too harshly – or if the net of punishment is cast too widely – there may be a backlash that plays into their hands.[66]

In contrast to his predecessors, Tutu brought a much more rigorous and inclusive approach to the investigation of historical injustice, moving beyond the broad strokes of "victor's justice" established in Nuremberg and generating safe spaces for survivors *and* perpetrators to tell their stories to the world and to one another. Tutu's major contribution to reconciliation politics is thus his explicit recognition of the limits of the Nuremberg model and the revisions he made to that model as such. To be clear, I am not suggesting that TRCs are alternatives to Nuremberg-like tribunals, but, instead, carefully considered, ideological modifications of them. The type of forgiveness that Tutu insisted upon in South Africa is in itself a manifestation of a moral order brought to life in the trials following the Second World War. While the "living body" of morality he wanted to corporealize was based on restorative principles, it was no less a case for substantiating the ethical claims made manifest by Nuremberg.

According to Archbishop Tutu, the Nuremberg paradigm functioned by "bringing to trial all perpetrators of gross violations of Human Rights and letting them run the gauntlet of the normal judicial process."[67] Tutu acknowledges that it was only because the Allies were the clear winners of the Second World War that they were able to assign participants to static roles, be they Nazi monster or enlightened prosecutor. As Tutu suggests, "The Germans ... accepted [their positions] because they were down and out and the victors, as it were, could kick the vanquished even as they lay on the ground."[68] Relative to Nuremberg, however, and much more in tune with the nuanced examinations of evil explored in works such as *Death and the Maiden,* Tutu's form of "justice" could not be informed by such a rigid dialectic as "good" and "bad." As Frankel points out in the quotation above, unlike in Nuremberg, survivors and perpetrators had to live and work together in post-apartheid South Africa – as citizens, as colleagues, and as neighbours. Not only would blanket statements about good and evil upset embedded power dynamics, but they would also do little to encourage viable, peaceable futures for South Africans. Tutu needed a commission that, like Chile's, moved away from retributive justice and focused instead on a restoration that did not leave perpetrators unaccountable.[69]

Retributive and restorative justice differ primarily in how they contain, or unleash, the human desire for revenge. Martha Minow lays out the distinction between the two in *Between Vengeance and Forgiveness: Facing History after Genocide and Mass Violence*: "Unlike punishment, which imposes a penalty or injury for a violation, restorative justice seeks to repair the injustice, to make up for it, and to effect corrective changes in the record, in relationships, and in future behavior. Offenders have a responsibility in the resolution. The harmful act, rather than the offender, is to be renounced."[70] While retributive justice appeals to a sense of justice based in reprisal and a Nietzschean sense of *ressentiment*, restorative justice asks survivors to put hate and anger aside with the Machiavellian promise of a better future for all.

In the context of state commissions, Tutu revolutionized restorative justice. Opposed to the retributive models that preceded him, and even the new "reconciliation" model developed in Chile, Tutu's TRC was empathy-driven, aimed at drawing in a sympathetic international audience and, more importantly, collapsing the emotional barriers between survivors and perpetrators that had been violently erected during apartheid. In this sense, what Tutu popularized with the South African TRC was forgiveness-based justice. With its emphasis on identification across survivor/perpetrator borders, forgiveness-based reconciliation deconstructed rigid distinctions between the self and the other by encouraging survivors and perpetrators to view the story from the perspective of the other. In these regards, one of Tutu's most resonant statements, aside from the title of his book itself (*No Future without Forgiveness*), is that "the only way we can be whole, healthy, happy persons is to learn to forgive."[71] Tutu presents forgiveness as the only model that will facilitate healing and reconciliation – a far cry from the punitive measures demanded by Nuremberg, and a brand new way to conceptualize the truth commission as a model of relationality.

The South African intervention into reconciliation politics is clearer if we collapse forgiveness into its discrete classifications. According to Everett Worthington, forgiveness can be broken down into three interrelated categories: hollow forgiveness, decision-based forgiveness, and emotion-based forgiveness.[72] To briefly summarize Worthington's distinctions, hollow forgiveness is that which is offered under societal duress when the victim actually feels no forgiveness at all. In this stage, one forgives in *logos* (rhetorical appeals) only, and even then, only because one is forced to; at the other end of the continuum, emotional forgiveness is offered freely, when the victim actually feels an end to their pain and resentment. Emotional forgiveness is akin to a release of the stress, anxiety, and hatred held against a perpetrator. In this stage, the body reflects the language; the forgiver feels no discrepancy between the words "I forgive" and their emotional state of being.

Finally, decision-based forgiveness, the most metaphysically complex of the three, falls somewhere between hollow and emotional. Decision-based forgiveness "is defined as the cognitive letting go of resentment and bitterness and need for forgiveness. However, it is not always the end of emotional pain and hurt."[73] This intermediate category between hollow and emotional suggests that forgiveness is not simply a black-and-white category – while there is certainly forgiveness and unforgiveness, there is also a curious combination of the two in which one can affect forgiving qualities while still holding on to one's pain and anger. This affect is not so much a lie, but rather a performance so personal that it actually works to suspend the disbelief of forgivers themselves, thus generating a split subjectivity in a single subject if simultaneously (un)forgiving.

The forgiveness Tutu required from South Africans must be classified as decision-based (and thus bifurcated, as opposed to whole), simply because even Tutu, the charismatic archbishop, could not demand that suffering individuals let go of their resentment toward a murderer or torturer, or the pain they felt over the loss of a loved one. Indeed, it is precisely at the point of the imperative that forgiveness always exceeds rationality: no matter what the reward (or punishment), forgiving is not a process that any individual, no matter what their authority, can compel a subject to undertake. Well aware of this, the archbishop was not obliging South Africans to forgive, which would amount to hollow forgiveness and only perpetuate fear and anxiety. Rather, Tutu encouraged South Africans to forgive by promising them a richer, healthier life when they did so: forgiveness, he writes, "is the greatest good, communal harmony that enhances the humanity and personhood of all in the community."[74]

When forgiveness is unpacked into a series of differently enacted stages, it is clear that Tutu was asking the victims of apartheid to act as if they had forgiven, to perform compassion and goodwill to the enemy without abandoning their physical and emotional pain. This is one example that fleshes out the ways in which recursivity functioned in Tutu's commission toward the construction of state morality: privileging decisional forgiveness, Tutu called for a performance of tolerance and compassion that clearly separates the action from the subject him/herself. What an individual does in this stage is not a reflection of an inner state of being, but is a contribution to an idealized moral order that promises to heal pain after the potentiality of the ideal itself is accepted.

By emphasizing the performance of forgiveness as a means to achieving a healthy, reconciled nation, Tutu evokes a classic religious formula developed by the seventeenth-century Christian philosopher Blaise Pascal, in which an individual performs an action (in Pascal's case, prayer) with the understanding that they will, given time, become that performance via the simple repetition of their actions. What makes Pascal's contribution to religious philosophy so interesting is that he does not begin with the idea that belief comes first. Rather, habit and ceremony maintain faith: "the external must be joined to the internal to obtain anything from God," Pascal writes, "that is to say, we must kneel, pray with the lips, etc., in order that proud man, who would not submit himself to God, may be now subject to the creature."[75] What Pascal is describing here is not simply a "fake it till you make it" performance of faith. Indeed, more profoundly, he is identifying recursivity as enacting a connection with the divine. Here, kneeling does not describe an inward, spiritual act; rather, it creates one in its (re)articulation. To take some liberty with Pascal's work, then, Tutu's translation of this principle – which, with its impossible appeal to forgiveness, is also dependent on a connection to the divine – would be: "take on the affectation of forgiveness and you will believe that you have forgiven."

Of course, what makes Pascal's and Tutu's insistence on recursivity different is that while Pascal calls for a specific action (kneeling down to pray), Tutu is asking that the South African people perform something that is much more abstract and difficult to capture in a single action or gesture. Indeed, because forgiveness (decisional and emotional) is such an abstract idea, Tutu needed subjects upon which survivors could model their forgiving behaviour. As such, he continually held up Mandela as a living testament to grace, contrition, and forgiveness. Tutu's reflections on the former president are pointed. In *No Future,* he writes about a moment when Mandela opened his home to his former torturers: "He [Mandela] invited his white jailer to attend his inauguration as an honoured guest, the first of many gestures he would make in his spectacular way, showing his breathtaking magnanimity and willingness to forgive."[76] Tutu's emphasis on Mandela's *performance* of forgiveness (his "gestures"), the expansiveness with which he was able to offer mercy to his former torturers, served as primary evidence to back up the thesis of his reconciliatory vision: no future without forgiveness.

Because of its exceptionally public nature and its dissemination through news, literature, and film, the South African TRC had a fundamental impact on the ways in which the international community understood and imagined reconciliation as a political possibility. In contrast to the Nuremberg trials, which built the stage on which South Africa then performed its morality, Tutu and South Africa reframed restitution and "victor's justice" within the contexts of restoration and forgiveness. This was a fundamental gesture toward reshaping the discourse by which states could talk about – or even conceive of – contending with violent pasts.

By conceiving of and implementing truth and reconciliation as a performed set of actions, Tutu also turned the TRC into a product: something that could be shipped across borders and overseas, taken out of the box, and unfolded in an entirely new environment. Following South Africa, "reconciliation" became a central term through which states engaged the theatre of regret via national commissions. Prominent examples include Sierra Leone's Truth and Reconciliation Commission (1999), the Peruvian Truth and Reconciliation Commission (2001), Ghana's National Reconciliation Commission (2002), Fiji's Reconciliation and Unity Commission (2005), the Truth, Justice, and Reconciliation Commission of Kenya (2008), and, of course, the TRC of Canada (2008).

Essential to recognizing Tutu's impact in shaping reconciliation as we understand it today is noting the centrality of forgiveness within that formula. In Tutu's model, and thus, I would argue, in the model Canada now sits with, "forgiveness" and "reconciliation" are inextricable terms and survivors must be willing to open their hearts, homes, and emotional well-being to their torturers. There is no future without forgiveness. Or, rather, there is no settler future without Indigenous surrender. This formulation opens up a number of uncomfortable and potentially dangerous situations that take on even more complex contours when set against the backdrop of settler colonialism. I devote Chapter 5 to unpacking those issues. Bringing Tutu into the conversation here, in Chapter 1, illustrates that forgiveness, much like transitional justice, has been built into the definition of reconciliation as it is employed today in places such as Canada. Deconstructing reconciliation in Canada, and, hopefully, replacing it with Indigenous epistemologies, means understanding the fundamental building blocks on which it has been (re)constructed.

Australia, 1991–Present: Council for Aboriginal Reconciliation (CAR) and Reconciliation Australia

Moving back a few years before the South African TRC was established, Australia illustrates how reconciliation, as a tool of international morality, can be recuperated by a settler colonial state. The TRCs in Chile and South Africa put in motion a particular new genre of Nuremberg ideology, re-centring moral politics around transitional justice and the rehabilitation of perpetrators. While not a TRC per se (there is no truth commission component to Australia's reconciliation movement), Australia's deployment of reconciliation parallels the model laid out by Aylwin in that it puts the emphasis of state intervention on the rehabilitation of society, with the purpose being the maintenance of existing power structures, which, in turn, limits the retributive authority of that intervention against perpetrators. Of course, in Australia, as in Uganda, the government that inflicted the wound is also the government attempting to suture it, which, as we have already seen, leads to some serious questions about ethics and intent.

In 1991, the Australian government unanimously voted to establish the Council for Aboriginal Reconciliation (CAR), initially branded to promote the "process of reconciliation between Aboriginal and Torres Strait Islander peoples and the wider Australian community."[77] This initiated a ten-year period of "official reconciliation," leading to the establishment of Reconciliation Australia in 2001, a non-profit organization that continues to "monitor Australia's progress towards reconciliation so that government, business, and the community can take on the responsibility to back up words with real commitment."[78] Conceived as a way to "address progressively"[79] Australia's Aboriginal/settler relations, Australian reconciliation has been passed to each incoming prime minister since and is an unavoidable fact of Australian politics.

From a bird's eye view, "reconciliation" is an integral part of Australia's political infrastructure. Aside from CAR and Reconciliation Australia, the country also hosts Australians for Reconciliation (AFR), the National Sorry Day Committee (NSDC), and the Reconciliation Action Plan, initiated by Prime Minister Julia Gillard in June 2011. On February 13, 2008, four months before Canadian prime minister Stephen Harper would do so, Australian prime minister Kevin Rudd issued a formal apology to the survivors of the Stolen Generations,[80] adding yet another layer to the state's ongoing performances of reconciliation and regret. In 2016, Reconciliation Australia released *The State of Reconciliation in Australia*, a ninety-nine page report summarizing and analyzing the country's quarter century of reconciliation projects between settlers and Australian Aboriginal and Torres Strait Islander peoples.[81] The intention of the report was "to spark a renewed national conversation about how, over the next 25 years, we [Australians and Aboriginal peoples] can move towards becoming a reconciled, just and equitable Australia."[82] Australia's history of reconciliation, which has generated an impressive number of policies and apologies, has produced a reconciliation infrastructure that runs deeper than any other in the world. As of this writing, it is a twenty-nine-year process. Depending on one's point of comparison, that is four, five, six, and in some instances even seven times longer than other reconciliation movements in the world.

Within that infrastructure, however, the largest, and for many the most moving, performance of reconciliation came when some 250,000 people walked across Sydney Harbour Bridge for the May 2000 "Reconciliation Walk."[83] The walk was organized so that both Aboriginal and non-Aboriginal Australians could show their support for Australia's reconciliation process, which was by this time almost a decade old. While there is some disagreement over the efficacy of a walk for reconciliation, many Australians saw the event as a foundational step toward better relations between Indigenous and non-Indigenous peoples. Reflecting on the event on its ten-year anniversary, Reconciliation Walk organizer Shelley Reys suggested that "many of the gains of the past 10 years can be traced directly to the walks of 2000 'because people were inspired to move.'"[84]

Aside from the large number of participants, the Reconciliation Walk is perhaps best remembered for a giant skywritten "Sorry" that was etched in the sky over the Sydney Opera House while the walk took place: indeed, the "Sorry" has become an iconic image in reconciliation media. Any online image search for the walk will produce photos of the skywriting, which dominates the skyline and looms over the crowd of walkers, like a giant, collective thought bubble. Damien Short notes that the gesture was not a government initiative but was financed by "a small North Queensland reconciliation group that had been deeply moved by the BTH [Bring them Home] report,"[85] connecting the display of regret to a wider public sentiment. Short, who attended the walk, notes that the gesture moved many to tears.[86] The grandiose moment quickly became part of the institutional memory as well: a photo capture of the image memorializes the event for the National Museum of Australia, serving as an imagistic introduction to the words Rudd finally composed for the official apology.[87]

Skywriting is pretty, but it doesn't last for long. As a spectacle of settler guilt and contrition, the "Sorry" contrail is an apt metaphor for Australian reconciliation specifically and settler reconciliation more generally. Whereas Tutu connected the discourse of reconciliation in South Africa to forgiveness, and thus to the role of the survivor in facilitating coexistence, in Australia, reconciliation, as established – at least partially – in this image, is connected to a discourse of apology, which centres perpetrator voices. As noted above, Australia did not offer an official apology to the Stolen Generations until 2008, but the sorry movement began a decade before that via the Sorry Books Campaign, organized by Australians for Native Title (ANT), a grassroots organization of Indigenous and non-Indigenous activists. The campaign was a direct response to the government's refusal to apologize to Torres Strait Islanders and Aboriginal peoples, and was thus a civil intervention into apology politics. The Sorry Books Campaign resulted in National Sorry Day, which, since 1998, has been held on May 26. According to Rosanne Kennedy, who writes on the social impact of the books, "Through the cultural medium of the Sorry Book, ordinary Australians expressed their feelings of regret, sorrow and compassion for the injustices that followed from European settlement, and particularly for the pain and suffering Indigenous Australians experienced as a result of government policies and practices of child removal."[88]

As I discuss in greater detail in Chapter 4, apologies provide a necessary role in drawing out lines of culpability and engaging perpetrators in the traditional dialectics of reconciliation: apology being one half of that dialectic (the perpetrator's), forgiveness being the other (the survivor's). That being said, the performance of a "Sorry" also has a way of distracting from the material facts of pain, anguish, and dispossession while centring settler guilt. An apology is not, despite the very real impact it can have on survivors, restitution unto itself.

In Australia, the performance and commodification of "Sorry" provided a space for settlers to vent guilt and shame without addressing the hard material realities of settler colonialism. Short, who has written extensively on Australian reconciliation and the politics of apology in Australia, argues that apology in Australia has done nothing to address Aboriginal peoples' sovereign claims to land or the fact that settler Australians enacted genocide to illegally claim those lands. Apology, in this circumstance, Short argues, "not only 'burie[s] a history of genocide' but it imagine[s] Australia as post-colonial when no meaningful structural or functional change to the colonial order has occurred."[89] The cynicism about Australian reconciliation is not limited to Australians. According to Jeff Corntassel, the attempts of civil society to compensate for the lack of a state apology via initiatives such as Sorry Books "failed to advance the project of reconciliation and may even have impeded it by fuelling a popular backlash."[90]

While "Sorry" captured the imagination of a country, and even the world, for a brief moment in time, it, like the contrail (which, it should also be noted, contains toxic pollutants harmful to the atmosphere), quickly faded, whisked away by the winds and absorbed into the literal and political atmospheres of Australia. Indeed, after Australian prime minister Kevin Rudd offered his apology, opposition leader Brendan Nelson delivered an address in which he "insisted that no generation can fully anticipate the long-term impact of its actions."[91] These neo-colonial remarks significantly undercut the message of reconciliation that both he and Rudd were attempting to convey – given that they effaced the ongoing effects of colonialism and severed the accountability of contemporary settlers. In response, Indigenous peoples and allies watching the proceedings outside on giant screens turned their backs "and began a slow, rhythmic clapping to drown out the rest of Nelson's speech."[92] As quickly as it was offered, the Australian apology was called into question.

The explicitly ephemeral nature of this apology can, in this sense, be directly connected to the meagre impact Australian reconciliation has had on the larger world of conflict resolution. Indeed, according to Short, "Australian reconciliation does not warrant a mention in any of the major texts on reconciliation despite the fact that it has been the longest running official process."[93] The lack of recognition that Short points out is due to the ephemeral nature of Australia's reconciliation politics. Because it does nothing to address the lived experiences of settler colonialism, Australian reconciliation is an empty signifier, devoid of transitional justice or forgiveness. But it is still instructive for us, given the way it is mobilized.

Indeed, when we avert our gaze from the skies, we see a very different idea of reconciliation on the ground in Australia. It is precisely the size of the apology performance that distracted from the material impacts of reconciliation for Aboriginal and Torres Strait Islander peoples in Australia. The 2016 reconciliation report found that "Aboriginal and Torres Strait Islander peoples still experience high levels of racial prejudice and discrimination. Thirty-three per cent of Aboriginal and Torres Strait Islander peoples had experienced verbal racial abuse in the six months before the survey."[94] Land dispossession remains at the top of the list of issues that continue to impact the lives and politics of Aboriginal peoples.[95] The report itself acknowledges that this fundamental issue remains buried beneath "a prevailing sense that Aboriginal and Torres Strait Islander peoples are responsible for their own disadvantage."[96] On the ground, at the level of lived experience in settler states, reconciliation is perpetually at risk of being levied against the people it claims to represent. Without acknowledgment of land claims, or the ongoing history of colonialism in Australia, this is unlikely to change.

As mentioned above, however, just because Australia's reconciliation has been mostly empty doesn't mean it isn't an important space for research. Like Chile and South Africa, Australia also made its own definitional contributions to reconciliation, which need to be folded into the genealogy I am collating here. By the time John Howard and his centre-right Liberal-National Coalition came to power in 1996, prominent land claims, such as *Mabo v. Queensland* (No.2),[97] had once again propelled Aboriginal rights in Australia into the international spotlight and put international pressure on Australia to adjust its official relationship with the Indigenous peoples it had murdered and displaced under *terra nullius*.[98] Thus, for his scene in Australia's theatre of regret, Howard and his government made a brash performative shift in Australian Aboriginal policy in order to demonstrate their commitment to international morality, while simultaneously working to protect colonial interests and resources. In order to enact this two-pronged colonial approach, Howard needed to revisit the language and put his own stamp on reconciliation. To that end, his government devised the phrase "practical reconciliation."[99]

Practical reconciliation was neo-liberal in intent, designed to redirect conversation away from the complex, and deeply fraught, sets of issues surrounding acknowledgment, apology, forgiveness, and redress toward outcomes that were easily quantifiable and could be checked off a relatively short to-do list. John Borrows itemizes that list and highlights its absurdity in his essay on practical reconciliation:

> The first [item on the list] is a shared commitment to improved living standards as part of providing equality of opportunity for all Australians. The second is an acknowledgement of the inter-related histories of Australia, where blame or guilt is not apportioned for past wrongs. The third objective is a mutual acceptance of the importance of working together and appreciating differences in a way that does not prevent people from sharing their futures together.[100]

As Borrows and others have already pointed out, practical reconciliation was a strategic colonial intervention into moral politics designed to undermine Aboriginal rights by focusing on ideas of formal equality and citizenship. According to William Jonas, the Aboriginal and Torres Strait Islander Social Justice Commissioner, writing in response to Howard, "Practical reconciliation ... strips Indigenous disadvantage of its historical context ... and admits no contemporary, ongoing consequences of this history. Consequently, there is nothing particularly distinctive about Indigenous disadvantage or about the response necessary to it."[101] In other words, practical reconciliation is reconciliation that actively ignores colonialism as the relevant context for the broken relationship. Under practical reconciliation, Aboriginal people's relationship to the state determined their rights. This form of recognition homogenized the public and precluded any special claims to land or history. The state maintained its colonial authority while simultaneously satisfying the public demand for contrition.

What Howard's government demonstrates is how, in a settler state, reconciliation can be mobilized as a tool of assimilation. Larissa Behrendt writes that Howard's practical reconciliation was little more than yet another assimilationist policy designed to eliminate the perceived "threat" of Aboriginal rights. Behrendt is not responding to Howard directly here, but rather reading his words through the lens of "practical reconciliation":

> The clear agenda, articulated more carefully and precisely by the Minister for Aboriginal Affairs, Phillip Ruddock, is one of assimilation and integration. This, of course, is not a new ideology, but a throwback to the paternalistic days when Welfare Boards and Aboriginal Protection Boards dictated the lives of Indigenous people and their children. It is an ideology that has been used in the past, did not work then, and has not only been rejected by Indigenous people, but has left a lasting legacy of disadvantage, trauma and family breakdown that is still plaguing Indigenous communities and families today.[102]

As Behrendt helps to illustrate, under the guise of moral benevolence and goodwill, reconciliation can be manipulated so as to reiterate the agendas of the settler state. Not only does this have the potential to reenact centuries-old colonial policy, but it can also inflict further harm under the auspices of healing and restoration. In much the same way I have argued that Uganda's commission is not an anomaly in the reconciliation genealogy, then, I contend that practical reconciliation does not represent an irregularity in settler reconciliation discourse. This is to say that while Howard's intervention in reconciliation politics is now muted beneath a more "progressive" culture of reconciliation in Australia, the neo-liberal, assimilative character of reconciliation in a settler state resonates deeply into its future development. "Practical reconciliation" – reconciliation that makes sense to a reigning colonial government – is, in many senses, a contradictory phrase.

Australia helps to illustrate precisely the grand scale on which the theatre of regret can operate in settler states as a means to delimit and control Indigenous claims for redress. The core of the practice (practical reconciliation) evokes regressive colonialist tropes designed to control Aboriginal peoples and flatten difference. Yet in spinning out its politics in the contexts of the new state morality, the settler government is able to couch neo-colonial objectives in the larger political order demanded by the Nuremberg trials. The giant "Sorry" in the sky provides a baseline from which to consider the reiteration of Nuremberg principles in and by settler nations. By contributing to the Nuremberg discourse, Australia participates in the recursive ideology that recuperates and maintains human rights and establishes states as just. State politics operate beneath the word "Sorry," which becomes the structuring element of the national symbol. However, like skywriting, "Sorry" gradually fades and is forgotten while material conditions – land claims, sovereignty, self-determination – remain unchanged. Furthermore, the fact that things remain unchanged is then mobilized against Indigenous peoples as an example of their innate deficiency, in spite of state benevolence.

In this sense, "Sorry" is weaponized insofar as the underlying conditions do not change. The scale of the performance demonstrates the commitment to perpetuating Nuremberg ideologies and the new international order, which demands this gesture as a sign of belonging to a larger notion of international morality but does little to change the conditions on the ground, acknowledge colonialism, or initiate transitional justice. The walk for reconciliation and the skywriting itself establish how grand and ostentatious this performance has become and precisely how large the gap between "reconciliation" and "justice" in settler states can be.

Canada, 2008–2015: Truth and Reconciliation Commission

The question of whether the TRC of Canada is or is not transitional justice continues to stymie movement toward Indigenous-centred reconciliation. To be clear, it is not transitional justice. What I hope to have illustrated in the first part of this chapter is that the TRC of Canada is not an isolated event: it exists within a larger international context of tribunals, truth commissions, and TRCs, and is shaped by the language and history of international morality. The "beginning" of reconciliation in Canada, therefore, always already extends beyond the boundaries of the state and the particularities of its history. Thus, while the TRC model brings with it a particular order and gravitas, when the system is transplanted into new, colonial spaces, it necessarily creates tensions between the global and local. While one foundational idea, such as forgiveness, may be perfectly suited to the South African context, that same idea may be entirely inapplicable, or even detrimental, to reconciliation in Canada. The following chapters contend with the problems that arise when the TRC model, as it was developed out of a variety of international contexts, is transplanted to Indigenous territories. For example, I explore the deep problem of forgiveness in Chapter 5. In closing Chapter 1, however, I feel it is necessary to provide a little more contextual detail on reconciliation in Canada and to unpack one of the more volatile issues lost in translation across Chile, South Africa, and Canada: transitional justice.

The TRC of Canada developed out of the Indian Residential Schools Settlement Agreement (IRSSA), which, with the support of all parties involved (the Assembly of First Nations, Inuit representatives, churches, and the Government of Canada), received final court approval in March 2007. The largest class action lawsuit in Canada's history, the IRSSA aimed to specifically provide redress for the survivors of Indian Residential Schools, a national network of boarding schools funded by the Department of Indian Affairs and Northern Development and administered by Canadian churches. As with the Stolen Generations in Australia, residential schools represent only a small portion of the colonial violence in Canada.[103] The TRC thus offers only a limited perspective on settler history, but it does, crucially, provide recognition of tragic events that, as I demonstrate more carefully in the next chapter, are heavily repressed in the Canadian social order.

Residential schools were in operation from the 1880s to the end of the twentieth century. The last school closed in 1996, so the events are "historical" in name only.[104] These schools removed – often forcibly – tens of thousands of Indigenous children from their families and communities to live, learn, and work in church-run schoolhouses with the intent of assimilating the Indigenous population under the banner of progress.[105] Indeed, Duncan Campbell Scott, head of Indian Affairs from 1913 to 1932 and one of Canada's Confederation Poets, built a political platform based on assimilation. In 1876, Scott wrote, "The happiest future for the Indian race is absorption into the general population, and this is the object and policy of our government. The great forces of intermarriage and education will finally overcome the lingering traces of native custom and tradition."[106]

Conditions in the schools were often deplorable. Children were undernourished (sometimes purposefully),[107] teachers had few and sometimes no credentials,[108] labour was regularly privileged over education,[109] and many, many students were physically, mentally, and sexually abused.[110] The level of education that the students received was also exceptionally low. They were being trained to be a servile class, and assimilation was thus seen as assimilation into a lower social order.[111] Students were also forbidden to speak their own languages in the schools, alienating children from their families and inflicting deep cultural rifts.[112] Anishinaabe Elder Fred Kelly remembers his experiences at St. Mary's Residential School:

> My first memory of my entry into the school is a painful flashback. For whatever reason, I am thrown into a kneeling position. My head is bashed against a wooden cupboard by the boys' supervisor. Instant shock, the nauseating smell of ether, more spanking, the numbness; sudden fear returns at the sight of the man. Was this discipline or just outright cruelty? This had never happened to me before. Where is my dad? Where is my mother? They're not here. Where are my three older brothers? Step in if they dare – they see what's happening, they watch in horror, but they are helpless.[113]

The TRC of Canada is just one of five pieces of restitution developed out of the IRSSA for residential school survivors and their families. The other four portions of that agreement are the Common Experience Payment (CEP), the Independent Assessment Process (IAP), Health and Healing Services, and a Commemoration Fund.[114] Announced in 2008 and closing in 2015, the TRC of Canada was chaired by lawyer and judge Murray Sinclair and assisted by two other commissioners, Marie Wilson and Chief Wilton Littlechild.

While skillfully driven by Sinclair and his team, the TRC of Canada was not without its hiccups. On October 20, 2008, only six months after receiving the appointment as the first chair of the commission, Harry Laforme, an Ontario court of appeal judge, resigned from that position. Laforme's reason for leaving was his inability to square his opinions on the matter with his two commissioners, attorney Jane Brewin Morley and Native health expert Claudette Dumont-Smith. According to the Canadian Broadcasting Corporation (CBC), Morley and Dumont-Smith wanted to focus on "uncovering and documenting truth," while Laforme wanted the emphasis to be on "reconciliation between aboriginal and non-aboriginal Canadians."[115] Even in that brief discussion, we can hear the resonances of the TRC genealogy: truth vs. reconciliation.

Because the commissioners failed to recognize the ultimate authority of the chair, Laforme asserted, the TRC was no longer able to move forward: "At the heart of it is an incurable problem," he wrote in a letter to Chuck Strahl, Minister of Indian Affairs. "The two commissioners are unprepared to accept that the structure of the commission requires that the commission's course is to be charted and its objectives are to be shaped ultimately through the authority and leadership of its chair."[116] After its initial committee collapsed, on June 10, 2009, the TRC appointed Sinclair, Manitoba's first Indigenous judge, to the committee along with Wilson and Littlechild. Sinclair served as the chair of the TRC through the remainder of its six-year mandate, championing both truth and reconciliation, and inciting settler Canadians toward education and improved relationships.[117]

Setting Sinclair's successful intervention aside for the moment, the internal divisions that led to the collapse of the initial TRC highlight a conflict at the heart of reconciliation in Canada: that is, the tension between truth and reconciliation. When examined in the larger history of TRCs, we can see that Morley and Dumont-Smith were committed to a South American model that forefronted the gathering of truth as the essential task of the commission. Laforme, on the other hand, was invested in a model of resolution and understanding that would bring previously divided groups together – which, of course, reflects more directly models in South Africa and Australia. That those differences in opinion were ultimately irreconcilable speaks to a central conflict implicit in the definition of reconciliation in the Canadian context: would the TRC of Canada be, like the one in Australia, beyond truth? Or would it re-centre truth telling and archiving, harking back to the TRC's foundations in Nuremberg? Sinclair's time as chair of the commission straddled this dialectic in such a way that the discussion between the two models contained much more grey area, but Laforme's resignation is instructive insofar as it lays out a key tension in the Canadian context of the TRC.

In locating the TRC of Canada within its larger genealogy, there are key and telling differences between the TRCs in Chile and South Africa and the TRC in Canada. The most glaring is that, in contrast to those in Chile and South Africa, the TRC of Canada was extra-governmental, meaning that it was created to exist beyond, or even counter to, the control and regulation of the state. Because this TRC aimed to address the violence committed against Indigenous peoples by a government that remained in power, the extra-governmental appointment was a necessary one to avoid a recapitulation of Amin's 1976 commission, in which the perpetrator was at once defendant, jury, and judge.

While the extra-governmental commission was thus a requirement for an independent investigation, it also threw into relief a rather vital and unavoidable point: that is, that the TRC of Canada was *not* a product of transitional justice, that it was *not* a handmaiden to major political reform, and that it was *not* an investigation into the specific crimes of perpetrators. Indeed, as TRC scholar and lawyer Ronald Niezen illustrates, the Truth and Reconciliation Commission of Canada was "victim-centred," meaning that it had "no range of authority that might lead to some sort of reckoning for the responsible or extend the information it receives beyond a focus on victim narratives."[118] This is all to say, that while the TRC of Canada provided a space in which to critique the modes of power that led to residential schools, it was never in a position to facilitate, in terms of infrastructure, concrete political change or transition into a new government.

As I have demonstrated above, Nuremberg principles have traditionally been used to enforce measures of transitional justice for states beset by violence – the primary examples being Chile and South Africa.[119] In transitional settings, the most immediate and material response to historical injustice is the removal of the government that perpetrated the crimes and the installation of a democratic administration. The succeeding truth commission or TRC is thus a way to both redress the past *and* facilitate a smooth changeover to new leadership. In settler states such as Canada, where the colonial government that inflicted the wound remains in power as the wound is being treated, we must, in good faith, keep reconciliation, truth, and transitional justice as mutually exclusive terms.

While it is certainly true, as Matt James points out, that political "transition" is often a murky terrain (for example, while Aylwin had power in Chile, he was still very much beholden to the previous Pinochet dictatorship),[120] in Canada there has only ever been a colonial government since confederation. This is not to say that there were no governments previous to colonization – indeed, since time immemorial there have been Indigenous governments on these territories – but rather that, in terms of the authority of the nation-state, government in Canada has remained constant and adhered to the legacy of settler colonialism. No transition preceded the announcement of the TRC and no transition followed it. In Canada as in Australia, reconciliation is not transitional justice.

There is a significant difference between transitional reconciliation, which has been at the core of the TRC model since its initiation in Chile, and what I am calling the theatre of regret, in which concrete political transition is never a part of the terms of conversation. As I illustrate above, with comparison across reconciliation movements in Chile, South Africa, and Australia, the fact of political transition (or lack thereof) plays a major role in shaping what the subsequent reconciliation will look like. On the one hand, transitional reconciliation is developed out of governmental transformation (or even revolution), resulting in the political mobilization of reconciliation to facilitate the shift of power. On the other hand, in the theatre of regret, when no significant shift in power has taken place and the fundamental core of political power remains untouched, reconciliation is founded on the promise of change and performances that convince the audience that while the government remains structurally and ideologically unchanged, it will now *act* differently.

To put this another way, without explicit political change to support it, settler reconciliation is performance only for the sake of performing; settler reconcilers differentiate themselves from the "traditional" TRC genealogy (which excludes Amin, of course) not by conceding the stage to new political actors, but by promising to take on different roles. According to Glen Coulthard, in settler colonial states "reconciliation must ideologically manufacture such a transition by allocating the abuses of settler colonization to the dustbins of history."[121] Australia helps to demonstrate this kind of reconciliation at work insofar as the message of reconciliation is loudly stated over a long period of time, but the content (that is, the lived conditions of Indigenous peoples) remains largely unchanged. To quote Ray Jackson, spokesperson for Aboriginal peoples in Australia, "the Federal Government continues to insult our Elders and Leaders. They continue to malign our true history. They continue to steal the land. All with impunity. Yet they talk of reconciliation."[122] In the theatre of regret, settler anxieties around the fact of Indigenous dispossession often result in performative over-compensations (such as giant, skywritten apologies) that facilitate settler moves to innocence and obscure more fundamental issues of sovereignty, self-determination, and land rights.

In the age of the theatre of regret, apology also benefits the state. In "Wrestling with the Past: Apologies, Quasi-Apologies, and Non-Apologies in Canada," Matt James identifies the symbolic capital of political apology and the ways in which Canada "has managed to extract unseemly political advantage from its participation in apology processes."[123] He builds this argument by measuring apologies offered by the Canadian government, including apologies to Japanese Canadians, residential school survivors (via Jane Stewart's "Statement of Reconciliation"), Italian Canadians, and Inuit families displaced during the "high Artic Exiles," against rigorous criteria developed out of the critical literature on state apology. According to James, an authentic apology, by which he means an apology that addresses and supports survivors and does not overly benefit the apologizer, must meet the following conditions:

> The apology must be recorded officially in writing
> The apology must name the wrongs in question
> The apology must accept responsibility
> The apology must state regret
> The apology must promise non-repetition
> The apology must not demand forgiveness
> The apology must not be hypocritical or arbitrary
> The apology must undertake – through ceremony and reparation – to engage morally with [the] wronged[124]

Applying these criteria against the apologies listed above, James concludes that, moving from Brian Mulroney's apology to Japanese Canadians in 1988, Canada has demonstrated "a trend of increasing deficiencies in recording the relevant words, naming the wrongs done, taking responsibility, expressing regret, seeking forgiveness, and providing adequate ceremony and publicity."[125]

Yet while the moral efficacy of Canadian state apologies has been steadily declining, the state's ability to cash in on the symbolic capital of those apologies has not. Referencing the sociologist William J. Goode's findings on the human tendency to give undue admiration for below-average performances, James notes: "This observation applies to the Canadian state's performance in the field of political apology."[126] And the trend continues. On November 28, 2017, Prime Minister Justin Trudeau apologized to Canada's LGBTQ communities for what has been referred to as the "gay purge": decades of discrimination against queer and trans peoples in the Canadian Armed Forces and RCMP. In 2018, a judge approved a class-action settlement for survivors (up to $175,000 individually, $110 million total) that had lost their jobs or been overlooked for promotion because of their sexual orientation. The story was widely reported in international newspapers, including the *New York Times*, and used as a platform to bolster nationalist rhetoric while distinguishing ourselves as the benevolent neighbour to the rough justice of the United States. For instance, R. Douglas Elliott, lead lawyer for the plaintiffs in the settlement, told the *New York Times* that "it's something we can be extremely proud of in Canada ... At a time when America is going backward and trying to reintroduce discrimination, we are moving forward and facing this historic injustice."[127] Just four days earlier, Trudeau had offered an apology to former students of residential schools in Labrador and Newfoundland, who were not included in Harper's 2008 apology. Trudeau's "sorry" came following a $50-million settlement from another class-action lawsuit. While certainly subtler than Elliott's remarks regarding the LGBTQ apology, the apology Trudeau offered to these survivors was aimed at reinforcing national pride, albeit couched in the rhetoric of reconciliation and Canada's bicentennial:

> All Canadians possess the ability to learn from the past and shape the future. This is the path to reconciliation. This is the way to heal the relationship between Indigenous and non-Indigenous people in Canada. Today's apology follows on the heels of a historic new approach to reconciliation between Canada and Indigenous peoples. And this year, as we reflect on 150 years of Confederation across Canada, we have an opportunity to pause – to think about the future we want to create, that we must create, that we will create, together, in the coming decades and centuries.[128]

Trudeau's appeal to "all Canadians" presupposes a reconciliation with Indigenous peoples, not based in self-determination or sovereignty, but in a liberal multicultural framework in which the settler state is the container and Indigenous peoples are the content. In this sense, "healing" becomes a measure of relegating violence against Indigenous peoples to the past (as something to "reflect" on), leaving the present-day, ongoing effects of settler colonialism unaddressed.

In this sense, Trudeau's remarks are actually quite similar to Elliott's in that they strive to define Canada as a more just society in its willingness to contend with its past. Indeed, by folding the bicentennial into his remarks, Trudeau frames this apology as a break in the colonial legacy from which Canadians can fortify a more just existence. In this way, Trudeau performs a political transition out of the residential school era rather than acknowledging his government's extension of settler colonial violence.

Indeed, building from Coulthard, I argue that because transition is, given its history with the TRC model, such a significant part of what reconciliation "is," it cannot be entirely erased from a settler paradigm. Rather, the resonance of transitional justice persists in the trace as reconciliation is reiterated across colonial borders. For instance, the apology offered by former prime minister Stephen Harper for Indian Residential Schools represents a particular performative choice for Canada, which both calls back to and obscures political transition simultaneously. I quote from Harper's apology at length to give a sense of the very careful language he and his speechwriters used in this historic apology:

> It has taken extraordinary courage for the thousands of survivors that have come forward to speak publicly about the abuse they suffered. It is a testament to their resilience as individuals and to the strength of their cultures. Regrettably, many former students are not with us today and died never having received a Full Apology from the Government of Canada. The government recognizes that the absence of an apology has been an impediment to healing and reconciliation. Therefore, on behalf of the Government of Canada and all Canadians, I stand before you, in this Chamber so central to our life as a country, to apologize to Aboriginal peoples for Canada's role in the Indian Residential Schools system.[129]

In this apology, which was offered to survivors and their families in the House of Commons, Harper makes sure to clearly distinguish his government from those that committed the crimes against Indigenous peoples. By doing so, he performs the transition that in other states founds the apology. In the passage I quote from above, Harper clearly delineates his party from those that refused to apologize by the absence of their formal statements of regret: "The government recognizes that the absence of an apology has been an impediment to healing and reconciliation." In earlier passages of the same apology he demonstrates a change in attitude from those who perpetrated the original offending legislation: "Today, we recognize that this policy of assimilation was wrong, has caused great harm, and has no place in our country." What Harper is essentially doing here is reiterating that political transition on which Chile and South Africa based their reconciliation initiatives as a nearly immaterial speech act: since there is no literal political transition, he performs one in the apology itself, differentiating himself from, or disavowing, the political power that he and his government have directly inherited. Sarah Maddison and Laura Shepherd identify this type of "weak" transition as a product of the misplaced temporality of transitional justice within the settler colonial paradigm. In confining violence to the past (that is, to previous colonial governments), Harper arbitrarily assigns transition to his cabinet while disavowing the ongoing effects of colonial power. Unless transition is understood as the possibility of "radical transition *within the established society*" [emphasis in the original], as Maddison and Shepherd argue, transitional justice only further obfuscates colonial violence and reifies settler colonialism.[130]

That the Canadian government is, in fact, engaging weak transition in its own paradigm of reconciliation is perhaps nowhere better evidenced than in the Supreme Court's decision on the 2017 Ktunaxa case, which was initially ruled on while I was in the midst of working on this manuscript. In 2012, the Ktunaxa Nation appealed to Canada's highest court after British Columbia refused to stop the development of a proposed ski resort on Qat'muk, land the Ktunaxa see as sacred. According to the Aboriginal Peoples Television Network (APTN), representation for the Ktunaxa "argued that charter of rights protections for freedom of religion must include not only spiritual beliefs, but also underlying sacred sites, in this case the presence of Grizzly Bear Spirit in Qat'muk."[131] The nine judges of the Supreme Court, however, unanimously agreed that the Canadian *Charter of Rights and Freedoms* does not protect sacred sites. The judges used the language of reconciliation to make this decision: "We arrive at these conclusions cognizant of the importance of protecting Indigenous religious beliefs and practices, and the place of such protection in achieving reconciliation between Indigenous peoples and non-Indigenous communities."[132]

The Ktunaxa case helps to illustrate what critics of settler reconciliation believed all along: namely, that "reconciliation," in the settler vocabulary, has been recuperated as a means to further abstract Indigenous sovereignty and self-determination while reifying settler authority over land. The language of the decision establishes that while the "idea" of Indigenous rights is protected by the Canadian system, reconciliation means that when it comes to land and development, Indigenous peoples will have to cede to the will of the state. The Ktunaxa decision makes plain that reconciliation in Canada is not transitional justice, inasmuch as the decision illustrates, unflinchingly, that the colonial state is the sovereign.

Given that political transition is only performed in Canada, reconciliation rests on a much different, and potentially unstable, political ground than in Chile and South Africa. Canadian reconciliation relies on a language and a history that cannot readily be transported to a colonial system and thus radically alters the trajectory of reconciliation politics at a global level. That is to say, whereas transition and reconciliation are mutually constitutive in Chile and South Africa, in Canada, Harper used reconciliation to validate the performance of transition, re-establishing the TRC legacy as simulacra. The performance of the TRC legacy in settler reconciliation is thus a transition that is distinct from political change – but nonetheless relies on the history of reconciliation as transition as a way to validate its existence.

Indigenous Critiques of "Reconciliation" in Canada

While it is intimately, and perhaps impossibly, entwined with Christian ideology and Western politics, the idea of reconciliation does not belong to Western theory alone. Arthur Manuel, Grand Chief Ronald Derrickson, Glen Coulthard, Audra Simpson, Dallas Hunt, Gina Starblanket, Billy-Ray Belcourt, Daniel Heath Justice, Hadley Friedland, Val Napoleon, Heidi Kiiwetinepinesiik Stark, and Leanne Betasamosake Simpson, among many others, have all produced rigorous and critical Indigenous frameworks through which to consider and critique the possibility of reconciliation in Canada: frameworks that are built in relation to the lands, stories, and peoples of the territories on which the concept is unfolding. Understanding reconciliation means listening to the peoples on whose lands that concept is being enacted and whose histories it claims to redress.

Napoleon and Friedland, for instance, investigate the power of story as a means to reconsider reconciliation as a resurgent iteration of Indigenous law. They use the TRC of Canada and its final report as leverage for an argument for Indigenous legal traditions. According to the TRC final report, "Aboriginal peoples must be recognized as possessing the responsibility, authority, and capability to address their disagreements by making laws within their communities. This is necessary to facilitating truth and reconciliation with Aboriginal societies."[133] Recognizing, facilitating, and building Indigenous law explicitly and materially positions reconciliation in relation to decolonization in that it interrupts the false logic of *terra nullius* and re-establishes Indigenous connection to land via legal traditions that date back thousands of years.[134] Establishing Indigenous law as a principle of reconciliation unsettles the founding legal principles on which the settler state is constructed and reconstructs Indigenous peoples as legitimate stewards of the land. Napoleon and Friedland argue that "Indigenous legal traditions are fundamentally about Indigenous citizenry, self-determination, and governance."[135] Stark illustrates that Indigenous diplomatic negotiation existed without settler interference and can be traced far before contact.[136]

Napoleon and Friedland's intervention into reconciliation in Canada is not a romanticization of pre-contact legal traditions but a direct and practical contention with the legal issues that Indigenous peoples are facing today and will continue to face in the future: "It is our belief that Indigenous stories should live out in the world with us today," they state in the final sentence of the essay, "fully and all the time."[137] Napoleon and Friedland bring stories into the present and future by engaging storytelling as a dynamic iteration of Indigenous law, which can both transmit historical knowledge and simultaneously respond to contemporary contexts.[138]

At the core of their argument is the assertion that Indigenous stories themselves were never meant to be static, lifeless objects. Rather, they are given meaning and life in their (re)telling – in the response and responsibility that open in the space between storyteller and audience: "Stories are not preserved by being passively passed on by infallible elders in some immaculate, if increasingly mysterious or obscure, form. Rather stories are part of a serious public intellectual and interactive dialogue involving listeners and learners, and elders and other storytellers – as they have been for generations."[139] These authors argue that Indigenous law is implicit to stories and cannot only be drawn out by close, careful reading, but can also be applied in ways that directly respond to contemporary issues while establishing Indigenous contexts for contending with those issues. Stories, they argue, provide the legal infrastructure to build citizenry, self-determination, sovereignty, and relationality, and, with these, perhaps also reconciliation.

In this sense, the work that Napoleon and Friedland are doing from their perspectives as legal scholars lands very close to what Indigenous literary scholars, such as Daniel Heath Justice, are thinking about when they situate story as a means to grapple with identity and our relationships to others. In *Why Indigenous Literatures Matter,* Justice suggests that

> our lives are incarnations of the stories we tell, the stories told about us, and the stories we inherit. They are both the process and the consequence of the transformations into the fullness of our humanity. Indeed, without those stories, without the teachings about the who, how, and why of us, something is profoundly, almost existentially amiss. We don't need to speak them to live them; even those not given voice are inextricably embraided in our sense of self. We know ourselves *only* through stories. The unstoried life is a terrible thing to comprehend, a soul-deep desolation.[140]

Justice, Napoleon, and Friedland argue that Indigenous stories extend well beyond entertainment and documentation. At the core of their arguments is the idea that stories hold fundamental and necessary roadmaps for locating ourselves in relationship to the land, in relationship to more-than-human kin, and in relationship to the other. Indeed, one of the primary questions Justice thinks we should ask of Indigenous stories is "what is it to become and live as a good relative?"[141] In this sense, Indigenous stories can do much more than narrate reconciliation or provide models of critique. They are maps for formally realigning our relationships to ourselves and those around us. They are models of praxis that centre Indigenous knowledges, traditions, and futures.

Story as relationship is a big part of Napoleon and Friedland's methodology. In their essay, they describe a law and story workshop that they organized, which illustrates a praxis of reconciliation as it develops out of legal engagement with Indigenous stories:

> Unlike a typical conference in which academics deliver papers while the audience sits and listens, in this workshop, academics, professionals, and Indigenous community members worked together in small groups to analyze ten Cree and ten Dene stories using the adapted legal analysis method with the help of a trained facilitator. These small groups then came together in two larger groups to collectively synthesize the principles identified through the legal analysis of the stories. Following the collective synthesis, the participants again divided into small groups and looked at the principles from the perspective of the women in the stories to promote consciousness of gender issues. Finally, using the synthesized legal principles and attending to gender and power dynamics, each group told the new story to the larger group.[142]

The workshop described above began with a bannock-making competition, in which academics, professionals, and Indigenous community members were grouped together and tasked with making bannock using unusual ingredients, such as almond milk and brown rice flour. The exercise was aimed at creating community and relationships between Indigenous and settler participants, while unsettling the expectations of "expertise" that pervade academic conferences.

With this community foundation in place, individual groups worked together to analyze the content and form of the stories using an "internal viewpoint" as an interpretive methodology. An internal viewpoint interpretation means reading the stories from the contexts, epistemologies, and territories of their inception: resisting non-Indigenous literary interpretation and Western models of analysis.[143] The goal of the workshop was to provide "an alternative access to Indigenous law that community members and members of the broader legal community can consciously apply in order to draw on intellectual resources for framing and resolving contemporary issues."[144] This is to say, out of collective readings of the stories arise Indigenous legal frameworks that are constructed not as the application of historical principles to contemporary contexts, but as grounded, living Indigenous legal engagement formulated out of active listening and community development. In this sense, Napoleon and Friedland not only offer an essential model for thinking about Indigenous legal traditions in the context of the TRC, but they also model an act of reconciliation: centred on Indigenous contexts, built from active listening and deconstructed power dynamics, and formulated in direct response to the fallacious legal structures of settler colonialism, namely *terra nullius*.

Aside from story, treaty processes and the relationships that arise out of them also bear fertile space for thinking about reconciliation from within Indigenous contexts. Treaty and reconciliation come from very different political contexts, but they are both grounded in relationality. Heidi Kiiwetinepinesiik Stark argues that, at their cores, "treaties are about making relationships."[145] Indeed, Stark's work illustrates that, if rigorously addressed from Indigenous perspectives, treaties, like stories, can serve as activation points from which to conceive our relationships to the other. "[Treaties] were not mere agreements that ceded one thing in exchange for another," Stark continues. "They carried commitments that did not end with the exchange of land for annuities. These agreements connected people. Treaties were a vision for what a multinational society could entail."[146] Inasmuch as treaties are about making respectful relationships, they are also about engaging with centuries-long practices of diplomatic negotiations that have been built out of the territories on which the TRC of Canada, and reconciliation itself, are now unfolding. Stark's work, for instance, illustrates the long-standing practices of Anishinaabe diplomacy and the formal practices through which those communities oriented themselves in relation to other peoples and nations.

This is only a piece of the large body of work that examines the effort Indigenous peoples have put into diplomatic processes. In his historical work on the Plains Cree, John Milloy writes, "Far from being the romantic wild riders of the plain, the Cree ... were engaged in a set of well-structured, inter-tribal relationships which were designed to ensure their security, to assist them in meeting the challenges of plains existence and to facilitate the acquisition of the good things in their world."[147] While settler colonialism and the myths of *terra nullius* work to delegitimize Indigenous law and diplomacy, there are detailed and sophisticated structures to draw from as a framework for reconciliation: "Indigenous peoples have always had governance," Kiera Ladner writes.[148] The question now is whether that governance can be read into contemporary reconciliation politics, and if doing so is even desirable (and, if so, for whom?). Stark addresses this question, building out of the notion of treaty as relationship, by looking into what she identifies as the three core principles of Anishinaabe treaty making: mutual respect, responsibility, and renewal. 1) Respect refers to holding the other in high esteem, speaking well of them, and treating them fairly; 2) responsibility refers to acting out of reciprocal obligation to the other and being accountable to previous agreements; and 3) renewal refers to the ongoing respect and responsibility that provide for the continuation of treaty and mutually beneficial relationship. Importantly, these principles are not human-centric. They are framed within a larger understanding of accountability to the renewal of the land and relationships with more-than-human kin.[149]

According to Stark, Indigenous treaties were built "as a living relationship,"[150] which operated far beyond the narrow confines of the treaty document into the relationships that developed before, after, around, and during the arrangement of the document:

> Treaties created relationships among nations. They established relationships of trust. That trust did not end with the completion of a written document; it merely began with it. However, it was the responsibility of all parties involved to maintain the relationships established through treaty making. The sustainability of these agreements was dependent upon each nation adhering to the principles of respect, responsibility, and renewal.[151]

Treaty, in the way Stark conceives of it from Anishinaabe tradition, is relational in the sense that it is about the actions, conversations, exchanges, supports, and hospitalities that occurred in, around, and through the written documentation named "treaty." Like the engagement with story that Napoleon and Friedland describe, "reconciliation," in this conception, would be derived from the ongoing processes of engagement with the object (i.e., engagement with the final report of the TRC or the ninety-four Calls to Action), rather than from the document itself.

Treaty is thus, for Stark, a verb rather than a noun. In this sense of treaty as verb, as action and engagement, I am again drawing from Justice, who also presses his readers to imagine relationality as an active, reciprocal process born out of responsibility and compassion. Justice formulates his conception of relationality in terms of kinship, but the resonances with Stark's work are illuminating: as with Stark's conception of treaty, "kinship isn't a static thing; it's dynamic, ever in motion. It requires attentiveness; kinship is best thought of as a verb rather than a noun, because kinship, in most Indigenous contexts, is something that's done more than something that simply is."[152] Like Stark, Justice asks us to consider the deep and ongoing modalities of care and attentiveness that are required in building and maintaining relationships, outside the stagnant interpretations of treaty rights, which he addresses directly:

> While the language of treaties all too often erases relational understandings and replaces them with the Eurowestern language of land-as-object, the guiding purpose behind the defense of treaty rights is as much (or more) about ensuring the ongoing maintenance of the ceremonies and rituals that ensure good relationships with the rest of creation as it is the defense of limited natural resources.[153]

The kinship model Justice unpacks acknowledges that relationships are not documents; they are acts of care and compassion that provide for sovereignty in ways that embrace the volatility of being in relation to the other, "opening room for the return of those models of self-determination that speak to the survival and presence of indigenous peoples, not simply the durability of individuals of Indigenous ancestry."[154] As Justice makes plain here, sustainable relationality is future-oriented, looking not only to the protection of land and resources, but also to care and cultivation, or, to use Stark's vernacular, renewal. The models of relationality that Justice and Stark offer here unsettle reconciliation in productive ways: they centre land and Indigenous epistemologies as means to evoke and engage relationships between Indigenous peoples and settlers in Canada; they place land and sustainability at the forefront of the conversations; and, building out toward one of the theses in this book, they lend support to the notion that reconciliation is a structure, not an event – which is to say that relationship cannot be confined to a final document, handshake, signature, or celebration. What Stark and Justice both offer is a model to conceive reconciliation as an ongoing network of trust and sustainability, oriented in relation to relationship and renewal.

That being said, in its unsettling, the emphasis on relationship and care offered in these critiques also refocuses reconciliation on some familiar TRC principles – for instance, the "love thy neighbour" tenets out of which Desmond Tutu built the South African commission.[155] Legal scholar Robert A. Williams Jr. writes that treaty provides "a way of imagining a world of human solidarity where we regard others as our relatives."[156] The principles of respect, responsibility, and renewal that Stark lays out in her work provide the means to conceptualize love, care, and human solidarity outside of the Christian framework that Tutu injects into the TRC model, but both Stark and Justice frame "neighbour love" as radical acts of care and relationality that hold up Indigenous diplomacy and therefore Indigenous ways of defining the neighbour as such. In appealing to the maintenance and respect of the borders defined in treaty, Stark and Justice, much like Napoleon and Friedland, provide decolonial relational frameworks, insofar as they reorient the maintenance of neighbour relationships in relation to the land, and privilege the knowledges and traditions that continue to spring from the land through and with Indigenous peoples.

If Stark and Justice provide the means to loop back into the larger, international, reconciliation discourse, they do so in a way that necessitates place-based analysis, not the overarching, universalist conceptions that are attached to Tutu's Christian superstructure. "Love thy neighbour," for instance, if it can, in fact, be translated into Anishinaabe contexts, must be rigorously read through protocols of respect, responsibility, and renewal if the concept is to be legible in this place and in relation to the peoples for which "reconciliation" is being named. Treaty provides a means to think about reconciliation insofar as it frames relationality in terms of established Indigenous diplomacy and protocol. As such, it provides tangible, respectful borders from which to conceive the universalist tenets of love and forgiveness that make up the larger discourse of the TRC as it arises out of the international context.

Finally, I put "reconciliation" in scare quotes in the header for this section because it is important to note that, because of the way the term has been co-opted by white settler Canadians, the term is replete with undertones of colonization and assimilation, and is therefore of limited or no use to many Indigenous authors. I am thinking specifically of writers such as Leanne Betasamosake Simpson, who in *This Accident of Being Lost* identifies reconciliation not as a gesture toward "harmony" between Indigenous and non-Indigenous peoples, but as a tool to be deployed strategically by Indigenous peoples, as a means to placate a settler class that would otherwise work against Indigenous peoples and their ways of life. For instance, in the short story "Plight," a group of Nishnaabekwewag called the Fourth World Problems Collective (FWPC) constructs a detailed plan to collect maple syrup from their territory, despite settler interference. The plan arises not only as a means to collect the syrup, although this is something they are learning as well, given that settler colonialism works to divorce them from the practice. Rather, the FWPC needs an elaborate plan to placate the settlers who otherwise might take offence at Indigenous peoples in "their" neighbourhoods. In order to facilitate syrup gathering, and existence on their own territories, the FWPC must "hand out ... flyers first. Have a community meeting. Ask permission. Listen to their paternalistic bullshit and feedback. Let them bask in the plight of the Native people so they can feel self-righteous."[157]

Reconciliation, when it comes up for the FWPC, is an extension of this list. It is yet another means to appeal to settler benevolence so that the FWPC might continue doing what their ancestors have always done on the land. In other words, "make them [settlers] feel better, and when reconciliation comes up at the next dinner party, they can hold us up as the solution and brag to their friends about our plight."[158] Reconciliation is, for the FWPC, useful only insofar as it can be mobilized strategically to advance resurgence and protect tradition. It works because reconciliation carries cultural capital for liberal white settlers, and evoking it provides opportunity for a performance in which "they can be part of the solution without doing anything."[159] This deployment of reconciliation is strikingly different to its uses in Chile or South Africa, but it gestures toward a means by which it can be strategically recast and reclaimed by Indigenous peoples in Canada, despite the ways in which it has been captured by colonial ideology.

Along with Simpson, who has done so much to challenge settler complacency in the TRC era, I am thinking here also of the work of young, queer Indigenous authors and poets, such as Billy-Ray Belcourt, who are rethinking the possibility of love and collectivity. Belcourt's inaugural poetry collection, *This Wound Is a World,* which won the 2018 Griffin Poetry Prize, is a profound and probing explication of (non)existence for queer Indigenous bodies in the violent wake of settler colonialism: "colonialism broke us," Belcourt writes in this collection, "and we're still trying to figure out how to love and / be broken at the same time."[160] These thirty-seven poems are not about reconciliation – the word never comes up in the collection – but they are about the struggle to love and be loved in a world that refuses to admit the existence of queer Indigenous bodies.

As the above quotation suggests, Belcourt's poetry works toward a being-together that is, in many ways, antithetical to the language of harmony and wholeness that pervades reconciliation discourse.[161] In the book's epilogue, Belcourt responds to Ann Cvetkovich and Karin Michalski's question "Is it possible to share the feeling of being lonely or alone as a way to make new forms of collectivity?," from *The Alphabet of Feeling Bad*, with the following: "*This Wound Is a World* insists that it is. It insists that loneliness is endemic to the affective life of settler colonialism, but that it is also an affective commons of sorts that demonstrates that there is something about this world that isn't quite right, that loneliness in fact evinces a new world on the horizon."[162] Much like Simpson, working against the popular discourse of reconciliation, *This Wound Is a World* offers an affective horizon attuned to the depression, alienation, and tears inflicted by settler colonialism and imagines a future in which those truths are not reconciled away, but remain productively, if not painfully, constitutive. This is a far cry from the Christian model of suffering and forgiveness propagated by Tutu and the TRC model that unfolds around him. It is a model of being "unbodied" and, in being unbodied, finding oneself in radical relation with the other as based in a shared precarity.[163]

The theme of radical relationality is evidenced again and again in poems throughout Belcourt's collection. For instance, in "If I Have a Body, Let It Be a Book of Sad Poems," he writes,

> If I have a body, let it be a book of sad poems. i mean it. indigeneity troubles the idea of "having" a body, so if i am somehow, miraculously, bodied then my skin is a collage of meditations on love and shattered selves.[164]

In these lines, Belcourt points to the ways in which settler colonialism renders Indigenous bodies less than, replacing history and human lives with stereotypes and Hollywood derivations of the "Indian." In re-bodying himself as a book of sad poems, the narrator in this passage imagines a (re)unification of "selves" that collectivizes brokenness qua brokenness. To build out of the psychoanalytic theory that Belcourt refers to in this same poem, the narrator of "If I Have a Body ..." gestures toward a modality of being, and of being with others, as an articulation of lack. From a Lacanian perspective, coming to terms with lack, or brokenness, is crucial to understanding self. In her reading of Lacan, Michaela Driver argues that "by listening to ambiguities, tangents, omissions, contradictions and other failed rhetorical constructions, we hear how subjects are experiencing fundamental lack as a presence they continue to circle in their own unique and creative fashion."[165] And while there is no cure for the condition of lack, in being attentive to it, in recognizing how it shapes human subjectivity, "we are freed momentarily from our illusions and the imaginary constructions that alienate us," that promise us, falsely, harmony and wholeness.[166] A theory of brokenness – a theory of lack – runs counter to the dominant discourse of reconciliation, which is variously defined as a process "providing a closure,"[167] or as a "truth that heals rather than divides."[168] Rather than looking toward wholeness and reconciliation, then, Belcourt's poetry articulates a community of care built out of the world of the wound and the affective potentiality of brushing against being and non-being.

While Belcourt's poetry compels us to imagine a world beyond the prevalent rhetoric and ideology of reconciliation, while it invites readers to imagine "this wound [as] a world," it is not an invitation for settler scholars to unearth, explore, and "discover" Indigenous pain and suffering. In this, Belcourt's poetry resonates deeply with Rebecca Belmore's *Apparition,* which is discussed in the Introduction. Indeed, a large part of what makes Belcourt's work antithetical to settler discourses of reconciliation, which imagine happy, harmonious relations between Indigenous and non-Indigenous peoples, is that it adheres to what David Garneau names as "irreconcilable spaces of Aboriginality"[169] – that is, "gatherings, ceremony, Cree-only discussions, kitchen-table conversations, email exchanges, etc. in which Blackfootness, Métisness, Indianness, Aboriginality, and/or Indigeneity is performed apart from a Settler audience"[170] – in which reconciliation, if we can call it that, is something produced only by and for Indigenous peoples. The penultimate paragraph of Belcourt's essay "Fatal Naming Rituals," which is addressed specifically to settler audiences, bluntly informs readers that "you are not invited into our tent. We are not yet at that point of hospitality. I will not tell you when this time has come."[171] The role of the settler in this discourse – which is *not* a discourse of reconciliation – is to unsettle the authority with which we lay claim to the description of Indigenous peoples and the description of colonial violence: "You need to read, to listen, and to write from someplace else," Belcourt tells settlers in the same essay, "from another social locus, a less sovereign one, a less hungry one."[172]

For both Belcourt and Simpson, authors who "break from colonial modes of storytelling," reconciliation does little, if anything, to contribute to the complex and elaborate worlds they imagine and (re)build.[173] And while white settlers so often turn to Indigenous authors and thinkers such as

Richard Wagamese and Chief Robert Joseph, authors who speak powerfully – and importantly – about the power of reconciliation, it is equally necessary to turn to authors who imagine otherwise. Authors who, in the midst of the theatre of regret, work against the compulsion of reconciliation and its primary mandates.

Conclusion

What I offer here, in Chapter 1, is a small but significant window into the trouble with reconciliation in Canada. I expand on many of these points in greater detail in the following chapters. The spectres of previous TRCs inevitably haunt its contemporary iterations – including the TRC of Canada. The history of TRCs also influences and limits the ways in which "reconciliation" can be mobilized to address Indigenous issues within a settler colonial state. Nuremberg, Uganda, Chile, South Africa, and Australia are all present, in varying degrees, in the reconciliation that now pervades Turtle Island and motivates Canadian political reform. The legacy, which I have begun to outline here, must be folded into analyses of the TRC of Canada or we risk overlooking the ways in which *form* can occlude and confuse *content,* thus precluding local contexts with universal mandates.

The historical through lines between reconciliation and transitional justice leave indelible marks on the TRC, which in Canada we see manifesting in dubious and potentially damaging ways. Being attentive to the history of reconciliation and the TRC allows us to be vigilant, aware of the traces that appear in their contemporary iterations and thus critical of their application. As I go on to demonstrate in the following chapters, Tutu's turn toward Christian models of forgiveness have left another troubling trace within the commission in Canada, as settler Canadians struggle for means to alleviate their guilt and, as stated in the TRC's mandate (Schedule "N"), "put the events of the past behind us."[174] I go into more explicit detail about the deep political problems that persist around reconciliation as forgiveness in Canada, particularly in Chapter 5. By teasing out the threads of reconciliation from its precedential successes and failures, we are better prepared to grasp how and why "reconciliation" fits into the puzzle of settler colonialism, but we also begin to formulate a working definition of what reconciliation "is" – not as floating signifier, waiting to be attached to the stray aftermath of historical violence, but as a political term with specific intents and consequences that have allowed it to persist and proliferate into present and future moments.

2

Listen to the Bones

Colonial Static and the Call for Reconciliation

The road to reconciliation is paved with g – dintentions.

– JOSHUA WHITEHEAD[1]

Weep for those who haven't yet sung.
Weep for those who will never sing.

– LOUISE BERNICE HALFE[2]

Joshua Whitehead's inaugural book of poetry, *Full-Metal Indigiqueer*, is a series of poems told through Zoa, a queer trickster figure rendered through the lens of technology. Whitehead combines cyberpunk tropes of the singularity, virus, and hacker in a narrator that inhabits and deconstructs the Western literary canon and popular media culture by infiltrating and rewriting the themes that define major works in either field. In doing so, Zoa re-centres queer Indigenous people within North American culture and makes space for voices that are typically relegated to the silence of the subaltern. "H3R314M" ("here I am"), the coded text that opens the book, and which also finds its way into a number of the poems, is the self-reflective compass by which Zoa locates themself within the labyrinth of literary and pop culture references that make up the book. *Full-Metal Indigiqueer* takes on a wide range of issues, from the oil sands and residential schools to Derridean archives and Lana Del Rey, to name a few. In the breadth of the book's scope, H3R314M is not a call for recognition or acknowledgment; it is an assertion of presence in the face of ongoing erasure. It holds space for Indigenous peoples in the past, present, and future, and it provides fresh, lucid perspectives on culture, technology, and politics in the contemporary moment.

The TRC is one of the spaces that Zoa works to locate themself within. In a number of poems, they unabashedly take on reconciliation and apology, often pointing to the failure of either to contribute anything to the recognition of queer Indigenous people. In the poem "you tell me you love me between two & three a.m.," for instance, Zoa informs the reader that "the road to reconciliation is paved with g – dintentions."[3] Here, Whitehead takes the phrase so often associated with the TRC ("the road to reconciliation") and, through the omission of letters in the additional clause ("paved with good intentions"), draws attention to the ways in which certain subjectivities are "paved over" when reconciliation depoliticizes intersectionality and re-inscribes colonial articulations of inclusion on Indigenous-settler relations. In this one line, Whitehead taps into a long history of Indigenous and queer erasure: national policy and legislation, such as the *Indian Act* and residential schools, for example, worked specifically to reduce Indigenous populations in Canada by assimilation and violent identity management. Erasure of queer Indigenous bodies was central to this project. Cindy Holmes and Sarah Hunt argue that, "inherent in [the colonial] project of erasure was the imposition of a binary system of gender which simultaneously imposed Indigenous rights and status along heterosexual lines and suppressed Indigenous systems of gender that went far beyond the gender binary."[4] By removing the *o*'s from the word "good" in the cited passage, Whitehead draws attention to the ways in which reconciliation risks reinstating this erasure and relegating queer Indigenous people to yet another "dint," or depression, of colonial legislation – hence "g – *dint*entions."

Pushing that reading further, however, the deleted *o*'s in this particular passage can also be read as zeros, which draws specific attention to the colonial binary that Holmes and Hunt reference – albeit here represented through the allegory of binary code, which is a patterned series of ones and zeros. There is an important double entendre here; the relationship between computer binary and gender binary is not coincidental. Anna Lauren Hoffmann writes that, "while issues of identity, data, and information systems seem to be – on one level, at least – an interesting conceptual or philosophical problem to ponder, they also expose the urgency of recognizing the very real and lived challenges these tensions and the rapid rise and adoption of data-intensive technologies and platforms generate for already vulnerable trans and queer populations."[5] Binary code is reflective of and instrumental in the reproduction of heteronormativity. In order for information to be stored in a digital archive, data is assigned a binary value, also known as a boolean, that is used to represent true or false statements: one is true, zero is false. The more concise (or "elegant") your code is, the more efficiently your program will run. Since personal data has been collected digitally in these systems, gender has been rendered into ones and zeros, which do not provide the space to store, or represent, data beyond "male" and "female." There is no "third space" in a boolean function, which might capture or subsequently represent (in a query made to that system) gender beyond the binary. Hoffmann identifies this failure as "data violence" in order to capture "the harm inflicted on trans and gender nonconforming people not only in government-run systems, but also the information systems that permeate our everyday social lives."[6]

Code, in its many valences, is a significant element of Whitehead's poetics. Zoa illustrates that "data violence" is also a form of deletion that recapitulates the erasure perpetuated by settler colonialism. Outside colonial and data binaries, and therefore outside colonial representation, Zoa is effectively disembodied – a ghost in the machine. Yet, rather than taking this as an impairment or an inscription of damage, Zoa mobilizes their position outside colonial representation as a weapon of decolonization, which renders them impervious to embodied attacks in the violent sphere of imposed colonial reality. Outside this space, Zoa informs the reader, "i have no fragility / like your body does."[7]

Holmes and Hunt help us to further articulate Zoa's ingenuity as the continuation of queer Indigenous resistance and resilience. In spite of settler colonialism's best attempts to erase them, Holmes and Hunt write, "Indigenous queers persisted."[8] Zoa's perseverance in *Full-Metal Indigiqueer,* their resourcefulness in the face of ongoing displacement and erasure, is encoded as evidence of the vitality and tenacity of queer Indigenous people within the delimiting systems of an oppressive settler state. In this, Zoa illustrates that not only have Indigenous queers persisted, but they have also played significant roles in the decolonial project. Holmes and Hunt define decolonization as "actively challenging or disrupting systems of knowledge that do not fully account for the lives of Indigenous people, queer and trans people."[9] In disrupting and deconstructing settler colonial culture and "code" via their presence as a disembodied singularity, Zoa works to make space for those whose lives have been erased or paved over by epistemic and material violence. While this space may be, in some sense, virtual, it nonetheless articulates a sovereign territory of resistance and resurgence. Zoa informs us that "this is the hypercyberrezsphere / where decolonialism has a chance / where survivance rests its head."[10]

In the sense that it fosters decolonization and recuperates survivance – Gerald Vizenor's articulation of active Indigenous presence within contemporary colonial reality[11] – Zoa's "hypercyberrezsphere" echoes Michelle Raheja's virtual reservation. According to Raheja, "Unlike Jean Baudrillard's notion of the virtual as simulacra, fake, and substitute for the "real," the virtual reservation is a supplemental arena of the possible that initiates and maintains a dialectical relationship between the multiple layers of Indigenous knowledge systems – from the dream world to the topography of real and imagined landscapes."[12]

Zoa's liminal existence as a resident of the virtual reservation affords the reader the opportunity to glimpse the ideological contours of the colonial "real" and thus render legible the grammars and syntaxes that work to erase and displace Indigenous bodies in the semiotic fields of settler colonialism. Whitehead illustrates this, for instance, by reading Milton's *Paradise Lost* alongside the death of a beloved aunt: "you cant make a heaven of hell / if the promise of heavens always been hellish to you";[13] in the poem "what I learned in pre-cal math," Zoa demonstrates their alienation from a literary canon defined by Shakespeare: "here im just a fractal of the indigenous curve / & this still isn't a social phenomenon / this is simple geometry, really";[14] in "to my mister going to bed," they further illustrate their incommensurability with colonial modernity, highlighting ways in which technology is used to consume Indigenous identity: "though i am machine / you cannot download me."[15]

To repeat, the lack of presence that Whitehead's narrator experiences, the inability of settler machinery to recognize or acknowledge them, is not a reiteration of deficit. It is hope, desire, and resistance in the curl of erasure. Whitehead takes up his narrator's lack, their (non)being, as a vehicle of agency and resistance. This agency functions within the realm of reconciliation and the TRC as well. In the poem "slay bells reign in suburbia," Zoa downloads "Charles Dickens software" as a means to critique "settler guilt" by balancing that guilt against the "precarity ... of day-to-day" existence for Indigenous peoples.[16] Directly at stake in this comparison is the fraught ideological space generated by the TRC, in which Zoa is able to inhabit the very fact of their non-existence – mobilizing the settler colonial tools levied against them (erasure and displacement) as a vehicle for deconstruction and rewriting: "i am the ghost of natives past; / the ghost of colonialism present; / the ghost of settlers to come."[17] Here, Zoa takes up the figure of present absence, this time via a hacked representation of a Dickensian ghost. Unlike *A Christmas Carol,* however, which depicts three separate spirts (past, present, and future), Whitehead's ghost is an amalgamation of all three – illustrating the continuity of Indigenous resistance while subverting the shallow colonial representation of the dead or dying Indian.[18]

As a figure empowered by the strength of both past and future relations, Zoa becomes the forebearer of a decolonial present, which rejects the futurity of the settler colonial narrative and teaches the TRC, not as a gentle reconvening of Indigenous-settler relations, but as something that those who cling to power and privilege should fear. Indeed, "run afeard in the wake of the trc," the narrator informs us, highlighting not the reconciliation initiated out of that event, but the Indigenous resurgence.[19] In this articulation, the "trc" is formulated as a harbinger of change, but one that is predicated, by Zoa, on the multitemporal permanence of Indigenous peoples on occupied territories.

Still, Zoa is not finished with the theatre of regret. They continue, closing the poem by taking aim at settler apologies: "i regard your apology as the deadest piece of ironmongery in this new trade / the wisdom of my ancestors in this extended simile / touch it, I dare you – this country's done for."[20] Here, Zoa identifies the apologies attached to the TRC as an iteration of currency in a new moral economy. The "dead ironmongery" of apology, referring to the emptiness of an economic signifier (i.e., a coin that does not carry the value its markings indicate), is trafficked by settler politicians (for instance, by Prime Minister Stephen Harper, who is also identified by Zoa as "settler scrooge"). For Zoa, this "new trade" is a systematic, and unidirectional, exchange of moral platitudes that recuperates and maintains the status quo while leaving "settler scrooge" in the position of wealth and power – even as he displays beneficence and goodwill after his encounter with the ghosts. Yet, in referencing the three spirits of Dickens's *A Christmas Carol* – the "extended simile" that Zoa notes in the line subsequent to "ironmongery" – Whitehead illustrates the power and potential of Indigenous peoples to resist and explode a colonially structured system of relationality, be it reconciliation or otherwise: "this country's done for," Zoa concludes. The false exchange that founds the authority of the settler state is exposed for what it is. The foundation is crumbling. Indigenous futures are reclaiming the past and present, and decolonial narratives are informing the geographies of the settler imaginary.

Acknowledgment: The First Step to Reconciliation

In the layered and complex ways that it grapples with Indigenous (non)representation, *Full-Metal Indigiqueer* provides a provocative and nuanced space to begin considering what is often established in conflict resolution literature as the first step on the "road to reconciliation": acknowledgment.[21] Zoa's challenge to settler colonialism, insofar as they are an entity existing (and thriving) outside colonial recognition, demonstrates the settler failure to register Indigenous experiences – even as figures such as Zoa mobilize that failure toward decolonization. For Whitehead, and Zoa, (non)representation is a superpower, insofar as it allows the Indigenous protagonist to infiltrate and subvert colonial machinery. For the settler colonial state, Zoa's challenge marks the enduring decline of empire. With Whitehead as a starting place, then, this chapter aims to slow down state and academic approaches to reconciliation's initial step – acknowledgment – a step that rarely, if ever, receives the critical attention of its more glamorized successors on the road, namely apology and forgiveness. By looking at acknowledgement critically, with an eye to what fails colonial systems of representation, we can critique the road to reconciliation from its foundations, thus providing the opportunity for more robust engagements with identity and the trauma inflicted by colonialism.

Moving on from Whitehead in what follows, I turn to the Cree poet Sky Dancer Louise Bernice Halfe as a means to further interrogate acknowledgment while extending the timeline of Indigenous resistance. Halfe's deep, moving, and multi-voiced poetry provides the complexity of language and form to unpack and meditate on the fraught nature of acknowledgment within the scope of settler colonialism. At its core, Halfe's work elucidates the labour and complexity of testifying to colonial violence. Much like Whitehead's verse, poems such as "Residential School Bus" and "Crying for Voice" make space for those whose voices are not registered in the colonial semiotic field, but they never do so at the expense of the agency of Indigenous peoples. Also like Whitehead's (in fact, I argue that Halfe's work is a large part of the reason why a new generation of Indigenous poets like Whitehead are now finding success), Halfe's poetry also speaks to the risks embedded in the act of creating Indigenous space – particularly in the presence of what I identify as colonial static, a phrase which I will go on to define below.

To begin, however, we need to ask: why acknowledgment? Why is this particular step necessary on the road to reconciliation? And why should

Indigenous peoples and allies be attentive to it? According to Nicholas Tavuchis, acknowledgment (what he identifies as "the call") sets the entire processes of reconciliation in motion. Without acknowledgment, Tavuchis argues, there is no ground for reconciliation to begin from: nothing from which apology or forgiveness might be offered, redress established, or reconciliation conceptualized. Tavuchis explicates what he means by "the call" when defining apology in his path-clearing text, *Mea Culpa: A Sociology of Apology and Reconciliation:*

> The proper and successful apology is the middle term in a moral syllogism that commences with a *call* and ends with *forgiveness.* The social processes that generate the sequence *cannot be activated until there is a call:* the attribution or nomination of an offense that can be negotiated not by an account or appeal to reason(s), but only through the faculty of forgiving. In other words, until the action in question is semantically and symbolically transformed into 'apologizable' discourse, it remains subject to other formulations and interpretations. [emphasis added][22]

For Tavuchis, "the call" is an acknowledgment of history that sets in action the processes of apology and reconciliation. "Wrongs" are not wrongs, per se, until they have been named as such. This would appear obvious if not for the fact that the naming of violence as such is not always a given, particularly when power inflects the translation of certain events into the national imaginary. In Canada, for instance, Japanese Canadian internment was, for decades after the injustice, labelled by the state as "relocation," stripping that event, in a linguistic sense, of the systemic and material violence that provided for it, a translation that, as Roy Miki has illustrated, had to be corrected before Brian Mulroney's 1988 apology.[23] More recently, high-ranking conservative politicians in Canada have disavowed the word "genocide" as applied to missing and murdered Indigenous women and girls. Until only recently, the Canadian Museum for Human Rights also refused the word "genocide" as it applied to Indigenous peoples in Canada, stating that it was not a museum's position to declare what is a genocide and what is not.[24] While the museum personnel/decision makers have since changed their stance, incorporating genocide into their representations of Indigenous peoples in 2019, their initial refusal demonstrates the ideological effects of the salt water thesis, which relegates colonial violence to countries overseas, rather than to the backyard of settler colonial nation-states.[25]

The examples cited above are about much more than squabbles over the definition of words. When governments refuse language that holds them to account the severity of historical violence, acknowledgment easily becomes part of the oppressor's tool kit rather than a means to facilitate change. Like Tavuchis, I argue that apology, forgiveness, redress, and reconciliation are all founded on survivor voice and agency, but I elaborate that acknowledgment must also be articulated through dense colonial structures of repression and disavowal. If the wrongdoing itself is not, or cannot be, heard, then the subsequent steps on the road to reconciliation will not respond to the specificity of the events in question. To paraphrase Whitehead, they will represent little more than potholes on the colonial superhighway. The wrong, genocide and land theft, therefore, needs to be heard before any further discourse – be it apology, forgiveness, redress, or reconciliation – can be ethically, logically, or rigorously pursued. In this sense, acknowledgment is a founding step that requires deep and considerable attention.

As a determinant of apology, forgiveness, and reconciliation, acknowledgment has been richly developed in the academic literature. However, because of the prevailing focus in that literature on reconciliation as it exists in transitional or postcolonial states, there has been little work committed to the distorting effects that settler colonialism can have on the process. Joanna Quinn, for instance, argues that acknowledging historical injustice is a necessary step in the movement toward forgiveness and reconciliation. According to her, individuals who constitute the community pursuing reconciliation "must first engage in a process of acknowledgement before any of the other steps take place."[26] Pushing claims about the quintessential nature of acknowledgment even further, Quinn suggests that acknowledgment is the most robust tool by which to measure the success of a truth commission, which she demonstrates through normative analysis of truth commissions in Haiti and Uganda. Quinn's argument for the necessity of acknowledgment in these case studies stems from a persuasive psychological point: that historical trauma never disappears. Such trauma cannot be repressed or ignored without causing further suffering and damage to all parties involved because, as Sigmund Freud famously demonstrated, the repressed always returns.[27] Acknowledgment, which in Quinn's analysis functions as a type of talk therapy, is the only way to bring these issues to the surface, where they might be dealt with in a healthy and productive manner. Unlike Tavuchis, who connects acknowledgment directly to apology, Quinn writes that "the effect of the progression of acknowledgement is to make possible both the act and the process of forgiveness."[28]

The difference in outcome for the two thinkers (apology for Tavuchis, forgiveness for Quinn) signals the diverse ways in which acknowledgment can be conceptualized: for Tavuchis, the initial step facilitates the role of the perpetrator and his or her ability to conceptualize an event toward a sincere demonstration of regret. For Quinn, acknowledgment provides survivors with the epistemic tools to move past resentment and hatred. Most importantly, however, is that both Quinn and Tavuchis identify a *teleology* of acknowledgment, the endpoint of which is reconciliation. In either case, acknowledgment is a threshold, a necessary point of inception.

Where my argument diverges from those advanced by Tavuchis and Quinn is not in the necessity of acknowledgment, but in its very possibility. I agree wholeheartedly with Quinn's psychoanalytic approach to the concept: historical trauma, if repressed, will only rise up and return to inflict greater damage on individuals, communities, survivors, and perpetrators. I write more on this in Chapter 5. Repression and wilful forgetting have for too long been the directive of the settler state and neo-colonial policy makers. Acknowledging the trauma of historical violence, whether through a truth commission, tribunal, or other means, is a crucial step toward reconciliation and/or decolonization because it makes visible what settler colonialism works to repress: the dehumanization of Indigenous peoples as a tool of nation building. In this sense, I follow from scholars such as Patricia Barkaskas, Sarah Hunt, and Gerhard Werle, who plainly state, "without truth, no reconciliation."[29]

My intervention into the theory of acknowledgment is more ontological than the pragmatic arguments put forth by Quinn and Tavuchis, which is to say that I question what the existing theory has to say about the individuals who are making acknowledgment possible. While Quinn and Tavuchis assume acknowledgment as a necessary step toward reconciliation, I am more concerned with the labour that is demanded of acknowledgment as a component of the politics of recognition – the work that falls on the shoulders of survivors under the false auspices that recognition from the settlers and the state will advance change or generate social justice.

In terms of labour, where the issue of acknowledgment becomes particularly fraught in Canada is in the question of who is asked to bear the weight of it. The devastating effects of bearing this load have been made plain to us in other national contexts. In his judgment on the case that challenged the conditional amnesty granted by the South African TRC, Ismail Mahomed, the deputy president of the Constitutional Court, clearly illustrates the difficulty of unearthing truth in the wake of historical injustice:

> Secrecy and authoritarianism have concealed the truth in little crevices of obscurity in our history. Records are not easily accessible, witnesses are often unknown, dead, unavailable or unwilling. All that often effectively remains is the truth of wounded memories of loved ones sharing instinctive suspicions, deep and traumatizing to the survivors but otherwise incapable of translating themselves into objective and corroborative evidence which could survive the rigours of the law.[30]

While Mahomed is referring to the South African context here, it is not much of a stretch to see the connections in Canada, particularly when it comes to witnesses and family testimony. What his judgment is intended to illustrate is the need for multiple sources of testimony to corroborate and piece together a traumatic history that, by its very nature, threatens to disappear if not properly acknowledged. It cannot be the responsibility of one cultural group to carry the load.

Of course, this raises an important question: if testimony is necessary for acknowledgment to take shape, who should be asked to take up this labour? In Chile and South Africa, perpetrator testimony was seen as an essential part of the TRC process, to such a degree that amnesty was provided for those offenders who came forward with their stories. Desmond Tutu writes emphatically about the necessity of perpetrator testimony in the South African TRC, highlighting the need for a distribution of labour: "had it not been for the amnesty process, all this would have remained in the murky crevices where apartheid hid such secrets."[31] The TRC of Canada, however, is "victim-centred," which means, most simply, that perpetrator testimony has been precluded from the historical record.[32] Schedule "N" of the TRC states clearly that "the Commissioners shall not record the names of persons so identified [as abusers, sexual or otherwise] unless the person named or identified has been convicted for the alleged wrongdoing."[33] According to Ronald Niezen, "Canada's TRC is the only truth commission to have so thoroughly extinguished the identities of possible perpetrators from its proceedings, preventing their names from even entering the record through survivor narratives, and maintaining their invisibility and anonymity all the way through the Commission's activities."[34] Matt James writes that "the commission's mandate precludes it from becoming a vigorous forum of investigation and accountability. The commission has no mechanism for inducing perpetrators, commanders, architects, or even bystanders, to come forward."[35] In other words, acknowledgment, in the rigorous sense determined in the TRC genealogy prior to Canada, is not a part of Canada's road to reconciliation. Truth, at least as it was defined in previous TRCs, is therefore already partial, and labour (i.e., the burden of proof) is distributed in such a way as to primarily benefit settlers.

It is difficult to ascertain precisely why perpetrators were excluded from testifying in the TRC of Canada, particularly given how important victim *and* perpetrator testimony is in many Indigenous justice practices and in the long genealogy of the TRC itself.[36] Schedule "N" offers no justification for the exclusion, nor has Murray Sinclair or any of the other TRC commissioners spoken at length to its omission. Konstantin Petoukhov, provides the most compelling answer as to why: simply put, perpetrator testimony does not easily fit within the Canadian legal framework within which the TRC operates.[37] In the Canadian justice system, perpetrators are discouraged from testifying by the threat of punishment. Under Section 11 of the *Canadian Charter of Rights and Freedoms*, any person charged with an offence cannot "be compelled to be a witness in proceedings against that person in respect of the offence."[38] More historical and legal research is needed to rigorously account for the ways in which the Charter is detrimentally impacting Indigenous peoples in the post-TRC era. While the point about perpetrator acknowledgment is buried deep within the language of the TRC of Canada, the *absence* of perpetrator testimony speaks volumes about the capacity for voice allowed for in this system. Read contextually, it should be noted that the exclusion of perpetrator testimony from the TRC of Canada is antithetical to the TRC model itself and puts undue pressure on survivors to bear the weight of testimony, which, as I will illustrate below via Halfe, has very real physical and emotional consequences.

Alongside the question of labour in acknowledgment, I also argue that, despite the *need* for acknowledgment, survivors are often not being heard for what they offer, at least not in any decolonial sense. There is a long history of settler colonial repression to support my point, which, put simply, is that Canada does not *want* to acknowledge its colonial history, even when the country is making loud and boisterous claims for reconciliation. History illustrates this, but so does the contemporary moment. Not so long ago, in 1988, eight years before the last residential school closed, Celia Haig-Brown wrote and published *Resistance and Renewal: Surviving the Indian Residential School*, one of the first academic texts to address the residential school issue by using direct testimony from survivors.[39] Haig-Brown is an education researcher who has done extensive work with Indigenous communities in British Columbia. She went on to teach early courses on Indigenous education at the University of British Columbia and Simon Fraser University, and is now a professor of education at York University. In 1988, however, despite her text being exceptionally researched and beautifully written, she couldn't find a publisher – because editors were concerned that the public wasn't ready for such a stark analysis of Canada's past.[40]

While searching for someone to publish her book, Haig-Brown turned to Randy Fred, residential school survivor and co-founder of Theytus Books, and asked him to write an introduction for her manuscript. After reading Haig-Brown's text, Fred was astonished by the way in which the general public still refused to acknowledge the reality of residential schools, even when these stories were sanctioned by the academy and a reputable researcher: "I was appalled, when first meeting with Celia to discuss publishing this book, to learn that some people who had read the manuscript believed some of it not to be true; the nuns *couldn't* have been that mean to those children."[41] What Fred points to in his socio-historical analysis of Haig's work is a problem of *reception,* in which the call, while being vociferously articulated, cannot – or will not – be heard by a settler community that understands the state as a benevolent, "civilizing," political structure. In Haig-Brown's case, it was not that no one was speaking the truth of residential schools (and many, besides her, were); it was that the public refused to hear that truth as such.

I identify this unwillingness, or inability, to receive the signal of residential schools as a function of what I refer to as "colonial static." Colonial static is the noise produced in a settler colonial state by ideological or settler-made disturbances. It is the media through which Indigenous testimony to historical injustice is distorted before being rendered into acknowledgment and "the road to reconciliation." Like radio static, colonial static intensifies or diminishes depending on location. Colonial static makes survivor testimony more difficult for both settler and Indigenous publics to receive – even if one is open to receiving it. Yet this static is also something that can be corrected (and something that allies can help to correct) by boosting the signal of survivor voices and identifying and dampening the sources of static that flare up in our daily lives. Comparing Haig-Brown's story to the post-TRC moment when the prime minister of Canada publicly acknowledged the damage caused by residential schools, we can see how colonial static has been reduced by the labour of survivors and their families. However, that does not mean it has been eradicated. There remains much work to be done before the signal can be considered clear, because colonial static is not a glitch in nation-state machinery; it is a defense mechanism devised to protect the interests and futurity of the settler nation.

Indeed, despite the shift we have recently seen in the politics of acknowledgment – for instance, from 1988 to the post-TRC moment – many settlers continue to publicly argue against acknowledgment. Colonial static is rife in these spaces. Frances Widdowson, for instance, has suggested that the public response to the TRC is a product of "postmodern relativism" and a plot to extract rent from the settler state in the form of compensation.[42] According to Widdowson, "residential schools were not the product of a malevolent plot to destroy the aboriginal population; instead, the decline of the fur trade and the development of an industrial economy meant that it became necessary to detribalize the aboriginal population and try to make them more productive."[43] As this quotation helps to illustrate, Widdowson's argument is grounded in a capitalist, "civilizing" narrative, which has a long-standing history in settler colonial static.[44] Suggesting that residential schools were a way to help "them" be more "productive" not only ignores the fact that the majority of these schools were little more than labour camps offering sub-standard education;[45] it also wilfully disavows the fact that, after the fur trade, many Indigenous communities were left looking for ways to support themselves because the land that had provided for them for thousands of years had been re-purposed for settler agendas. Residential schools, in this sense, can only be understood as systems of "productivity" insofar as they kept Indigenous peoples from interfering with settler nation building, resource extraction, and primitive accumulation.

Like Widdowson, Ken Coates, in an article published in *The Dorchester Review,* argues that scholars have been myopic in their attention to the trauma of residential schools: "Not all students left the residential school broken," Coates argues. "In fact, there are amazing stories of resilience and agency in every school."[46] According to Coates, what he sees as the single-story narrative of colonialism has led to "an account of residential schools [that] is not sufficiently nuanced," meaning, in sum, that it does not hold up the beneficence of settlers and the "gift" of civilization.[47] Crystal Fraser and Ian Mosby handily dismantle this opinion, so I will turn the argument over to them:

> Unfortunately, Coates offers few suggestions for what a more "nuanced" history would look like. And readers of his essay might be forgiven for

> asking: how do you add nuance to a system that forcibly removed children from their families, that used violence and coercion to eliminate Indigenous languages and culture, and that ... allowed thousands of children around the country to not only suffer from hunger and malnutrition for decades but, in one particularly egregious case, subjected nearly 1,000 students to a scientific experiment without their knowledge or consent?[48]

Both Coates and Widdowson seem unable to hear, or they purposefully tune out, an astonishing breadth of evidence confirming that residential schools inflicted immeasurable harm and even death on extremely vulnerable populations. They are wed to the idea that colonialism is ultimately beneficent and that Indigenous populations are at a deficit and therefore in need of a paternalistic structure to set them right. What is at stake in these opinions is a litmus test of what acknowledgment actually looks like in much of Canada: colonial static amplified as a means to reaffirm the necessity and authority of the capitalist nation-state.

What colonial static is, and how it functions, is connected to a larger theoretical field of acknowledgment that needs to be drawn into this conversation before I move to analysis of Halfe's poetry. When Tavuchis argues that by "respond[ing] to the call *after* the offense by apologizing, we are seeking reconfirmation of our credentials as members" [emphasis added],[49] he is drawing directly from a Hegelian framework of recognition, which, in the Western episteme, provides a theoretical core for subjectivity. To quote Hegel in *Phenomenology of Spirit*, "self-consciousness exists in and for itself when, and by the fact that, it so exists for another; that is, *it exists only in being acknowledged*" [emphasis added].[50] As we can see from this short excerpt, for Hegel, recognition and acknowledgment are intertwined with the ability to know oneself as a subject within a field of mutually assured subjectivity.

Yet, there is even more at stake here when we apply Hegel's acknowledgment to an Indigenous studies framework. For Glen Coulthard, the foundation of Hegel's recognition (and, by proxy, acknowledgment) is also the possibility of human freedom. That is to say, in order to become a self-determining subject, individuals must not only see themselves as self-determining, but must also be recognized by another self-determining subject as such: "It is through these reciprocal processes and exchanges of recognition that the condition of possibility for freedom emerges."[51] Coulthard's critique of the politics of recognition, however, which he expands through detailed engagements with Charles Taylor and Frantz

Fanon, takes issue with how Hegelian recognition posits reciprocity and mutual respect as the baseline for freedom. In Coulthard's reading, the foundational Hegelian dialectical case, that of master and slave, is not built on reciprocity at all, but extraction. What the master wants from the slave, Coulthard argues, "is not recognition but work."[52] In other words, the crux of acknowledgment as an extension of recognition is capital and the Marxist definition of alienation that accompanies it, which leads to the dehumanization of "slaves" and the recuperation of power, resources, and land for the "master."

For Coulthard, the politics of recognition break down precisely in this movement between master and slave or, in the terms of his argument, between the Canadian government and Indigenous peoples. Further, however, and more germane to the operationalization of settler colonialism, the primary extractive target of the master is not labour – it is land. Not just land in terms of resources, but also land in terms of home and belonging. From this position, Coulthard argues that "rather than leading to a condition of reciprocity the dialectic [within the settler colonial framework] either breaks down with the explicit nonrecognition of the equal status of the colonized population, or with the strategic "domestication" of the terms of recognition leaving the foundation of the colonial relationship relatively undisturbed."[53]

The point here is that recognition is, before it even begins, a failing mediation point in Indigenous-settler relations, given that it does nothing to unsettle the structures of power implicit in settler colonialism – namely, who controls land and resources, and who gets to determine "belonging." Recognition, in this sense, does nothing to return subjectivity to Indigenous peoples; it operates to reify colonial power.

In the discourse of reconciliation, acknowledgment stands in for recognition in that it speaks precisely to the reciprocal processes of exchange that guarantee the subjective experience of the other – in this case, the experience of historical injustice as repressed or erased by the state and testified to by residential school survivors. As such, Coulthard's critique is just as cutting within the contexts of these scholarly debates. It is particularly incisive insofar as acknowledgment, too, is caught up in the master/slave dialectic, with the burden of proof – in a TRC that does not include perpetrator testimony – placed squarely on the backs of survivors, who are charged with making legible the violent history of residential schools. What the "master" wants in the discourse of acknowledgment, however, is not work or resources – at least, not directly. Rather, what the settler state wants out of acknowledgment in the Canadian configuration of reconciliation is a recognition that recuperates and maintains its authority and sovereignty, not in spite of, but *because* of historical injustice.

The Canadian state seeks recognition from residential school survivors on the basis that it is in the moment of acknowledgment that Canada can distance itself from the past while affirming its starring role in the theatre of regret. Rather than an act of reciprocity or mutual exchange, what is returned from the labour of the testimony shouldered by survivors and their families in courageous moves toward acknowledgment is an articulation of what Eve Tuck identifies as a "damage-centered" narrative, which frames Indigenous communities "as sites of disinvestment and dispossession."[54] That is to say, what is at the core of acknowledgment for the settler state in the contexts of residential schools is an articulation of brokenness framed through the windows of pity and/or guilt. In acknowledging survivors and their families as "damaged," settler acknowledgment, as the translation of historical injustice through colonial power, works to justify the state's paternalistic relationship to Indigenous peoples and validates the existing colonial origin story in which Western civilization saves Indigenous populations. In other words, the politics of acknowledgment carry the possibility of initiating "spaces saturated in the fantasies of the other," as Tuck puts it, while precluding opportunities to imagine Indigenous futurities rooted in hope and desire.[55]

Reading acknowledgment alongside Coulthard and Tuck, we can see that the narratives perpetuated by authors such as Coates and Widdowson have direct, lived impacts. First, most prominently, they are felt in the (most often Indigenous) labour required to refute their claims and subsequently realign acknowledgment so that it accurately reflects the past. Second, in order to push back against those who seek to defend residential schools, or to suggest that "they weren't all bad," as Coates does, those who repudiate residential school apologists are often put in the awkward position of having to resort to "damage-centred" facts to make their case heard. Or as bell hooks puts it, survivors, within the scope of this discourse, are positioned to "only speak from that space in the margin that is a sign of depravation, a wound, an unfulfilled longing. Only speak [their] pain."[56]

Tuck illustrates that these types of damage-centred narratives are tolerated, despite the pain induced in their (re)telling, because there is an assumption that they will eventually effect change. Or, to put it another way, advocates for social justice suppose that the labour and pain invested in challenging colonial static will eventually result in a period when those narrative will no longer exist. While we can hope this might be true, there is no evidence that this future will ever appear. In fact, as Dallas Hunt argues, "state-sponsored reconciliation efforts on colonial contexts tend to require that Indigenous peoples 'reconcile' themselves to their continued colonization."[57] Given that the structural change on which acknowledgment is premised is, at least in the settler state, an ever-receding horizon, we are compelled to ask, as Tuck does, if the costs perpetuated by damage-centred narratives are worth the price of that debate?[58]

Following from Tuck, who calls for a moratorium on damage-centred research, I think that the answer to this question has to be no. This is not to say that the violence and genocide inflicted in residential schools should be left unsaid – I stand behind Barkaskas and Sarah Hunt's call for truth before reconciliation as discussed earlier – but rather that Canada's politics of acknowledgment must also acknowledge the strength, resilience, resurgence, and love that emanates from survivors, despite the state's best efforts to repress and diminish those ways of being. This is not the same as saying "not all residential schools were bad." It is saying, steadfastly, that residential schools caused immeasurable harm, and yet Indigenous cultures, communities, and languages persist and flourish in spite of them. In this sense, acknowledgment in Canada needs to better reflect the complexity of what Gerald Vizenor called "survivance" in residential schools – that is, the survival and resistance that nurtured the strong and resilient Indigenous communities and people that exist today: poets such as Whitehead and Halfe, the activists who organize global movements like Idle No More, the leaders and grassroots community members who make the very fact of a Truth and Reconciliation Commission in Canada possible, and many more.

Acknowledgment that centres hope and desire, to borrow once again from Tuck, is a means to "depatholog[ize] the experiences of the disposed and disenfranchised ... so that people are seen as more than broken and conquered."[59] Acknowledgment that not only looks back on colonial history, but which also emphasizes the present and futures of Indigenous peoples, is a means of initiating a "road to reconciliation" outside the cold, dead grasp of settler colonialism. As I illustrate below via Halfe, Indigenous testimony reframes acknowledgment not as an iteration of the politics of recognition, but as a sovereign articulation of resilience and futurity that cuts through colonial static and makes space for desire and hope in the process.

"This Chosen Walk Is a Blizzard Whiteout"

In her long-form poem *Blue Marrow,* Sky Dancer Louise Bernice Halfe illustrates the threat of colonial silence as it haunts the margins and white spaces of her books, her individual poems, and her experience as a Cree woman. Halfe articulates the labour of choosing to bear witness through the metaphor of a snowstorm: "This chosen walk is a blizzard whiteout / My Creeing alone in the heavy arm of snow."[60] Here, the whiteness of the snow, as it surrounds the narrator and dampens her voice, stands as an apt allegory for the density and deadening effects of colonial ideology. As with my static metaphor, a snowstorm is helpful for visualizing the ways in which colonial thinking permeates the air we breathe and blankets the land we walk on – even as another reality sleeps beneath it, waiting for the thaw. Indeed, the violence of colonialism resonates all around Halfe's narrators: violence against Indigenous peoples, violence against Indigenous children, violence against the land, violence against Indigenous women. In the way she articulates these violences through the colonial whiteout, Halfe provides evocative spaces throughout her oeuvre from which to further consider the problem of acknowledgment and the resurgence of Indigenous voices in a post-TRC Canada.

During her distinguished writing career, Halfe has breathed life into silence and refused the single-story narrative of Indigenous damage. As a residential school survivor herself, for more than twenty-five years she has used Cree poetics to delicately craft voice out of the unheard: out of the ongoing violence of Canada's settler colonial history, and out of the repression administered in Canadian residential schools. Halfe, like her narrators, hungers for voice in a system designed around narrative famine. Perhaps more than any other poet in Canada, in her struggle against the whiteout she captures the dangers that lurk in the quest to break colonial silence.

That said, while it bears witness to the unheard, and holds space for those who can no longer speak, Halfe's poetry also makes plain the love and healing that Indigenous peoples – particularly Indigenous women – dedicate to sharing language, stories, culture, and history.[61] For instance, the narrator of *Blue Marrow* entreats her ancestors to "*pê-nîhtaciwêk nôhkomak* / Climb down, my grandmothers / *pê-nânapâcihinân* / Come heal us."[62] The stories that the grandmothers subsequently tell after being called are not simply of the pain and death caused by residential schools and colonization. They do not only emphasize damage. They also hold up resistance, love, and hope, and an Indigenous future other than the blizzard whiteout.

Take, for instance, the following story told by the grandmothers, which emphasizes radical defiance in the face of Christianity and assimilation:

> There are Holy iskwêwak – nôsisim, all over.
> We were the ones who burned down the jesuits'
> church, trilled, danced, and laughed through the night.
> We watched those cabins eaten by our flames. We
> were the ones, nôsisim, who hid the Bundles,
> held council when we learned how those brothers
> lifted their skirts to spill their devils into our son's night.[63]

In this passage, the grandmothers centre Indigenous resistance in the face of colonial violence. The story relayed holds up the strength of Indigenous peoples and the powerful will of Indigenous women to mobilize against colonization and patriarchal violence: burning down the church, organizing against sexually abusive Jesuits, and storing the "Bundles" – the language, culture, and knowledge of the community – for future generations and storytellers.

For Halfe, making Indigenous histories available to ears that are unwilling or unable to hear them has always been a key component of her work. Halfe was one of a handful of Indigenous poets published in the first collection of Indigenous writing to directly contend with the legacy of residential schools. This anthology, entitled *Residential Schools: The Stolen Years,* featured essays, poetry, and creative non-fiction by now prominent Indigenous authors and activists such as Harold Cardinal, Maria Campbell, Janice Acoose, and Phil Fontaine, as well as Halfe. Her four poems included "The Residential School Bus," which depicts life inside these institutions. The following excerpt captures the loneliness and silence that permeated the cold night in the schools:

> Somewhere
> someone
> in the huge dorm
> sobs quietly.[64]

Punctuated by purposefully vague descriptors ("somewhere," "someone") that are sequestered in single lines of verse, "The Residential School Bus" depicts a cold, antiseptic space that strips Indigenous children of their identity and connection to place; they become no one, existing nowhere, in a space that encodes assimilation and muffles tears. While bodies and people take up a large portion of the space in this poem, silence is the primary character. The only mention of sound lies in the final line, the "quiet sobs," and in an earlier reference to an "echo" in a "long white empty hallway." The entire poem feels as if it is taking place in an oversized vacuum. The silence is dense, palpable, smothering, and, as indicated in the colour of the hallway, white, but out of it Halfe traces the outlines of resurgence in the voices that lead out of the darkness toward the possibility of healing rooted in the truth of these experiences.

Indeed, poems such as "The Residential School Bus" played a significant role in changing the way settler Canadians imagined residential school history. In this same collection, Cree Métis author Janice Acoose points out that entering stories such as Halfe's into Canadian discourse is necessary not only to educate settlers and Indigenous peoples about repressed history, but also, more importantly, to affirm the reality of survivor experiences for survivors themselves. According to Acoose:

> As a child, I tried to tell anyone who would listen about those night visits to our dorm, the cruel punishments, and the deadly threats, but *my voice was silenced* by my family's fears, the community's pressure, and the church's power. As a result, I grew up believing that what I felt, heard, and saw was not real! [emphasis added][65]

Acoose's writing speaks to the way in which testimony, acknowledgement, and "the real" are intertwined. Being silenced as a child, unable to make her experiences heard, Acoose was no longer certain if the abuse committed against her had actually happened. Her courageous admission to that fact speaks to the way in which the discourse of reconciliation is in constant conversation with the past. In these spaces, acknowledgment works on a deeply subjective level that is inextricably intertwined with the production of "truth," which is to say the colonial static that directly influences what can or cannot be heard – by settlers and survivors both.

Acoose's testimony also illustrates how, as Dori Laub argues, bearing witness to historical violence "testifies to an absence."[66] Or, to put it another way, in order for testimony such as Acoose's and Halfe's to be made knowable, survivors must have the strength and resilience to render legible what the larger population, and sometimes even family, has decreed to be impossible, or non-existent. In this sense, Laub argues, testimony is "a dialogical process of exploration and reconciliation of two worlds – the one that was brutally destroyed and the one that is – that are different and will always remain so."[67] Bearing witness to historical injustice means shouldering the burden of producing truth in a world that rejects it, and it can therefore be a deeply lonely and isolating act.

Acoose helps to illustrate the density of the static that surviours speak through. Cindy Holmes and Sarah Hunt clarify where that static originates from and how to target it. With regards to conceptualizing acknowledgment through settler colonialism, Holmes and Hunt provide lucid context for Halfe's poetry, locating violence as clearly existing *exterior* to Indigenous communities and pushing back against theories that would centre damage in those communities or Indigenous individuals. Holmes and Hunt begin stringently from the position that research on violence in Indigenous communities must *begin* with the open acknowledgment of settler colonialism. In an extensive literature review covering fifteen years of academic research on violence and Indigenous communities, the two researchers found that analysis of settler colonialism as a determinant of Indigenous health was almost always missing. Without this essential context, they argue, violence by and against Indigenous peoples is naturalized – that is, it is seen as ahistoric and apolitical: "public discourse naturalizes violence within Indigenous families and blames Indigenous people."[68] Further still, however, they elaborate that naturalizing Indigenous damage is not simply a methodological oversight. It is a function of settler colonial ideology: "a central tool of colonialism."[69] It elides the histories of settler violence and perpetuates the myth of "savagery" in Indigenous peoples, which in turn legitimates (non-consensual) state intervention and bolsters narratives of wardship and Crown protectionism.

What is at stake in Hunt and Holmes's argument is orientation. They insist that we turn our attention away from the damage-centred narratives that pervade mainstream discourse and look instead toward the source of violence: settler colonialism. Building on research by Margo Greenwood, Sarah de Leeuw, Nicole Marie Lindsay, and Charlotte Reading, Holmes and Hunt argue that an imperative starting point for all research concerning Indigenous peoples and violence is colonialism: "Colonialism is the most fundamental determinant of health for Indigenous people in white settler colonial states" and its ongoing influence continues to impact the well-being of Indigenous peoples across Canada.[70] Without acknowledging the founding context of violence, researchers and residential school apologists perpetuate racist narratives of settler colonialism that naturalize violence within Indigenous communities and relegate Indigeneity into stereotypes that serve the benefit of the settler state.

In this sense, it is not just the history of violence that Halfe's narrator grapples with in *Blue Marrow.* The blizzard whiteout of which she speaks is the never-ceasing demand to endure the *ongoing* violence of settler colonialism. This is to say that, despite a trend in reconciliation discourse that frames violence against Indigenous peoples as a problem of the past, damage must instead be understood in direct relation to the ongoing articulations of settler colonialism and the effects of intergenerational trauma.[71] Indeed, without directly acknowledging the contexts of settler colonialism, the lived experiences of many Indigenous people today are framed as community and individual problems rather than the product of the entity (the settler state) that now proclaims apology and begs forgiveness. Working against this static requires reframing the narrative goal posts and taking aim at systemic determinants of health and well-being: if a survivor's inability or unwillingness to testify to historical injustice is determined to be a symptom of poor health, then the cause must be identified as settler colonialism and its ongoing effects.

Moving past damage-centred research also means looking forward and backward to resistance and resurgence. Holmes and Hunt make plain that, "as long as there has been violence, there has been resistance."[72] Halfe's work is a beautiful manifestation of Indigenous women's strength and a testament to the possibility of healing: "I must pass all that I possess," the narrator, *âcimowinis,* informs us in the opening pages of *Blue Marrow,* "every morsel to my children. / These small gifts."[73]

That being said, while she holds up a long history of Indigenous women's resistance, Halfe is also careful to outline the labour and cost of that resistance. The emotional energy and risk required to undertake the labour of voice is conveyed in a vignette from *Blue Marrow,* relayed by âcimowinis, "Keeper of the Stories." In this excerpt, an Indigenous mother relays an event in which she and her children attended the family reunion of her white husband. Each member of her husband's extended family "has brought a book they've lovingly compiled," and as the settlers convene, they reread and, in doing so, re-substantiate the "heroics" of the colonial project, burying the narrator's Indigenous history beneath a blizzard of colonial snow:

> Laughter and wonder
> as fingers move across the atlas. This is where
> great-granddad Arne crossed on the barge.
> This is where great-great-granddad travelled
> and preached the law of the land where his
> wife Isobel taught the little savages to read.[74]

It is not a coincidence that each member of the white settler family carries a book in this passage. According to the Crow Creek scholar Elizabeth Cook-Lynn, "the invasion of North America by European peoples has been portrayed in history and literature as a benign movement directed by God, a movement of moral courage and physical endurance, a victory for all humanity."[75] As the passage from Halfe illuminates, those stories are told and retold (and retold) in canonized literature, film, and oral history. Settlers, like myself, carry these stories with us, both knowingly and not, and the blizzard emanates out of us in the moments when settler narratives begin to orbit one another.

Of course, the (re)telling of this "benign" narrative is anything but benign. Told and retold, settler stories of courage and endurance naturalize and glorify systems that displace, dehumanize, erase, and silence Indigenous peoples – even when, as in Halfe's story, Indigenous people are in the room when the stories are told. Bearing witness to this erasure time and time again is what positions Halfe's work as an act of refusal, a call to justice and redress with, as Warren Cariou points out, an emphasis "on the necessity of present action."[76] The labour of this work is enough to drain all of the breath from one's body, as the narrator in *Blue Marrow* goes on to demonstrate. On the car ride home from the reunion, she attempts to tell her children the stories of their Indigenous ancestors, those who had been buried beneath the colonial narrative: she shares stories of resistance, love, and deprivation. The task is immense, however, and she only has so much in her to give when faced with the scope of the narrative shared at the reunion. She finally surrenders to exhaustion: "My breath / won't come anymore. / I stare / at the wheatfields."[77]

As I argue above, acknowledgment, as constructed in the literature, is rooted in a Hegelian articulation of recognition that suggests that survivors can elicit freedom from the past by receiving and returning the truth of a violent history. What this exchange presupposes, however, is a fair and reciprocal exchange between subjects, which Halfe demonstrates is rarely the case, even among family. What acknowledgment theory has not yet considered, in this sense, are the contexts of colonial static, or what Roland Chrisjohn and Sherri Young call the "Standard Account."[78] According to these authors, "what the Standard Account is designed to do is manage how all of us interpret the abuse."[79] That is to say, the Standard Account operates like a filter, straining out the voices that might undercut the benevolent state narrative that settler Canadians connect their identities to while subsequently formulating a version of acknowledgment that obscures, rather than unveils, truth.

Writing in 1997, well before a TRC discourse began to develop in Canada, and even before Tavuchis published *Mea Culpa,* Chrisjohn and Young were already developing a theory of acknowledgment in relation to residential schools. They define the Standard Account as a single-story narrative that "disposes neatly of all problems associated with Indian Residential Schooling. There is a statement of initial motive, a recognition of responsibility, an exoneration of victims (Aboriginal Peoples), and the expression of a determination to tackle present manifestations of existing, unintentional injuries with all the armamentaria of modern social science. In short, the Standard Account is an act of contrition."[80]

For Chrisjohn and Young, the Standard Account is a means of theorizing the ways in which Canada delimits Indigenous claims for redress and restitution within the boundaries of a particular discourse of regret for "unintentional" harms, which can be boiled down to a phrase such as "we are so sorry that this happened. We didn't mean it to turn out like this." The Standard Account functions as a disavowal of colonial violence primarily because "it is not a logically coherent set of beliefs," meaning that its "solutions" displace or fail to address the cause of residential schools while simultaneously claiming the grounds for change.[81] For instance, proponents of the Standard Account will acknowledge the harm caused by residential schools and advocate for the healing of Indigenous communities, while doing nothing to address colonialism as a determinant of Indigenous health. This important omission thereby pathologizes survivors rather than addressing the sickness at the heart of the settler colonial project.

The Standard Account is also not simply a product of interpretive error; it has a socio-political function as well. Chrisjohn and Young go on to argue that "while logically incoherent, the Standard Account is ideologically consistent," which is to say that this way of acknowledging residential schools begins in service of protecting and maintaining the settler state and non-Indigenous ways of life.[82] By relegating the violence of residential schools to the past and centring the sickness caused by them in Indigenous people and communities, the state is under no pressure to structurally redefine itself. Or, to put it in the language of conflict resolution, the acknowledgment that might serve as the impetus for transitional justice is displaced and disavowed. In order to support this position, Chrisjohn and Young argue, settlers will often resort to the argument (as contemporarily evidenced by Widdowson and Coates) that not all residential schools were bad. One of the most paradoxical examples of this vein of argument is that residential schools provided students with the skills they needed to later challenge these schools. Chrisjohn and Young unpack the absurdity of this defence: "We are asked to believe that these schools *did good by doing bad*. We are asked to forget they did what they did. We are asked to agree that the ends justify the means" [emphasis in the original].[83]

"A Recipe for Voice"

Fully aware of the ways in which the Standard Account has attenuated Indigenous testimony about colonization and residential schools, one of Halfe's primary projects as a poet has been identifying and sharing what Laura Ann Cranmer identifies as a "recipe for voice":[84] that is, a means for making Indigenous stories heard within the claustrophobic space of the "blizzard whiteout." One of the first poems in Halfe's inaugural book of poetry, *Bear Bones and Feathers*, is entitled "Crying for Voice," which begins,

> I must pull frog
> pry its webbed feet
> from snails in
> my throat.[85]

Opening with the image of a "frog in the throat," an idiomatic expression for loss of voice, the narrator of "Crying for Voice" acknowledges that she must find a way to clear the obstructions that have lodged themselves in her body: a visceral means of depicting the ways in which the silencing effects of colonialism become embodied, impeding speech from within.

After "invit[ing] weasel to untangle / [her] braids,"[86] she then begins to list her recipe, a concoction of duck, rabbit, fish, and fresh blood, as well as some other surprising ingredients, which I will turn to in more detail momentarily: "Boil bible and tripe / clean of grass."[87] Halfe depicts a relationship to culture and healing via food in much of her work and the connection to the pleasure of eating plays a profound role in shaping her poetics. For example, in *Blue Marrow*, âcimowinis "yearns to eat. Rabbit, deer, moose / nose, porcupine, beaver, muskrat, prairie / chicken."[88] The relevance of the animals in both recipes can be read as a connection to freedom found in the bush, and an escape from the nutritionally bereft meals served at residential schools; meals which, as Ian Mosby has proven, were purposefully tampered with in order to "demonstrate the effects of nutritional interventions into the diet of an already malnourished population."[89]

In "Crying for Voice," however, after finally completing and consuming the recipe, there is a notable change in the narrator's tone and the direction of the narrative. The effects of the food become notable in the structure of the poem itself. Between the fifth and sixth stanzas, the narrator becomes distinctly more aware of her body and the sensations within it. From the first to final stanzas, she shifts from having a frog in her throat to finding "mosquitoes up [her] nostrils," which, while probably equally uncomfortable on a literal level, not only clears the throat and draws attention to her memories, but also disturbs the distinctly Western idiom that initially impedes her speech. While the narrator remains "blocked" in some ways, it is via a metaphor of her own making – centred in the breath, but distanced from the throat and voice. Freeing herself from the Westernized cliché and using her own metaphors to describe her condition, the narrator locates, if not an antidote, then at least a salve for the voice built out of the lands and waters of her home, which resonates through the remainder of the poems in the text.

As readers, we encounter this bold, pointed, and often humorous voice in the diversity of poems that make up *Bear Bones and Feathers.* For instance, in "My Ledders," the narrator, here speaking a "rez english" that Halfe develops throughout *Bear Bones,* composes a letter to the Pope, making plain her frustration with the Catholic Church and its interference with Indigenous ways of being. Reflecting on the Jesuits, the narrator writes, "dese men, pope, don't know what / tobacco mean, what suffer mean, / ... I so dired of all dis *kimoti,* pope."[90] Compared with the narrator in "Crying for Voice," the narrator here speaks truth to power in her own distinct voice while drawing on her own language to emphasize a point ("kimoti" means "stealing" in Cree). In this sense, the recipe that opens the collection can be seen as a formula for testimony, which not only clears the throat, but also makes space for other Indigenous speakers, authors, and poets to bear witness.

The recipe for voice evoked in "Crying for Voice" is conjured once again in *Blue Marrow.* That the recipe is drawn out across texts illustrates the continuity between the author's works and the ongoing development of a formula for expression and testimony. At the midpoint of *Blue Marrow,* the narrator, who, like the narrator in *Bear Bones,* is searching for access to her own voice and the voices of her ancestors, calls on her grandmothers to climb down and share their healing stories with her. The grandmothers agree, but with a condition: "*We do not talk until we are fed. / You've wanted us yet you ignore us. Dream us. Feed us.*"[91] Upon this demand for food, âcimowinis offers the grandmothers a strikingly similar recipe for voice to what is found in *Bear Bones:*

Saskatoon moose nose sturgeon soup
Indian popcorn bannock lard
laced bowels bible tripe duck
neck bones deer steak goose roast
cottage cheese cream tea
corn rice raisin strawberry-pudding.[92]

While the two concoctions are not exact replicas (illustrating again how the recipe for voice is dynamic and can be adapted for context), there are at least two important similarities that bear critical reflection. Amid a list of traditional foods in both poems, the word "bible" appears. Both recipes also lead to the same outcome, voice and testimony, and both connect the narrators to their ancestors and their own bodies. How then are we to interpret the interruption of traditional food items with one of the most blatant symbols of colonization, the image so often associated with the trauma and repression inflicted on colonized populations, particularly in residential schools? On one hand, the bible, as an ingredient, can be read as a means to signal the ways in which Indigenous children were forced to consume Western religion in church-run residential schools with Christian mandates.

On the other hand, it is also important to note that "bible" is lowercase in both instances, which strips the word of its authority as a proper noun and contributes to erasure as it is buried, rendered almost unnoticeable, among the other ingredients in the recipe. Méira Cook offers an insightful interpretation of the word "bible" in these regards: "Positioned as a rude interruption to the flow of memory and appetite that the list initiates, the 'bible' is buried in the inner organs (between 'bowels' and 'tripe'), a fitting reminder that the missionary enterprise colonized the bodies as well as the minds and souls of the converts."[93] While I agree with Cook's interpretation, it should also be noted that "bible" is never a dominant signifier in Halfe's recipes. Embedded in the formula, Halfe mixes in ingredients from her home and culture, dampening the influence of religion and limiting its culinary influence on the final meal. Indeed, from the first recipe to the second we see how deeply "bible" has been buried beneath traditional remedies, indicating that the recipes are doing their job – that the "taste" of religion, while still seasoning the recipe in some oblique, lowercase sense, is becoming less and less present as the recipe is shared, revised, and remade.

Of course, the bible is not the only embodied silence that Halfe must contend with in her struggle to testify to colonialism and her ancestor's histories, but it does offer a productive metaphor through which to read the poet's engagement with the effects of colonization. While there are Cree words throughout all of Halfe's work (and Cree glossaries), the narrators primarily share their stories in English, which creates its own "frog in the throat." While, on one hand, English is a vehicle for testimony and a means of transmitting trauma and love, on the other hand, it compels her narrators to mobilize the very language that was used as a tool of oppression. Halfe makes the double bind of English explicit in *Blue Marrow,* as the narrator, and perhaps Halfe herself, is confronted with the inevitable problem of disseminating her stories in a language other than Cree:

My words get in your way.
I feel your sting.
My printer refuses to feed my leaves.
A squirrel stakes out
the sink.
I feed him my apple.
My printer sins.[94]

It could be that the "you" in this passage identifies the non-Cree reader of the text, the individual who is unable to "hear" the Cree words Halfe inserts into all of her poetry. In this sense, the narrator would be identifying how the loss of that language, loss that comes through the residential school system that worked (and failed) to eradicate it, interferes with her audience's ability to interpret the text and bear witness to the testimony it is offering.

However, this interpretation assumes a non-Cree readership and risks eliding significant portions of Halfe's audience – namely Cree readers. It is therefore much more likely that the "you" in this passage refers to any reader of the text, Cree-speaking or not. In this case, the matter of "words getting in the way" is directed more specifically at the effects of the written word, including the centripetal force of the poetic signifier, which, the further it is removed from the care and protection of the poet, becomes more and more open to the threat of misinterpretation. In this sense, the "words get in the way" insofar as the narrator struggles to relay, to any audience, the specificity of her experience within a colonial system that sucks up meaning like a vacuum in a sandbox, leaving the authorial intent – to convey the truth of Indigenous experiences within the whiteout of settler colonialism – alienated in the movement from testimony to the written word.

This point about "words getting in the way" warrants further reflection, not because I want to highlight the sway that settler colonialism holds over poetic interpretation, but because I want to categorically emphasize the kinds of work that Halfe continually puts into her poetry and testimony. Halfe's poetics both critique and reflect anxiety over the (im)possibility of accurate acknowledgment in a system in which words fail. This anxiety is well-founded, and Halfe's willingness to explore it as a part of her poetics can be educational, particularly in the contexts of reconciliation.

One of the most illuminating examples of the problem of acknowledgment, which I am defining here as a problem of reception and static, is found in the video recording of Halfe's reading at the 2007 Words Aloud Spoken Word Festival, commissioned for the Words Aloud documentary series. Halfe begins with a series of poems from *Bear Bones and Feathers* that, notably (considering that the Canadian federal government had just finished litigating the Indian Residential Schools Settlement Agreement), deals with the genocidal history of Canada's residential school system and recent apologies from the Catholic Church. Before beginning the reading, Halfe provides her audience with a strong personal opinion on the state of acknowledgment and reconciliation in Canada. From the podium, she tells the audience:

> This is the story of the residential school and as many of you know there is a settlement going in Indian country, which to me isn't sufficient, because it will never heal the wounds of my community. *This country doesn't know what happened there.* What I'd like to do is to show you and leave you to think about it. [emphasis added][95]

Turning then to a copy of *Bear Bones and Feathers,* Halfe goes on to read "Returning," a powerful poem about going back to visit a residential school after being free from it for years. She follows "Returning" with a reading of "Der Poop," a shorter poem that, with the rez english also used in "My Ledders," mocks the Pope's apology to residential school survivors: "sorry mean dat i don't need yous church / and yous priest telling me what to do / sorry mean dat i free to dalk to *Manitou*."[96] As Halfe admits before her performance of "Der Poop," "I was quite ticked when the Pope said 'I'm sorry.'"

The poet's anger, although it is couched in humour, is readily apparent in the poem itself. The possibility of apology is roundly mocked and derided, based specifically on the fact that acknowledgment has failed: that the country, and the pope, "*don't know what happened there*." There is unintentional evidence from the Words Aloud festival to back this claim up, found in the video that was produced of her reading. In the title card made for "Der Poop" in that recording, the poem is listed as "Dear Pope," missing entirely the joke that the poem rests on.[97] This "translation" not only strips the poem of much of its vitriol, rendering it a more polite, anglicized version of the original verse (an unwitting recapitulation of residential school censorship), but it also testifies to Halfe's anxiety about "words getting in the way." In this reading the signifier itself ("Pope") interferes with how the audience receives the narrator's testimony, proving the poet's opening point about the knowledge gap between Indigenous peoples and settler Canadians. What the videographer's error demonstrates is that even when survivor testimony is offered loudly, powerfully, with humour and dramatic flair, this does not guarantee that its audience will hear it as such. "The words get in the way," and the first step toward reconciliation is suddenly not as sturdy as the weight borne by the road to reconciliation requires. Indeed, literally sanitizing the shit out of residential schools is another way of twisting acknowledgment to the benefit of the settler state.

"Listen to the Bones"

While Halfe emphasizes the difficulty of testifying to colonial violence, she never admits defeat, and her willingness to revise and republish, to continue generating poetry and essays, demonstrates an ongoing commitment to the possibility of change. According to Warren Cariou, "*Blue Marrow* is not only a poem but also an elaborate ceremony, designed to call the spirits of the Grandmothers to come forth and tell their stories in order to heal the present generation."[98] The ceremony that Cariou identifies here is also a call to action. In Halfe's insistence that we "see the blood" and "listen to the bones"[99] – in other words, that we, as readers, bear witness to the violent histories of settler colonialism – she compels us to read beyond the limitations of colonial static and the Standard Account and respond to the material conditions of testimony and acknowledgment. What makes Halfe's poetry particularly relevant to the discourse of acknowledgment is that it is never reified or limited to one body or text. âcimowinis, for instance, while serving as the primary narrator for *Blue Marrow*, is positioned as "Keeper of the

Stories": not an owner or a benefactor of testimony, but a witness proliferating history.[100] Multiple perspectives move within and through her, thus rendering her "Cree-ing" varied and pluralistic. âcimowinis tells the reader,

> I bring to you
> these Voices I will not name. Voices
> filled with bird calls, mountain goats.
> I do not recognize who speaks.[101]

As this passage helps to illustrate, Halfe's acknowledgment of colonial violence is derived from a community of voices that exceeds the Western conceptions of the solitary author. By refusing to name the voices, the narrator also refuses to have these stories rendered into a consumable artifact, which might be recuperated into a colonial narrative. To acknowledge, in this sense, means to bear witness to a collective of perspectives, many of which cannot testify themselves, while standing as steward and keeper of a precarious history.

Halfe's attentiveness to the dynamic nature of community voice, and the ethics of bearing witness with and for these voices, is evident in her poetry, but it is also apparent in her publishing practices. When Coteau Books approached her about republishing *Blue Marrow* (five years after it was first published by McClelland and Stewart), she immediately saw it as a way to re-vision and re-voice the poem. In the acknowledgments for the second edition of *Blue Marrow* she writes, "I was given an opportunity to revisit the text in new ways, and I am deeply appreciative of the vision that resulted from this."[102] While both texts were released under the same title, and contain roughly the same content, the two versions of *Blue Marrow* have a number of editorial changes that compel readers to question their immediate reactions to the text and the validity of the tools they might use to unpack it. Most importantly, the differences between these two texts ask us to consider how we as readers – and witnesses – might contribute to the proliferation of testimony and how this, in turn, inflects what acknowledgment is and what it can do as a decolonizing methodology.

There are a number of production and language changes between the first and second editions of *Blue Marrow* that deserve close attention. The Coteau edition includes a new cover, added sections of poetry, in-text glosses, and a seven-page Cree-to-English glossary at the end of the text. In the context of acknowledgment, the latter two changes, particularly the glossary, are of special importance, as the glossary necessitates a different interaction with the long poem and the ways in which Halfe compels her readers to "listen to the bones." To quote Halfe herself, in a phrase used at the beginning of *Blue Marrow,* the glossary, a feature that she has included in all her published works subsequent to the Coteau edition of *Blue Marrow,* presents readers with a new way to "ride English," prompting continuous movement across the landscape of the poem that unsettles the colonial language as a necessarily oppressive vehicle for thought, and re-centres a Cree poetic voice within it.[103] With the glossary, rather than simply receiving meaning from both the Cree and English words, readers are asked to help produce meaning through a particular bodily interaction with language and the materiality of the text. The words are made alive in the ways they compel the reader to trace them through the poetry and to illuminate their dynamic meanings in relation to context.

This engagement with language creates an energy in the text that makes the reader an active witness of Halfe's poetics. Samantha Nock outlines dynamic witnessing in her essay "Being a Witness: The Importance of Protecting Indigenous Women's Stories":

> Too often we think that the act of listening is equal to the act of witnessing. Listening is passive. We can listen, however your ability to listen lets you, while making to-do lists in our heads, thinking of what we are going to have for dinner, or what we are going to say next. When we witness a story we are not only present physically, but emotionally and spiritually, to hold this story in our hearts. When someone tells us their story, that story becomes a part of us. When you witness someone's story, be it a comedy or a tragedy, you are carrying a part of that person with you now. You have entered a very specific and powerful relationship that exists between the storyteller and the witness.[104]

By tracing words to the glossary and back in *Blue Marrow,* readers give new life to Cree words and the poetry itself by connecting it to larger webs of meaning that spread out like the tendrils of a spiderweb through words, lines, and pages of the poems. We become witnesses to colonial violence and residential schools in that we are called to be keepers of that knowledge and active participants in the production and proliferation of its meaning. In other words, we become part of a relationship evoked by the power of poetry.

Building witnessing into the written word is a key feature of Indigenous poetics. The Anishinaabe critic Niigaanwewidam Sinclair writes, "Indigenous poetics are the intricate and intellectual acts of gifting words full of breath, rhythm and expression in the hopes that they will be accepted in a world constituted by language."[105] Being a witness via *Blue Marrow* means carefully and compassionately carrying, and caring for, the bundles of breath that Halfe has gifted into a world in which colonial violence is still defined by absence. It means being willing to speak with those stories and against the systems that attempt to erase the fact of colonial violence. In bearing witness to Halfe's poetics, we commit ourselves to resisting colonial static and ensuring that these histories are not ignored, refuted, or silenced.

The active witnessing implicit to the second edition of *Blue Marrow* becomes more apparent when interpreted via comparative analysis across the McClelland and Stewart and Coteau publications. The first edition provides little or no gloss for the Cree language sections. This in itself has served as a primary point of analysis for Halfe scholars, who draw attention to the ideological importance of the poet's choice *not* to include a glossary. For instance, according to Méira Cook, the absence of a glossary in the McClelland and Stewart edition "is an editorial choice that signals [Halfe's] acknowledgment that she is not writing predominantly for a white, English-speaking audience."[106] For Cook, a Cree readership is identified and produced by the narrative voice, which both implies and creates a Cree literary community while simultaneously estranging non-Cree readers.

Similarly, Shelley Stigter argues that "since no glossary is included, Halfe leaves the reader to rely on context to gain understanding, or he/she must do outside research."[107] For Stigter, the lack of a glossary has very real effects on how the text is read, informed by the additional work the non-Cree reader must do in order to understand the richness and subtlety of the narrative. Both Cook and Stigter argue that the alienation generated by the Cree words in *Blue Marrow* are a productive element of the text's poetics. In sum, the argument advanced is that by estranging the reader who cannot read Cree – who, it must be remembered, may in fact be Indigenous or even Cree (though perhaps not a fluent reader/speaker) – Halfe incites a more involved interaction with Indigenous culture and the history of colonization. In order to make this point, both Cook and Stigter appeal to an inside/outside binary to define the geography of the text. According to Cook, "the untranslated word ... situates a trope of incomprehensibility that functions to mark the non-Cree outside, as opposed to [the reader's] habitual mode of fluent language use in the North American context where the linguistic currency is English."[108] In other words, the *form* of *Blue Marrow,* in its first edition, plays a primary role in conveying how information is received.

Through the lack of a glossary, the colonizer/colonized dichotomy is inverted. It is the non-Cree reader who is pushed outside a familiar space (i.e., the book itself) and forced to be uncomfortably aware of their difference in what is now rendered an uncanny landscape.

There is a call to action implicit in the readings that Cook and Stigter offer: the non-Cree-speaking reader is compelled to move outside the text and learn more about Cree language and culture as opposed to passively receiving information, or just skimming over non-English words. However, what this interpretation overlooks is the fact that the publishing world is often already alienating to many Indigenous readers and storytellers. Who Cook and Stigter would seem to be directing discomfort toward then are the non-Indigenous audiences with ingrained assumptions about text and language: audiences who would seek to recognize Cree words by making them legible within a certain poetic schematic.

By turning to Stigter, we can further flesh out the particular notion of recognition that she and Cook are identifying. For instance, Stigter looks at Halfe's use of the words "amisk" and "iskotwêw" to illustrate her point. According to Stigter's reading of the passage, the reader is left to guess, through context, the meanings of the words:

> This passage shows not only dialectic separation of Cree and English, it also carries cultural meaning regarding the medicine bundles that is not made explicit ... Since cultural meaning is not clarified for the non-Aboriginal reader, the connection of the medicine bundles to the animals is lost upon them. The dialectic [between culture and knowledge] then becomes more apparent.[109]

In other words, Halfe's use of Cree displaces non-Cree readers (incorrectly identified above as "non-Aboriginal readers") and actually compels them away from the text and toward the "outside research" she mentions earlier, here identified as supplementary study. The "call out" of *Blue Marrow,* then, in this reading, is quite literally a call-out, a demand to the reader to move outside the text and into secondary sources in order to gain access to the bundles stored for safekeeping in Halfe's work. As both Cook and Stigter agree, as long as readers are willing to do their cultural homework, the lack of a glossary in the first edition revitalizes Cree voices and challenges the non-Cree reader's propensity to view the text as something they can control or know in its entirety. The first edition of *Blue Marrow* thus becomes a way to disrupt the smooth flow of discourse that maintains the colonial status quo, generating the space for Cree voices to be heard and studied in context. In this sense, the text itself becomes a form of medicine: a dose of decolonial culture to soothe colonial wounds, which both the Indigenous and non-Indigenous readers can gather into their own medicine bundles. This reading is useful in unsettling the category of acknowledgment, given that it emphasizes the labour that must be incurred *outside* naturalized colonial structures to move toward a culturally contextualized understanding of events.

With the addition of a glossary, however, the more recent edition of *Blue Marrow* cannot be said to compel its readers to go outside the text in the same ways Cook and Stigter suggest. Rather, any reader can simply flip to the back of the book or refer to in-text glosses. This means that the "guessing" that Stigter identifies as a critical aspect of *Blue Marrow*'s semiotics is no longer an explicit issue. As such, the call to action attached to that kind of reading, the demand to move outside the text in order to learn, can no longer be said to be a direct imperative. For better or worse, the glossary in the second edition of *Blue Marrow* makes for a much more contained entity. For instance, in reading the passage cited above, the reader can almost immediately learn the Cree meaning of "amisk" and "iskotwêw" without putting the poem down.

It is on this point of acknowledgment and engagement that I would like to dwell, if the reader will bear with me for one moment's more close reading. What I have attempted to illustrate in the beginning of this chapter is that a significant part of the difficulty with acknowledgment is not simply that Indigenous testimony is repressed, but that it is not taken up in a meaningful way and therefore left to stagnate in a colonial system that primarily wants to recuperate power. Indigenous peoples do not require non-Indigenous recognition for events, or language, to be meaningful. However, acknowledging the history of settler colonialism – for non-Indigenous people who truly wish to engage and for Indigenous people who want to further their knowledge – means shaking language free of the calcifying effects of colonial logocentrism and engaging with the complex and philosophically rich meaning embedded in Indigenous languages.

For Halfe, who welcomes audiences that come willing to learn, words need movement to be brought to life, but that movement does not necessarily mean "outside research." Like brackish water, a stagnant word hints at sickness and contamination, becoming more an agent of harm than an envoy of healing. In Halfe's poetry, a word is brought to life by the readers' movement through the text. Not only are words that make an appearance in later poems informed by earlier contexts, but readers are also compelled to move backward through *Blue Marrow* to see how new understandings of language can inflect earlier representations. By adding a glossary to the second edition of *Blue Marrow,* Halfe amplifies this process by asking readers to move back and forth through the poetry, encouraging them to "grow" the Cree word in relation to the English contexts in which it is planted. To push this idea a little further, the glossary in *Blue Marrow* makes readers aware of their bodily interaction with a text as a material object that requires a specific performative interaction with its content. Suddenly pages, spelling, and word order become vital aspects of the readers' ability to negotiate the poem, and the "foreign" word becomes a living form that is (re)activated as readers map out meaning as they move back and forth through the poetry.

Through the emphasis on its materiality – which compels readers to interact with its meaning making – the second edition of *Blue Marrow* encourages readers to experience their own subjectivity in their reading of the poem. To put it otherwise, borrowing from Anishinaabe Elder Mary Lou Fox, the second edition compels us to recognize that "we do not create a language, but we are created within it."[110] Indeed, with the aid of the glossary, Cree voices are witnessed in more active terms in the Coteau edition of *Blue Marrow;* readers are created as key components in the composition of acknowledgment, as opposed to being passive recipients. Once engaged, made living through interaction, language reveals its intimacies and secrets, adding richness, depth, and complexity to voice and the concept of acknowledgment. Indigenous words are rich, vital pools of knowledge that both bear witness and testify to the past.

This reading resonates through Indigenous literary studies, particularly in the focus on language. Leanne Betasamosake Simpson writes that "Indigenous languages carry rich meanings, theory and philosophies within their structures. [Indigenous] languages house our teachings and bring the practice of those teachings to life in our daily existence."[111] In this context, it is important to note that in the way it calls for readers to bear witness, the glossary in *Blue Marrow* challenges the idea that meaning in Cree language is something that necessarily exists outside the text itself. By emphasizing the importance of the *lack* of a glossary in the first edition, Cook and Stigter tacitly make a case that presupposes "outside research" as the primary hermeneutic tool for investigating Indigenous texts. The alienating effect of language forces readers out of the poem in order to discover the meaning Halfe is working with, rather than asking them to draw out meaning in relation to the poetry itself. This is not to disparage historically contextualized analysis, which can be a necessary part of the work of reading Indigenous literature. It is to suggest, however, that the Coteau version of *Blue Marrow* is not only about how culture and history shape language; it is also about how audience interaction and Halfe's poetics shape language itself. Clearly, the engagement with language that Halfe introduces will be different for different readers. Those with Cree heritage and language will convene with the text in a different way than an Anishinaabemowin speaker, although there will likely still be resonances in the decolonial contexts. Settler scholars, on the other hand, will most likely bring with them a dense genealogy of English-language poetics, which pose the threat of "the words getting in the way." Even so, I would argue that Halfe generates a material space of activation through which to unsettle these genealogies and to welcome rigorous engagement with Cree poetics.

Indeed, Halfe's poetry is deeply moving, by which I mean it shakes and unsettles Western limitations of language. From this point, internal, close readings of *Blue Marrow* can be just as applicable as the cultural or historical analysis that Stigter and Cook emphasize in their interpretations of the first edition. Close reading affords the space to reflect on the fact that many English-speaking Cree readers may be learning about their language for the first time from Halfe's books, which, in turn, provides for more nuanced and accountable interpretations of the calls to action implicit in the text. The glossary also creates space for non-Cree Indigenous readers, who want to engage the text and the Cree language as a poetics of testimony. Finally, it makes space for non-Indigenous readers, who might not yet know about secondary Cree sources, to begin a journey toward the acknowledgment of colonial violence. For example, using the glossary in *Blue Marrow,* the reader learns that the Cree word "wêpinâsowin" can mean at least five different things at once: something thrown in the wind, a flower print, material that flows in the wind, an offering, or a flag.[112] It is up to the reader to use the text to understand how and why each definition fits the passage in question, which facilitates learning and illustrates the depth of the language. But the glossary also asks the reader to enact a performance of wêpinâsowin in their reading, adding another layer of meaning to the word and the complexities of language as Halfe deploys it.

As we fan through the pages of the text looking for meaning, *Blue Marrow* itself becomes a material that flows in the wind, a poem caught in the breeze of our own interpretive process. The "play" of language that Halfe evokes with words such as wêpinâsowin adds a new vitality to the word, not as a set or stagnant meaning, but as a process that can be continually (re)animated and (re)developed by considering the page and our interactions with it in relation to its structure, not only its cultural or even textual implications. Simpson draws attention to the power of the process of connecting to Indigenous culture and land through language: "this learning through the language provides those who are not fluent with a window through which to experience the complexities and depths" of Indigenous cultures.[113] I would add that learning through the language holds the same potential for the acknowledgment of colonial violence. Halfe's playful use of the glossary thus brings Cree language to life in the ever-present moment of its reception – as opposed to relegating meaning to the past. Imbued with multiple meanings from the glossary and one's bodily interaction with the text, wêpinâsowin, for instance, is no longer a foreign signifier, impenetrable and stagnant to the non-Cree-speaking audience, but a vital, complex and volatile element of the book, which bodies and languages set into motion. wêpinâsowin is acknowledged as a rich, dynamic, and living voice, and *Blue Marrow* is thus a means of recognition that sets reciprocity as a praxis for engagement.

Conclusion

What Halfe's poetry has always demonstrated is not only the cultural and political challenges implicit in hearing Indigenous voices within colonial systems, be they in a book of poetry or at a TRC hearing, but also the many ways in which these challenges are being opposed and overcome, particularly by Indigenous women and queer and trans folk. If acknowledgment is necessary in order to even *begin* the reconciliation process, we need to resist the temptation to reify it. Making the call "knowable" (or recognizable) so that settler society may subsequently move on to apology and forgiveness elides the depth and complexity of the voices in this structure and the work of individuals like Halfe and Whitehead who labour – and will go on labouring – to make them heard, with or without settler witnesses.

Halfe is certainly cautious of the ways in which her work might be (mis)interpreted, but her readiness to republish *Blue Marrow,* to revise and revitalize her call to action, also demonstrates her willingness to continue to challenge the "whiteout" of settler colonialism with ongoing love, resistance, and resurgence. In making acknowledgment a continuous and reciprocal practice, Halfe not only provides an alternative means to struggle against settler colonialism, but also brings new vitality to the Cree language, allowing it to be heard as testimony against the system that works so hard to silence it and as a deeply philosophical and dynamic language. This, in turn, creates space for the next generation of Indigenous poets, such as

Whitehead, to further press the boundaries of recognition and representation, and to critique the ways in which these ideas play out within the context of a TRC. Apology and forgiveness, to which I will turn in subsequent chapters, would not be possible without the work in acknowledgment that she, Whitehead, and other Indigenous authors, activists, and performers have been doing – and will continue to do – alongside the TRC.

3

To Acknowledge, but Not to Accept

Critical Reflections on Settler State Apologies

> *"Sorry, sorry, sorry, sorry,"* says Coyote.
>
> – THOMAS KING[1]

Near the end of *Green Grass, Running Water,* Thomas King, via Coyote, offers an extended and rather empty apology to anyone who may have been offended by the preceding chapters of his novel. After deconstructing, interrupting, and outright mocking some of the West's most cherished cultural foundations, including the story of Genesis and the heroic narratives of the settler nation, Coyote offers a half-hearted "sorry" to the *Green Grass* audience:

> "Wait a minute," said Ishmael. "Wait a minute. Before we begin, did anyone offer an apology?"
> "Wasn't Coyote going to do that?" said Robinson Crusoe.
> "Apologize for what?" says Coyote.
> "In case we hurt anyone's feelings," said Hawkeye.
> "Oh, okay," says Coyote. "I'm sorry."
> "That didn't sound very sorry, Coyote," said the Lone Ranger. "Remember what happened the last time you rushed through a story and didn't apologize?"
> "Yes," said Ishmael. "Remember how far you had to run?"
> "Oops!" says Coyote. "I am *very* sorry."

"That's better," said Hawkeye.
"I am really *very, very* sorry," says Coyote.
"That's fine," said the Lone Ranger. "It sounds very sincere."
"*Sorry, sorry, sorry, sorry*," says Coyote.
"Okay," said the Lone Ranger. "We believe you."
"Hee-hee," says Coyote. "Hee-hee."[2]

Written at the time that Canadian churches were offering their own apologies to the survivors of residential schools (1991–94 saw the issue or publication of four church apologies), Coyote's emphatic repetition of sorry here – "*sorry, sorry, sorry, sorry*" – which, likely not coincidentally, matches the number of church apologies, reflects the social climate in which King was writing (what the apology scholar Roy L. Brooks has famously dubbed "The Age of Apology").[3] It also demonstrates King's deep understanding of what other critics have called the "new global morality,"[4] and the way in which the language of regret and contrition has been embedded in political discourse.

More importantly, however, because Coyote is not apologizing in order to heal or minimize hurt in this scene, but rather to protect himself from further persecution, King draws special attention to the ways in which apologies can be deployed as a means of self-interest.[5] Coyote's desire to avoid being "run out" of the scene, which Ishmael draws attention to here, is a humorous yet apt comparison of the ways in which many politicians shape their discourse in response to public opinion in order to stay in office, all the while affirming their own sense of being moral agents without doing the hard work required for facilitating structural change.

Apology is the crown jewel of state reconciliation. Once the call has been initiated and the perpetrator acknowledges their role in the crime, apology is the first step toward securing a new relationship between parties. According to Nicholas Tavuchis, "in its purest expression, an apology clearly announces that I have no excuses for what I did or did not do or say. I am sorry and regretful. I care. Forgive me."[6] A good apology exposes the vulnerability of the apologizer, allowing survivors to overcome their reproach and begin the process of forgiveness. For Tavuchis, apology is "the tension between sorrow and forgiveness that is transcended by reconciliation."[7] However, in this chapter I want to challenge the notion of the "purest expression" of apology (also known as a sincere apology) in order to expose the ways in which blind faith in sincerity can be deployed strategically *against* the subjects that an apology claims to redress. King's Coyote provides a fertile place to begin this conversation.

King's comic critique of apology in the scene above is better understood if analyzed within the context in which it was conceived. Published in 1993, *Green Grass* was written during a time when "I'm sorry" was just beginning to make its political emergence. According to Aaron Lazare, author of the 2005 text *On Apology,* the rise in public apologies began in the early 1990s, when a number of legal articles were published on "the role of apology in both civil and criminal law, analyzing how it functions during trial and pre-trial mediation."[8] Papers such as "Advising Clients to Apologize" and "Legal Consequences of Apologizing" demonstrated how apology could actually facilitate the defendant's position, leading to shorter legal battles, out-of-court settlements and even lower payouts for wrongs incurred.[9] Following this legal work, "the formerly forbidden idea that physicians should apologize" began to emerge in the medical literature,[10] and the practice was implemented in certain hospitals with positive effects for doctor-patient relationships (and hospital bottom lines).[11] Indeed, as the *New York Times* reports, once health care providers began to sink under malpractice costs and consumer demand for redress, prominent medical centres, like Johns Hopkins and Stanford, began trying a "disarming approach" – namely, offering "earnest apologies and fair compensation."[12]

In sum, elite communities were gradually establishing apology as something with the potential to be friendly to the wrongdoer, with the ostensible goal of generating healthier grounds for healing and restitution. With law and medicine serving as testing grounds, space was cleared for apologies to be mobilized politically. In 1993, South African president F.W. de Klerk apologized for apartheid; later that same year, Japanese prime minister Morihiro Hosokawa apologized for suffering caused by Japan in the Second World War; and on March 26, 1998, U.S. president Bill Clinton apologized for American inaction during the 1994 Rwandan genocide in what became one of seven apologies from Clinton during his two terms in office (including his apology for lying about his relationship with Monica Lewinsky).[13]

In Canada, where King was living and working at the time, the political efficacy of the apology was also being tested by the churches. On August 17, 1986, the United Church of Canada officially apologized to Indigenous peoples for past wrongs inflicted by the church. Delivered by Reverend Robert Smith, the moderator of the United Church at the time, this apology acknowledged the role the church had played in the destruction of Indigenous culture. Smith was responding to a request from Indigenous peoples in the United Church to speak to that institution's role in the residential school system. He offered these words at the 31st General Council in Sudbury, Ontario:

> We tried to make you be like us and in so doing we helped to destroy the vision that made you what you were. As a result, you, and we, are poorer and the image of the Creator in us is twisted, blurred, and we are not what we are meant by God to be.[14]

The United Church's apology marked a national shift in Canada's discourse of regret. Smith's words formed the basis of a long string of "sorries" that would eventually arrive at Prime Minister Stephen Harper's apology to the survivors of residential schools – delivered in the House of Commons in 2008, twenty-two years later. While Smith's 1986 apology is an important benchmark for how and why large institutions apologized to Indigenous peoples in Canada, it also set a precedent for how Indigenous communities could respond to these apologies. However, because apology analysis is so often focused on the apologist, as opposed to the survivor, these types of responses are frequently overlooked or overshadowed, which is why I take those responses up here.

Notably, it took two years and one day for the Native Circle Conference (NCC) to consider and respond to Smith and the United Church. At the 32nd General Council of the United Church of Canada, Edith Memnook, an Elder and representative for the NCC, publicly acknowledged but did not accept the apology. In her statement, she told the council:

> The Native People of The All Native Circle Conference hope and pray that the Apology is not symbolic but that these are the words of action and sincerity. We appreciate the freedom for culture and religious expression. In the new spirit this Apology has created, let us unite our hearts and minds in the wholeness of life that the Great Spirit has given us.[15]

The NCC's delayed response and Memnook's carefully crafted statement speak to a number of important ideas on Indigenous approaches to apology for colonial violence. First, by waiting just over two years to offer its response, the NCC demonstrated that such an issue deserved close consideration and that an extended amount of time was necessary to reach a conclusion. Second, while the council and Memnook *acknowledged* the United Church apology in their response, they refused to *accept* it on the grounds that they needed more time and further proof in order to determine whether "these are the words of action and sincerity." In other words, while the NCC recognized that the church was taking a step toward healing and reconciliation, the apology itself (i.e., the words in the prepared statement) was not enough to guarantee its sincerity.

The NCC's response to the United Church indicated that they appreciated and respected the church's attempt and that the council would not actively work against the apology. Indeed, Memnook's reply is compassionate and patient. However, in order for the apology to be accepted as sincere, further evidence and action were needed to support the claims that Smith had made. The time, reflection, and discussion given to deliberating on Smith's short statement demonstrated that responding to an apology was not something that should be rushed or forced. By privileging "acknowledgment" over "acceptance," the NCC emphasized the need to continue studying, discussing, and researching the apology rather than just "moving on." To put it differently, apology must be considered over the expanse of the *longue durée*. Like reconciliation itself, it is a structure, not an event.

Coyote's apology at the end of *Green Grass,* written in the wake of the United Church's apology and Memnook's response, reflects and reinforces the approach determined by the NCC by playing sincerity off as comedy. In the space of a few lines, Coyote goes from not appearing sorry at all, to his interlocutors guaranteeing that his apology "sounds very sincere," to him giggling at their naïveté. The joke is, of course, the performative nature of sincerity and the ways in which that performance can be mobilized by the perpetrator toward specific ends. King's critique notwithstanding, however, sincerity is still a significant part of what makes an apology function as such. According to Susan Alter in a paper commissioned by the Law Commission of Canada, "an apology must sound natural and sincere, as if it comes from the heart of the wrongdoer and not from the pen of a lawyer or an indifferent third party."[16] In a special report as Acting Ombudsman for the Province of British Columbia, Howard Kushner writes that "a sincere apology can heal wounds, restore dignity, and encourage forgiveness."[17]

In Coyote's apology, however, sincerity is deployed as a performance within the theatre of regret. Time for proper consideration of his remarks is closed off immediately, so there is no further discussion of the *need* for apology, which his interlocutors identify at the beginning of the passage, nor a closer examination of Coyote's emphatic insistence that he *is* sincere and therefore should be taken at his word. It is by taking up the mantle of sincerity that he convinces those around him to proceed without careful consideration: to take his apology as truth without evidence.

The brevity of the scene resonates with what the apology industry in Canada was becoming at the moment of *Green Grass*'s publication. Indeed, despite the important precedent set by Memnook and the NCC, "sorries" were, with almost the same rapidity that Coyote spits them out, being fast-tracked through the system by both churches and government officials in Canada. After the 1986 apology from the United Church, the 1990s saw five apologies to survivors of residential schools: four from churches – including a re-apology from the United Church[18] – and the first from the Canadian government (Jane Stewart's Statement of Reconciliation), which would set the tone for the "string of apologies" that the Canadian government would offer to various groups (including Chinese Canadians, Japanese Canadians, and Indo-Canadians) in the following decade.[19] In the limited space between these "sorries," there was little time for the reflection and debate that are needed to initiate the genuinely transformative politics of reconciliation that Memnook demonstrated as precedent. And while many spoke out against their validity, no group stepped forward to "acknowledge but not accept" these apologies or to stave off guaranteeing their sincerity in some public or formal fashion.

Indeed, in this period of time, as Roland Chrisjohn and Tanya Wasacase point out, "so many people ... embraced the government's own characterization of their words ('truth,' 'reconciliation,' 'apology,' and so on) and deeds ('mistakes,' 'forging new partnerships,' et cetera) at face value" that the language of reconciliation was reified within the specious logic of logocentrism:[20] that is, a word such as "apology" was made stable and guaranteed by explicit meaning in the external world. By the time Harper gave his 2008 apology, the space for debate and analysis around "apology" was all but foreclosed. Perhaps as evidence of this, Harper's statement of regret was referred to by his government as a "Full Apology": a sorry that covers all ground, leaves no wound unhealed, and thus needs no further thought, conversation, or deliberation. The "full apology" presumed that all outstanding matters were now closed – the apology *was* the action.

As King illustrates in *Green Grass,* without the proper space for reflection and careful consideration, "sorry" becomes a way of deflecting persecution and promoting self-interest. Seizing the moment to his own advantage, Coyote is able to escape the wrath of his would-be persecutors and play one last trick on his interlocutors (this is the final "hee-hee" of many that punctuate the passage). Thus, reflecting the current political climate of apology, "sorry" here is determined by King as a tool more useful to the perpetrator than to the survivor(s) it addresses.

Coyote's apology raises some important questions for us within the discourse of reconciliation: How applicable is the Coyote model of apology to the "sorries" we have recently seen from the Canadian government and which Canadian leaders continue to proffer? Are states benefitting from their own sorries? How? Has "sorry" become what Sky Dancer Louise Bernice Halfe identifies as "med-sin" or can apology still do the work of healing and reparation that scholars such as Tavuchis suggest it can?[21] Following Memnook's lead, it may be beneficial for proponents of reconciliation to step away from acceptance and consider moving closer to acknowledgment of apology, locating the spaces to critically examine "sorry" rather than attempting to guarantee it.

The "Statement of Reconciliation"

On January 7, 1998, Jane Stewart, then minister of Indian Affairs and Northern Development, offered the Statement of Reconciliation as part of the unveiling of *Gathering Strength: Canada's Aboriginal Action Plan*. The media coverage almost unanimously declared the Statement to be a sincere apology. The morning before Stewart's address, the *Globe and Mail* published an article entitled "Natives Finally Get Ottawa's Apology: 'Deeply Sorry' for Residential Schools," which stated that the Statement of Reconciliation was "the first time the government [made] a clear apology" for residential schools.[22] After the Statement was delivered, *ABC Newslink* reported that "the Canadian Government has apologized to Indigenous people for actions that have had a negative political, economic and social impact on its Aboriginal society."[23]

However, while the media was ready to guarantee the apology as sincere, Indigenous peoples and their representatives were not as sure. Matt James writes that "the Native leaders present [at Stewart's apology] dismissed the Statement as an inadequate response to both Canada's unjust treatment of Aboriginal peoples in general and to the legacy of residential schools in particular."[24] John McKiggin, a lawyer for former Indian Residential School students in Nova Scotia, openly challenged the media's position: "The statement of reconciliation does not apologize for government actions. It recognizes the pain. It doesn't admit responsibility for that pain."[25] According to Paulette Regan, a former resolution manager for Indian Residential Schools Resolution Canada and senior advisor for the National Truth and

Reconciliation Commission, many Indigenous people consider Jane Stewart's Statement of Reconciliation to be "a completely inadequate response, lacking the moral authority or political legitimacy of a public formal apology made in Parliament by the prime minister."[26] The tension between the two interpretations of the same speech – apology on the one hand, (non)apology on the other – might compel reconciliation scholars to ask precisely what constitutes a sincere statement of regret for the colonial violence inflicted on Indigenous peoples and whether it is indeed possible, or even desirable, to apologize for settler colonial violence. Who has the power to guarantee a proper apology? What are the performative elements required to ensure it is received as sincere? And what are the subsequent actions that might guarantee its sincerity after it is delivered?

A direct comparison between Stewart's and Stephen Harper's statements creates the space for us to investigate what a "proper" apology looks like in Canada. To begin, the Statement of Reconciliation is built out of the rhetoric of acknowledgment and recognition, which I cover in the previous chapter. Stewart began by arguing that "it is essential that we deal with the legacies of the past affecting the Aboriginal peoples of Canada, including the First Nations, Inuit and Métis. Our purpose is not to rewrite history but, rather, to learn from our past."[27] Difficulties in doing so notwithstanding, Stewart's primary point here is that the state needs to be able to hear colonial violence as such (i.e., beyond the Standard Account) and act specifically toward redressing what they learn.

Stewart then goes on to specifically identify how Indigenous peoples were negatively affected by historic policy, which I quote at length in order to afford readers a better sense of her tone and pacing:

> Sadly, our history with respect to the treatment of Aboriginal people is not something in which we can take pride. Attitudes of racial and cultural superiority led to a suppression of Aboriginal cultures and values. As a country, we are burdened by past actions that resulted in weakening the identity of Aboriginal peoples, suppressing their languages and cultures, and outlawing spiritual practices. *We must recognize* the impact of these actions on the once self-sustaining nations that were disaggregated, disrupted, limited or even destroyed by the dispossession of traditional territory, by the relocation of Aboriginal people, and by some provisions of the Indian Act. *We must acknowledge* that the result of these actions was the erosion of the political, economic and social systems of Aboriginal people and nations. [emphasis added][28]

The language of recognition and of acknowledgment that Stewart offers here is identified by apology experts as being "at the centre of apologies."[29] Indeed, it is difficult to assert that an apology is possible without this fundamental element. If the call for restitution has not first been heard, the apologizer's sorry is most often considered empty. Acknowledgment is effective in this instance insofar as Stewart marks a separation between Canada's actions in the past and the government's ostensible commitment to renewed Indigenous-settler relations.

If any critique of the Statement of Reconciliation is to be taken seriously, however, we must recognize that acknowledgment in and of itself is not enough to guarantee the sincerity of an apology. To reiterate, McKiggin argues that Stewart's statement was not an apology because while she *recognized* historical wrongdoings, she did not admit any *responsibility* for them.[30] Indeed, in a close reading of the section quoted above, it is difficult to locate any particular perpetrating agent in Stewart's remarks due to her use of the passive voice. The following sentence is particularly troubling in this regard: "We must recognize the impact of these actions on the once self-sustaining nations that were disaggregated, disrupted, limited or even destroyed by the dispossession of traditional territory, by the relocation of Aboriginal people, and by some provisions of the Indian Act." While there is a subject in this portion of the speech (the royal "We"), it acts only as an observer to historical violence. The "We," which often stands in for the "I" in state apologies, simply looks over the disaggregation, disruption, and dispossession of traditional Indigenous territory, careful not to implicate a direct subject in the bloodshed.

Stewart seems to detach any state agency from this violence, spuriously designating the "relocation of Aboriginal people" and "the Indian Act" as actors. In doing so, she elides the "We" (the white citizenry and government, including religious and educational authorities that aided and abetted these violences for generations) that was behind relocation and the *Indian Act*, erasing responsibility and allowing her to embrace the all-important rhetoric of acknowledgment while simultaneously distancing herself and her government from responsibility. When the language is parsed, it becomes clear that what is really at stake in the "statement of reconciliation" is performative regret, which, I should add, is not in itself without value. As I will argue below, as a speech act, an apology, even an empty apology, has the potential to effect material change on a lived environment. A *performance* of apology can still be mobilized by the recipient toward political and material change. However, this analysis still presupposes the labour of the survivor, and when the history of empty apologies is added up, it is difficult to argue that the ends support the means.

Using ambiguous pronouns to disavow agency is certainly not a new tactic in the history of apologies offered to Indigenous peoples in Canada. In her analysis of formal apologies presented by Canadian churches to Aboriginal people, Janet Bavelas identifies passive voice as one of the primary grammatical fallacies in almost all of the statements. As the above passage from Stewart illustrates, passive voice is the most common way to apologize without apologizing – or to (non)apologize – because it acknowledges the past while tacitly disavowing responsibility for it. Passive voice puts the agent in the background by describing an action, using verbs, and even identifying an agent. Yet, as Bavelas points out, "even if there is an agent present, there is a subtle shift of focus to *receiving* the action rather than doing it" [emphasis in the original].[31] In four of the six apologies that Bavelas looks at in her study (Anglican 1993, Catholic 1991, Oblate 1991, and United, 1998), "not one of the 18 clauses describing an offense was in active voice"; rather, "the church (or 'we') [acts] as agent."[32] As in Stewart's statement, the active agent is always slightly removed from being directly involved in the violence. When an agent is included, the apology is carefully constructed so as not to directly implicate any specific individual or group. Thus, paradoxically, "the Church" or "the system" stands in as perpetrator while simultaneously denying the existence of a specific executor.

Thus, while Phil Fontaine, then National Chief of the Assembly of First Nations, quickly accepted the Statement of Reconciliation, many saw it as Mitch Miyagawa did: as a means to "whitewash the ways in which Canadians still benefit from the past, stripping the apologies of remorse. Rendering them meaningless. Forgettable."[33] It is no coincidence, then, that Stephen Harper's "Full Apology," offered almost a decade after Stewart's Statement of Reconciliation, would tactfully avoid employing the word "sorry" to the same degree in its own movement toward reconciliation.

I will discuss Harper's apology shortly, but it is perhaps necessary first to pause here and reflect on this word "sorry" and how it was being used in Canada and the international community at the time. As King indicated in *Green Grass, Running Water* (even before Stewart presented her statement), the ways in which "sorry" was being inscribed in Canadian discourse were already specious and cause for concern. Indeed, the overuse of "sorry" in Canadian culture has become a significant part of our cultural identity, to the point of being an international joke. That being said, the Canadian "sorry" isn't always about repairing relationships or even cracking wise. A

2010 study by Carrie Barr and Jackie Gillberry found that when Canadians say "sorry," we are "more interested in impressing others and in advancing through making personal connections in their career and everyday life and therefore are more open to saying 'sorry' to keep the relationship positive."[34] In other words, "sorry" is, in the sense that Erving Goffman once defined it, often an "empty gesture" for many Canadians, an everyday ritual that allows us to "position ourselves strategically in relation to ... social facts" – in this case a patriotic adherence to expressions of regret.[35]

The insistence on "sorry" in a Canadian cultural context helps to shed a different light on its political usages, particularly in relation to residential schools: it is a term that resonates deeply for Canadians and therefore offers a particular political leverage inasmuch as it carries with it a sense of national identity (much like hockey or universal health care). But as King, as well as Barr and Gillberry illustrate, just because "sorry" is used with more regularity in Canada, that doesn't mean Canadians are more committed to reparations. Indeed, the overuse of "sorry" can also be attributed to a mode of transit – a means by which individuals negotiate relationships in order to move progress forward, rather than as a means to slow down, address, and redress the past.

This point is certainly not lost on Indigenous authors in Canada, who, long before the TRC, sharply critiqued the culture of apology that is tied in so closely to Canadian identity. In the play *Burning Vision,* Métis playwright Marie Clements offers a scathing critique of the word "sorry" that casts light on the often-vacuous ways it is deployed toward Indigenous peoples and peoples of colour. Awarded the 2004 Canada-Japan Literary Award, *Burning Vision* draws out powerful alliances between Japanese and Indigenous communities, unpacking the cultural history of the uranium that was mined from Dene territory to be used in the atomic bombs detonated over Japan.

Stitching together stories and characters in ways that transcend space and time, Clements illustrates the ways in which racialized bodies are dehumanized and rendered the enemy by the settler colonial state. But even as this dehumanization occurs, these characters look toward future allyship and the possibilities for reconciliation *outside* a white, liberal framework. For example, the Métis character, Rose, proposes beginning a relationship with a Japanese man named Koji. In the way that Clements sets up the pairing, it might appear that the two are at odds, given that Koji represents part of the settler population that displaced Indigenous peoples, and given that the uranium used for the atomic bombs dropped on Japan was mined from her territories. Still, Rose asks him, "If you make me yours do we make a world with no enemies?" To which Koji responds, "if we make a world, we will make one where there are no enemies?"[36] According to Rita Wong, "the mutuality implied by [Rose and Koji's] parallel lines suggests that affiliation can be stronger than common enmity, though of course this possibility remains a question."[37] That is to say, Rose and Koji come to represent the potential of a reconciliation that contends with historical injustice, but which does so *against* the backdrop of settler colonialism instead of through it.

Exploring relationality outside of colonial frameworks is a key part of the complexity and intrigue of *Burning Vision*, but apology does not figure within that rubric. In opposition to how it is conceptualized in mainstream discourse, for Clements, apology is a means of distancing subjects, not drawing them closer. The "sorry" offered in *Burning Vision* comes from the character "Fat Man," who occupies a small home with a young Indigenous boy named "Little Boy." "Little Boy" and "Fat Man" are, of course, references to the atomic bombs dropped on Hiroshima and Nagasaki in 1945, which together killed over 210,000 people. Wong points out that while Fat Man is an allusion to violence undertaken in the Second World War, he also stands in for the *War Measures Act*, which, as I discuss in Chapter 4, was mobilized against Japanese Canadians and Indigenous peoples.[38] Inasmuch as he is a split signifier, with one foot in destruction and one in reparation, Fat Man's apology is similarly loaded, representing harm through an expression of healing. The character Rose, however, is quick to point out his duplicity and the danger implicit to his, and all Canadians', performances of regret:

> Half the time we don't even know what we are sorry about, it just squeaks out of our sorry gaps before we're even clued into the conversation. Well, I'm sorry. YOU'RE all so sorry. You have to know when to be sorry. You can't really be sorry for something you don't want to remember can you ... But it's alright ... everybody's sorry these days. The politicians are sorry, the cops are sorry, the priests are sorry, mining companies, electric companies, water companies, wife beaters, serial rapists, child molesters, mommy and daddy. Everybody's sorry. Everybody's sorry they got caught sticking it to someone else ... that's what they are sorry about ... getting caught. They could give a rat's ass about you, or me, or the people they are saying sorry to. Think about it ... Don't be a sorry ass, be sorry before you have to say you are sorry. Be sorry for even thinking about, bringing about something sorry-filled.[39]

In this passage, Rose points out that the word "sorry" as it has been, and is being, employed in Canada has been stripped of the meaning it may have held as an expression of sorrow.

Like King, Clements is drawing specifically on the political climate of the time and the ways in which "sorry" had permeated international discourse. The Anglican Church apologized for residential schools in 1993, followed by the Presbyterian Church in 1994. In 1998, the United Church offered their second apology, "Apology to Former Students of United Church Indian Residential Schools, and to Their Families and Communities," and Stewart's Statement of Reconciliation in 1998 came almost exactly one decade after former prime minister Brian Mulroney's apology to Japanese Canadian internment camp survivors (and almost exactly one decade before Harper's apology). In 2001 The Missionary Oblates of Mary Immaculate offered "An Apology to the First Nations of Canada by The Oblate Conference of Canada." Published in 2003, out of these sorry contexts, *Burning Vision* makes a compelling case that "sorry," which in Canada developed as a political concept in relation to harms committed by the state against Japanese Canadian and Indigenous peoples, no longer facilitates healing and reconciliation. Rather, she suggests that it allows the perpetrators to continue their harmful narratives under the pretense of regret and contrition. Chrisjohn and Wasacase put it this way: "What Indigenous peoples and Canadians-at-large have been subjected to in the entire run-up to the apology for residential schools and the creation of the Truth and Reconciliation Commission has been *rhetoric,* a concerted effort to manipulate our perception and understanding of what is happening" [emphasis in the original].[40]

What I understand Chrisjohn and Wasacase to be suggesting here is that "sorry," in the way it is formulated as rhetoric, is not meaningless. Rather it is meaning-full, just not in the way we expect. "Sorry" is a word that perpetrators/settlers know we can use to get out of trouble. It is a word that shuts out survivors and entrenches systems of violence. Indeed, what both King and Clements illustrate in their work is that "sorry" can no longer be fully trusted as a way to heal historical injury. In this "Age of Apology," when the word has become discursively fashionable and even financially advantageous, "sorry" becomes the domain of the trickster, a word that cannot and should not be taken at face value.

Moving from Stewart's Statement of Reconciliation to Stephen Harper's "Full Apology," offered to the survivors of residential schools on June 11, 2008, we can identify the ways in which the state has employed its own trickery to redefine "sorry" for neo-colonial and neo-liberal purposes. Indeed, Stewart's Statement marked the end of the political efficacy of "sorry" in Canadian discourse and ushered in a new rhetoric of apology, carefully reconstructed to protect certain financial interests and maintain the legitimacy of the state. In order to fully understand Stephen Harper's apology, which forms a load-bearing pillar of the TRC of Canada, it needs to be read against and with the apologies offered by Stewart and churches. Harper's apology, which I will turn to now, is embedded in a cultural history of "sorry" that informs and directs the shape of his discourse.

The "Full Apology"

In contrast to Stewart's Statement of Reconciliation, what is most striking about Harper's apology is the way he subtly shifts the discourse away from "sorry" toward the more robust phrase "we apologize." While "sorry" is still used in his address, "apology" is the rhetorical focus, most obviously illustrated by the title the Conservative government gave the speech after the fact: "Prime Minister Harper Offers Full Apology on Behalf of Canadians for the Indian Residential Schools System."[41] The word "sorry" is used twice in his speech, but it is largely overshadowed by the focused use of "we apologize," which is uttered six times in the address, with four occurrences in one paragraph. Again, I quote at length here to give the reader a sense of the very deliberate and carefully constructed language Harper employed:

> To the approximately 80,000 living former students, and all family members and communities, the Government of Canada now recognizes that it was wrong to forcibly remove children from their homes, and *we apologize* for having done this. We now recognize that it was wrong to separate children from rich and vibrant cultures and traditions, that it created a void in many lives and communities, and *we apologize* for having done this. We now recognize that in separating children from their families, we undermined the ability of many to adequately parent their own children and sowed the seeds for generations to follow, and *we apologize* for having done this. We now recognize that far too often these institutions gave rise to abuse or neglect and were inadequately controlled, and *we apologize* for failing to protect you. Not only did you suffer these abuses as children, but as you became parents, you were powerless to protect your own children from suffering the same experience, and for this *we are sorry*. [emphasis added][42]

The four repetitions of "we apologize" here, in contrast to the single utterance of "we are sorry," are indicative of the shift away from the latter phrase toward a new performance of regret. Whereas "sorry" was once the phrase to be repeated again and again, as indicated by King in his comic repetition of the word, "we apologize" now takes on that role under Harper's regime.

The reason for this shift can logically be seen as the upshot of the overdetermined use of "sorry" by Stewart and the Liberal government. To put it differently, per Clements, in Canadian state apologies, "sorry" as an expression of grief and sorrow had been overdetermined by deceit and bad-faith politics. Thus, in order to make his statement viable, Prime Minister Harper had to employ a new discursive approach, using language that would convince the audience of his sincerity and desire for reconciliation.

At first glance, Harper's apology seems to be much more intimately engaged with the politics of apology and the theories that sustain it. To begin with, he attempts to engage on a cultural level by using Indigenous languages to express his regret. Rather than simply saying "sorry" in English, he also includes expressions of regret in Cree ("Nimitataynan"), Anishinaabemowin ("Niminchinowesamin"), and Inuktituk ("Mamiattugut"). This creates a system of inclusion that has the potential to explode Western definitions of "sorry." According to Anishinaabe Elder Fred Kelly, "we must ... insist that the Aboriginal peoples have meaningful participation in the design, administration, and evaluation of the reconciliation process so that it is based on their local culture and language."[43] By including Indigenous languages in his apology, Harper makes a small yet significant gesture toward clearing space for Indigenous traditions within a primarily Western discourse, inviting alternative expressions and interpretations of "sorry" with the potential to undo Western delineations of apology. Sincere or not, by introducing Indigenous languages into his speech, the prime minister destabilizes the state's apologetic discourse, if only by introducing a tiny crack to be exploited by attentive readers with knowledge of these languages and the cultures they come from.[44] For instance, "Niminchinowesamin" can also mean to "have regret" or "to be disappointed,"[45] which has the potential to profoundly alter what Harper is attempting to convey regardless of intent.

Further, like Stewart before him, Harper makes sure to acknowledge the damage that colonial practices and residential schools inflicted on Indigenous peoples and communities:

> The government now recognizes that the consequences of the Indian residential schools policy were profoundly negative and that this policy has had

> a lasting and damaging impact on aboriginal culture, heritage and language. While some former students have spoken positively about their experiences at residential schools, these stories are far overshadowed by tragic accounts of the emotional, physical and sexual abuse and neglect of helpless children, and their separation from powerless families and communities.[46]

This portion of the speech is compelling not only because Harper demonstrates that the Canadian government, which is represented as the perpetrating agent here, acknowledges the damage it wrought on Indigenous people, but also, more importantly, because it recognizes the narrative that sustained these schools for so long: that is, the perverse fantasy that these schools actually benefitted Indigenous children and that many of these children had positive experiences in them (also known as the Standard Account). Here, Harper makes clear that while this may be the case in a select few instances, those few positive accounts of residential schools are deeply overshadowed by the schools' destruction of language, culture, and family.

Finally, Harper evokes what is probably the single most important issue in contemporary apology debates: sincerity. Nearing the end of the speech, he claims that, "the Government of Canada *sincerely apologizes* and asks the forgiveness of the Aboriginal peoples of this country for failing them so profoundly" [emphasis added].[47] While the word "sincerely," attached to "apologizes," seems to act in the same way as other modifiers (or "upgraders," as apology theorists in the social sciences call them),[48] the abundance of critical work done on "sincerity" necessitates that it be given due critical attention. As I have already illustrated with the examples of Coyote and Stewart, upgraders are an important part of a convincing apology: Coyote insists that he is "*very* sorry," while Stewart proclaims, "We are *deeply* sorry." By upgrading the term through modifiers, "sorry" is given more import and made to appear more heartfelt.

The logic of this is somewhat silly, of course, as King points out by exaggerating Coyote's use of "very" through repetition and emphasis via italics. There is no reason to accept that individuals are any sorrier, or feel any deeper sense of regret, simply because they can modify the language of their apology's expression. However, there is something to be said for how the performance of an apology makes it easier for the intended recipient to accept it. Obviously, the bare signifier, standing on its own without any performative compliment, seems robotic and indifferent. If I were to apologize to my partner for forgetting her birthday simply by walking up to her and saying, "I'm sorry" in straight monotone while staring at her blankly, it is unlikely that my apology would be accepted. As Coyote helps to demonstrate, "I'm sorry" becomes meaningful when it is dressed up appropriately. Indeed, if you look back at the opening quotation from *Green Grass,* Coyote's "sorry" does not "sound sincere" until he fancies it up with emphasis, upgraders, and repetition, after which it is taken as sincere.

In general, we define a good apology by its ability to communicate regret and contrition. According to James V. Scott, "what most people are looking for in an apology is sincerity. They want the apology to come from the heart. They want to know that the offender feels something, that they 'give a damn' about the damage they have done."[49] Most critics agree that in order for an apology to be successful – with success measured by the acceptance of the apology – it must be free of deceit, hypocrisy, or duplicity and must express a certain probity in intention. In other words, to use the liberal-humanist language that continues to be applied to apology discourse, a proper apology must "come ... from the heart of the wrongdoer and not from the pen of a lawyer or an indifferent third party."[50] An apology that forgoes this crucial element of sincerity risks causing further injury and negating the possibility of reconciliation. Dugald Christie puts it this way: "An insincere apology is a dangerous matter. It can result in the arousal and not the abatement of passions."[51]

Using "sincerely" as an upgrader, Harper evokes the central element of the "proper" apology and fulfills his promise to offer a "Full Apology." By utilizing this specific word in conjunction with "apologize," he explicitly connects his apology to a larger critical discourse and tradition, which helps to guarantee the legitimacy of state regret. What the logic of sincerity insists upon, however, is that the audience, or, more specifically, the survivors of historical injustice, collapse the distinction between *saying* that one is sincere and actually *being* sincere, which opens up a dramatic space for deceit. Indeed, one of the main difficulties with apology is that this sort of faith is built into its structure. Tavuchis, for instance, argues that apology itself is impossible: "An apology, no matter how sincere or effective, does not and cannot *undo* what has been done. And yet, in a mysterious way and according to its own logic, this is precisely what it manages to do" [emphasis in the original].[52] In the sense that it is "impossible," that it sets out to achieve the unachievable, an apology demands certain devotion to its healing potential and to its built-in sincerity. Both the perpetrator and the survivor must believe in the possibility of a new and better world and the impossible possibility of healing unhealable wounds, but this belief is always part of a larger relational dynamic. "We apologize" is expected to be the start of a new relationship in which further structural change takes place. It cannot simply be a placeholder for white guilt.

If we turn to the academic literature, apology is presented as some sort of magic word, a speech act par excellence, which, if properly evoked, can change lives. Tavuchis, for instance, leans on the "mystery" of apology accomplishing the impossible. Other thinkers make similar claims. For instance, Howard Kushner argues that "apology is but one word, but it is one word that can make all the difference for those who need to hear it."[53] Kushner's remarks strongly resonate with those of Tavuchis and the notion of the impossible possible. In the way it is afforded singular powers as a speech act (something which I will explore in more detail shortly), "apology" has been imbued with a mysticism that can account equally for both the healing potential it carries and the ways it is abused by insincere apologists.

While, on one hand, the implicit belief that society has in the word "apology" can itself account for the healing potential of the word (what some might call the placebo effect), on the other hand, this same belief can cloud critical facilities, distracting from the mechanisms that drive it. Chrisjohn and Young illustrate that the explicit emphasis on healing and therapy in the Canadian discourse of reconciliation is "another rhetorical manoeuvre designed to obscure ... the moral and financial accountability of Euro-Canadian society in a continuing record of crimes against humanity."[54] To assume that the rhetoric of healing and apology is not being applied strategically against survivors is to egregiously underestimate the depth and complexity of the imperialist system and what may well be the literal impossibility of apologizing for colonial violence.

Reading Harper's apology closely, then, within the political and social discourse in which it was offered, it is difficult not to assert that this mysticism is what is being deployed in Canada. To return to an earlier point, what is most important to reflect on here is the shift that the prime minister makes away from the use of "sorry" to the more robust phrase "we apologize." This is an important semantic detail, insofar as "I'm sorry" has become overdetermined, a statement that the global community now associates with duplicity and the self-interest of the one offering it.

On a purely rhetorical level, by using "apology" directly (and repeatedly) in his own statement, Harper makes it difficult for his critics to assert that the "Full Apology" was of the same order as Stewart's. But the word "apology" has its own special qualities, which need to be unpacked in order to lift the veil on its supposed "magical" qualities. Doing this also sheds light on the ways in which Harper negotiates the "Full Apology" within the confines of the Canadian system. The linguist J.L. Austin is exceptionally helpful in setting out the differences between Stewart's and Harper's apologies. In one of his final seminars in *How to Do Things with Words*, Austin distinguishes specifically between the phrases "I'm sorry" and "I apologize" as a way to flesh out his ideas on the behabitive, a speech act by which an attitude is changed or adapted. Austin's text is a study of the word as a performative, an examination of what words *do* once they are uttered – such as marrying a couple or naming a ship – rather than what they report. As the seminars in the text progress, statements of regret, such as "I'm sorry" and "I apologize," play a vital role in the development of Austin's theory, providing the space for him to highlight the nuances of the performative and what it accomplishes.

According to Austin, there are three semantic orders of expressing regret: I apologize, I am sorry, and I repent. For him, "I apologize" is a performative utterance; "I am sorry" is half report, insofar as it can describe an inner feeling and perform reconciliation; and "I repent" is merely a report.[55] The distinction between "I apologize" and "I am sorry" is of key importance to reconciliation scholars, not only because of the way these two phrases have been employed in Canadian discourse, but also because of the subtle yet important distinctions Austin identifies between them. Most significant here is Austin's notion of the behabitive, which he develops with the use of "I apologize." According to Austin, "behabitives include the notion of reaction to other people's behaviour and fortunes and of attitudes and expressions of attitudes to someone else's past conduct or imminent conduct."[56] To put it differently, "we apologize" is not simply an act of telling an audience something, rather these specific words also alter their reception of that telling. This is where the possibility of expressing regret in a meaningful and material way lies: in changing attitudes that open people and communities up to new possibilities of truth and facilitate material change. Apology, in this sense, bears witness to the extent that it is an ongoing act of listening coupled with relational response.

For Austin, the test that proves the difference between these two similar statements of regret ("I am sorry" versus "I apologize") is the fact that the former "could be literally false."[57] For instance, I can say "I am sorry" for the damage caused by residential schools without being or even feeling sorry. In the sense that it is a half report, "I am sorry" already has the potential to be a lie. However, saying "I apologize" cannot be clearly distinguished as a falsehood. "I apologize" does not report or describe anything and it is not simply true or false. Rather, "the uttering of the sentence is, or is a part of, the doing of an action, which again would not *normally* be described as, or as 'just,' saying something" [emphasis in the original].[58] In other words, the latter statement of regret is a performative: it puts a particular kind of idea into motion rather than simply describing an inner state of being. Indeed, as Austin points out, translating "I apologize," as opposed to "I am sorry," into its present participle further demonstrates its active quality: "I am apologizing" is an accepted turn of phrase, while "I am sorrying" is just ungrammatical.

What the *act* of "I apologize" depends on, then, is not the truthfulness of the speaker, but rather the way in which it commits both the speaker and the audience to like conduct. In this sense, "I apologize" can be insincere (or infelicitous, as Austin puts it) insofar as it is rejected as a performance by the players involved. If "I apologize" does not enact a change in behaviour or attitude from the apologist, then it is insincere – not because the speaker is falsely reporting on their inner feelings (indeed, there is no descriptive variation of "I apologize"; I can *be* sorry, but I cannot *be* apology), but because it fails to set in motion what it portends. In this sense, Austin's analysis provides a possible means to interpret the logic behind Harper's shift to "we apologize" from Stewart's "we are deeply sorry." By deploying "apology" as opposed to "sorry," Harper negates the possibility of critics directly levying claims of falsehood against him and his government. This is because the onus of the second official apology lies not on whether Harper and other government officials actually *feel* sorry for the damage inflicted on Indigenous communities but in whether the statement can generate a positive change in behaviour and belief, resulting in improved conditions for the survivors (rather than just an ambiguous feeling of sorrow or guilt).

The "mysticism" of Harper's apology, if we follow from Tavuchis's theory of impossibility, derives from this crucial point. In a generous interpretation, we can argue that by utilizing "we apologize" rather than "I am sorry," the prime minister is not simply reporting on his innermost feelings, but rather attempting to inflect a kind of change of attitude on the part of the government he represents. Equally important, the apology, if received as sincere (and he emphasizes it should be), is a speech act that potentially alters his audience's perceptions of an event.

For Austin, this is precisely what the behabitive accomplishes. In using "apology," as opposed to "sorry," Harper attempts to recast a national understanding of the mistreatment of Indigenous peoples, not as something that may have been ultimately beneficial – the skewed colonial perspective that dominated well into the twentieth century – but as a tragic error, a violent and devastating procedure that "has no place in our country." As such, the "Full Apology" is not just a report on the government's inner feelings of regret for colonial practices (feelings that can never be proven to exist anyway), but an attempt to inflect a certain measure of change in Canada's collective history. Notably it also pulled the residential school system out of the larger assimilative and colonial policies of Canada, thus rendering it unique and anomalous rather than symptomatic. Read from these contexts, there is possibility in the Harper apology insofar as it opens up an opportunity for material change through the nature of the behabitive. And while neither the Harper government nor the subsequent Trudeau government acted on this potential, we need to be prepared to think critically about the fleeting gap the apology may have opened, and to read the apology against what we might assume to be the intentions of the apologizer.

Ultimately, what makes the behabitive successful, or felicitous, as Austin puts it, is the speaker's ability to engage with certain performative rules. It is perhaps easiest to understand Austin's conceptualization of apology as behabitive with some help from the language of theatre itself. A "happy or "felicitous" speech act is one that allows an audience to adequately *suspend their disbelief,* to comprehend the performance as sincere. As in any good play or film, in order for this to happen the actors and circumstances must be appropriate, suitable language must be used, and it must be delivered at the appropriate time. The performance must also be enacted fully and completely. This is not to say that audiences are obligated to enter some hallucinogenic state in which they can no longer differentiate between reality and representation, but, rather, that the act itself does not offer any interruptions or glitches that might draw attention to its performative quality. As Clements so aptly puts it in *Burning Vision,* "we want the unreal real thing"[59] – an apology that is obviously scripted and connected to specific political interests, but which conforms to the rules of performance that allow the audience to disavow its supporting context(s).

Indeed, for Austin's conception of the behabitive, this disavowal is of particular importance in apology when the audience enters the theatre of regret already suspicious of the performers' motives. As Miyagawa argues, political performances of regret are seen by many survivors as a way to "whitewash" apologies, making them empty gestures.[60] In the "Age of Apology," in which audiences are hyper-aware of the potential for affectation, if an apology is to be effective – authentic or not – it must operate within a convention that interferes with the recipients' ability to maintain their skepticism. In this sense, "breaking the fourth wall," or actually drawing attention to the inadequacy of apology, can be a significant gesture to building trust, which, in turn, facilitates the reception of meaningful expressions of regret. An apology that reflects on what it can't do, despite its sincerity, opens up spaces for conversation, through which the recipients of the apology can help to shape and craft the response in a way that respects their needs and boundaries. It makes apology dialectic – though not in tangent with forgiveness, as in the Christian formulation, but rather with history and with testimony. This does not mean that there is no end to apology. It means that apology happens with and for its subject(s) within a system aimed at expanding conversation, not narrowing it down.

However, rather than taking the opportunity to "break the fourth wall," Harper's apology actually engages with the performative elements that allow settler audiences to suspend our disbelief – a suspension that has some disturbing implications. Assuming Stewart's Statement of Reconciliation as a backdrop, or as a way to *not* apologize, Harper was able to draw in his audience by employing at least four important performative measures to guarantee the sincerity of his "Full Apology."[61] First, he offered the apology himself. Stewart was an important government official (then minister of Indian Affairs and Northern Development) but not a top figure in the Canadian government, so when she offered the government statement rather than the prime minister of the time (Jean Chrétien, who is also famous for co-authoring the 1969 White Paper), her words were not given the weight that a delivery from the nation's top official would carry. Second, Harper chose the right stage. While Stewart's Statement of Reconciliation was offered on the grounds of Parliament Hill, Harper stood in the House of Commons, evoking the history and authority of that space, and thus making the apology seem that much more important to the history of Canada while integrating it more firmly into the national imaginary. Third, he used the pronoun "you," directly addressing residential school survivors and Indigenous peoples more generally. And finally, as illustrated above, he included Indigenous languages in his apology, which directly addressed the audience and the history he was attempting to redress.

I have already established above that an apology is received as felicitous when the sincerity of the speaker is convincing – which can be quite difficult to measure. By evoking the above performative measures in his "Full Apology," Harper generated the sincerity necessary to guarantee his statement as a behabitive, and thus allowed for what National Chief Phil Fontaine called "the accomplishment of the impossible."[62] However, insisting that Harper is truly sincere simply because his performance appeared to be is to forget the radical disconnect between being and saying that is implicit to the behabitive. Uttering "we apologize" is not a report on the speaker's emotions or feelings of regret; rather, it is an attempt to alter attitudes and behaviour. In this instance, the speaker's "being" should not come into question – despite the temptation to make that link.

It is equally fruitless to levy arguments for or against the truth of Harper's statement in order to defend or oppose it. In fact, such arguments have the potential to cloud precisely what is at stake here. In appealing to the behabitive rather than a constative report, Harper opens up potential for change in his apology, while Stewart forecloses it. Whether one believes he is being "true" or not is beside the point: it is in the performance itself, which can be either true or false, that the potential for change arises. By registering this "Full Apology" in the national discourse, Harper invites his audience – and his government – to reimagine Indigenous peoples and history and to forge new relationships inflected by this re-conceptualization. Intent notwithstanding, insofar as Harper opened up the potential for change via the performative there existed, if only momentarily, a potential for reconciliation that existed outside his control.

That said, the gap between being and saying that is opened up by the behabitive also provides an auspicious space for insincerity.[63] Insofar as this speech act is no longer connected to a state of being, there is potential for a radical disconnect between a speaker's utterance and their intentions. Because we, as audiences to apology, so often fall into the trap of collapsing the performative with the constative, thereby identifying a change in attitude as the truth of the remarks, the behabitive can operate as a veil behind which insincere apologists can carry out their own interests and agendas. Or, to put it differently, to insist that the behabitive is actually an indicator of a speaker's intent is to radically disavow the fact that performance can be evoked by prevaricators with self-serving ends.

The most obvious place to begin this type of reading in Harper's apology is through continued close reading of the word "apology," the semantic lynchpin of his statement. Here, rather than looking through the lens of the performative, I shift my analysis to emphasize the economic significance of "sorry." The word "apology" itself, particularly in Canada, is caught up in an intricate political/financial web, which requires further attention in order to fully contextualize his apology. According to Tavuchis, the word "apology" is nearly inextricably associated with guilt and fiduciary responsibility. As such, saying that you are sorry opens one up to justified financial attack and public shaming: "Given these cultural and judicial facts of life," he writes, "to apologize sincerely is a potentially stupid and costly gesture."[64] In light of this, we should be suspicious of how and why Harper – who notably ran on a neo-liberal platform based on austerity and free market principles – would put to use a word that might directly implicate his cabinet in a form of welfare state provisions. Drew Hayden Taylor perhaps captures this skepticism best when he writes, "You would think the residential school system would be something the Conservatives would admire."[65]

One clear way to reconcile the Conservatives' fiduciary platform with their willingness to apologize is to read the apology into the larger legal and political contexts of the time. Looking at the legal literature surrounding apology at the time of the "Full Apology," we can see how it might be possible for an apology to support neo-liberal principles and fiscal conservatism. For instance, in 2006, British Columbia passed the *Apology Act,* which abstracted financial liability from expressions of regret and sorrow.[66] BC's legislation was quickly followed by Saskatchewan's *Evidence Act,* which operates under similar pretences.[67] By 2008, just before Harper's "Full Apology" to survivors of the residential school system, apology legislation was either in effect or being considered in more than half of Canada's provinces and territories, including British Columbia, Saskatchewan, Alberta,[68] Manitoba,[69] Nova Scotia,[70] Newfoundland and Labrador,[71] and the Yukon.[72] Ontario quickly followed suit in 2009.[73]

Lawyers were also calling for federal changes to the use of apology in Canada at this time. In 2007, Russell J. Getz, a prominent BC lawyer and legal counsel for the Ministry of the Attorney General, wrote a paper calling for a "Uniform Apology Act," which "provides that an apology is not admissible in civil proceedings for the purpose of proving liability and that an apology is not an admission of liability."[74] In this paper, Getz cites evidence from malpractice suits in which 37 percent of those surveyed said they would not have sued if they had been given an apology. Building from this evidence, Getz argues that Canada-wide apology legislation would "encourage people to engage in the moral and humane act of apologizing after having injured another."[75]

The legal extraction of liability from apology is of no small consequence to the TRC. According to Getz, the fiscal responsibility attached to apologies actually stymies healing and reconciliation because it de-incentivizes the words by putting finances at stake.[76] By extracting financial liability from the definition of apology, then, it is assumed that more wrongdoers will be willing to admit their mistakes and express their contrition. This, in turn, would lead to a society more invested in relationships and their repair. The idealist logic sounds nice, but in practice it abstracts apology from its material implications, increasing the potential for a perpetrator to apologize without fear that the apology could make them legally or financially responsible for their actions. According to Getz, "In general, apologies are morally desirable,"[77] and thus, according to his logic, governments should be doing all they can to break down barriers to their release. However, by emphasizing morality, one can also strategically evade fiduciary responsibility and the material impacts of historical injustice.

Idealist claims like the one Getz makes, which privilege morality over materiality, are difficult to challenge because they put those who might oppose an Apology Act in in the awkward position of appearing brutish and uncompassionate. However, what Getz and others like him do not acknowledge in the push toward moral accountability is the stark reality behind legislation of this sort: namely, that by untethering the apology from fiscal responsibility, survivors can no longer use the former to recoup the land and capital that they have lost due to the event the perpetrator is apologizing for. Indeed, for Getz, the apology takes on a false materiality of its own – "an apology is a form of compensation," he argues.[78]

By taking up a nearly unassailable "moral" position, which strategically substitutes words for resources, the argument for an idealist apology tacitly severs the link between apology and claims for land and resources, thus negating the possibility of Indigenous peoples being properly compensated for colonial tactics, and offering them instead an intangible form of healing that maintains the status quo. Indeed, Christie argues that "the proposed *Apology Act* [and, I would argue, all the apology legislation that is now in place in Canada] is primarily designed to save the government money, particularly with respect to Aboriginal claims."[79]

Apology legislation of this sort benefits the cynical and hurts the empathetic. Christie supports this argument by reflecting on the needs of injured parties to receive financial compensation for healing: "A sixty-year-old woman, whose life has been devastated by childhood abuse from a person she trusted, likely will not recover with a mere apology. She may need years of painful counselling from a clinical psychologist so that she and her family can come to terms with what has happened."[80] Christie is obviously referring here to the many Indigenous survivors who went through severe psychological trauma in residential schools. Suggesting that an apology can enact the work of psychological treatment – which, at 130 dollars plus per hour, demands a stable bank account – denies the complexity of this trauma and elevates the need to a level not even the most profound speech act can reach.

In my view, however, Christie does not push his argument far enough. It is not simply that these survivors need financial redress in order to begin healing, something that the government has provided (in the form of $1.9 billion in restitution), but that they have also been denied access to the land and resources that sustain their way of life. By suggesting that an apology can somehow take the place of land, not to mention the culture and language that stem from it, is not simply an egregious miscalculation. In a very real way, apology becomes an essential piece of ensuring that land and resources remain firmly under settler domination. It is a way to perpetuate settler colonial privileges and maintain control of the resources that put Indigenous peoples at a disadvantage in the first place. Indeed, critics must be willing to move even further past Christie's final point, in which he asks for "compensation *and* meaningful apologies,"[81] and start to think of compensation as a part of the very definition of apology, as opposed to a separate and independent form of redress.

It is no coincidence, then, that Harper's slew of apologies to the survivors of Canada's racist and colonial policies was offered when apology legislation was in place or being considered in more than half of Canada's provinces and territories. Those remarks include apologies to survivors of residential schools, Chinese Canadians impacted by the head tax, and Punjabi immigrants on the *Komagata Maru* who were refused entry to Vancouver. By offering these statements when "apology" and "compensation" were being separated into distinct terms in the official Canadian vernacular, Harper was able to utilize the more semantically powerful terminology without fear of making his government financially liable.

In sum, when read within the larger legal and political discourse of the time, Harper's apology should be viewed as a failed endeavour of the same order as Stewart's Statement of Reconciliation. Indeed, read contextually, it becomes clearer that the same financial conservatism – aimed at distributing as few resources as possible to Indigenous peoples – was at play in both Harper's and Stewart's statements. In fact, Harper's apology is even more insidious. In both cases, a deeper reading reveals an "unconscious" self-interest behind the manifest display of contrition, which should be enough to compel researchers and critics to initiate deeper and more critical studies of all apologies offered at a state level, despite what might appear to be positive steps in semantic presentation and performance. In other words, Harper's use of apology, despite its potential as a speech act, should be put under the same microscope that King calls for in his comic presentation of the word "sorry." Indeed, such a comparison offers disturbingly similar results. Like

Coyote's, Harper's apology is rooted in a deeper discourse of self-preservation and self-interest that shields itself behind the rhetoric of regret and contrition.

Finally, there is one more "text" that needs to be considered if we are to determine the sincerity of the 2008 address. On September 25, 2009, at a press conference during the G20 summit in Pittsburgh, Prime Minister Harper made a statement that retroactively inflected how his apology should be read. While trying to impress on members of the media and fellow world leaders exactly how irresistible he believes Canada is, Harper made the following remarks: "We also have no history of colonialism ... So we have all of the things that many people admire about the great powers but none of the things that threaten or bother them."[82]

In these remarks, Harper appeals to a long-standing rhetorical tool of the settler colonial: the "blue water rule" or "salt water thesis," which aims to abstract colonialism from nation-states such as Canada and the United States. The salt water thesis was originally adopted by the United Nations in 1952 as Belgium relinquished colonies in Africa. This put pressure on the United States to "decolonize" and allow for the self-determination of Indigenous peoples living within its colonial borders. In order to negate this pressure and continue with settler business as usual, the United States pushed for a definition that in order for decolonization to occur, colonies must be "separated from the colonial power by a substantial body of water, preferably an ocean."[83] The UN adoption was supported by many UN member states with Indigenous peoples within their borders. In essence, the salt water thesis means that colonization is only ever external to the nation–Canada state; it can never occur internally, which was fundamentally what Harper was stating in his remarks.

However, while the salt water thesis might hold water in the UN (pun intended), it makes little or no sense to colonized people living in the United States or Canada, who experience the effects of Canadian colonialism in their daily lives. As a result, Harper's remarks rightly outraged both Indigenous peoples and their allies, and called into question the validity of the earlier apology. Shawn Atleo, who was National Chief of the Assembly of First Nations at the time, released the following statement to the *Georgia Straight*, pointing out how Harper was contradicting himself:

> I have spoken with the Minister of Indian Affairs and urged him and the prime minister to meet with First Nations in good faith to address this matter and, equally important, begin the work of reconciliation that lies ahead.

> The prime minister stated in his apology to students of residential schools that, "There is no place in Canada for the attitudes that inspired the Indian Residential Schools system to ever prevail again." The prime minister must ensure that such commitments inform every statement and action.[84]

By directing attention to the apology, Atleo rightly points out that these two "texts" need to be read alongside one another. By insisting that Canada has "no history of colonialism," Harper effectively dismissed his earlier commitment to acknowledging the horror of residential schools.

There are at least two ways to unpack the contradiction Harper sets up here. The first is simply to insist that the apology and the comments offered at the G20 are entirely incommensurable, that the second deconstructs the first and exposes the duplicity of the prime minister. While this is an important and necessary reading, it risks foreclosing a deeper analysis of how apology is now being defined in the Canadian political sphere. Rather than deconstructing the apology via this supplement, it is more challenging and informative to try to read the two texts together as complements, not contradictions. This is not an attempt to justify Harper's racist and egregiously false remarks at the G20, but, rather, an attempt to understand how he could arrive at a place where such a comment would make sense, particularly in light of his recent string of apologies, which seemed to be an open acknowledgment of Canada's colonialism.

Harper's 2008 and 2009 remarks can be cogently read together if we are willing to read his initial apology as a type of erasure. In this sense, one could ascertain that Canada has no history of colonialism because the Conservative government used the 2008 apology to delete this history from collective memory, and, to borrow a line from *Burning Vision,* "You can't really be sorry for something you don't want to remember can you?"[85] In this reading, by offering a "Full Apology," the government was essentially recasting the national perception of colonial violence. By redressing it in its entirety, or at least by saying that it was "fully" redressed, there were no longer any wounds to point to, no explicit markers that could confirm that Canada is a product of genocide and imperialist policies. Apology, in this sense, acts as a means of camouflaging the past, hiding the damage and bloodshed that might drive away potential investors.

By reading Harper's seemingly preposterous remarks at the G20 against his House of Commons apology, we are compelled to acknowledge the way apology is being defined at the state level. Offered as a closed space, a complete narrative, "we apologize" is yet another way to disavow or dis-remember a violent colonial past while clearing the space necessary to construct a new, more congenial history in which Canada, fantastically, has "all of the things that many people admire about the great powers but none of the things that threaten or bother them." Following from Clements, if the act for which one is apologizing is forgotten, or even rendered invisible by "sorry," the apology itself is probably moot, an empty gesture designed to control public opinion by playing into the theatre of regret.

Indeed, to bring Canada's two apologies to survivors of residential schools together once more, where both Stewart's and Harper's statements ultimately fail is in their steadfast attempt to close the debate. Stewart simply starts on the wrong foot, offering her "apology" under the rubric of reconciliation. Following Tavuchis, the process is backward. Logically, reconciliation can only be defined as such if both parties agree to it and feel safe and comfortable. By placing reconciliation ahead of apology, Stewart tacitly implies that the latter has already been accepted, that the wrongs she outlines in her rather short statement are the only ones that need to be addressed, and that this portion of the conversation is now closed. Similarly, Harper attempts to end the dialogue by offering what he calls a "Full Apology," a narrative that, rightly or not, drew a full circle around the boundaries of discussion and foreclosed any new debate or appeals to the past.

Incomplete Apologies?

Taking our cue from Stewart and Harper, we should be attentive to the fact that the Canadian concept of "apology" is slowly being reformulated as a means to control narrative and protect the interests of the status quo. In the last section of this chapter, I would like to offer a brief critique of what might be called the "deconstructive" or "postmodern" approach to apology, which comes up regularly in the academic literature. According to Carl D. Schneider, the statements of regret that have the most potential for reconciliation do not attempt to offer a full account of the wrong in question. Rather, the proper apology acknowledges its own limitations: "I don't know what I can say except I'm sorry for what I did. I'm sorry – that's all I can say."[86] Tavuchis makes a similar point: "To apologize is to declare voluntarily that one has *no* excuse, defence, justification, or explanation for an action (or inaction) that has 'insulted, failed, injured, or wronged another.'"[87] In this line of thinking, it is incompleteness that makes a truly sincere apology: the recognition of its impossibility.

The notion of an impossible apology resonates loudly with a Derridean approach to the discourse of reconciliation, which is skeptical of the idea that apology or forgiveness can be rendered into a political program. For Derrida, state-level apology and reconciliation depend on a sovereign to organize them; both concepts require "the power necessary to organize a trial, an applicable judgement or, eventually, acquittal, amnesty, or forgiveness."[88] Derrida longs for reconciliation that does not require sovereignty, but he also wonders how this might be possible, inasmuch as it requires a guarantor. Apology theorists working out of the Derridean paradigm solve the problem of sovereignty by usurping the government with the "figure" of the aporia, an unresolvable internal contradiction. In this configuration, a "healthier" apology is one that recognizes its own "impossibility" rather than pretending to offer a full and complete account for a historical injustice (as in the Harper instance) or demanding acceptance. To argue this differently, a Derridean apology "is" only insofar as it deconstructs its own meaning in its utterance.

This difficult point is made more lucid with an example. A provocative illustration of a deconstructive apology comes from Tavuchis's interpretation of Albert Speer's famous statement of regret. Speer was one of the only Nazi leaders to admit his guilt at the Nuremberg trials, during which he was charged with war crimes. Speer apologized to the court, admitting that he was culpable, but that he had no knowledge of Hitler's crimes against humanity. When sentences were handed out in 1946, Speer received a relatively light punishment of twenty years at Spandau Prison in Berlin, where he reportedly tended to a small garden and wrote *Inside the Third Reich.* In that memoir he wrote, "Whether I knew or did not know, or how much or how little I knew, is totally unimportant when I consider what horrors would have been the natural ones to draw from the little I did know ... *No apologies are possible*" [emphasis added].[89]

Speer's statement of regret deserves its own kind of definition. It cannot rightly be entitled an "apology" per se, at least in the sense outlined above, because it explicitly acknowledges the impossibility of that term. On one hand, if an apology is something that can heal or make up for the past, Speer admits that his words are incapable of the task. On the other hand, to assert that Speer's statement is not an apology at all, and therefore is not fraught with the same difficulties I have attempted to unpack, is also to miss the point. Indeed, although he says he cannot apologize, it is in the act of "not apologizing" that Speer perhaps makes his apology viable. To make this point clearer, one need only think of Speer actually saying nothing (as many Nazi perpetrators did). If "no apologies are possible," then nothing can be said, but by saying that he *can't* apologize, Speer in fact offers a more possible apology simply because he does attempt the unattainable, therefore allowing his audience to suspend their disbelief and trust in his sincerity. Indeed, according to Tavuchis, "most critics praised his [Speer's] candour in writing about the responsibility he bore for Nazi excess."[90] To be clear, this is not to say that Speer was in fact regretful of his actions – indeed, there is plenty of good evidence to the contrary – but that his delivery of apology was more conducive to a reception as such.[91]

Speer's words are a primary example of what can only be properly called the (non)apology – which must be differentiated from the disingenuous apology and the non-existent apology. The (non)apology is a statement of regret that can be read as acknowledging its own impossibility and in doing so actually allowing it to be possible for its audience. There is an obvious theoretical advantage to sanctioning this type of statement. In making explicit its limitations, the (non)apology engages with Austin's logic of the behabitive, allowing for radical changes in beliefs about and attitudes toward the perpetrator, while still allowing for a healthy measure of uncertainty and skepticism from the recipient. Marking the apology as incomplete does not detract from its sincerity, rather it opens the space for dialogue between perpetrator and survivor and thus sets a foundation for material change based on a dialectic that is not dependent on a Christian model of forgiveness. The incomplete apology, in its acknowledgment of its limitations and its failure, resists political and juridical rationality and the stabilizing discourse of neo-liberalism because it resists closure. Within settler colonialism, it opens a possibility for truth to the extent that it requires an ongoing encounter with the colonial history that the state works to deny.

Still, while Speer's (non)apology offers a more robust theoretical approach to the concept, we should still be wary of how the "deconstructive" approach might function in the world of politics. If one is willing to admit that apologies can be read deconstructively, and thus represent a more politically viable and compassionate way to express regret, one must also be willing to admit that apologists can engage with deconstruction in order to perform a "sincere" apology as part of a political strategy. Indeed, by privileging the deconstructive element of Speer's "apology," Tavuchis overlooks one of the most problematic elements of the officer's remarks: namely that "how much or how little [he] knew, is totally unimportant."[92] In focusing on the "impossibility" of the apology, Tavuchis simultaneously allows Speer to distance himself from the realities of Nazi persecution. His knowledge of the events, and thus his ethical responsibility for them, is maintained as secondary to his "sincere" statement of regret. In order for the (non)apology to be viable, it requires persistent vigilance and a commitment to truth over reconciliation.

Conclusion

Although I am wary of this type of analysis, I don't want to suggest that the (non)apology is unproductive. Rather, I argue that we must be cautious when employing it, and that we remain accountable to its lack of closure as a type of politic. This is no small feat in a settler colonial environment where closure is demanded, where "get over it" is a rallying cry, the "full apology" is a mode of regret, and TRCs are mandated with a five-year timeline. "Get over it" is essentially what Frances Widdowson is arguing when she writes that "a certain amount of 'cultural loss' was inevitable if aboriginal people were to survive in the modern context."[93] "Get over it" is what Rex Murphey is insisting when he argues that "Natives need to tone down the anger" and that "going all radical, hitting the racial/racist buttons and constant invocations of empty pseudo-academic framings of 'colonialist, settler, imperialist' mentalities do nothing but burn time."[94] "Get over it" is behind what Canadian Senator Lynn Beyak was asking when she insisted that the public look for the "good" in residential schools and argued that "none of us are leaving, so let's stop the guilt and blame and find a way to live together and share."[95]

The following is Chief Justice Murray Sinclair's response to the Canadian public's demand that Indigenous peoples "get over" residential schools:

> Because this is about memorializing those people who have been the victims of a great wrong. Why don't you tell the United States to "get over" 9/11? Why don't you tell this country to "get over" all the veterans who died in the Second World War, instead of honouring them once a year? ... until people show that they have learned from this, we will never forget, and we should never forget, even once they have learned from it, because this is part of who we are. It's not just a part of who we are as survivors and children of survivors and relatives of survivors, it's part of who we are as a nation. And this nation must never forget what it once did to its most vulnerable people.[96]

The (non)apology refuses to "get over it." It holds space for memory and pain, but also for healing, education, and truth. The (non)apology acknowledges that survivors have not, and maybe cannot or should not, get over it. The (non)apology holds space for grieving and healing to continue, with no foreseeable endpoint.

There is also a history of the (non)apology in Canada for us to look back on for guidance. In his 1988 apology to Japanese Canadians, Prime Minister Brian Mulroney appealed to the impotence of his words as a means to convey his sincere regret to that community: "We have all learned from personal experience that as inadequate as apologies are they are the only way we can cleanse the past so that we may, as best we can, in good conscience face the future."[97] The use of "cleanse" here should rightly cause us to pause, and by no means should Mulroney be held up as the example par excellence of apology, but there is still a lesson to be taken from this statement. Indeed, Matt James argues that Mulroney's words are "closest to the criteria for authentic political apology" in Canada's sorry history.[98]

Rather than suggesting that an apology can be "full" or complete, as Harper would later do, Mulroney leaves a small space open for unrest, discontent, and the presence of the past. Aside from his reference to the inadequacy of apology, this all-important gap is also illustrated in the sentence's only dependent clause, "as best we can," which interrupts the smooth flow of the "cleansing" narrative. In this interruption, Mulroney affirms the potential of apology while recognizing that the pain and the trauma of internment can never entirely heal. The shift in discourse from Mulroney to Stewart and finally to Harper, which has taken place over thirty years, illustrates how this important gap has been closed in official apologies. Statements of regret are now labelled as "full," complete circles of discourse that annex the past and strive to revise history through acceptance, all while simultaneously maintaining settler colonial ideologies and an unequal distribution of resources.

If reconciliation is to be born out of apology, thus bringing two narratives (Indigenous and settler) together without the latter colonizing or absorbing the former, TRC researchers need to continue to search for these types of gaps, and this will require space and time that will necessarily exceed any five- (or even six-) year mandate. Without proper consideration, apology can be tactically deployed to serve state interests. Staving off acceptance for acknowledgment, as Memnook and the NCC did two decades before the TRC of Canada, can help to open up this space and provide for more critical and compassionate insight on state apologies. The (non)apology, as resistance to the neo-liberal discourse of closure we see in apologies like Harper's, also represents a discourse of unsettling and provides an essential opening toward truth.

4

Redress as a Gift

Historical Reparations and the Logic of the Gift

> The gift of Indigenous philosophies is not found only in the challenges it poses to conventional conceptualizations of philosophy, but, perhaps even more importantly, in the alternative logic and vision it offers to today's global economic order.
>
> – RAUNA KUOKKANEN[1]

In 1998, as apologies for Indian Residential Schools began to proliferate and the Canadian government offered the first official "sorry" to Indigenous people, Nalo Hopkinson published *Brown Girl in the Ring,* a dystopic, futuristic novel set in Toronto. *Brown Girl in the Ring* imagines the downfall of the Ontario government as the upshot of settler redress and explores the realities of "dystopia" for Black and Indigenous peoples. Hopkinson is a Canadian author of Jamaican descent, Indigenous to the Caribbean, and is well regarded for her provocative and political strain of speculative fiction and her literary engagement with Caribbean history and language. She has been specifically noted for her contributions to what Grace Dillon calls "Indigenous scientific literacies" and the ways in which her novels speak to potential allyships between Indigenous and diasporic peoples.[2] Indeed, Dillon writes that Hopkinson's novels are "meditations on Indigenous contact with colonial power" that actively work to undo the "dreamwork" of imperialism.[3]

For the purposes of this book, *Brown Girl in the Ring* is instructive in how it teases out the implications of redress within a settler colonial society committed to the notion of Indigeneity as a threat. The novel is told from the perspective of Ti-Jeanne, a young woman of Jamaican descent and a new mother grappling with the power of her ancestry and culture. The plot is structured on the financial collapse of the Ontario government, which results in the evacuation of settler peoples and settler law from the country's largest city, rendering it what the remaining occupants call a "doughnut hole": a colonial power vacuum in the centre of Canada.[4] In Hopkinson's Toronto, only the poor and disenfranchised are left to roam the streets. Violence and crime are pervasive, but so is a new, anti-capitalist way of life based on trade and the strength of community. Far ahead of its time, *Brown Girl in the Ring* engages redress and reconciliation in prophetic ways, centring Indigenous land claims and imagining Indigenous laws, protocols, and peoples in the future while exposing the settler fragility connected to redress and restitution.

Brown Girl in the Ring is a beautifully written, fun, and engaging novel with a deep political message. In 2008 it was included in Canada Reads, a popular annual literary competition hosted by the Canadian Broadcasting Corporation that pits Canadian novels against one another in a best-of-five competition. It is a valuable text in reconciliation studies because it imagines a future built out of a settler colonial fear of redress, while providing readers with an opportunity to project Canada's TRC onto future horizons. *Brown Girl in the Ring* is a book that imagines a radical alternative to the reconciliation being trafficked in settler government discourse today: an alternative premised on the collapse of capitalism and the downfall of the state initiated by Indigenous rights and title. The book projects redress as an inevitability, the collapse of the settler state as irrevocable, and the future presence of Indigenous peoples as a given. And while it is a dystopia, it raises the question, dystopia for whom? The answer is that it is not a dystopia for Indigenous peoples or peoples of colour, but for a settler society that only understands its existence within the frameworks of late capitalism and settler colonialism. In that "dystopia," then, there is a radical glimmer of hope for reconciliation on Indigenous territory found in the death of capitalism and the collapse of the settler state that is built out of it.[5]

The plot of the book – i.e., the cause of Toronto's economic collapse – is built around the fictionalized redress of the Teme-Augama land claim, a real-life event that was prominent in the courts and in the press when Hopkinson was writing *Brown Girl in the Ring*. As the novel begins, Hopkinson introduces several newspaper headlines that trace Toronto's decay as a result of the Teme-Augama pursuit for justice and set out the context for the ostensible dystopia. The headlines have been cut and pasted onto a wall, graffiti style, in someone's attempt to draw a genealogy of the city's collapse:

> TEMEAGAMI INDIANS TAKE ONTARIO TO COURT; AMNESTY INTERNATIONAL FUNDS TEME-AUGAMI ANISHNABAI LAND CLAIM
> FEDERAL GOVT. CUTS TRANSFER PAYMENTS TO PROVINCE BY 30%, CITES INTERNATIONAL TRADE EMBARGO OF TEMEAGAMI PINE
> JOBLESS RATE JUMPS 10%: TEMEAGAMI LAWSUIT IS FUELLING ONTARIO RECESSION, SAYS LABOUR MINISTER
> CRIME AT ALL-TIME HIGH BUT BUDGET CUTS FORCE ONTARIO PROVINCIAL POLICE TO DOWNSIZE
> TORONTO POLICE THREATEN MASS WALKOUT: JOB TOO DANGEROUS, NOT ENOUGH BACKUP, SAYS UNION
> JOBS LEAVE TORONTO: 7 LARGEST EMPLOYERS RELOCATE, SAY TORONTO'S NOT SAFE
> TORONTO CITY HALL MOVES TO SUBURBS: SAFER FOR OUR EMPLOYEES, SAYS MAYOR
> HUNDREDS KILLED IN RAPID TRANSIT CAVE-IN: TORONTO TRANSIT COMMISSION BLAMES FEDERAL CUTBACKS TO ITS MAINTENANCE BUDGET
> CAVE-IN PROTEST SPARKS RIOT: THOUSANDS INJURED, DEAD
> RIOT COPS LAY DOWN ARMS, ARMY CALLED IN: TORONTO IS "WAR ZONE," SAYS HEAD OF POLICE UNION[6]

The causal chain represented here incorrectly identifies the Teme-Augama as the root cause of dystopia, a trick of settler colonialism in which Indigenous *responses* to colonial violence are misinterpreted as the *cause* of subsequent disrepair. This disavowal perpetuates settler colonial ideology by re-enacting *terra nullius* as the erasure of erasure itself – that is, the historical elision of the genocide initiated by settler colonialism.

Critics fell into a similar trap in their reviews of this novel. For instance, Gordon Collier wrote that "Hopkinson's *Brown Girl in the Ring* is set in a Toronto of the future whose economic infrastructure, along with that of Ontario, has collapsed *as a result of litigation by native peoples*" [emphasis added].[7] What Collier misses in this analysis is that Teme-Augama redress in the novel is a direct response to settler colonialism. A more comprehensive reading, then, attentive to Canada's colonial history, would identify colonial land theft as the backdrop to the dystopia of *Brown Girl in the Ring,* rather than Indigenous peoples' responses to that theft. Or, to put it another way, the collapse of Toronto in *Brown Girl in the Ring* is predicated on the theft of Indigenous land and resources – not the Teme-Augama's just claims for recompense. In this sense, the "dystopia" that underlies the novel's plot can be read as the beginning of Indigenous restoration, or the onset of decolonization. Indeed, "left without the comforts of Western technologies, the remaining populace returns to traditional Indigenous farming and husbandry in order to survive. Grandmothers reclaim old memory and dispense 'bush medicine,' because federal, provincial, and city aid no longer exist."[8]

Fact is never far from fiction in Hopkinson's work, just as good dystopian fiction brushes the speculative against the real. *Brown Girl in the Ring* presents a fictional extension of the actual negotiations over n'Daki Menan ("Our Land"), traditional Teme-Augama Anishnabai land located about four hours north of what is now known as Toronto. According to colonial bureaucrats, the Teme-Augama Anishnabai (TAA or "Deep Water People") are signatories of the Robinson-Huron Treaty (1850), which in the eyes of Canadian law, extinguished their title, thus providing the basis for nationalized resource extraction in n'Daki Menan.[9] Since at least 1920, that territory has been logged extensively for red and white pine, displacing hundreds of Teme-Augama people while providing a major source of revenue for the Ontario government. There is also a long history of colonial violence attached to n'Daki Menan. In 1978, the Province of Ontario sued the TAA and "attempted to secure a declaration from the courts that would prove once and for all that these lands were Crown lands."[10] Years later, after a number of blockades, which resulted in the arrest of Teme-Augama Second Chief Rita O'Sullivan, the Supreme Court of Canada finally ruled that a Teme-Augama signature on the Robinson-Huron Treaty was irrelevant (1991), as the First Nation had adhered to it nonetheless.[11] Thus, the Crown had outstanding legal obligations to the First Nation and could not proceed with resource extraction without acknowledging treaty law.

In 1992, when less than 1 percent of original old pine growth remained on n'Daki Menan, Ontario's minister of Natural Resources agreed to start formal treaty negotiations with the Teme-Augama – who had by that time been seeking redress for the expropriation of this land for 125 years. Treaty processes ground to a halt in 1995, however, when a provincial judge lifted a land caution, opening the territory to mining for the first time in two decades. By 1996, Indigenous peoples and their allies (namely, environmental activists) protested incursions into traditional territory with direct action, setting up road blockades and other types of protest – including the destruction of a logging bridge near River Valley. Ontario entered into negotiations with the Temagami First Nation (TFN) and the TAA in 2000. In 2002, three years after *Brown Girl in the Ring* was published, the parties reached a tentative agreement, which included 127 square miles of land and $20 million in financial compensation.[12]

In the world of *Brown Girl in the Ring,* land negotiations with the Teme-Augama Anishnabai continue into the fictional with financial support from Amnesty International and international donors. The Canadian government in the novel is found to be illegally extracting resources from n'Daki Menan, leading to the expanded redress claims noted in the newspaper headlines quoted above. By extending the real-life legal battle into fiction, Hopkinson projects and amplifies settler colonial anxieties over Indigenous land claims and draws explicit attention to settlers' tenuous occupation of stolen land, an anxiety that is thrown into explicit relief via the figure of redress. Indeed, by incorrectly identifying redress, and from it the Teme-Augama, as the source of Toronto's collapse, settlers in Hopkinson's novel effectively position Indigenous peoples as the primary threat to state sovereignty, and redress becomes another means of pinning blame on Indigenous peoples for the ongoing histories of colonialism. As speculative fiction, *Brown Girl in the Ring* is thus a realization of the repressed settler fear surrounding Indigenous sovereignty and the rightful claim to land, a "threat" that settlers can no longer ignore due to international pressure from the United Nations and the repercussions of illegal resource extraction.

Brown Girl in the Ring confirms that reconciliation in Canada does not begin, nor will it end, with Indian Residential Schools. The country has a long history of colonial violence, which, in keeping with the international moral turn, it began to redress in the wake of the Cold War and it continues to redress at the time of writing. But aside from financial restitution, what does redress give to the people living in what is now known as Canada? What does it take? Does it have the potential to radically change the settler colonial environment, as in *Brown Girl in the Ring,* or can it only recapitulate and reaffirm the status quo and state ideologies?

Hopkinson's novel provides unique insight into the settler anxieties that circulate around redress and restitution by illustrating that the very idea of the colonial "utopia" is dependent on the theft of Indigenous land and the ongoing refusal of Indigenous rights. In this sense, *Brown Girl in the Ring* offers a radical depiction of redress, not just as compensation for a historical wrong (which, as I illustrate below, is the Canadian government's primary definition), nor even as a return of land. For Hopkinson, redress is a potentially fatal blow to the settler colonial order: a blow that has the potential to render capitalism inoperative and drive settlers from the land, providing the space for a return to Indigenous ways of being in decolonization coded by the settler population as apocalypse.

For Hopkinson, redress, at its most authentic, is the death of capitalism. I offer *Brown Girl in the Ring* as a starting point to this chapter in order to highlight a parallel narrative to the sanitized discourse of redress that the Canadian government has adopted. Dallas Hunt identifies the latter as the "hermeneutics of reconciliation": settler-inflected redress that guarantees the futurity of settler colonialism. For Hunt, who develops his theory out of a careful reading of a variety of settler speculative fiction (sf) pieces, state-sponsored reconciliation contributes to the ongoing erasure of Indigenous peoples because it requires "that Indigenous people 'reconcile' themselves to their continued colonization."[13] The hermeneutics of reconciliation is founded on the notion that Indigenous-settler relations are solvable and without conflict and therefore require none of the difficult labour that goes into dismantling racism and white privilege, let alone negotiating cultural difference and Indigenous sovereignty. In contrast, Hunt posits Indigenous sf as a means of forecasting Indigenous futures grounded in Indigenous laws and ways of being, which extend (and even thrive) in the wake of the collapse of the settler state. Insofar as it imagines the downfall of the settler government in Toronto, *Brown Girl in the Ring* helps to illuminate precisely the kind of antidote Hunt imagines, because Hopkinson's novel opens a space from which to imagine new possible futures and new trajectories of reconciliation, which do not guarantee settler futurities and which centre Indigenous peoples and ways of knowing.

To address the question of redress, and the acts of giving and receiving that it entails, this chapter takes up the logic of the gift, developed and practised by Indigenous peoples since time immemorial. Gift theory has been developed by a wide array of philosophers, poets, and critical theorists. I will be focusing on the work of Roy Miki, Rauna Kuokkanen, and Dara and Patrick Kelly, all of whom think specifically about the logic of the gift in relation to Indigenous epistemes. In deconstructing the logic of the gift and applying it to the difficult question of redress, this chapter examines the capacity of redress to build community and facilitate relationships outside of the colonial/capitalist framework. Hopkinson provides one model from which to interrogate redress within a settler framework: as the onset of the apocalypse. This chapter imagines another model of redress: as a gesture of obligation that functions outside capitalism. Below, I make a case for the gift, in relation to redress, building from its potential to create and maintain community and restore meaningful relationships.

Redress as a Gift

Redress as a gift raises compelling questions about financial recompense as a relationship. Those questions include: what does it mean to consider redress as a gift (rather than a penalty), and what might this shift in rhetoric afford us as scholars of reconciliation? What does the gift teach us about relationality? And how might its logic allow us to reformulate accountability to the other? In this chapter, I attempt to add new dimension and depth to the ways in which we can consider redress as a gift by building out of one of the more poetic moments in Roy Miki's *Redress: Inside the Japanese Canadian Call for Justice*. I bring Japanese Canadian perspectives into this chapter and the next in order to highlight the existing allyships developed between communities that contend with reconciliation in the contexts of white supremacy and settler colonialism. We must be willing to investigate the grammars of redress as they have been inflected within the settler colonial boundaries of Canada since the Nuremberg trials, and we must also be willing to ask how the state's historical attempts to recuperate redress might impact Indigenous sovereignty in the wake of the TRC. In addressing redress as a gift, we are afforded insight into the ways in which settler Canadians conceptualize redress – not as compensation, but as a threat to the capitalist foundations of the settler colonial nation-state. With the idea of a gift, we also open up the opportunity to rethink reconciliation as a discourse of responsibility and reciprocity – outside of the strictures of obligation and debt.

Miki's work offers a provocative activation site from which to begin this type of analysis. Miki is a Japanese Canadian author and educator who was involved in the 1988 Japanese Canadian redress movement as a frontline activist, poet, and academic. His work in *Redress* is vital to understanding how the genres of reconciliation and redress have developed within the Canadian state prior to the TRC, and the question of the gift is central to this work – particularly in Miki's ability to transcend the quantitative analysis that is so easily pinned to redress. With only three pages of *Redress* remaining, Miki "returns us to the question of redress as a gift."[14] Here, he not only asks his readers to conceive of redress as a gift, but also asks us to return to the notion, suggesting that "redress as a gift" has a historical basis that readers might draw on in order to clarify the inner workings of reparation in both its histories and its futures. What Miki is evoking in his use of the word "gift," and in his insistence that his readers "return" to it, is a notion of *reciprocity* and the relationship building that occurs between survivors and perpetrators in the ongoing attempt to act responsibly in relation to the past. As he explains to Guy Beauregard in a 2009 interview, redress is "both a loss and a gain."[15] In other words, it is not a unidirectional endowment; redress is a site of social engagement through which reconciliation can be articulated as a relationship dependent on deep listening and a bonded relationship to the other. In this sense, for communities receiving redress, it also means giving something up. What is a gift in the terms of restitution then? Is it even possible? Is it desirable?

Within the context of redress, the idea of the gift appears out of place because redress and reparation are so often conceptualized as compensation for a wrong or loss as opposed to something given out of benevolence or affection demanded by the logic of the gift. It is difficult to argue that any offering from the State is proffered without cost when it seems evident that governmental gifts are rooted in precise political considerations, not goodwill. Indeed, Rauna Kuokkanen argues that in order for the gift to be maintained as such, it must be abstracted from systems of exchange (for instance, a credit, loan, or social obligation). Once it requires "gratitude, another gift, or a return of the favour," the gift is made impossible.[16] I will come back to Kuokkanen and the impossibility of the gift shortly, but for now it is important to note that there is a deep history of the gift as reparation that supports Miki's analysis. This history is rooted not in systems of exchange but in the onset of responsibility and the facilitation of a relationship.

In order to unpack redress as a gift, however, we need to return to World War II, or more precisely to the aftermath of the genocide inflicted by Nazi Germany. Germany has a unique and troubling history of reparations that, in many ways, sets the benchmark for the modern world. As Daniel Vernett so aptly puts it, the Germans are "unsurpassed both at the crime and at repenting for it."[17] While there was deep national debate about how to remember the Nazi past, by the end of the 1980s a "culture of contrition" was shared across Germany.[18] This shift began, in earnest, in 1952 when Chancellor Konrad Adenauer and the Bonn government signed the Luxembourg Agreement, "the first major executive statement of responsibility and remorse, delivered at a time when Germany was largely still mired in amnesia."[19]

In order to address the unprecedented contexts of reparations they were contending with out of Luxembourg, Adenauer and the Bonn Government designated the particular kind of redress they would be providing as *Wiedergutmachung* (which loosely translates to "moral reparation"). This word was aimed specifically at separating compensation from traditional understandings of military indemnity and "victor's vengeance." *Wiedergutmachung* emphasized relationship as a necessary element of reparation and reconfigured payment not as an exchange for loss, but as the perpetrators' "acceptance of one's own destructiveness and guilt."[20] Along with the Nuremberg trials, the *Wiedergutmachung* model revolutionized the ways in which international communities conceived of payment for historical injustice, insofar as compensation here was rooted directly in human rights principles.[21]

In Desmond Tutu's own need to distinguish redress from "victor's justice," the moral reparations developed out of Luxembourg were adapted as a foundation for the South African TRC.[22] Like Adenauer, Tutu saw the necessity of overturning the dry fiscal model of compensation and endowing redress with a more compassionate, human element: "reparation is as balm," Tutu writes in *No Future without Forgiveness*, "an ointment, being poured over the wounds to assist in [survivors'] healing."[23] As both Adenauer and Tutu help to illustrate, the *Wiedergutmachung* model throws into relief exactly what makes reparation such a difficult discourse to conceptualize, implement, and analyze: arguments about redress are often flat and divisive because of the difficulty we have conceptualizing morality within a fiduciary framework. Indeed, the fact that this discourse is substantially less discussed than other elements of reconciliation, such as apology and forgiveness, is not a coincidence. Economics are often elided in the conversations surrounding reconciliation because what governments are "giving" in redress is presumably payment for the loss of land, life, and culture. Not all social situations (and few political ones) have the conceptual depth to make room for the cognitive load required to process financial transactions as an exchange for life. Economic principles are incompatible with certain socio-political interactions because economics signify calculation and self-interest in situations that defy a calculus.

In the case of reparation, the exchange of money suggests that a loved one, home, or material contribution to the future can be assigned a numeric value. Many survivors are thus, rightly, quite unwilling or unable to allocate this valuation. Daniel Levy and Natan Sznaider eloquently point out the demoralizing effects of financial redress for genocide:

> Honor and money, like fire and water, cannot exist together. They are the circulatory media of two very different systems of behavior that are distinguished in both our historical memory and in social theory. Economic behavior is supposed to be self-regarding, rational, and calculative. Honorable behavior is supposed to be undertaken without thought of gain, to be based on intrinsic values, and to be other-regarding. In common parlance, to act honorably is to override one's personal interest and to act on principle. But restitution, by its very nature, must mix the two together.[24]

Suggesting an equivalency or calculus for the loss of land or the life of a loved one is in bad taste, to say the least, and it almost always results in strenuous public outcry. In 1952, as Adenauer's government secured the reparation package to be delivered to Israel, survivors and witnesses around the world were appalled that the horrors perpetrated in Auschwitz and Dachau could be quantified or compensated for in any way – particularly monetarily. Massive demonstrations were organized in protest against the initial dialogue between German and Jewish officials. In Tel Aviv, 40,000 people protested the reparation talks with Germans by raising their right arms en masse and stating, "If I forget thee, O murdered Golah, let my right-hand wither. I swear never to relent, never to rest until our six million murdered brethren have been avenged."[25] Thus, while the international community demanded some reparative material for the unthinkable damage the Germans had inflicted, extending these reparations as such was an impossible gesture. To put it differently, money, while a necessary aspect of reconciliation, was simultaneously marked as taboo within that same discourse.

As Kuokkanen illustrates, this too is the logic of the gift: "The pre-condition of the gift is that it not be recognized, for once it is, it ceases to be a gift and becomes something else (a credit, or a loan, or an obligation)."[26] For Kuokkanen, the gift is therefore impossible because as soon as we need a reason to give it (for example, obligation, debt, etc.), it ceases to exist as what it pretends to be – that is, an act of unselfish offering to the other, without demand or duty. Of course, as Kuokkanen demonstrates, reasons for giving in a Western framework are inextricably intertwined with colonialism, capitalism, and patriarchal attitudes, which have the tendency to frame the logic of the gift in a particular discourse. The consequence of this being that gift theorists often overlook or disregard the ways in which Indigenous communities have engaged gift economies relationally (rather than as systems of debt) for thousands of years.

Indeed, just because the gift might be rendered impossible when framed in Western discourse does not mean that it is unreasonable or without value. Building from the aporia of the gift she finds in Jacques Derrida's analysis of the gift, in which the logic of the gift calls out for acknowledgment, return, and responsibility, Kuokkanen identifies the impossibility of the gift as a socio-political touchstone through which ongoing systems of community building and reciprocity are developed. In fact, she connects the impossibility of the gift to the response-ability of the giver – that is, one's capacity to hear and act on the needs and desires of the other: "one could argue that reason as hospitable receptivity signifies a certain openness beyond control. Reason as the capacity to receive might also be able to receive the gift responsibly, with a response and therefore also reciprocity."[27] In this sense, the impossibility of the gift demands a return that does not fulfill an obligation or debt but rather opens up an enduring relationship built out of the persistent necessity of being in relation to the other. The "well-being of the social order" is core to what Kuokkanen identifies as the Indigenous logic of the gift, in which priority is placed on relationship, not debt.[28]

Much like the logic of the gift that Kuokkanen identifies, *Wiedergutmachung* exists only in its impossibility as such – in its failure to take up a demand that cannot be ignored. In 1952, the need for a conception of restitution that extended beyond the exchange of cash was played out specifically in the Luxembourg Agreement, which established German-Jewish reparations in the wake of the Second World War. Nicholas Balabkins refers to these payments "as the innovation of this century, a *res nova,* a *sui generis,*"[29] not only because they embodied the largest payout for human injustice in world history (roughly 3.5 billion DM), but, more importantly, because they represented the first time a "nation had ever made payments to another for material damages on a collective basis."[30]

On a global stage, *Wiedergutmachung* established compensation for historic wrongs as a new means to facilitate interstate relations between perpetrators and survivors and between perpetrators and the international community. That being said, determining *how* to give these reparations was just as much at stake as determining the amount. The *sui generis* character of *Wiedergutmachung,* identified as such in the way it instituted compensation as an essential element of interstate relations, altered the face of reparative practices and generated a new ideological space through which modern redress movements, such as the TRC, could be read. The inflated global emphasis on morality brought on by the Nuremberg trials, the stage on which Adenauer and his government were made to play out *Wiedergutmachung,* necessitated the moral conversion of cash. Any official proceeding that appeared to be based on a cost-benefit analysis would not be seen as a moral action at all, but as a miserly counting of coins. As such, "morality" and "compensation" became deeply complicated terms, being both inextricably intertwined and, at the same time, mutually exclusive.

What was at issue for Adenauer and his government, then, inasmuch as they believed that "the soul of Germany depended on reconciliation,"[31] was not simply how to give reparations to Jewish people, but, in a much more complex sense, how to give them in a way that de-emphasized economic exchange and highlighted the establishment of a changed and ongoing *relationship* between parties. In other words, furthering the logic that evolved out of Nuremberg, "reparations" needed to be endowed with another meaning aside from (but also including) cash settlement. In order to be accepted by the Jewish community, compensation needed to be at least partially divested of the value of its *content* – i.e., its monetary significance – by converting that significance to the value of its *form* – i.e., the fact of reparations themselves. Or, to borrow from Pierre Bourdieu and the logic of the gift he propounds, reparations had to be "misrecognized ... disguised, transfigured, in a word, euphemized,"[32] in order to maintain any "value" whatsoever in a moral economy.

It is in the moral conversion implicit in reparations, from content to form, from recognition to misrecognition, from economics to relationship, that we can begin to think of one way in which reparations and the gift fit together. The *sui generis* quality of German-Jewish reparations is historically conceptualized by reparations scholars as a "symbolic gesture of amends."[33] However, the logic of the gift allows for further insight into the psychic mechanisms behind the symbolic gesture – that is, the unsaid processes that facilitate the act of giving *qua* reparation. This is to say that the logic of the gift provides for the use of calculation in the fraught and unquantifiable space of historical injustice while simultaneously generating a space for new relationships to unfold. It was only by effacing the distasteful elements of equivalency in reparation that Adenauer was even able to broach the concept of reconciliation in the wake of such a horrific loss of life. To the extent that the Bonn government was in the business of providing redress to Jewish survivors, the economic purpose of its assistance needed to be elided – although not disappeared – from the process. This amounts to a more radical divination of the desires and need of the injured party: not only "what do you want?" but, more importantly, "how do I give it to you in a way that communicates a compassionate understanding of our fragile relationship?"; or, *how do I give giving?*

So how does "redress as a gift" allow us to contend with the fundamental impasse between "honour and money"? How does one conceptualize giving and receiving in the wake of unreasonable loss, grief, and anger? It is no coincidence that Bourdieu argues that gifts are "sometimes intended to set the seal on alliances or reconciliations,"[34] but what is the logic that unfurls here, and how is it connected to Canada's unique history of redress? In what follows, I dig deeper into the implications of the honour/money binary and demonstrate the spaces in which the two brush against and inform one another. The logic of the gift, as unpacked by Indigenous scholars such as Kuokkanen and Kelly and Kelly, provides the epistemic space to do this work.

If redress is a gift, then we must be willing to look for what that gift erases and what it calls for in return. I don't think that "money" and "honour" are mutually exclusive terms in the redress vernacular; rather, I argue that one supports the other in complicated and often insidious ways that distract from the roles that economics play in facilitating a public understanding of morality. On the one hand, asking for money risks rendering the call for apology false. Currency makes it impossible to render sincere appeals for moral recompense because it attempts to make quantifiable that which cannot be counted. But on the other hand, some form of compensation is necessary for an apology to respond to the economic damage inflicted during historical injustice – and which survivor communities are forced to live out. Economic disparity, by which I mean not only loss of property, resources, and access to jobs, but also the loss of land and the repression of culture, is not the only effect of historic injustice, but it does play a significant role in how we understand and quantify that violence. Indeed, it is absolutely imperative to note that the perpetrators of genocide, particularly within settler colonialism, almost always see economic prosperity as the ends to the means, whether that prosperity comes through cultural appropriation, cheap labour, or primitive accumulation. Thus, to *not* consider redress is to ignore the material deprivations of historical injustice and the physical, emotional, and mental impacts of perpetrator theft: impacts that would not be as acute if the survivors hadn't been forced into material poverty in the first place. As such, financial compensation is, in some small way, a material improvement in physical conditions, which can have a significant impact on other aspects of survivor health, healing, and well-being.

Just as important, however, is the need to extend the conversation around redress beyond the unidirectional discourse of compensation, and more specifically beyond what the state gives as redress to communities impacted by historical injustice, such as residential schools and Japanese Canadian internment. Compensation ignores the complex systems of responsibility and reciprocity enacted in the act of giving redress, most particularly what is given back by the communities that receive it and what is implied in the act of giving as a relationship for which the gift is only the onset: "the gift creates community and social ties whereas markets interrupt them," Kuokkanen reminds us.[35] Reframing redress as gift therefore opens new possibilities for reconciliation, beyond the hermeneutics of reconciliation that Dallas Hunt identifies, and toward a future that does not guarantee settler, or market, futurities.

Japanese Canadian Redress, 1988

After the 1941 Pearl Harbor bombing, Japanese Canadians and their families were forcibly removed from their homes and interned in camps in the interior, away from the coast, ostensibly as a means to protect against a fifth column insurgency from the "Japanese" (a racialized designation that elided the fact that most of those interned were born in Canada and therefore Canadian). The government confiscated the possessions and property of almost all of these families, auctioning them off for a fraction of their value to white settlers, and dispersed the families into labour camps in the interior of British Columbia and across Canada. This diaspora fundamentally redistributed the Japanese Canadian population, at times separating families and often putting children at risk in racist and violent environments, a fact of white supremacy that echoes across the residential schools that were operating at the same time.

The Canadian government initiated the forced removal of Japanese Canadians under the *War Measures Act,* first enacted on August 14, 1914, which allowed for the internment of Canadian-born and naturalized citizens who believed that their citizenship would protect them from persecution.[36] The *War Measures Act,* as conceptualized in political theory, was an exercise in state sovereignty, insofar as, in deploying it, Canada was able suspend law and act against its citizens in order to maintain its authority as lawmaker. As a tool of settler colonialism, by which I mean a process that facilitated white settler possession over land and resources, the *War Measures Act* gave the Canadian state the power to render racialized citizens as "bare life." As such, Japanese Canadians were evacuated of the rights guaranteed by the state and the UN and left entirely vulnerable to Canadian white supremacy, losing land, property, and freedom of movement in the process.[37]

In the way it has been levied to secure white settler ownership of land and resources, the *War Measures Act* should be read as a tool of settler colonialism. Insofar as this chapter and the next aim to illustrate how the impacts of settler colonialism extend beyond Indigenous communities – and thus how the discourse of reconciliation can evolve pluralistically yet from the same foundation – I want to elaborate on that point here. Part of what I suggest in these chapters is that settler colonialism intersects with white supremacy toward the settler colonial "logic of elimination" that facilitates white settler belonging in territories that we in fact occupy as colonizers.[38] While racialized settlers also benefit from stolen Indigenous land, whiteness functions as a structure of power through which "belonging," at least in a colonially informed juridical sense, is secured or disavowed – which Japanese Canadian internment attests to. Because, in Canada, reconciliation must be understood as a reaction to, and a redressing of, both settler colonialism and white supremacy, reading the two ideas alongside one another provides a more rigorous methodology through which to analyze the culture of redress as it unfurls in this country.

The *War Measures Act* provides a productive site through which to establish a firm meeting point between settler colonialism and white supremacy, given that it was leveraged against both Indigenous peoples and Japanese Canadians. While research by Ann Gomer Sunahara establishes how the *War Measures Act* disenfranchised Japanese Canadians, there is less research on its impacts on Indigenous peoples.[39] However, some documentation does exist illustrating that the same act was also used to confiscate Indigenous land and facilitate government ownership of unceded and treaty territories. In his research on the *War Measures Act* and Indigenous land theft, P. Whitney Lackenbauer quotes Mrs. Beattie (Mary) Greenbird, an Elder of the Kettle and Stony Point band, who reports that white men sold off her community's inheritance using that very legislation, despite the fact that the treaty they operated under made no mention that the government could "take Indians' land without their consent."[40] Lackenbauer goes on to argue that "the *War Measures Act* offered a straightforward solution to a pressing dilemma that not only assured immediate freehold control over the reserve for the duration of the war without Indian consent, but also seemed to secure land for a postwar district camp."[41] Untangling the effects of the *War Measures Act* from the Japanese Canadian redress movement, therefore, means addressing the ways in which settler colonialism levies sovereignty and white supremacy against racialized bodies as a means to control access to land and resources and to reproduce the status quo.

What is revealed by the *War Measures Act* is the deeply seeded racism that undergirds Canada's genealogy as a sovereign power. For instance, the Geneva Convention expressly forbids governments to intern their own citizens, insofar as internment is "a legal act applicable only to aliens."[42] Gomer Sunahara points out that this means that, lawfully, the Nisei – children born to Japanese parents in Canada – could not be interned. Rather, in the political doublespeak of Orwell's *1984,* they were "detained at the pleasure of the Minister of Justice."[43] As Gomer Sunahara puts it, "their legal status was equivalent to that of a criminal under psychiatric care."[44] The semantic "play" in the distinction between internment and detainment illustrates that under the *War Measures Act,* government officials were able to translate illegal actions into discourses of grey areas and doublespeak. Thus, the word "internment" readily became "detention," allowing officials to skirt the legality of the Geneva Convention; similarly, Japanese Canadians were referred to as "Asiatics" or "Orientals" in order to construct them as alien to the nation's (white) identity; and "evacuation," which denoted safety and protection, was the term used to describe, and simultaneously ignore, the deportation, dispersal, and disenfranchisement of racialized Canadian citizens.[45]

The substitution of vague, indirect language played a quintessential role in the Canadian government's ability to carry out illegal measures against its own citizens. It was through the spurious act of translation that fear and racism became "the language of bureaucratic efficiency,"[46] and Japanese Canadians were stripped of legal protection, just as white settlers benefitted from their displacement. This piece of legislation was deeply rooted in settler colonial principles that provided for the dispossession and dispersal of racialized peoples while simultaneously providing the colonial government with further control of Indigenous land and resources.

On September 22, 1988, nearly fifty years after the *War Measures Act* was enacted against Japanese Canadians, Canadian prime minister Brian Mulroney and National Association of Japanese Canadians (NAJC) president Arthur Miki (Roy Miki's brother) sat down to sign the Japanese Canadian Redress Agreement, one of the world's largest and most comprehensive restitution accords, which both echoed the Nuremberg trials – in that they both made war crimes public and attempted to redress historical injustice – and helped to establish what the principles of restitution looked like when applied to *national* conflicts. Hired by the NAJC, the respected accounting firm Price Waterhouse (now PricewaterhouseCoopers) valued losses to Japanese Canadian families at $443 million. When an agreement was reached, internment survivors each received $21,000 in redress money. Another $12 million was given to the NAJC to support the community and promote human rights, and $12 million was given to establish the Canadian Race Relations Foundation, with an aim of eliminating racism.[47]

Aside from the cash settlements, the agreement also cleared the names of any Japanese Canadians convicted of violations under the *War Measures Act* and returned Canadian citizenship to any Japanese Canadian who had had it revoked between 1941 and 1949. All in all, the Japanese Canadian redress movement is viewed as one of the most successful reparation movements in international history, not simply because of the fiduciary justice meted out, but also because of the ways in which it gave back to Canada's socio-political fabric. According to Miki, Japanese Canadians "gave their wartime experience as a gift to the official history of the nation."[48] Redress, offered at a critical time in Canadian history – namely, concurrent with the passage of the *Multiculturalism Act* (1988) – encouraged a vital revaluation of Canadian citizenship that mediated the emergence of a new Canadian identity. As Miki puts it, "the receivers had become the givers."[49] The logic of the gift had played out as a historical relationship between the NAJC and the state that facilitated Canada's reputation as a moral leader in a neo-liberal global economy trading in post–Cold War benevolence and intra-state justice.

The Gift of Japanese Canadian Redress

A large part of the success of a redress movement is not the size of the offering but, more importantly, the ways in which both parties, perpetrators and survivors, are able to overcome the aporia that arises between material reparation and affective responses to the quantification of human life. Assuming that there is a desire for an ongoing relationship and that survivors are willing to put their trust in a government that has historically lied and reneged on its promises, the logic of the gift can form the basis for an equitable redress movement insofar as it develops a responsibility between giver and receiver based on an ethic of reciprocity. That is, the *givers* conduct themselves in relation to the desire of the other and openly acknowledge what is returned on the delivery of compensation, financial and otherwise.

The Japanese Canadian redress movement helps to illustrate how this formulation of redress operates on the ground. It also provides a cautionary tale about the ways in which that return can be recuperated into settler state mythos. By locating redress as a gift – not just a payment for loss of life and land but a reconfiguration of the Canadian state – the NAJC transcended the economic shibboleth of reparation (honour vs. money), without doing away with the need to financially compensate survivors. What Canada took away from Japanese Canadians during the Second World War – their homes, their possessions, their families, and, in many cases, their lives – can never be returned. The success of the 1988 Redress Agreement was thus its ability to compensate, commemorate, and critique, leading to financial reparation, a legacy of Japanese Canadian activism, and a deconstruction of the racist legislation built into Canada's internal human rights policies. One of Miki's most important points throughout *Redress,* however, is that while what the Canadian government gave to Japanese Canadians is significant, what is more important, and what had more of an impact on Canada's socio-political order, was what Japanese Canadians *gave back.* In the sense that the Redress Agreement changed how Canada understood Canadian citizenship – outside of race – the import of redress as a gift must be understood, and critiqued, in what Miki identifies as "a healing of the democratic system – and, by implication, of the nation."[50]

I have already argued that gifts are caught up in their own reciprocal economies. The same logic can be applied to redress. Indeed, the self-interested logic of the gift is built right into the discourse of redress and reparation. In redress, the survivor is at risk of being positioned by the redressing party, usually the state, as an empty signifier through which "generosity" must pass in order for the latter party to appear moral. In the theatre of regret, perpetrators are called on to acquit themselves of historical injustice through restitution, which ostensibly allows them to re-enter the global economy as a cleansed subject. In what Eve Tuck and K. Wayne Yang would identify as a "move towards innocence," survivors become the vehicle through which that transaction takes place, which reifies the power of the state while effacing survivor agency.[51]

Idi Amin's Commission of Inquiry, which I discuss in more detail in Chapter 1, helps to demonstrate how, in giving reparations, the perpetrating state gives itself access to an international system of exchange that has become contingent on the appearance of morality. If Uganda were to continue in international trade, Amin had to arrange a truth commission to appease the international community and lift trade embargos. Uganda was unable to participate in the global economy, because the state had been deemed immoral within the relatively new context of the Nuremberg trials. By going through the performance of morality, Amin regained trade rights without changing the political conditions for which he was being held accountable. In this framework, the Amin survivors become the signifier through which a violent political economy was recuperated and re-circulated. This foundational truth commission illustrates how the emphasis of "morality" is placed on the reward of auto-recognition for the perpetrator, rather than the political conditions of those being redressed. What redress as a gift makes clear is that Amin's position is fundamental to the TRC process – not an exception to the rule.

In order for the 1988 Japanese Canadian redress movement to be successful, according to Miki, "it had to present a cogent argument for redress and it had to do so in a language, tone, and mode of presentation that would both educate readers and draw them into the drama of redress as a current issue."[52] In my reading of Miki, this "cogent argument" hinges on an articulation of "redress as a gift" for both the state and the Japanese Canadian community, and on the return that accompanies any gift economy as surplus value. In fact, Miki's text is almost entirely about exposing the reciprocity implicit in the Japanese Canadian redress movement, and therefore overturning the projection of "generosity" that settler states such as Canada – perhaps particularly Canada – seek to propagate via compensation. By addressing redress as something that can and should be reciprocated, Miki directly engages with the power dynamics of the gift, taking Japanese Canadians from the role of passive receivers to the more politically efficacious position of givers. In doing so, he demonstrates how the NAJC created a space for successful reparation and how grassroots groups can strategically deploy reconciliation against the status quo and colonial politics.

At its base, the reciprocal success of Japanese Canadian redress is linked to the critique and reconstitution of Canadian citizenship, which, until the Redress Agreement, was contingent on race and empowered by the *War Measures Act*. Writing with a nod to the neo-liberal turn of the new international morality, Miki argues that the "call for redress could be of 'use' in *giving* value to Canadian citizenship" [emphasis added],[53] which is to say that redress represented an economic benefit for Canada in a global economy defining itself in opposition to *realpolitik* and (back) toward the morality and compassion derived out of the Nuremberg trials. The language of citizenship, implicit in Miki's use of the concept of the gift, is directly connected to the *War Measures Act*, which allowed the colonial government to strip citizens of their rights arbitrarily and with no more justification than race. In their move toward redress, the NAJC was banking on a definition of compensation, resonant with *Wiedergutmachung,* that would allow all Canadians to consider the value of national belonging. Put simply, in return for reparations, Japanese Canadian redress gave the state back a more rigorous and ethical definition of citizenship, one based in nationality rather than race. This exchange gave Japanese Canadians a larger stake in redress because it contributed to *all* Canadians' sense of citizenship, and thus of the safety and belonging provided by Canadian sovereignty. In this act of reciprocity, the NAJC was able to interrupt the appearance of pure benevolence from the Canadian state and render Japanese Canadians active agents in a system of exchange – as opposed to empty signifiers through which the state recuperated morality.

The unseemly upshot of this, however, which Miki clearly lays out for us, is the ways in which Canada was thus able to recuperate internment, via redress, into financial leverage: "In retrospect, then, Japanese Canadian redress was woven into a complex negotiation process – an event that redeemed the nation at a time of shifting formations and that brought to political resolution the historical injustices endured by Japanese Canadians."[54] Which is all to say that "redress as a gift" operates at a number of complex levels and articulations within the Japanese Canadian movement: both elevating Japanese Canadian agency in a system that historically has worked to efface survivors, and also bolstering Canada's identity (on which it prides itself) in an international economy that trades in morality.

Of course, the Japanese Canadian history of redress should raise massive concerns when mapped onto the TRC of Canada, not only in how it provides a cautionary tale about the ways in which white settlers recuperate historical trauma into cultural and financial capital, but also in the ways redress and reconciliation are caught up in state nationalism. Indeed, for better and for worse, nationalism is at the heart of the 1988 Redress Agreement. In her book of the same name, Patricia E. Roy defines the Japanese Canadian redress movement as "the triumph of citizenship," arguing that the redress movement made Canada and the Canadian constitution a stronger and more robust system based on inclusion.[55] Roy's book is premised on the notion that Japanese Canadians were so successful in their call for justice because the principle of citizenship, as defined both nationally and internationally, superseded racism. Citing *The Penticton Herald,* her primary argument is that "citizenship in Canada must have meaning, not alone for folk of Japanese ancestry but for all of us."[56] Miki argues a very similar point, although with a more nuanced critique of the ways in which Canada was able to monetize redress for the state in "the emergence of the new global economy."[57]

The centrality of nationalism to redress and reconciliation should not come as a surprise given the international history of the TRC. For instance, Priscilla Hayner points out "that each [Commission] is nationally rooted, unique to each place, and reflects a process of national ownership."[58] Similarly, Jennifer Matsunaga argues that, "while its individual instruments incorporate victim-centred approaches, transitional justice is itself inherently nation state-centred."[59] At stake in truth commissions in Chile and South Africa, for instance, was a reconciliation of singular national identity that had been torn apart by racism and ideological differences. Finding peace was thus a means of reclaiming national identity and strengthening nation-state sovereignty.

Hayner and Matsunaga are instructive in defining the local parameters of reconciliation in Canada. Indeed, in terms of national ownership, the Japanese Canadian Redress Agreement constructed a definition of redress in Canada that is almost entirely grounded in multicultural values and settler state citizenship, leaving little room to conceptualize Indigenous sovereignty and self-determination. Of course, many Indigenous peoples, including residential school survivors and their families, reject or are deeply critical of citizenship in a colonial state because citizenship has, since at least the imposition of the *Indian Act,* been a means of assimilating Indigenous peoples while insisting that they abandon sovereignty and the right to self-determination. To be enfranchised as an Indigenous person in Canada, for instance (at least until 1981), meant to forsake legal and cultural identities as an "Indian" as well as claims to land and heritage. Individuals were involuntarily enfranchised for serving in the army, for obtaining a university education, and even for leaving their reserve for long periods of time. The violence of citizenship is also directly connected to gender. Women were enfranchised for marrying non-Indigenous men and if their Indigenous husband died or abandoned them. Citizenship was a tool of oppression, not liberation. If redress is synonymous with citizenship, then, as it has been defined through Japanese Canadian redress and recuperated by the settler state, it will continue to enable settler colonialism, to the extent that it re-enacts, out of a performance of regret, a long and damaging history of assimilation.

There is certainly pressure from the Canadian government, and even from within the TRC itself, to follow in the path of Japanese Canadian redress and deploy the TRC as a means to define a stronger, more inclusive state. The first line of Schedule "N" reads: "There is an emerging and compelling desire to put the events of the past behind us so that we can work towards a stronger and healthier future."[60] Without first addressing how settler colonialism and power are at play within any definition of "us," though, the "stronger and healthier" future posited here risks recapitulating the liberal, multicultural state of Canada's recent history rather than holding up the sovereign, self-determining nations within Canada with which Canadians and the Canadian government interact. This type of redress, to borrow from Glen Coulthard, is about rendering Canadian law consistent so as to protect Crown sovereignty over land while providing security for capital investment and the continuing development of state infrastructure.[61] It is not about finding ways to upset the power balance that structures giving and receiving in the settler state. As a gift to the state, by which I mean what is returned to Canadians from redress payments, redress always bears the risk of benefitting the state more than the survivors it claims to recognize, even as conservative pundits spread fallacious rhetoric about "handouts" and the "victim industry."[62] For all the work and change that the NAJC accomplished, for all the good that came out of the redress movement, Indigenous peoples and allies must remain attentive to what was lost and what can continue to be extracted in the bifurcated movement implicit in redress as a gift.

Gifts, Rewards, and Lotteries: *Where the Blood Mixes*

Understanding the depths of what Indigenous peoples are asked to give in relation to redress adds further dimension to the gift economies that Miki addresses in *Redress* and the trepidation he expresses over state recuperation of returns. Nlaka'pamux actor and playwright Kevin Loring provides a provocative activation site from which to continue thinking through the gift of redress in his award-winning play *Where the Blood Mixes*. This play was first produced in 2008, just as the TRC of Canada was getting underway: "on the very day we opened at Magnetic North [a theatre festival in Vancouver]," Loring writes, "the Conservative government officially apologized for the atrocities committed at the Residential Schools."[63] In terms of its historical contexts, then, as well as the content it examines, *Where the Blood Mixes* provides an important counterpoint to the redress narratives offered by the Canadian state – narratives in which healing and redress are stable and easily discernible signifiers made legible by what it means to give.

In terms of narrative, *Where the Blood Mixes* tells the story of Mooch and Floyd, both survivors of Canada's residential school system, now middle-aged men living in a small, unnamed, community. The two men spend most of their time in the local pub, which is run by a Shum'ma (white person) bartender named George. The primary action is derived from a newspaper article announcing that the Canadian government will be providing compensation for residential school survivors. George is the one who breaks the news to Mooch and Floyd: "people are getting compensated. I guess the government and the church are finally going to compensate people for what happened at those Residential Schools."[64]

While never named specifically as such, the compensation announced in *Where the Blood Mixes* alludes to the two forms of redress offered to residential school survivors under the Indian Residential Schools Settlement Agreement: The Common Experience Payment (CEP) and the Independent Assessment Process (IAP), both of which were announced in the fall of 2007. Under the CEP, survivors could apply for a lump-sum payment ($10,000 plus $3,000 for each year they attended a residential school). To receive the CEP, survivors needed to prove that they attended a registered school.[65] A total of $1.6 billion was paid out under this model. In contrast, the IAP is reported to have paid out $3.1 billion in redress. How surviours were asked to go about collecting money under the IAP was quite different than the CEP:[66] here, survivors had to prove they had been subject to sexual or physical abuse under the definitions provided by Schedule "D" of the Indian Residential Schools Settlement Agreement, such as serious physical or sexual abuse committed by priests, nuns, staff, or other students. Survivors could also claim the IAP if school employees of the government or church committed acts leading to serious psychological harm.[67] Dollar amounts were specifically attached to the amount and type of harm caused. In this sense, the IAP was directly linked to testimony and the recollection of difficult truths, what the *Washington Post* pointedly labelled a "pay-for-pain" model.[68]

Where the Blood Mixes helps to draw out some of the consequences attached to the redress model employed by the state for residential school survivors. Floyd is quick to point out that the compensation offered to survivors will only be distributed when they give over their truths to the TRC. When queried about the size of a potential payout, Floyd, alluding to the IAP, responds, "It depends on how bad it was, eh. Most people are getting about fifteen grand. If it was real bad, you get lots more."[69] In the way Floyd describes it, redress is positioned not simply as a government payout, but as a painful exchange for truth. And while compensation means that Mooch and Floyd will be able to make minor improvements to their lives – "you could even pay off your bar tab," George tells them – there is also a significant catch: "you gotta talk about it ... That's the thing, eh? You gotta talk about what happened."[70]

Indeed, speaking truth does not always lead to justice, and it cannot always be directly equated with healing. Christine Fiddler describes the IAP system as "[survivors recalling] every memory of pain inflicted upon him or her, while filling out a form."[71] In the wake of the CEP and IAP, there is now significant data to support the damage caused by these processes. The Aboriginal Healing Foundation (AHF) reports that due to the procedures required by the CEP, study groups have reported that the "application process triggered negative reactions." The AHF continues, "While for some these triggers led Survivors to seek counselling and were later seen as a step along their healing journey, for others the pain was unbearable and led to a relapse of addictive behaviours or thoughts of suicide."[72] The Assembly of First Nations 2012–2013 Annual Report further notes that the Healing Centre programs operated via the Indian Residential School Resolution Health Support Program "have experience[d] a demand in services resulting from the IAP deadline as well as the TRC and Commemoration events, all [of] which trigger trauma that requires treatment provided by the Centres."[73] Scholarly attention has also been paid to the damage generated by the TRC's redress models. Ronald Niezen argues that the IAP has "the effect of clarifying, but at the same time heightening and making uncomfortable the associations between financial compensation and traumatic experience."[74] Niezen quotes one survivor who, when asked his opinion of the IAP, said, "I found it abusive. 'How many times did you get raped? That's another $5,000.' It's demeaning. It didn't work."[75]

Building out of the damage caused by residential school redress – in the exchange incurred at the site of transaction – Loring's play makes a vital contribution to redress discourse by providing a space for the social explication of how compensation impacted survivors and their communities. As an illustration of the distress caused by the "pay-for-pain model," *Where the Blood Mixes* draws our attention to the fact that the demand that one produce grief and pain in order to receive redress contributes to a folding of experience in which the time and space of the abuse becomes omnipresent. Indeed, for Mooch, it is impossible to contain the abuse suffered in residential schools in the past. Trying to recall the timeline of his own abuse, he stammers, "It happened yesterday, it happened today, it'll happen tomorrow. Every day is every day."[76] Compensation for Mooch and other survivors is deeply fraught because the politics of redress do not go far enough in considering the bifurcated agency of the system, as both agent of healing and harbinger of suffering, or, as Sky Dancer Louise Bernice Halfe puts it, as "med-sin."[77]

The implications of the pain induced by compensation are echoed across *Where the Blood Mixes*. Loring shows how many survivors rightfully don't want to talk about their experiences because of the trauma it potentially reawakens. When Mooch starts a conversation about his time in the schools, Floyd repeatedly tells him: "I don't want to talk about this."[78] For Floyd, bearing witness to residential schools represents a higher cost than the compensation that doing so can provide for. It is no accident, then, that when George initially reads the details of the compensation package out to Floyd and Mooch, Mooch hears the word "compensation" as "constipation."[79] For Mooch, who understands government redress in relation to his friend and fellow survivor Floyd, compensation is not necessarily a means of facilitating truth telling, or even healing via talk therapy. Rather, it can have quite the opposite effect, insofar as the call for testimony that redress induces can further complicate feelings about sharing that reawakens traumatic experiences, which in turn stymies their release. This "constipation" then leads to further suffering and illness, which Mooch, and the audience, bear witness to specifically in the development of Floyd's storyline. For Loring, if there is an answer to the question of redress as a gift in *Where the Blood Mixes,* it is configured in much the same way that Marcel Mauss and Bourdieu define it in the gift: as expenditure and violence. Mauss writes that "the form usually taken is that of the gift generously offered; but the accompanying behaviour is formal pretence and social deception, while the transaction itself is based on obligation and economic self-interest."[80] In Floyd and Mooch's conception, what is owed in the system of exchange that circles around redress in the TRC is testimony, and testimony, as Shoshana Felman so aptly puts it, can "penetrate us like an actual life."[81]

Yet for Loring, what redress does, as a system of exchange, is even more complicated and potentially more damaging given the plurality of economies that circulate around it. While exchange is deeply problematized in *Where the Blood Mixes,* Loring also draws out the connecting tissue of another metaphor for restitution: redress as lottery. This connection is first made in the scene described above, in which George announces the government's compensation package to Floyd and Mooch. Directly after George shares the news, the stage directions read, "*Floyd and George stare at Mooch who begins to feverishly open his pull-tabs.*"[82] The pull-tab machine plays a prominent role in *Where the Blood Mixes,* and it is carefully positioned in proximity to compensation throughout. In my analysis, it stands as metonymy for redress, insofar as it represents the arbitrary nature of the tiered system: survivors who attended day schools, for instance, were not eligible to receive compensation under the CEP or IAP; neither were Métis survivors or survivors who attended residential schools in Newfoundland and Labrador.[83] Intergenerational survivors were also never eligible to apply for redress, despite the demonstrated impacts the schools had on those individuals' lives.[84]

Finally, as Floyd pointedly reminds us, those who suffered most in residential schools will never have access to the compensation money made available by the state because "most of the people that went to [those] school[s] are dead now!"[85] Thus, while redress, like the lottery, is positioned by Loring's non-Indigenous character (George) as a windfall, "winning" comes at great risk and cost to those who choose to engage in the game. The inequity of both systems, redress and the pull-tabs, is made plain when George tells Mooch, "If you just saved the money you spent on those things you'd be rich. Instead you spend all your money ... on those goddamn pull-tabs hoping to win back a little bit of what you spent."[86] Thinking specifically of the testimony that is owed to the CEP and IAP systems, it is possible to tease out the connections Loring is drawing here between pull-tabs and compensation for residential school abuse: namely, what goes in is not necessarily worth what comes out. Opposed to redress as gift, then, Loring frames redress as gamble: that is, a process not governed by goodwill or attentive relationality, but by odds and chance, with the ultimate payout benefitting the settler government.

Loring's conception of redress as lottery resonates deeply with settler Canadian articulations of redress culture, which are often unable to exceed the logics of capitalism, including exchange, debt, and financial reward. For instance, Michael Ignatieff, former Liberal candidate for prime minister of Canada and a prolific reconciliation scholar in his own right, has argued repeatedly and thoroughly for a culture of reconciliation that is mediated through reward. According to Ignatieff, "people don't need lectures on tolerance. They need institutions that guarantee the security bargain between ethnic groups that will allow tolerant behaviour to be rewarded."[87] By suggesting that people should expect a "reward" for "tolerant behaviour," Ignatieff ignores the "unprofitable" debates on hospitality and friendship and suggests instead that survivors and perpetrators direct their attention toward the financial gain of "getting along." His argument, like the pull-tab model of Loring's redress, privileges the economic over the social – eliding lived experience in the process – and takes for granted the fact that morality and compassion must be mediated through the invisible hand of the market.

Pushing this reading of Ignatieff further, in relation to Loring, provides insight into the capitalist frameworks that underpin reconciliation and Canada's relationship to redress as a gift. At first glance, Ignatieff's argument responds to shallow reconciliation arguments that rely heavily on the rhetoric of "peaceful coexistence" and "loving thy neighbour," which he rightly argues shifts conversation away from the wronged communities' need for basic infrastructure and economic stability in the wake of historical injustice. In general, this argument looks to undo the idealism that surrounds reconciliation and redress discourse and centre material responses to historical injustice as the road forward. This is an important gesture: one, at face value, that I endorse. That being said, Ignatieff's argument has nothing to do with Canada. He is a salt water thesis humanitarian, for whom "colonization" (and reconciliation) is something that happens "over there," not in Canada's backyard. As such, his line of argumentation on reconciliation is not legible when placed in the context of the TRC of Canada.

Indeed, despite the international reputation Ignatieff built opining on the topic of reconciliation, when it comes to the TRC of Canada he has been almost entirely quiet.[88] Further, we also need to be attentive to the ways in which Ignatieff neglects to indicate who gives the reward in his formulation, because the absence of a giving subject is instructive when attempting to understand how morality and economics are folded into his argument. In suggesting that survivors should be compensated for displaying forgiveness and tolerance, but failing to point out that it is governments and capitalist systems that supply this compensation, Ignatieff ignores both the ideology and power dynamics that are generated through the act of reward, as well as who ultimately stands to benefit from parties buying into that system.

The capitalist ethic underpinning his argument is, of course, that the invisible hand of the market will solve contradictions rather than open up new problems and questions. If the government can financially incentivize coexistence, it will, in turn, facilitate its own economic growth while bolstering nation-state sovereignty. Indeed, the chief imperative for Ignatieff is not promoting conversation and encouraging reciprocity (in fact, he suggests that such debate is superfluous).[89] Rather, he aims to protect the freedom of citizens while removing the things that might obstruct exchange in the free market. In classic liberal formulation, then, redress is positioned as a complement to Smithian economics, which suggests that capitalism will cure society's ills, if only given leave to do so – or if only the most vulnerable continue to play the game.

Liberal conceptions of redress, because they are based in a notion of redress as a reward and do not develop reciprocity beyond a vague notion of tolerance, risk putting recipients in a position of lasting obligation in which they will continually have to "be good" in order to fulfill their debt to the state. Whereas the reciprocity implicit in the gift is rooted in community and social connection, market principles centre the individual. Indeed, in this formulation, until recipients have returned the social obligation implicit in the gift (also known as *hau,* a concept I will turn to shortly), they are obliged to show their gratitude toward the giver, or as Bourdieu puts it, "show regard for him, go easy on him, pull his punches, lest he be accused of ingratitude."[90] If the terms of return are not adequately outlined beyond tolerance, the balance owed on redress will always lie just beyond the means of the recipient. In this framework, one can never be "good" enough to live outside the edicts prescribed by one's creditors; one must continually subscribe to, or at least be tolerant of, a set of laws that are not one's own in order to repay the benevolence of the social contract. Thus, in the debt it tacitly prescribes to Indigenous peoples, this form of redress reiterates deeply embodied forms of settler colonialism: the reification of settler colonial power dynamics, including wardship, and the guaranteed futurity of the settler state.

All of this is not to say that Loring, in *Where the Blood Mixes,* is suggesting that healing through redress is impossible, but, rather, that he does not see recovery as something which can be derived from a financial relationship with the state. Indeed, while redress is announced early in *Where the Blood Mixes,* the reward never arrives in the hands of either Floyd or Mooch. Redress is only ever a receding horizon in this play. As a result, the reconciliation and redress that are found in the community come from the testimony and truth sharing that occur between friends and family, as opposed to that which is exchanged with the settler state for reward or redress. Reconciliation is, for Floyd at least, an ongoing relationship and kinship that exists outside settler mediations and financial interventions. Indeed, the moment that Loring himself, in the afterword to *Where the Blood Mixes,* identifies as the "reconciliation scene" of the play is an intimate moment shared between Floyd and his daughter Christine, who was taken from him as a child, presumably as part of the Sixties Scoop.[91] It is in speaking his truth to Christine, sharing with her the effects of residential schools and the impact they had on him and his family, that Floyd is able to find some semblance of peace and healing. In his final words in the play, Floyd shares his desire to meet his grandson, Christine's son, and to rebuild a world with them, with or without compensation. After thanking Christine for coming home, the final stage directions have father and daughter standing hand in hand, "illuminated in the light of the new day."[92]

Rather than reward, then, redress and reconciliation are configured in *Where the Blood Mixes* as relationships and kinships configured, and reconfigured, among Indigenous peoples as they work through the trauma inflicted by residential schools and settler colonialism. This is not to say that money is not owed to survivors, or that the settler state does not have a responsibility to those who were stolen away from their families. Canada has a moral and fiduciary duty to redress these people. It is to say, however, that redress does not have to be, and perhaps should not be, only the signifier through which truth and healing are articulated.

Indigenous Articulations of the Gift

Loring's work is an affective nexus through which to consider the potential damage of a state-directed redress movement that does not progress beyond compensation and therefore never seriously engages redress as a relationship. If there is reconciliation in *Where the Blood Mixes,* and Loring suggests that there is, it is to be found in the existing relationships and care of Indigenous communities. The logic of the gift, as defined by Indigenous scholars, provides more context from which to think of redress as a relationship and the gift as a disruption of settler debt and exchange. While this is not a solution to the neo-liberal implications of state-directed redress as reward, it does provide a compelling site from which to unsettle the question of redress as a gift, which Miki productively introduces. Indeed, the call to consider the gift in the TRC framework has already been made, but the Canadian state has yet to adequately address it. For instance, Bruce Granville Miller has argued that if reparations are to have a specific, decolonial impact on Indigenous communities in Canada, the logic of the gift needs to be taken apart and reassembled from contexts specific to Indigenous communities: "local, bottom-up efforts at reconciliation, through apology or reparations and that take culture seriously, may better serve local needs and convey a more satisfying message than those derived from top-down rituals alone."[93] For Miller, the gift provides a vital point of access to consider reconciliation, but Canadian redress operates "in an idiom that neither reflects indigenous sensibilities nor conveys an appropriate message" and is therefore, in fact, incurring more structural damage in the very act it attempts to extend as reconciliation.[94]

The idea of redress as a gift resonates in Indigenous communities as well. Carrier Elder Dr. Maggie Hodgson also calls for the gift to be taken seriously in the TRC culture of Canada. She writes that in her "traditional ceremony of the Potlatch, when we wrong people, we have to gift them, along with all of our clan members who have to gift them as well. It is intended to teach about respect, and it also teaches that abuse not only hurts the person but also the collective."[95] Hodgson's analysis illustrates how gift giving is embedded in her traditional practices of reconciliation and how the logic of the gift can provide a rich and vital place to begin to think about respect and responsibility. In gifting those who have been wronged, both the perpetrator and their community are called on to restore relationship through exchange. As a communal act, the perpetrator is identified as part of a larger group and is called back into the circle via reciprocity, but this requires that the perpetrator, and their community, acknowledge the wrongdoing and make themselves vulnerable to those they have harmed.

Hodgson helps to begin to illustrate how the logic of the gift, as Rauna Kuokkanen refers to it, has a deep history in Indigenous cultures around the globe. While it may have been introduced to academic discourse by Marcel Mauss, the Indigenous peoples from whom he took the idea (namely the Haïda, Tlingit, and Maori) have been practising a nuanced, relationship-oriented form of gifting since time immemorial. Now a cornerstone topic in continental philosophy, anthropology, sociology, and even business, the logic of the gift continues to provoke reflection on systems of exchange that transcend European capitalism and generate new, human community-centred models of relationality that connect to land and non-human kin.[96]

Of special importance in the logic of the gift is the identification of *hau*, a "spiritual mechanism ... which obliges us to make a return gift for a gift received."[97] According to the Maori sage Tamati Ranapiri of the Ngati-Raukawa, from whom Mauss developed a significant portion of his gift theory, *hau* is a signification of the return value that a gift carries once it has been given: a value that must eventually find its way back to its point of origin in order for ethical, and healthy, systems of exchange to take place. Reciprocity, in this sense, is about returning the "intangible" spirit of goodwill, love, and relationship that is attached to, and a consequence of, the gift. It is not necessarily a return of a material thing, but of that elusive element of relationality that makes the gift what it is. That is to say, in giving, one creates an obligation to relationship and an ethic of reciprocity that facilitates community and builds relationships based in an ethic of care and responsibility to the other – or, more precisely a response-ability: the framework necessary to position oneself in relation to the other via ongoing networks of exchange.

In the context of reconciliation, gift theory must hold up Indigenous knowledge keepers and centre gifting as an act of relationship building that undoes much of the antagonism at the core of Western conceptions of the gift, as described by Mauss and Bourdieu. Specific to this, Kuokkanen has written extensively on the logic of the gift as it applies to Indigenous cultures across the globe. For her, "gift giving ... is based on the values of care, cooperation, and bonding. It is other-oriented, and it gives directly to the needs of others."[98] While the logic of the gift should not be applied uncritically across all Indigenous cultures, it does have real and resonant histories in many communities. Kuokkanen argues that the gift "binds collectives together,"[99] and therefore "it could be suggested that in Indigenous societies, the gift is one of the most important organizing principles around which values and perceptions of the world are attached."[100]

As opposed to Mauss – who maintained that the gift is an act of repressed violence – Kuokkanen is more concerned with the "circular reciprocity" of Indigenous gift giving, in which "responsibility is commonly regarded as an integral part of being human and inseparable with one's identity."[101] This notion of giving as relationship with and accountability to the other provides for an epistemological space for redress that transcends reward and quantification and invites a more radical exchange of love, responsibility, and attentive listening. Kuokkanen's analysis therefore illustrates the centrality of the gift to Indigenous philosophies and highlights the ways in which gifting generates connections and responsibility to community and to the land. In these contexts, the gift "exceeds the realms of both economy and exchange" and is instead intimately connected to one's accountability to family, kin (both human and more-than-human), community, and the environment.[102]

Like Kuokkanen, Dara Kelly and Patrick Kelly, of the Stó:lō Nation, also argue for the logic of the gift as a means to disrupt settler colonial capitalism. In their analysis, gifting emphasizes reciprocity and relationships: "What is exchanged [via the gift] transcends the tangible and explicit, and additionally, implicit actions and behaviors have impacts on the strength and quality of relationships that are bound by reciprocity."[103] For them, the logic of the gift is directly connected to the practice of Stl'eáleq (potlach gifting traditions) and centuries-old traditions of Stó:lō witnessing and gifting protocol. As for Kuokkanen, for Kelly and Kelly the logic of the gift is less about *hau* than it is about the maintenance, production, and reproduction of healthy communities and interactions across communities, even when those relationships are severely hindered by settler colonial governments and racist legislation, such as the potlach ban: "at the heart of the gift economy," they write, "is the people, and the wealth that drives the economy can be measured by the wellness and wholeness of the people who come together."[104] In the system of giving that Kelly and Kelly unpack, economics can only be quantified insofar as wealth is directly reflected in the community, not only in individual well-being, but more specifically in the strength of the relationships that hold communities together and allow them to thrive and grow.

Of course, one cannot simply recuperate the gift into a system such as redress without looking at the long history in which Indigenous peoples were punished and incarcerated for engaging gift cultures in settler states. Indeed, it is vital to note the long-standing fear of the gift that Canada has expressed and the violence it has levied toward Indigenous peoples as a result of this fear. A significant reason why it remains so difficult to conceptualize the gift within a national framework of redress is that it has long represented a threat to the capitalist order of settler colonialism, standing as an open threat to the promises of individual wealth and property ownership made by a capitalist system. According to Kelly and Kelly, Indigenous gift economies endangered the settler state because they "were deemed to be an impediment to the successful introduction and adoption of British European exchange philosophy."[105] The logic of the gift was, in other words, antithetical to the colonial and patriarchal systems that undergirded the settler state.

There is no separating redress as a gift from the violence inflicted on Indigenous peoples and their economies under settler colonialism. As the colonial project unfurled in Canada, laws were rapidly established to repress gift economies as they occurred in Indigenous communities. The potlach ban, which was in effect in Canada from 1884 to 1951, and legally enforced under section 149 of the *Indian Act,* made the practice and ceremony of gifting criminal in Indigenous cultures across Canada. Those who were caught participating in potlaches were subject to up to six months of jail time. Indian agents and church officials closely monitored Indigenous communities, which continued to practise gifting ceremonies underground and share the traditions of the potlach with younger generations. Agents of the state had the power to seize material and ceremonial objects, which were then often shipped to museums for provincial and federal collections. According to the U'mista Cultural Centre, which repatriated many of the objects stolen from the Kwakwa̱ka̱'wakw during the ban, "the opponents of the potlatch could only see the custom as a wasteful, immoral and heathen practice, an impediment in the road of progress."[106] Through strength and perseverance, many communities, such as the Stó:lō and Kwakwa̱ka̱'wakw, among many others, have been able to revitalize the protocols and social structures that provide for gift economies like the potlach, "but the economic impacts were devastating and ... exchange systems have yet to fully recover."[107] Despite the will of the settler state to destroy it, and sixty-seven years of legalized repression, the logic of the gift remains a central means through which Indigenous peoples galvanize community while generating ongoing systems of reciprocity that feed healthy relationships within and between nations and across arbitrary colonial borders.

As the history illustrates, there is much to attend to when considering the translation of Miki's simile onto the TRC of Canada. Articulating redress as a gift means de-emphasizing compensation while holding up the relationships that are initiated and maintained via the gift. However, through the window of these relationships, thinking of redress as a gift also means carefully accounting for, and working against, the power dynamics that frame what it means to give in the wake of genocide and historical injustice. In the case of settler colonialism and the Canadian history of the potlach ban, this means being specifically attentive to how the logic of the gift is caught up in the very systems of oppression that the state now claims to redress. Residential schools played an active role in the repression of gift economies, forcibly removing children from community and ceremony and forbidding the practice or sharing of culture within the schools themselves. For settlers, or the state, to uncritically take up redress as a gift would therefore be a continued act of violence and appropriation.

What is at stake for settlers, then, is what it means to receive a gift that we are neither owed nor that we deserve. It means being open to what Kuokkanen identifies as the impossibility of the gift: of receiving without the calculus of debt or exchange. Commodifying the gift, or folding it into the logic of the settler colonial state, makes this impossible. This is evidenced plainly in the case of Japanese Canadian redress, in which Canada recuperated what Japanese Canadians gave back to Canada in exchange for the Redress Agreement: an exchange that Roy Miki openly laments. Redress is possible as a gift only when the logic of exchange is disrupted, or when the calculus of debt and countergift give way to a privileging of relationship and the active maintenance of a healthy social order. In this sense, the gift of redress cannot belong to the settler state, because it cannot guarantee the futurity of settler colonialism. Rather, being attentive to the gift, or recognizing the Indigenous gift as such, means settlers must attend to the colonial systems in which we receive it and acknowledge the impossibility through which it is given.

Rachel Flowers, writing about the gift of Indigenous women's love and the right to refuse to offer it, makes clear that the gift is not a given: "If our gift is received and respected, then the gift binds people together in an ongoing relationship of reciprocity and responsibility. When this gift is rejected or abused, expect our sadness, our resentment, and our rage."[108] Accepting the gift as a relationship and working with Indigenous peoples to undo the frameworks that seek to monetize and exploit it is a difficult, but necessary, task. That task begins with unsettling the heuristics of compensation and reward that permeate redress discourse – heuristics that recast settlers and settler governments in the position of benefactors. Flowers makes plain that there is potential in the gift, but that misinterpreting, ignoring, or mishandling it, will not lead to reconciliation. Rather, it will deepen the divide between settlers and Indigenous peoples.

If there is room for the gift in redress discourse, it is in what it represents as an aporia within settler colonialism. Indeed, for Kuokkanen, at the core of Indigenous conceptions of the gift is the radical disruption of settler capitalism and an implosion of the relational ambivalence implied by monetary exchange. The logic of the gift accomplishes this insofar as it productively blurs the space between honour and money while emphasizing instead relationship and reciprocity as the core ethic: "The gift paradigm disrupts the global capitalist, patriarchal world order by not following its rules and values. It pays close heed to the problematic nature of individualism, which is not only a value opposite to that of the gift but is also linked to the colonization of Indigenous peoples."[109]

Because the gift offers a new way of mediating relationships while simultaneously threatening the colonialist economic order, Kuokkanen, drawing on Jacques Derrida, labels it as *pharmakon,* which means, simultaneously, both medicine and poison. Although the gift, as Kuokkanen conceives it, may be a threat to colonial governments and the capitalist agenda, that means it may also, simultaneously, be medicine for those like Hopkinson and Loring, Kuokkanen, and Kelly and Kelly who imagine otherwise. Indeed, as *pharmakon,* the threat of the gift that Canada's (failed) potlach ban worked to repress can be determined as a peril to settler colonialism, which is dependent on transnational capitalism and primitive accumulation. As an example, consider *Brown Girl in the Ring,* in which Hopkinson structures the dystopic collapse of Toronto on the settler state's obligation to redress the Teme-Augama Anishnabai. In this instance, one way of reading redress as gift in *Brown Girl* is as the *pharmakon* of economic collapse or the gift of dystopia. Redress is a gift, in this sense, in its potential to disrupt or impede or even explode the smooth flow of settler capitalism on Indigenous lands. Or, to put it another way, it is a gift because it is a threat and a threat because it is a gift.

Counter to Hopkinson's radical articulation of redress as a gift – amounting in the collapse of the capitalist settler state – there are also more moderate ways to think about the *pharmakon* in relation to settler economies. Kelly and Kelly, for instance, argue for the disruptive potential of the gift via a case study of Stl'eáleq as taken up by BC First Nations in relations with BC Hydro. BC Hydro is an electrical utility and a Crown corporation headquartered in Vancouver, British Columbia. In the early 1990s, BC Hydro established an Aboriginal relations department in response to "250 expired right-of-way agreements" with BC First Nations, which were drawing attention to the meagre compensation Indigenous peoples had received for use of their land for hydro development.[110] These groups were advocating for renewed agreements that offered fair, market-level rents for hydro development on their territories. In order to address concerns from First Nations, BC Hydro implemented an Indigenous cultural awareness program that included direct engagement and relationship building with those nations.[111] Working with the utility to expand relationship building, Indigenous Elders and knowledge keepers proposed that BC Hydro should host a Stl'eáleq, to which leaders and Chiefs would be invited, with specific support from the Sqwxwó:mex (Squamish) Nation. The goal of the Stl'eáleq, for BC First Nations, was to "test whether the corporation was serious about sustainability."[112]

While Kelly and Kelly identify the Stl'eáleq at BC Hydro as a success, they do not subscribe to the notion that the gifting ceremony indelibly altered the state of Crown economics, or even that BC Hydro meaningfully took up Indigenous practices of material reciprocity. However, they do point to the potential of the gift to disrupt the smooth flow of settler capitalism when deployed within a settler financial system. Under the terms I am operating with in this chapter, the gift as *pharmakon* demonstrates, in this situation, the potential to slow down the persistent machinery of settler capitalism and the imperialistic desire to quantify and monetize Indigenous-settler interactions. By introducing the Stl'eáleq to BC Hydro as part of a business relationship, Kelly and Kelly argue, the logic of the gift productively interrupts the capitalist order and makes space for new ways of thinking about economic prosperity for Indigenous peoples alongside state infrastructure. In this sense, they write provocatively of the puzzling nature of the gift as it is introduced to capitalist frameworks: "Stl'eáleq was an unconventional expense, particularly from the perspective of the accounting department that did not have a cost code for 'potlach' and the company's business analysts, who did not know how to estimate return on such an investment."[113] Here, the gift is illustrated as irreducible to the settler calculus; the relationship that sits at the core of Stl'eáleq resists capitalist quantification while nonetheless inviting reciprocal exchange across Indigenous and settler communities. It may not collapse the entire colonial/capitalist system, as in *Brown Girl in the Ring,* but Stl'eáleq makes space for Stó:lō peoples and epistemologies in the colonial order in that it represents an aporia within a colonial machinery built out of the horizontal integration of figures.

Redress as a gift, in this formulation, is both medicine and poison, or "med-sin" as Halfe puts it:[114] poison to the extent that it represents a potential disruption to the capitalist order, and medicine as it potentially makes space, on a variety of scales, for Indigenous peoples and epistemologies. In a state-determined reconciliation calculus framed in systems of debt and "reward," the gift offers the potential to imagine – as Hopkinson does in her speculative fiction – a reconciled future that does not guarantee the survival of settler colonialism. Reward and compensation are particularly about the maintenance of the capitalistic-colonial patriarchy. They not only advocate for a system of healing that takes the object of harm as the instrument of restoration, but, as Miki demonstrates, they also aim to recuperate the power of those instruments by claiming that ostensible healing as evidence of their necessity. An example of this is that the settler state, when properly attuned, is necessary to guarantee the protection and health of its citizenry. This is ideology writ large: objects of violence, such as settler colonialism, re-articulated *ad nauseam* as bastions of liberation.

Conversely, as medicine, the logic of the gift is about centring relationships and the ethic of care that provides for their development and maintenance. It is about undoing systems of colonial capitalism and making space to centre Indigenous ways of knowing and being in relation, perhaps even reconciling. What the logic of the gift brings to the myriad and complex conversations about redress in Canada is a means to critically and compassionately reformulate the calculus of compensation, which infects a settler discourse that, first, cannot get over itself as the beneficent giver of gifts and, second, refuses to acknowledge what it continues to take from Indigenous peoples – including the cultural and financial capital it receives as a result of the TRC. At its foundation, however, redress is a gift (and therefore a *pharmakon*) only insofar as it is an impossibility within the capitalist, patriarchal order of settler colonialism. It is gift inasmuch as it represents a threat to that order and therefore a disruption (or, in Hopkinson's formulation, an implosion) of the machinery that undergirds the settler colonial state.

Conclusion

Miki's suggestion that his readers return to the question of redress as a gift offers fundamental insight into the need for an acknowledgment of redress as a reciprocal exchange rooted in relationality and outside of capitalism. Reconceptualizing redress as a gift reframes reparation as something that both takes *and* gives, that both receives *and* offers, and is thus a system of gain *and* loss – therefore opposing any notion of finitude or wholeness.

When approached carefully, as a category unto itself, redress illustrates the subtle shift that takes place in the movement between apology and forgiveness – the space in which survivors can find agency beyond the passive role of recipient, and perpetrators are potentially compelled to acknowledge the vitality and resilience of those owed recompense. In order to realize this shift, however, the *return* of the gift is what needs to be of primary importance when addressing modern redress movements. What is *given back* by communities, such as Japanese Canadians or Indigenous peoples, is where the focus must be turned. Simply enumerating the details and importance of what is given only affirms the state as a benevolent entity, thus eliding the power dynamics and deeply emotional exchanges that can occur within the rubrics of redress and reconciliation. Of course, this all depends on a community, such as internment or residential school survivors, being willing to make that return – to give back to a system that has historically worked against their interests. There is obviously no obligation to do so. If redress as a gift means opening up a relationship, it is contingent on settlers and the settler state to honour what it means to receive, if it is offered, and thus to listen and cultivate response-ability.

In *Brown Girl in the Ring*, Nalo Hopkinson projects a future in which the redress of Indigenous peoples is apocalyptic. Insofar as redress structures

Hopkinson's dystopic reality, this novel can be read as the return of the repressed, the bubbling up of disavowed settler anxiety over the illegitimacy of their claims to land and resources. Yet, at the same time it exposes settler fragility, Hopkinson's critique of redress also offers a new way to approach the arguments levied against reconciliation by fragile settler pundits. In the universe of *Brown Girl in the Ring,* the collapse of capitalism and settler colonialism is, for settlers, a dystopia, but for many Indigenous peoples and peoples of colour it represents a new, decolonial beginning filled with possibility and hope. It represents a space outside the violence of settler colonialism, and it projects a future that centres Indigenous ways of being and refuses to guarantee settler futures. Hopkinson offers a truly radical articulation of redress in *Brown Girl in the Ring,* one that strips land of settler colonial rule and ideology and returns it to Indigenous stewardship. This is not the only direction redress can take in Canada, but it is an important reminder that redress need not (and perhaps should not) hinge on the continuation of settler colonialism.

5

An Exercise in Forgiveness

Confronting the Risk of Forgiveness and Empathy

> You will never have my forgiveness as long as land dispossession, domination and violence are present in the lives of Indigenous peoples.
>
> – RACHEL FLOWERS[1]

> Are we to forgive endlessly, "as to an idiot in the house"?
>
> – JOY KOGAWA[2]

For Richard Wagamese, the Anishinaabe author, journalist, and residential school survivor, forgiveness is "a thousand-pound word."[3] Hailing from the Wabaseemoong First Nation, Wagamese is the author of twelve novels and the recipient of multiple literary awards, most notably for the 2012 work *Indian Horse.* He was also a prolific essayist and journalist, writing Indigenous issues columns and music reviews for the *Calgary Herald.* Wagamese died at the age of sixty-one in March 2017, leaving behind a rich legacy of critical and creative writing, which literary critics have only just begun to investigate.

Forgiveness and reconciliation were deeply important concepts in much of Wagamese's writing. In fact, during the TRC he advocated strongly for the healing potential of reconciliation as it applied specifically to Indigenous peoples. In an essay published by the Aboriginal Healing Foundation (AHF) entitled "Returning to Harmony," Wagamese writes about what reconciliation and forgiveness might mean for Indigenous communities as a way to overcome the pain caused by residential schools and forge new, respectful Indigenous-settler relations:

> It is a big word, reconciliation. Quite simply, it means to create harmony. You create harmony with truth and you build truth out of humility. That is spiritual. That is truth. That is Indian. Within us, as nations of Aboriginal people and as individual members of those nations, we have an incredible capacity for survival, endurance, and forgiveness. In the reconciliation with ourselves first, we find the ability to create harmony with others, and that is where it has to start – in the fertile soil of our own hearts, minds, and spirits.[4]

Wagamese's words in this moving essay point to the potential for Indigenous peoples to find peace and renewed relationships from acts of forgiveness and reconciliation. Throughout the essay, he looks to the possibility of reconciliation as an articulation of harmony, which he clarifies as a self-oriented process of looking outward to the other, with the ultimate aim of benefitting intergenerational residential school survivors and Indigenous youth. In this sense, forgiveness is a self-interested reciprocal act that begins at home.

Forgiveness is welcome, for Wagamese, if not necessary, because it provides the space to overcome the "simmering anger and resentment" he carried with him from residential schools. Steeped in these emotions, he writes, "my life was slipping away on me and I did not want to become an older person still clinging to [such] disempowering emotion[s]."[5] In this, Wagamese's perspective on forgiveness resonates with forgiveness scholars such as Trudy Govier, who argues that "forgiveness and reconciliation appear as necessary in order to preserve humanity."[6] Yet, against the universalist tendencies of reconciliation, Wagamese articulates forgiveness as a specific Indigenous ontology that residential school survivors can pass on to the next generation in order to foster resurgence and sovereignty. He develops this point more fully in the essay "Truth and Reconciliation," published in his collection *One Story, One Song:* "We owe these kids [intergenerational survivors] more. We owe them our truths. We owe them our apologies. We owe them a commitment to our healing, however hard and bleak that journey might be. We owe it to them to become an empowered people who have learned the importance of forgiveness."[7]

As these two essays, "Returning to Harmony" and "Truth and Reconciliation," help illustrate, Wagamese advocated for forgiveness across his career, not because of what forgiveness affords settlers (e.g., the alleviation of guilt and national shame), but because, for him, forgiveness provided a necessary space for Indigenous healing and community building.[8] Indeed, as Glen Coulthard notes – even in his argument against reconciliation and for resentment – Wagamese articulates forgiveness as a means to "decrease the likelihood of reproducing internalized forms of violence," and he does so pointedly, with attention to the care and well-being of Indigenous peoples.[9]

Like Desmond Tutu, who famously argued that, in South Africa, there could be no "future without forgiveness,"[10] Wagamese articulates forgiveness as an ontology of possibility and hope. This definition, which privileges the well-being and sovereignty of survivors, is much different from classical definitions of forgiveness, aimed at reconciliation between survivors and perpetrators. For instance, in *Forgiveness and Reconciliation,* Everett Worthington defines forgiveness as "a process by which unforgiving emotions are replaced by positive other-oriented emotions producing an affectively less negative, neutral, or more positive state, and an associated change in motivations away from unforgiving motivations toward more conciliatory or reconciliatory motivations."[11] For Worthington, forgiveness begins in relation to the perpetrator with the end goal being the closure of an existing rift between parties (i.e., with reconciliation).

For Wagamese, however, the upshot of forgiveness, while it may exist in relation to settlers, has little to do with attending to settler shame or guilt, but has everything to do with empowering Indigenous communities. This definition of forgiveness is anchored in a nuanced adherence to truth and the ways in which Wagamese holds up the refusal to forgive in his creative work. In both of the essays I quote above, truth is the primary mandate – truth before apology; truth before forgiveness; truth before reconciliation. Forgiveness, in this sense, necessitates a return to Indigenous peoples. When Jacques Derrida asks in *Cosmopolitanism and Forgiveness,* can we "forgive whoever does not know how to give?," he is identifying the very problem of exchange that lies at the heart of forgiveness.[12] Forgiveness itself, Derrida argues, is an act of remitting debt. For Wagamese, that debt is truth, and it is owed not by survivors but by settlers, many of whom demonstrate their unwillingness to give up their racist epithets and increasingly nuanced moves to innocence.[13] Within this transaction, then, refusing to forgive is a justified and moral decision, just as unforgiveness is a means to building strength.

While his essays are instructive, the depth and nuance of Wagamese's engagement with forgiveness is found in his creative work. Those who are familiar with Wagamese's novels know that forgiveness is never won easily by his characters and that truth is always a battle fought through difficult circumstances. *Medicine Walk,* for instance, tells the story of Franklin Starlight (Frank), who is called by his estranged father, Eldon Starlight, to take a difficult journey through the backcountry, looking for a place for Eldon to die and be buried in the warrior's tradition. Along the way, Eldon shares his stories with his son. For both Eldon and Frank, repressed truth is the hard kernel on which the plot of the novel turns. Eldon circles around it and draws his son into his life in the moments surrounding its silence. Their walk together is significant because Eldon has spent almost an entire lifetime hiding the difficult truths of his life – namely, his role in the death of his wife – from his son, Frank, and from himself. Eldon buries his truths with alcohol and sex and is only able to share them with Frank in his final hours as he dies from cirrhosis of the liver. "Truth ain't never easy," Frank's surrogate father, "the old man," who raised him when Eldon was unable to, tells him. "Especially one you had hung up in you a long time."[14] While sharing the truth that has been "hung up in you a long time" is a difficult and perhaps even admirable act, it does not necessarily amount to forgiveness for Wagamese. Sharing truth, if it is anything, is the possibility of a new beginning for Frank – a way to move forward, now with a more complete understanding of his family's story – but it is a far cry from reconciliation. Indeed, the devastation of repressed truths, and the ways they can lay waste to individuals and families, is made pointedly obvious in *Medicine Walk,* which circles around at least three truths that Eldon is unwilling or unable to share: 1) leaving his mother to an abusive boyfriend; 2) his role in the death of his best friend; and 3) his role in the death of his wife, Frank's mother. Eldon's inability to process these events, and his need to repress them, has driven him to a life filled with alcohol, which in turn alienates him from his son.

While Eldon's trauma is real and his drinking is undoubtedly a form of self-medication, having an absentee father is no less damaging or painful for Frank. Raised by a non-Indigenous man (the previously mentioned "old man"), Frank has a limited connection to his Indigenous heritage, given that his guardian, while a loving and kind man, "can't teach [him] nothing about bein' who [he is]."[15] Frank has been hungry for a connection to his past and to his people, but his few encounters with Eldon over the years were bitter, injurious events consumed by Eldon's alcoholism and his avoidance of reality. If there is a fourth truth Eldon is repressing, it is how he has failed his son, something he wishes to rectify in the final moments of his life. Their definitive walk together (the titular "medicine walk"), at the end of which Frank will bury his father, is thus construed by Eldon as the act of recompense that Wagamese first articulates in the "Truth and Reconciliation" essay cited above: "I owe," Eldon tells Frank when questioned about the purpose of their trip together.[16] More than seeking forgiveness, which is another part of the journey, Eldon's story is thus also about a fiduciary responsibility to truth and the knowledge that he holds in debt for the next generation.

One of the stories Eldon feels that he owes Frank is the story of how he killed his best friend, Jimmy, a man from the Blood nation, when the two were soldiers in the Korean War. While they are out on patrol, Jimmy is badly wounded and loudly calling out in pain. In order to avoid capture, which would undoubtedly be brought on by his friend's screams, Eldon has to end Jimmy's life by slipping a knife between his ribs. The death is quick, and Eldon escapes unharmed, but the moment haunts him. Until he tells his son of this traumatic event, Eldon has never shared the story with anyone, carrying it in silence for all of his adult life. When he finally reveals the details of Jimmy's death to Frank, he also identifies it as the first truth that led him to alcohol. As such, it represents a key piece in Frank's story as well, given the impact his father's drinking has had on his own life.

That said, close reading of the context surrounding this painful scene reveals that this truth is not Eldon's alone: it is also connected to the larger structures of settler colonialism and capitalism and the impacts they have had on Indigenous communities via displacement and land theft. Indeed, building up to the story about Jimmy, Eldon tells Frank of the ways in which he was disconnected from the land and Ojibwe ways of life due to settler incursion onto his traditional territories. As a result, his immediate family lived in extreme poverty, and the need to find a job – at any cost – became the driving element of his young life. Eldon tells Frank that "your grandparents and them like them just followed the work and tried to make out the best they could. We camped in tents or squatted on scrublands no one wanted or in deserted cabins and sheds and such. Never no proper home."[17] The fact of settler colonialism and the destitution it inflicted on many Indigenous communities via the violence of erasure and displacement extends to the war itself, which, as Eldon says, promised "no more bustin' a nut for peanuts no more";[18] fighting a war for the settler government, to protect settler interests, would provide an opportunity to alleviate his family's poverty. In the background of Eldon's story about murdering his best friend is thus the larger narrative of structural violence and the desolate positions Indigenous peoples were put in as their lands were stolen and wars were fought over the filched sovereignties of empires. For Wagamese, while the burden of this violence is borne entirely by the individual, in this case Eldon, the cause is much more nuanced and structural, directly implicating a settler state that removed Indigenous peoples from their lands and thus obstructed their ability to provide for and support families.

Forgiveness, too, is caught up in the history of settler colonialism in *Medicine Walk*. Wagamese's writing is deftly nuanced and structural violence is articulated only as a backdrop to Eldon's story, artfully woven into the narrative so that the careful reader might intuit the larger colonial narrative that Eldon is unwillingly caught up in. For Eldon himself, however, theories of settler colonialism have no concrete bearing on his actions or on his perception of the death of Jimmy. He is immersed purely in the guilt of his own culpability and his inability to share his truth – absorbed in his own guilt to such a degree that it has made him sick and unable to make himself available to his son. Finally, however, having confronted the truth of Jimmy's death by releasing it into the world with Frank as his witness (a role that Frank, it should be noted, is loath to take up), Eldon finally finds it in himself to ask Frank for forgiveness: "you figure you might be able to forgive me, Frank?"[19] And while Frank listens carefully to his father's story, and even empathizes with his pain ("musta been hard ... carrying Jimmy all this time"), he does not forgive.[20] He tells Eldon directly, "I ain't the one that has to."[21] Frank's refusal to forgive here is pointed. In testifying to Jimmy's death, Eldon looks to Frank, his unwilling witness, for absolution. Forgiveness is configured as a release for the perpetrator and Frank stands in as the intermediary, bestowed, by Eldon, with the power to grant that release.

What is at stake in this moment is the transfer of debt, from father to son, for the emancipation from guilt and shame. Yet, despite Eldon's obvious suffering, Frank refuses to take on that debt, even when his father clarifies that he is not asking his son for forgiveness for everything, meaning all the pain that Eldon caused *him,* his son, but for this singular act: "I mean about Jimmy." Frank's response is plain and direct: "I mean about him too."[22] Here, casting his feelings for his father aside, Frank identifies his inability to forgive a perpetrator for the suffering caused to another human being, or to forgive a history in which he played no active role. While his father calls for forgiveness as a means to ease his own pain as he moves toward death, Frank will not give what he sees as not his to offer. Further, Frank's *un*forgiveness here, while perhaps not precisely resentment, is a refusal to embody a system of relationality that flattens or reduces the debt of truth that his father owes him. He will not forgive at this point because while this story helps to clarify his father's illness, Eldon still owes him the story of his mother.

Careful reading of this inaugural forgiveness passage in *Medicine Walk* provides the textual context to render Wagamese's calls for forgiveness and harmony in his critical writing more robust: if it is medicine that perpetrators seek from survivors – or if it is harmony that settlers seek from reconciliation – that medicine can only come at the behest of hard, often decimating truths. Even then, after those truths have been shared, there is no guarantee that survivors can, will, or even should provide the healing that perpetrators desire. It may not be theirs to give. They may have no desire to give it. The truth may not be equal to the debt owed. Inversely, while Indigenous peoples may indeed have an enormous capacity for forgiveness, as Wagamese suggests, there is no debt owed by survivors in exchange for perpetrator truths. Forgiveness is never a given, and those who request it must be prepared to own, and even die with, their guilt.

What *Medicine Walk* helps to clarify is that in order for forgiveness to be valid, it must be the sovereign domain of the survivor. Yet it can be exceptionally difficult to maintain forgiveness as a sovereign and self-determined act within the hegemonic rubric of settler colonialism. Martha Minow writes that "forgiveness is a power held by the victimized."[23] Of course, that power is often upset when held within the Venn diagram of colonialism, patriarchy, and class that leverage structural power to extract forgiveness, often as a means to bolster national agendas. The question thus becomes how to maintain forgiveness as the domain of the survivor, how to hold mercy as a power that cannot be recuperated or demanded by the perpetrator.

Interpreted from a critique of power, the tendency toward forgiveness in the TRC has already raised red flags for a number of Indigenous studies scholars, who push for alternative modes of engagement rather than clemency and mercy. Coulthard, for instance, has argued that resentment (which can also be articulated as unforgiveness) is the most viable response for Indigenous peoples in the face of colonial violence. He writes, "It would appear that the emergence of reactive emotions like anger and resentment can indicate a breakdown of colonial subjection and thus open up the possibility of developing alternative subjectivities and anticolonial practices."[24] In other words, unforgiveness is a means of producing identities that can interrupt the smooth flow of settler colonialism. Building on Coulthard's work, Rachel Flowers sees the growing demand for Indigenous forgiveness, facilitated by the TRC and the theatre of regret, as yet another assimilative strategy of the settler state, aimed at repressing justifiable Indigenous rage. For Flowers, "Indigenous peoples' resistance to the calls for forgiveness is a legitimate rejection of a new relationship [reconciliation] that is simply the old relationship dressed up in new clothes."[25] For Flowers, forgiveness feeds into a system of power that elides the fact of stolen land and shelters the colonial structures complicit in the ongoing fact of settler colonialism.

While Wagamese's argument *for* forgiveness would seem to run counter to the positions taken by Coulthard and Flowers, through my reading of *Medicine Walk* I would argue that Wagamese complicates the structures of power through which forgiveness is articulated in order to reclaim it for survivors as a possibility guaranteed by refusal. In addressing forgiveness as a discourse of power, Wagamese's work brings further nuance and complexity to reconciliation discourse by overturning the false choice of forgive/don't forgive. Indeed, unforgiveness is a kind of power for the survivor in *Medicine Walk*. It does not refuse so much as it negates. It holds space in that it deflects the false choice of forgive/refuse to forgive and resists the will of the apologizer from whom the request for forgiveness emanates. In this sense it is an aporia, what Derrida identifies as "the difficult or the impracticable, here the impossible, passage, the refused, denied, or prohibited passage, indeed the nonpassage, which can in fact be something else, the event of a coming or future advent."[26]

As Frank helps to demonstrate in *Medicine Walk*, to hold the aporia with forgiveness means to reject the authority, or authoring voice, of the one who asks (or demands) forgiveness and thus to hold space for a radically different, self-determined choice. While Eldon's story about Jimmy is a significant scene of unforgiveness in *Medicine Walk*, it is equalled and rendered more compelling by Frank's second decision to not forgive, which comes at the novel's conclusion. The final story that Eldon shares with his son is about the death of Frank's mother, who passed away during childbirth. This is the truth that Frank has been waiting for throughout the medicine walk and the reason he even agrees to accompany his father in the first place. The story Eldon finally reveals proves what Frank had always guessed: that his father was out drinking on the day of his birth. Because he was not home, Eldon was too late, and too drunk, to get Frank's mother to the hospital when he found her, hours later, collapsed on the floor. In Eldon's estimation, she dies because he was not there for her. This is Eldon's deepest and most painful truth, which lies at the core of his suffering.

Soon after he shares this final story with Frank, Eldon dies and Frank buries him at the site that he requested as a final resting place. Frank then returns home to the old man, where he attempts to pick up his life in the wake of his biological father's death and with the newfound knowledge about his mother. Perhaps sensing his son's unwillingness to embrace forgiveness, as demonstrated in Frank's response to his initial request for it, Eldon does not ask Frank for forgiveness a second time. However, the old man is able to ask if Frank was ever able to forgive, giving the reader a window into the aporia that Frank encounters and braves in his relationship with Eldon:

> [Frank] regarded everything solemnly. "I don't know as he [Eldon] ever got what he wanted in the end," [he] said.
>
> "Whattaya think that was?" the old man asked.
>
> They stopped and they both put a foot on the bottom rail of the fence and gazed out across the acres. The kid shook his head. "Don't know. It's all jumbled up in there. Maybe I was s'posed to forgive him."
>
> "Do ya?" the old man asked.
>
> "Don't know that either. Kinda like a thousand-pound word to me right now."[27]

Configured quite differently from the initial request for forgiveness in the novel, Frank's encounter with the concept here, at the conclusion of *Medicine Walk,* leaves much more space for reflection and possibility, but it cannot be easily read as an act of forgiving. Forgiveness is, Frank concludes, "a thousand-pound word," one weighed down with so much history, including the fact of colonialism, and with so much pain and suffering that it feels impossible to lift, or to bestow on one person. Yet, in contrast to his response to Eldon's direct request for forgiveness, when questioned about forgiveness by a third party, Frank seems to find some solace, and suffering, in ambivalence, in the aporia, neither refusing to forgive nor willing to explicitly offer up the medicine his father seemed to crave. If forgiveness exists in *Medicine Walk,* it is only as an (im)possibility, as an almost unbearably heavy concept that must be carried by the individual left in its charge and decided on in their own time.

It should also be noted that the question of forgiveness, which Wagamese skilfully illustrates here, cannot be caught up in the system of debt tacitly enunciated in Eldon's request for it. Indeed, Frank considers the possibility of forgiveness at the end of the novel in the absence of the one who requested it. While he certainly knows much more about his father and his circumstances now, it is Eldon's absence that allows for this possibility, which is to say that in the absence of its subject, (un)forgiveness becomes something that is for the survivor alone. Indeed, for Frank it is no longer a question of medicine for Eldon but for himself, should he choose to take it up – an action that Wagamese never confirms or denies.

Wagamese's decision not to close with forgiveness in *Medicine Walk,* to leave it open, like a wound, speaks worlds about how he is grappling with the concept in the essays on reconciliation he produced for the AHF and *One Story, One Song.* While Wagamese's forgiveness is no doubt a potential path toward healing and empowerment, it is never an imperative for survivors or their families. Indeed, to insist on forgiveness, to request it from those who have been harmed, would be to undermine truth and the primacy Wagamese gives to that concept throughout his work. If forgiveness is something that Wagamese thinks survivors should take up, he also recognizes it as a deeply personal and often painful journey that individuals must undergo, and quite possibly refute or negate, on their own, and in their own time.

As I will illustrate in this chapter, there is much to be learned from Wagamese's work when placed in relation to the TRC genealogy and the Christian insistence on forgiveness that pervades it. In what follows, I look deeper into the demand for forgiveness as it has been articulated via the TRC. And using Joy Kogawa's novel *The Rain Ascends,* I interrogate the damage that this demand for forgiveness can inflict on survivors and their families. Then, through a reading of Eden Robinson's short story "Queen of the North," I illustrate the illegibility of forgiveness in the syntax of settler colonialism. Through these narrative touchpoints, which grapple with Canada's two big reconciliation narratives (Japanese Canadian redress and the TRC), I reject the academic assertion articulated by Trudy Govier that "however terrible his or her atrocities might have been, a perpetrator should never be regarded as entirely lacking potential for positive moral change."[28] Rather, I would argue that this kind of reasoning, which develops out of a very specific TRC genealogy, bolstered by Christian ideology, creates physical and psychological harm in survivor communities and obscures the socio-political contexts of settler colonialism and white supremacy.

Forgiveness in the TRC Context

If forgiveness, that "thousand-pound word," is contingent on time, careful consideration, and the right to refuse, as Wagamese suggests, this has not been reflected in its historical use in the TRC. Indeed, within that genealogy, forgiveness is positioned less as a choice and more as an imperative. Archbishop Desmond Tutu built the South African TRC specifically from mandates of the Catholic Church and the Christian tradition of forgiveness, in which mercy and suffering are imperative to salvation.[29] As the title of his book *No Future without Forgiveness* suggests, Tutu's version of forgiveness is not a suggestion but an ultimatum, the singular means to reconciliation: "The only way we can be whole, healthy, happy persons," Tutu tells us, "is to learn to forgive."[30] There is, and I reiterate this point here because we need to acknowledge how deeply embedded this idea is, *no future without forgiveness* in the TRC paradigm that Tutu constructed and that Canada has inherited. That alone should give us pause.

If we return to the research on forgiveness, however, it shows that the repetitive, unconditional, and unending process of forgiveness called for in Tutu's model of the TRC may simply be too much to ask of survivors who have little reason to believe in the fidelity and goodwill of the perpetrators of violence against them. Even if one is told to forgive by an authority such as Tutu – even if one deeply wants to forgive – forgiveness is not simply a choice, and even if it were, it would not always be a desirable one. Tutu's brand of Christian forgiveness, which insists on the unending, repetitive act of offering mercy, "not just once, not just seven times, but seventy times seven, without limit," is at risk of undermining the diversity of emotions (including resentment), politics, and resistances that individuals and communities bring to a TRC.[31] It is not simply that people should or should not forgive, but that they are made aware of the labour, pain, and trauma that can accompany forgiveness as a product of a Christian system that naturalizes and glorifies suffering.

The type of forgiveness that Tutu calls for – and the ideology of forgiveness I argue stems from the TRC structure – is based on the normalizing assumption that the "goodness" of a community or state can be enhanced through practices of mercy and empathy, and that choosing to forgive will always be better for the whole. For Tutu, choosing forgiveness, or allowing oneself to experience forgiveness, was the only way that South Africa could continue to exist in the wake of apartheid, and the only way that communities, families, and individuals could hold themselves together in the wake of such terrible and widespread violence. Thus, when Tutu asserts that "there is no future without forgiveness," he is claiming that survivors, and the new, anti-apartheid state, would be unable to exist and thrive if survivors were unable to "get over" the pain and thirst for vengeance that festered within them. Since apartheid began, he notes, people have "been choking with a lust for revenge,"[32] and he asserts that it is only by neutralizing those feelings or finding some means to overcome them that there will be any chance for his country to continue. When Tutu writes, "The only way we can be whole, healthy, happy persons is to learn to forgive,"[33] this is not a subtle or indirect statement; forgiveness is an absolute imperative for him, as well as for the survivors and the democratic state.

What must be made clear, however, is that Tutu's insistence on forgiveness is contingent on the survivor's acceptance of, if not outright desire for, the suffering that accompanies the act of giving mercy. In the Christian tradition, which Tutu draws from directly (his suggestion that survivors forgive not once but "seventy times seven," is a direct quotation from Matthew 18:22), true forgiveness can only be achieved via the anguish of the forgiver, whose suffering guarantees the value of the mercy and humbles the forgiver. According to Douglas White, author of *Forgiveness and Suffering: A Study of Christian Belief*, "the worth of forgiveness is measured exactly by the intensity of the suffering inflicted by the offender. That is the cost of forgiveness; and in the nature of the case, it is a cost borne by the injured person, and not by the wrongdoer."[34] When this type of suffering is linked to a system that demands unending forgiveness, the result is constant and continual anguish for those survivors who are paradoxically prescribed forgiveness as the only means to healing. In the context of residential schools, which were operated by Christian churches, the potential for suffering is potentially doubled, given that survivors are asked to embrace the system that inflicted their initial suffering and to carry that suffering on into a practice of "healing."

While there is no one in the pulpit calling for forgiveness quite as explicitly in Canada as in South Africa, the insistence on Christian formulations of mercy still rings throughout the TRC of Canada. In 2010, Kenny and Louise Blacksmith, Cree ministers from the Cree Nation of Mistissini of Quebec, organized the "Forgiveness Summit," with events in Vancouver and Ottawa.[35] The summit, which received little attention outside religious communities, culminated with Blacksmith presenting a "Charter of Forgiveness" to Minister of Indian Affairs Chuck Strahl, which proclaimed the necessity of forgiveness in the healing process.[36] To quote the Blacksmiths, who channel Tutu in this document, "Forgiveness is a necessity in order to achieve a full restoration of our integrity of our inner self, families, communities, people and nations."[37] Their words resonate heavily with the South African insistence on forgiveness. As in South Africa, forgiveness is presented as the only means for survivors to find healing and to progress down the road to reconciliation.

In response the Assembly of First Nations (AFN) quickly released a statement identifying the summit as independently organized, thus distancing themselves from the ideology that the Blacksmiths were evoking.[38] Chief Justice Murray Sinclair has also removed himself from the forgiveness narrative, telling Nancy Macdonald of *Maclean's* magazine, "I don't know that I've ever felt that I needed to forgive anybody. My sense of commitment to this country is strong enough for me to see that this is a wart on our existence, and we need to come to terms with it."[39] Sinclair and the AFN's rebuttals aside, the message of forgiveness that has attached itself to the discourse of reconciliation seeped into the language of the TRC of Canada as the commission drew to a close and released its final report.

The fact that forgiveness found its way into the language of reconciliation in Canada (primarily via settlers) illustrates just how difficult it is for burgeoning TRCs to navigate outside the structure of feeling generated in the genealogy of reconciliation. On December 15, 2015, newly elected prime minister Justin Trudeau once again "sincerely apologized" for residential schools and "ask[ed] the forgiveness of the Aboriginal peoples of this country for failing them so profoundly."[40] A few months earlier, in May 2015, the Catholic archbishop of Ottawa, Terrence Prendergast (who also attended the Blacksmith summit), released a letter entreating his parishioners to look to the past and ask for forgiveness.[41] Writing specifically to Indigenous communities, he proclaimed, "We face the past and sincerely ask for forgiveness. Your awareness of this history, your presence at events, and your prayers will help the Church express its genuine desire to work with Aboriginal communities to build a shared future of mutual respect."[42] Notably, to come back to Wagamese, forgiveness here comes at the request of settler perpetrators – the church and the state – even as it is refused by Indigenous groups like the AFN and the TRC commissioners. As such, the recipients of its good effects (i.e., the release of guilt, the clemency of mercy) are also always the perpetrators, rather than survivors and their communities.

In any TRC, forgiveness is given form by the political contexts it arises out of. In South Africa, under a Catholic archbishop, forgiveness was explicitly connected to the Christian tradition and mobilized in a way that supported transitional justice and Nelson Mandela's platform with the African National Congress (ANC). In order for Mandela to build a democracy in the wake of apartheid, he needed to shed light on the violence that had been committed under that regime, but without inspiring further retribution.[43] Forgiveness provided the conceptual space to undertake this: the violence of apartheid was exposed, but the population was prompted to move past it with the promise that doing so would be best for the community and the burgeoning democracy. Forgiveness thus became a means to facilitate transitional justice and the move away from racist, totalitarian rule.

In Canada, however, where (as I argue in Chapter 1) transitional justice is not, and has never been, part of the equation, forgiveness carries with it the threat of erasure and the continued disavowal of colonial history. This is because without the future promise of real political change, forgiveness is attached only to the notion of *getting over* the past, or, even more drastically, *forgetting* history. Indeed, according to Lewis B. Smedes, forgiveness is "the editing of your own memory."[44] Whether this is true in all cases ("forgive but not forget" is, of course, a recognizable cliché), forgiveness is historically and semantically connected to the need to "move on."[45] This reasoning lines up all too uncomfortably with a specific strain of settler colonial rhetoric that insists that Indigenous peoples need to "get over" the past and acclimatize themselves to the colonial reality.[46]

While it operates almost entirely under the same principles, forgiveness has an entirely different political meaning when it is shifted from one TRC context to the next. Indeed, it is not too much of a leap to see how a Christian model of forgiveness, such as the one effectively mobilized by Tutu in South Africa, feeds into a colonial model of disavowal and assimilation when taken up in the colonial, Canadian context and, hence, why the AFN, for instance, might be suspicious of its deployment on Indigenous lands. In South Africa, forgiveness was the price to pay for a transition out of apartheid and a means to move toward a new political consciousness in the country. In Canada, however, in the absence of serious political transition, forgiveness is potentially more aligned with forgetting the past and assimilating with a state order whose functionality and authority are based on the erasure of colonial histories and violence committed against Indigenous peoples.

It is not my intent in this chapter to persuade survivors to either forgive or not forgive. As Wagamese helps to illustrate, that choice (and the refusal to choose) rightfully belongs to survivors themselves. Rather, I hope to show in this chapter that the TRC, as a genre of conflict resolution, is still conceived out of the imperative of forgiveness – not as a choice, but as a sentence. And, as such, forgiveness poses an emotional and physiological threat to the disempowered, for whom it is primarily offered.

In what follows, I turn to the acclaimed Canadian novelist and Japanese internment camp survivor Joy Kogawa to flesh out the consequences of forgiveness as it persists in the Canadian imaginary. In this analysis, I step away from the TRC model momentarily, not only because Kogawa's work is, in my view, one of the most robust and sustained literary reflections on the problem of forgiveness, but also because it takes place within the new space of forgiveness opened up by the Japanese Canadian Redress Agreement. From Kogawa, I return to Indigenous literature, this time to Haisla and Heiltsuk author Eden Robinson, who, read alongside Kogawa, provides further evidence for unforgiveness, or resentment. My intent here is to bring forgiveness into the conversation using a scholarly and critical approach, thus driving a wedge into a process that is, in many ways, assumed to be foretold and given. I also bring an important piece of Canada's reconciliation culture, Kogawa's novel *The Rain Ascends,* to bear on the TRC.

The Rain Ascends

Joy Kogawa's third novel, *The Rain Ascends,* is intimately concerned with the dangers of the Christian model of forgiveness and offers a deeply rigorous space in which to consider the effects and dangers of forgiveness as a tacitly accepted necessity and/or demand. *Rain* is Kogawa's third novel, published to little critical acclaim (particularly in comparison to her first two novels, *Obasan* [1981] and *Itsuka* [1993]), first by Vintage in 1995 and later, with revisions, by Penguin Canada in 2003.[47] Read as an extension of her ongoing engagement with Japanese Canadian redress, or as the final book in the *Obasan* trilogy, *Rain* is a torrid reckoning with the political moment of forgiveness that comes after apology and redress. In many ways *The Rain Ascends* is a litmus test for the hold that forgiveness as an imperative of reconciliation has on Canada and Canadians in the era of the theatre of regret.

Kogawa came to prominence and later eminence in Canada with the publication of *Obasan,* which chronicles the removal, internment, and diaspora of a Japanese Canadian family during the Second World War. She was one of those children who was removed, along with her family, from their Vancouver home, and *Obasan* is the semi-autobiographical account of that history – the first literary representation of the removal in Canada to make it to print.[48] *Obasan* quickly became a standard in the Canadian literary canon, and the novel is now taught in high school and university classrooms across the nation as well as overseas.[49] As Kogawa's biographers have noted, *Obasan* has also played an essential role in educating Canadians about Canada's racist past.[50] In 1988, when Prime Minister Brian Mulroney offered an official apology to Japanese Canadians in the House of Commons, National

Democratic Party (NDP) leader Ed Broadbent read an excerpt from *Obasan,* solidifying the novel's place in Canada's reconciliation history.[51] Kogawa's second novel, *Itsuka,* continued the story of *Obasan* and moved the redress narrative forward, following the protagonist, Naomi Nakane, as she becomes involved in the Japanese Canadian redress movement. Unlike *Obasan, Itsuka* is a deeply procedural novel, which provides insight into the systems and people that provide for redress and make reconciliation a possibility.

Kogawa's final novel, *The Rain Ascends,* moves away from Japanese Canadian contexts to investigate an issue no less germane to the redress movement: forgiveness. The novel, which did not receive the same public and critical acclaim that *Obasan* and, to a lesser extent, *Itsuka,* did, was initially perceived by critics to be a dramatic break from Kogawa's oeuvre.[52] Unlike those earlier novels, *Rain* is told from the perspective of a white Anglican woman, Millicent Shelby. While the novel contends deeply with violence and social unrest, race politics almost never enter into the conversation, at least explicitly, although (as I argue below) they are implicit in the context of the novel. Rather than looking at the Japanese Canadian experience, the plot of *Rain* centres on Millicent's father, Barnabas, an Anglican priest who is revealed to have used the power of his station to sexually abuse hundreds of young boys. The foundation of *The Rain Ascends* is built on Barnabas's pedophilia and Millicent's struggle with the demand to forgive (as she has been taught by the church) an unforgiveable act.

In its shift from Japanese Canadian internment and redress, *Rain* is striking in its frank treatment of the sexual abuse of children and its damning condemnation of the church for its role in enabling and sheltering perpetrators. In this move, the novel also creates space to think of Kogawa's work in relation to the sexual violence committed by priests in Indian Residential Schools and the violence directed at children and vulnerable communities under the cloak of forgiveness and reconciliation.[53] Indeed, while in many ways *Rain* might seem to be a step away from her early work, Kogawa's third novel continues to develop themes that the author has invested in throughout her writing: most particularly, violence, the repression of minority voices (particularly women's), and communities' struggles against trauma.

The Rain Ascends is most productively read as an extension of Kogawa's first two novels. Canadian literature scholars before me have already made this argument. From a thematic perspective, Benjamin Lefebvre convincingly argues that *Rain* can and should be read as the final book in the *Obasan* trilogy.[54] Drawing on the work of Shoshana Felman and Dori Laub, he argues that Naomi's trauma in *Obasan* and *Itsuka* is "incomplete," because trauma itself, such as that inflicted by internment, is "unconcludable" and therefore always in excess to the confines of a single narrative. He therefore reads Kogawa's oeuvre as narratives that circle around the traumatic core of internment, which necessarily plays out in all sorts of representations in the author's attempts to grapple with it. Lefebvre quotes Kogawa herself to elucidate this point: "To every story there is an after-story, and to every life an afterwards. Beyond each punctuation point, each period, are further questions and more bends in the road than we can imagine."[55] In this sense, Lefebvre argues, *Rain,* like *Obasan* and *Itsuka,* is a further pursuit of the myriad questions opened up by the trauma of her family's internment during the Second World War. To flesh this out further via Felman and Laub (who offer productive accounts of literature as the possibility of testimony to traumatic events), Laub argues that bearing witness to trauma is ongoing because testimony itself is "a dialogical process of exploration and reconciliation of two worlds – the one that was brutally destroyed and the one that is – that are different and will always remain so."[56] Retelling (and retelling and retelling) a story is thus a means to come to terms with the irreducible gap between the world that has been destroyed and the one we are forced to live with. Or, in other words, to reconcile what is inherently irreconcilable. It is in this sense that literary testimony takes on the impossible, and Felman argues that "literature becomes a witness, and perhaps the only witness, to the crisis within history which precisely cannot be articulated."[57]

Building on the idea that bearing witness to trauma in literature will always be in excess to a singular narrative or perspective, I take Lefebvre's argument that *The Rain Ascends* is another chapter in Kogawa's ongoing attempts to grapple with the history of Japanese Canadian internment, and I push that argument further to suggest that *Rain* is Kogawa's deepest point of reflection on the trauma and alienation that come after redress and apology in the pressure to forgive. How, *Rain* asks, does an individual even attempt forgiveness in the wake of an unforgivable act? What does it mean, on an emotional, psychological, and physiological level, to forgive someone who has caused unspeakable harm? And how does it feel to exist in a culture that expects – or demands – that forgiveness be offered in the wake of such violence?

As a literary centre of indeterminacy, the character of the priest, Barnabas, is embedded with the histories of colonial, racist, and patriarchal violence that operate with and through very particular legacies of forgiveness and reconciliation in Canada. In this sense, Kogawa deftly and presciently draws attention to the impossible act of forgiveness that both Japanese Canadians and Indigenous peoples are forced to confront beneath the mantle of white supremacy and patriarchy. Indeed, read alongside the history of residential schools, Barnabas provides a striking corollary to the priests, nuns, and "educators" who sexually abused hundreds if not thousands of Indigenous students in the residential school system, and who remain protected from prosecution due to the "no naming names" clause in the TRC. What Barnabas helps to illustrate are the processes by which offenders and sexual predators insulate themselves from accountability via settler colonial structures of power, including forgiveness, which work to dehumanize vulnerable populations while perpetuating systems of authority that benefit white men. In this sense, Barnabas's culpability also provides valuable, and disturbing, insight into residential school abuse, given that perpetrator testimony was excluded from the TRC.

Indeed, the omission of perpetrator testimony runs deep in the TRC of Canada. Ronald Niezen points out that "Canada's TRC is the only truth commission to have so thoroughly extinguished the identities of possible perpetrators from its proceedings ... maintaining their invisibility and anonymity all the way through the Commission's activities."[58] Unlike in South Africa, where perpetrators were encouraged to testify by the promise of amnesty, there is no perpetrator testimony through which to articulate the truth of residential schools. The power that Barnabas wields, as a white man and as a man of faith, to not only abuse the vulnerable but also cover up his actions even after they are made public, is a vital testament to the white heteropatriarchy that governs justice in the colonial state and perpetuates systems of violence and the silencing of victims in Canada. As Felman illustrates, indeterminacy is, in fact, the nature of literature that testifies to trauma. It begins with someone who testifies to absence and articulates "what we do not yet know of our lived historical relation to events of our times."[59] Given that perpetrator testimony is excluded from the TRC of Canada, *Rain* renders the trauma of abuse from a perspective other than that of the survivors, adding at least a modicum of the testimonial equilibrium evidenced in previous TRCs. At the same time, *Rain* traces the unarticulated violence that is inflicted beneath the sublime narrative of forgiveness and provides insight into the psychosomatic trauma that circulates from perpetrator violence.

Kogawa's reflections across her work provide invaluable insight into the political implications of forgiveness, extending and nuancing Canada's genealogy of reconciliation while offering a psychological roadmap for those who, due to redress or the TRC of Canada, are under similar pressures to forgive. The protagonist of *Rain,* Millicent, contends with a forgiveness in which one must "rush headlong, impetuously, desperately, through the terrible light of our fears and our truths, glancing neither to the left nor to the right, till at last we come to the Mercy seat."[60] As this quotation helps to illustrate, the forgiveness at stake in *Rain* demands recognition, even at the expense of truth and vulnerable communities. It is a forgiveness built out of the mythos of the TRC model (as instantiated in South America) and echoes across vulnerable communities in Canada.

In what follows, I attempt to unpack at least some of the complex issues surrounding forgiveness that are addressed in *Rain,* looking specifically at the demand to forgive and the violence inflicted by a forgiveness that exists first and foremost as an ideological imperative. After analyzing the mythos of forgiveness in *The Rain Ascends,* I turn to a short story by Eden Robinson, "Queen of the North," to examine the preposterous translation of forgiveness into the grammar and syntax of settler colonialism. *The Rain Ascends* and the TRC deserve to be put into conversation because they share the same claustrophobic space of forgiveness perpetuated by a state – Canada – that traffics specifically in morality. Locating links between communities, geographies, and individuals clarifies how this ideology operates, and thus how it can be confronted and perhaps even overturned. What is integral to my reading, then, is also the allyships that can be drawn across reconciliation movements in Canada to work to dismantle racism, white supremacy, settler colonialism, and patriarchy.

Charles Barnabas Shelby (referred to as Barnabas) is patriarchy writ large in *The Rain Ascends.* He is an Anglican clergyman, musician, and the community pillar in a small, primarily white, town. Initially, his daughter Millicent, who narrates the story, represents Barnabas as a warm and caring man with a deep sense of community. She dwells on the number of important contributions he has made, including the establishment of "three new centres of music and healing," and she emphasizes the love and respect that people there have for him.[61] As the narrative unfolds, however, the reader learns that Barnabas has used his position in the church and as a proprietor of healing to sexually abuse hundreds of young boys, many of them from his own community and at least one from his own family. Faced with the horror and atrocity of his actions, Millicent is finally forced to ask, "What monstrous mockery of faith was it that allowed him to experience forgiveness without turning from his sin? Or was forgiveness just his word for licence?"[62]

As this passage suggests, silence plays a large role in how forgiveness is configured (and undone) in *Rain.* Millicent is unaware of her father's transgressions until he returns home unexpectedly from an Anglican mission. He appears to be quite ill. Initially the reasons for his early homecoming are kept secret from the young girl, who is still in grade school at this point. She is told only that her father is "suffering from an enlarged heart," and that he has a "heart condition,"[63] crude metaphors for his actual "condition," which is shortly revealed to be his unwillingness to control his sexual impulses toward children. (These metaphors, not coincidently, echo the euphemisms that were used to protect the Canadian state when it illegally interned Japanese Canadian citizens during the Second World War, supplanting "internment" with "evacuation," for instance).[64] Just before Millicent is to return to school, however, a delegation of church representatives arrives at the family home to speak with Barnabas. It is at this point in *Rain* that the idea of forgiveness as suffering is introduced into the narrative and established as the central plot of the novel. The meeting is held behind closed doors, but Millicent, and through her the reader, is aware enough to understand that her father has been charged with some sort of crime. Others in the family are more aware of what is happening. While the delegation is speaking to Barnabas, Charlie, Millicent's older brother, rushes into the den where the meeting is taking place in an attempt to defend his father from the charges levied against him. Moved by the young boy's love for his father, the rector warden leading the meeting is compelled to offer some form of consolation, which he finds in the Christian rhetoric of suffering and forgiveness. He tells Charlie and the rest of the family, "Your father has confessed. He has repented. And it's an exercise now in forgiveness that faces us all."[65] In this phrase, "exercise in forgiveness," Kogawa captures the essence of the practice of forgiving as deep emotional and relational labour. The exercise in forgiveness is the arduous and often painful work that those affected by the perpetrator, such as survivors, and those who are close to the perpetrator, like Millicent, are required to take up on an ongoing basis, as Tutu writes, "not just once, not just seven times, but seventy times seven, without limit."

In what follows, this exercise in forgiveness also proves to be a philosophical and physiological test of the limits of reconciliation, pushing Millicent to the far boundaries of justice, mercy, and compassion. Coming out of an Anglican home, the exercise in forgiveness is her moral métier, the only compass by which she knows how to guide her actions. Indeed, throughout almost the entirety of *The Rain Ascends,* Millicent will cling to the idea that "Forgiveness is everything ... It's what we're here for."[66] Yet the obligation she feels to forgiveness and the moral demand of mercy will prove to be her undoing, leading to the collapse of some of her closest relationships, the distrust of her community, and her own mental and physical instability.

What does it even mean to require forgiveness for an unforgivable act such as child abuse? This difficult and emotional theme is not new to Kogawa's work; in fact, it makes an appearance in all three of her novels, with the most critical attention being given to the abuse of the young *Obasan* narrator, Naomi, at the hands of Old Man Gower, a white neighbour who takes sexual advantage of the girl in the lead-up to the family's removal from British Columbia. Naomi represses this memory, but it comes back to her when she testifies to the trauma of internment, thus linking the two traumatic events: "The one secret that emerges even now, curious as an infant fern, a fiddlehead question mark asking with its unformed voice for answers still hidden from me."[67]

The urgency of this repressed truth and the desire to make it legible is articulated again in *Itsuka*. Here, Naomi, now a grown woman, recalls a threat that occurred when she was working on the beet farm, one of the primary work camps Japanese Canadians were relegated to during internment. At the beginning of this novel, Kogawa introduces a stranger who lurks outside the pool hall, reading passages from the Bible out loud to anyone who will listen. But despite his Christianity (which foreshadows the coming of Barnabas in *Rain*), the threat of sexual abuse permeates this character: "It's also whispered about that he cornered a girl behind the rink and fondled her."[68] When Naomi is at work later in the story, this same stranger watches her from the road, and when she sits down to rest he is suddenly "lurching towards [her], a five-dollar bill in his thick hand, his eyes so wide they are bulging."[69] Before Naomi or the reader can fully understand his intent, however, the girl collapses in dizziness and pain, soiling herself, causing her uncle and brother to come running across the field to help her. Naomi's abuse is never described in *Itsuka,* given the fact that the narrator is incapacitated. However, it is not difficult to see the ways the trauma of her experience with Old Man Gower may have spilled out of the pages of *Obasan,* into the sequel, and finally into the pages of *The Rain Ascends,* just as Lefebvre identifies trauma in Kogawa's work always being in excess to the confines of a single narrative. It is an event that exceeds representation and that requires the reader to instill their belief in the narrator, who must testify against an absence: the silence that protects white men against the monstrosity of their actions in a colonial structure of truth.

The question mark that arises in Kogawa's work, in *Obasan's* fragile figure of the fiddlehead, draws attention to the indeterminacy of the abuse inflicted on Naomi as it signifies within the larger contexts of internment, settler colonialism, and white supremacy. As Felman puts it, "the meaning of testimony is not completely known, even by its author, before and after its production, outside of its articulation, of its actual writing."[70] For Felman, this leaves space for the critic to read with the author toward uncovering truths that exceed authorial intent. Yet, this is difficult interpretive terrain for a reader to traverse. Obviously, child abuse is a difficult thing to read and/or write about, and critics have struggled to make sense of the reoccurring trope in Kogawa's work. Many Kogawa scholars have attempted to metaphorize it, reading sexual abuse as an allegory for internment, which has the unintended effect of distancing their readings from the literal and specific violence of that crime. Cherry Clayton argues, for instance, that the sexual abuse against children in Kogawa's novels is "a kind of an analogy" for the relationship between Japanese Canadians and the Canadian government.[71] Clayton's analysis echoes that of Ann Gomer Sunahara, who opens *The Politics of Racism* by stating that internment "left Japanese Canadians in a state of trauma that has been compared to that of a rape victim."[72] Similarly, Donald Goellnicht makes the case that Old Man Gower's abuse of Naomi, and the quiet that surrounds the event, is an allegorical representation of minority silence following a traumatic event. Goellnicht writes that "Kogawa has effectively linked a particularly female condition of sexual silence to her more general concerns with the condition of minority silence."[73] Goellnicht's assertion is that racial and sexual silence are part and parcel of the same imperialist, patriarchal order, which opens a productive space to consider the mechanics of imperial power and their application to the racialized other.

That said, while reducing the space between rape and internment via metaphor may capture necessary attention and highlight the psychosomatic effects of interment, it also risks distracting from the structural conditions, determined by the settler state, that provide for the abuse of the defenceless. By this I mean that sexual abuse also needs to be read literally in Kogawa's work. It is a material consequence of a racist and imperialist government superstructure that deliberately works to separate families and disrupt the communities that traditionally protected the most vulnerable, including children.

In their research on the implications of violence within a settler colonial system, Cindy Holmes and Sarah Hunt make plain that colonialism purposely erodes Indigenous governance and kinship, and therefore facilitates a space in which heteropatriarchal violence is wilfully ignored, if not sanctioned:

> Kinship networks within many Indigenous cultures normalized gender fluidity as individual roles and relationships arose in relation to the diverse needs of local realities within non-nuclear family structures. Colonialism has interrupted these networks through the imposition of a heteropatriarchal family model resulting in wide-ranging and harmful impacts on the health and well-being of Indigenous families and communities.[74]

As Hunt, Holmes, and Amy Piedalue illustrate elsewhere, "sexual violence is a tool of colonialism," which enacts and reinforces racialized bodies as less-than-human. Within this system, in certain spaces – for instance, residential schools or internment work camps – structural violence is "concealed through the naturalisation of these spaces as degenerate,"[75] which is to say that the bodies that occupy them are not protected by the same (colonial) rule of law that protects the white citizenry.

By dissimulating culture, community, and, most importantly, home, under colonial ordinances such as the *Indian Act* and the *War Measures Act*, the Canadian state generated spaces of naturalized violence that explicitly put children at risk. By marking Indigenous and Japanese Canadian bodies as "degenerate" (whether through the savage/civilized binary or via the false threat of "fifth column" insurgency) and by restricting the movement of these groups with literal spaces of exception (residential schools, and work and internment camps), Canada founded spaces that facilitated, if not invited, violence and sexual abuse. The TRC final report confirms this:

> The failure to develop, implement, and monitor effective discipline sent an unspoken message that there were no real limits on what could be done to Aboriginal children within the walls of a residential school. The door had been opened early to an appalling level of physical and sexual abuse of students, and it remained open throughout the existence of the system.[76]

What is at stake in the child abuse scenes in Kogawa's novels is thus not only a metaphor for cultural injustice but also a direct depiction of the physical and psychological damage inflicted on individuals as a result of structural violence informed through the dissimulating structures of settler colonialism and white supremacy. Not only is sexual violence a metaphor through which racism and white supremacy can be read, it is a material product of the colonial nation-state.

In *Rain,* Kogawa adds further depth to the structures of violence addressed throughout her work by illustrating how those structures are facilitated by the theatre of regret. Indeed, *Rain* is a political novel based in an international culture of reconciliation. That fact becomes somewhat buried as the novel progresses, but it is established early and pointedly in the opening chapters. In Millicent's world, forgiveness, as connected to the TRC model, is sublime: a sense of mercy that recuperates compassion out of suffering, no matter how terrible the crime or the perpetrator. The sublime then effaces the trauma that the individual (i.e., the survivor) must endure in order to enact forgiveness, generating a culture of forgetting that is justified out of the emotional high of divinity and a deeply Christian sense of the idealist universal good.

For Millicent, sublime forgiveness is established as the moral baseline for her "exercise" narrative via a story about forgiveness in South America, the home of the first TRC. I will provide a more detailed reading below, but to set this passage up, Eleanor and Stephannie are Millicent's sisters-in-law, each of whom represents one half of the debate for forgiveness in the novel: mercy on the one hand, and punishment on the other. What follows is the story that Stephannie shares as proof of the sublime nature of forgiveness:

> I do not recall the name of the merciful man. But I remember who told the story. It was Eleanor's much-travelled sister, Stephannie, who had returned from a trip to South America. As she spoke, her lips trembled, her eyes filled with tears. She had brought blessed news from the south. Good news. Mercy was still in the world.
>
> Once upon a time, so the story goes, a dying man looked upon his killers and said, 'Father forgive them, they know not what they do.' The man in South America was following a tradition.[77]

It is no coincidence that the story Kogawa provides as a basis for Millicent's understanding of forgiveness is attached explicitly to South America. As I demonstrate in Chapter 1, that continent has its own special place in the TRC genealogy as a political birthplace for reconciliation, which continues to shape how we think about and enact TRCs today. In particular, Argentina and Chile have played essential roles in the development and proliferation of the truth commission model, with Chile providing the primary model for Tutu and the South African TRC.[78] Priscilla Hayner identifies

South America as ground zero for the TRC genealogy, given the timely ability to meet human rights demands in the 1980s. It is only through South America, Hayner argues, that the TRC becomes a "known and attractive entity – thought of as a piece of the solution for places like South Africa, Guatemala, and Malawi."[79]

This is all to say that Kogawa's reference to South America at the beginning of *The Rain Ascends* is linked to a specific history of reconciliation and the divine, Christian tradition it rests on. Indeed, the particular "tradition" referred to in the quotation above is inextricably intertwined with the mythos of the merciful survivor, which finds its instantiation in the figure of Christ, marked in the above passage with a quotation from Jesus himself, as found in Luke 23:34. In taking on the "exercise in forgiveness," then, Kogawa artfully positions Millicent's quest for mercy within the complex international contexts of the TRC writ large, and thus radically expands on the breadth and depth of an argument against forgiveness that, at first glance, might seem to focus on the perspective of a single white woman.

One of the things that makes the South American story in *Rain* unsettling, however, is not the act of grace it portrays, but the fact that it is not attached to any specific actor. As Millicent narrates it, the story her sister-in-law recalls is not connected to a particular person ("I do not recall the name of the merciful man"). Rather, divine mercy is attached to an ephemeral religious ethos, giving it the false appearance of the transcendent and universal. In abstracting forgiveness from a particular individual, then, the storyteller renders mercy as a capital "T" Truth that extends far beyond subjectivity into the ether of an idealist imperative, where reconciliation discourse so often takes refuge.

There is more to be unpacked in this passage, however. In this abstraction of mercy, Eleanor also falsely locates herself in the place of the suffering subject, as captured in the tears that punctuate her telling. In her performance of grief, the emotional subjectivity of the particular forgiving body (i.e., that of the survivor) is erased and replaced. Eleanor is thus an apt metonym for the ways in which the suffering inflicted by forgiveness for crimes against humanity is deflected away from the subject of abuse and recuperated by the Christian West. That Millicent's own engagement with forgiveness is premised on an "exercise" rendered out of the TRC and recuperated into the white performance of suffering speaks volumes about the ways in which a very particular forgiveness narrative unfurls in Canada – via the transmission of reconciliation stories overseas. Indeed, it is in the ways Kogawa depicts forgiveness as a social modality based in the collapse of space – between a global audience and an individual, between witnesses and survivors, and, most radically, between perpetrator(s) and survivors – that she offers the most profound insight into the potential violence of forgiveness and the threat of empathy, to which I will now turn.

Empathy and the "I" of the Enemy

At stake in Stephannie's forgiveness story, which is, notably, relayed to the reader third- if not fourth-hand (via the forgiver, Stephannie, Eleanor, and then the narrator herself), is how forgiveness presents the space to take up the positionality of the other, with or without the socio-political or land-based contexts that provide for it. We see how forgiveness creates the space to fold subjectivity into Eleanor's own reaction to the story: "As she spoke, her lips trembled, her eyes filled with tears." Even here, with the use of the pronoun "she," Kogawa demonstrates how the space between the triad of the forgiving man, Stephannie, and Eleanor collapses. Is it Eleanor's lips that tremble? Stephannie's eyes that fill with tears? The who is less important than the fluid transmission of suffering and mercy enabled by the sublime affect of forgiveness. Kogawa is canny in her deployment of empathy throughout *The Rain Ascends,* even drawing the reader into the fraught space of forgiveness through her use of the second person: "He may not have heard you. You repeat yourself. He would not want to know why you were up all night. He would want it all to go away. So would you. Yes. So would you."[80]

In its conditioning of subjective space, *The Rain Ascends* takes on a question central to forgiveness studies: the question of empathy as a means of knowing the other and even occupying their positionality. Empathy, in this sense, means engaging a wrong from the other's eyes or, if we consider it in literary terms, the "I" of the other. This is the "I" that serves as the transformative foundation of so many literature classes: the invitation to step out of the limited space of self and to experience the world from another person's point of view. It is through empathy, Everett Worthington argues, that "one sees the other as having acted in a way as human beings do, out of his or her own perceptions; there may even be the recognition that what he or she did is something one has done or could well do."[81] For Kogawa's oeuvre, this is not an insignificant space. Indeed, the perceived induction of empathy in her work played a major role in the critical success of her first novel.

According to Kogawa biographer Arnold Davidson, *Obasan* "enable[s] us to become, in imagination, a member of a Japanese Canadian family, and to experience the internment and dispersal of Japanese Canadians, during and after the Second World War, through the narrator's intense memory of a childhood troubled by the disruption of her community and family life."[82] It is in the possibility it presents (for non-Japanese Canadian readers) to inhabit the space of the other, Davidson argues, that the novel's aesthetic and political power lies. It is important to note that Davidson assumes a white readership here. While empathy can be a powerful and even transformative process for the audience of some stories, seeing through the "I" of an architect of violence can also be an exceptionally emotional and physiologically damaging event, particularly for those who are personally connected to those histories.

Testimony from translators at the South African TRC helps to illustrate this point. Authors writing out of those contexts have been able to pinpoint the vulnerability evoked by occupying the "I" of a victim or perpetrator of violence. For instance, Antjie Krog, a white South African journalist who spent months bearing witness to and writing about survivor testimony to apartheid, writes that "it is difficult to interpret survivor hearings ... because you use the first person all the time. I have no distance when I say 'I' ... it runs through me with 'I.'"[83] Tutu makes a similar point about the "I" in *No Future without Forgiveness,* highlighting the damage that can be incurred by inhabiting the first-person perspective in the reconciliation process. He reflects on the role translators played in the hearings and the ways in which they were asked to embody violence: "It was particularly rough for our interpreters," Tutu writes, "because they had to speak in the first person, at one time being the survivor and at another being a perpetrator."[84] The impacts of inhabiting these spaces are made plain by Krog in *Country of My Skull:* "My teeth are falling out. I have rashes. After the amnesty deadline, I enter my house like a stranger. And barren. I sit around for days. Staring."[85]

Kogawa is just as descriptive in the picture of pain she paints for Millicent in her attempt to occupy the perspective of her father:

> I have been staying awake for too many nights, listening to the termites nibbling at the paper walls. My brittle arms can no longer hold up the roof. I've been trying hard to speak with father. With each failed effort the weight of silence grows. Some days I feel I can hardly move at all – one foot in the slough of loathing, the other in the glue of love. I'm stuck. I'm wretched with knowing and not knowing.[86]

As Krog, Tutu, and Kogawa all demonstrate, stepping into the "I" of the other in the wake of historical injustice is aimed particularly at collapsing the seemingly irreducible distance between self and "enemy," inviting no small amount of pain and discomfort into the world of the individual attempting to empathize. In this sense, forgiveness also provides for the theoretical space to imagine the collapse of the boundaries between self and other, survivor and perpetrator, with potentially damaging consequences. From this perspective, the process of forgiving can be seen to literally welcome suffering and distress into survivors' subjective spaces, deeply troubling the insistence, often born out of stories attributed to the TRC, that forgiveness promotes healing and wholeness.

Kogawa's exercise in forgiveness, however, refuses any easy movement into the space of the other by unpacking the consequences of forgiveness and the empathy that mobilizes it. Indeed, ultimately, forgiveness in *The Rain Ascends* is guaranteed as an ethical act only when it comes subsequent to the perpetrator's confession and lamentation; it is not necessary in any and all situations. Millicent's father, for instance, not only negates his own accountability for his monstrous actions; he actually mobilizes forgiveness as a means to protect himself from persecution, even appealing to the Christian rhetoric of unlimited forgiveness to justify his crimes. When Millicent finally summons the courage to confront her father and demand he account for his actions, asking, "Do you think you have been forgiven, Father?" Barnabas will only reply that "God came into the world to save sinners, and I am a sinner."[87] Here, by suggesting that forgiveness acts as a safety net between him and the hard ground of real moral depravity, Barnabas makes it clear that while he might be willing to admit that his actions were wrong, he has also been relieved of his responsibility for those actions by giving in to a divine power, thus granting himself the space to continue to inflict suffering while projecting moral character.

For Millicent, who herself suffers throughout this novel in her attempts to reconcile the demand for forgiveness with the unforgivable acts of her father, grace ultimately unfolds in the decision to *not* forgive. In the end, she learns that the suffering inflicted by forgiveness on survivors and their families is untenable. By the end of the novel, as Millicent comes to accept the full extent of her father's crimes, she is unable to remain in the state of suffering demanded by unlimited forgiveness. Confronted by the bishop of her own church, she refuses to hold on to the spurious idealism of the Christian tradition and ultimately revokes forgiveness as an ontology and epistemology: "Are we to forgive endlessly?" she asks, quoting Arthur Miller's

After the Fall, "as to an idiot in the house?"[88] Millicent's final position on forgiveness here is not so much resolute as it is exhausted: she is no longer physically or emotionally able to carry the demands of unlimited forgiveness (Tutu's "seventy times seven, without limit"), nor is she able to hold up the responsibility to her community that it requires, even if it will lead to a larger notion of healing, which is never proven to be the case. Christian forgiveness requires for Kogawa, a divine stupidity: shutting oneself off to the pain and suffering of mercy's material effects in the blind hope for a messianic future. Ultimately, when forgiveness is proven to serve the perpetrator and to uphold the status quo, it can no longer be a viable choice for Millicent. What she identifies as the "world-altering labour of befriending the enemy,"[89] the core of the sublime forgiveness story that Eleanor shares with her at the beginning of the novel, is ultimately demonstrated to be an exercise in maintaining the structures of power that precipitate violence against the most vulnerable and recuperate the authority and control of the most powerful.

What both Tutu and, to a lesser extent, Trudeau and Prendergast ask of survivors in their independent calls for forgiveness is that survivors accept the suffering implicit to forgiveness in exchange for democracy and an empowered nation-state. Whether that exchange is equitable is still very much in question in Canada. Forgiveness, as defined by Worthington, is an "other-oriented emotion,"[90] meaning that survivors are most likely to overcome feelings of resentment and vengeance if they can accurately identify the perspective and emotions of the perpetrator. In other words, by locating oneself in relation to the offender via the process of empathy, a survivor is more likely to see their perpetrator's actions as human and therefore deserving of mercy. In enmity relations, rehumanizing the other means not only acknowledging the good in a person or group that one has (often quite justifiably) been conditioned to see as evil, but also acknowledging the evil, or the potential to be evil, that exists in oneself.[91]

Thus, in order for forgiveness to take place, the forgiver must be willing and able to understand the perpetrator from within the innermost spaces of their own perspective; hence the "empty chair technique" that is so often deployed in psychology initiatives concerning reconciliation, in which survivors are literally asked to imagine themselves in the space of the other. Worthington utilizes the "empty chair technique" as a means to instrumentalize this empathetic movement, during which survivors sit across from an empty chair and literally imagine themselves occupying the space of the other: "The enactment in the empty chair," he writes, "allows the view of the other person to become more affiliative. Empathy is developed for the other person."[92] Forgiveness, in this sense, is spatialized in the movement between bodies and psyches that collapses strict delineations of "self" and "other." This level of understanding requires a certain psychological over-proximity, in which survivors must put themselves into the subjective space of the enemy and cede, to some degree, the sovereign boundaries of the self.

Clearly the empathetic movement implicit in this model of forgiveness has dangerous personal and political ramifications that throw into relief the value of forgiveness offered in exchange for a reinforced colonial order. Indeed, in opposition to Western scholars of forgiveness like Worthington, who argues that "empathy is morally neutral,"[93] I would argue that on top of, or in relation to, compassion, the empathy model of forgiveness implies a certain menace: in the act of empathy, survivors are at risk of being subsumed by the other and losing track of the boundaries and borders that define difference – for instance, race, gender, sexuality, etc. Without critical interrogation and intersectional analysis, empathy thus risks replicating Canada's historical assimilation policies, particularly those advanced in residential schools, which actively sought to reduce the difference between settlers and Indigenous peoples by assimilating Indigeneity into the settler state.[94] Rejecting empathy, refusing to take up the position of the other, can thus also be articulated as a means of asserting sovereignty and self-determination while interrupting historical legacies of assimilation. *The Rain Ascends* demonstrates precisely how fraught empathy is as a space for healing. "Queen of the North," which I will turn to next, provides further insight into forgiveness and empathy as illegible spaces.

"Queen of the North" and the Impossibility of Forgiveness

When Millicent finally admits that "too much has been hidden for too long under the rubric of the confessional," she speaks not only to her father's long history of abuse, but also to the abuse that has been perpetrated against children by members of the church in Canada more generally, most particularly in residential schools.[95] Kogawa traces the outline of residential school sexual abuse in *The Rain Ascends* when Millicent, finally interrogating her father on his crimes, asks, "Were they Native children?" Barnabas neither confirms nor denies his daughter's query, but the question is significant given the rampant sexual abuse that proliferated in the residential school system that was run and directed by churches, including the United, Catholic, Presbyterian, and Anglican (Barnabas's home denomination) churches.[96] Indeed, BC Supreme Court Justice Douglas Hogarth wrote, "The Indian residential school system was nothing more than institutionalized pedophilia."[97] Sexual abuse was rampant in residential schools, as evidence from the TRC now confirms, and its victims were many.[98] In many instances, the abuse was known by those in authority, but action against it was slow in coming, if it existed at all.[99]

As early as the 1880s, adults charged with the care of children in the schools were being formally accused of sexual abuse. In 1886, Jean L'Heureux, an Indian Affairs translator and recruiter, was accused of the sexual abuse of Indigenous children under his care. School officials recognized that he had committed these crimes, but no formal action was taken until 1891, when he was allowed to resign.[100] The summary of the final report of the TRC of Canada, *Honouring the Truth, Reconciling for the Future,* concludes that "when it came to taking action on the abuse of Aboriginal children, early on, Indian Affairs and the churches placed their own interests ahead of the children in their care and then covered up that victimization. It was cowardly behaviour."[101] Indeed, after L'Heureux, sexual abuse in residential schools only grew more rampant. Grollier Hall, for instance, a residential school in Inuvik, opened its doors in 1958. Between that opening and 1979, there was not one year in which a dormitory supervisor did not sexually abuse a student.[102] All of these supervisors were later convicted of sexual assault, although many not until years later.[103] I cite *Honouring the Truth* at length here in order to emphasize the violence and trauma residential school caregivers were allowed to inflict on Indigenous children:

> Joseph Jean Louis Comeau, Martin Houston, George Maczynski, and Paul Leroux all worked at Grollier Hall ... All were convicted of abusing Grollier Hall students. William Peniston Starr served as director of the Gordon's, Saskatchewan, residence from 1968 until 1984. Prior to that, he worked at a series of schools in Alberta and Québec. In 1993, he was convicted of ten counts of sexually assaulting Gordon's school students. Arthur Plint worked as a boys' supervisor at the Alberni residential school for two five-year periods between 1948 and 1968. In 1995, he pleaded guilty to eighteen counts of indecent assault. In sentencing him to eleven years in jail, Justice D.A. Hogarth described Plint as "a sexual terrorist."[104]

Eden Robinson's short story "Queen of the North" is constructed from the contexts of residential schools and sanctioned violence against Indigenous children, committed by men and women like Barnabas. Robinson is a

Haisla and Heiltsuk author from Kitamaat, British Columbia, known for her deep, rich storytelling, her literary depictions of her home and her culture, and her flair for the horrific. To this last point, she cites Stephen King and Edgar Allan Poe as two of her primary influences.[105] But unlike King or Poe, Robinson's horror is often grounded in the traumatic reality of colonization and the intergenerational effects it has on Indigenous peoples, particularly Indigenous youth. "Queen of the North," for instance, which went on to form the basis of her award-winning novel *Monkey Beach,* is fully immersed in these truths, focusing particularly on the devastating effects of sexual abuse as it occurred in residential schools and the ways in which that abuse can proliferate across communities even when those schools have been shut down.

Aside from the fact that both stories contend with the sexual abuse of children, I am putting "Queen of the North" and *The Rain Ascends* into conversation here as a means to further reflect on the possibility of translating forgiveness into the TRC of Canada. "Queen of the North" is a story about forgiveness, but only inasmuch as Robinson measures forgiveness against the repression of truth. Testifying to the ongoing trauma of residential school ruptures any discourse that looks to harmony and reunification, and therefore forgiveness is inarticulable in "Queen of the North." Patricia Barkaskas and Sarah Hunt argue that the truth of survivors "disrupts the notion that we have entered an 'Age of Reconciliation' and challenges us to consider how we will meaningfully address the ongoing colonial project in Canada."[106] This is to say that there is no room for reconciliation, let alone forgiveness, in a world in which the violence of residential schools and settler colonialism is ongoing. For Barkaskas and Hunt, and, I would argue, for Robinson, truth provides the conditions under which forgiveness is even comprehensible. What "Queen of the North" demonstrates, then, is how far from comprehensibility we are when the possibility of truth continues to be filtered through colonial narratives.

In the way it contends with truth, "Queen of the North" needs to be considered as further evidence *against* forgiveness. In this, I am borrowing from Marlene Brant Castellano, who asks what I see as fundamental questions of forgiveness within a reconciliatory framework: "Can the proponents of reconciliation assure ... reluctant parties that the universe is indeed friendly? That it is safe to forgive and reach out a hand of friendship? That friendship will even be welcomed?"[107] If the damage inflicted by residential schools is structurally embedded – and not a matter of individual "bad seeds," as Robinson helps to illustrate – the answer must be no. If violence continues to be ascribed to Indigenous families without interrogation of settler colonialism, the answer must be no. If truth goes unsaid because Indigenous women and girls fear what their testimony will mean for them and their families, the answer must be no. Forgiveness without truth is an invitation to further harm and the reaffirmation of the status quo, a theme that Robinson expertly narrates through a nuanced engagement with testimony and intergenerational violence.

"Queen of the North," set in Kitamaat Village in British Columbia, is told from the perspective of Adelaine, also known as "Karaoke," a name given to her after a night in which she refused to relinquish the microphone of a karaoke machine. Adelaine is a young Haisla woman who lives at home with her mother and who spends a large portion of her time in the story (aside from a short sojourn in Vancouver) fighting and partying. While the majority of the short story is told in the present tense, Robinson deftly integrates flashbacks from Adelaine's memory into the narrative development, which gradually illustrate and develop the repressed trauma that the protagonist contends with throughout. The story itself ends with an explicit and traumatic reveal about sexual violence. It is a reveal that confirms Nabokov's insistence that "one cannot read a book: one can only reread it."[108] The suffering released at the end of "Queen of the North" compels the reader to look back and (re)read the barely submerged trauma that pushes against the surface in each and every paragraph of the short story.

That trauma at the centre of "Queen of the North" concerns the sexual abuse inflicted on Adelaine by her uncle Josh. The fact of this abuse is noted at various times throughout the short story by the aforementioned flashbacks, but, importantly, it is never rendered explicit in Adelaine's world; that is, she never speaks it aloud. The reader learns of it in bits and pieces as the story progresses, primarily through Adelaine's internal monologue and, finally, in its abrupt eruption at the story's conclusion. Fearing the reprisal that sharing her trauma might bring, particularly how it might damage her relationship with her boyfriend, Jimmy, she keeps this truth inside. Robinson makes Adelaine's adherence to silence, even when she knows breaking it might save her, a prominent part of the character's development as well as the story's plot.[109] When Jimmy invites Adelaine to speak, stating "You're quiet tonight," she quickly retreats into quiet, even as her desire to speak urges her forward: "I almost told him then. I wanted to tell him. I wanted someone else to know and not have it locked inside me. I kept starting and then chickening out. What was the point? He'd probably pull away from me in horror, disgusted, revolted."[110] Adelaine's fear of giving voice to her trauma here illustrates and adds further complexity to the complications of speaking truth within a colonial structure of violence, which, operating under a false narrative of Indigenous deficiency, works to assign blame to the victim, their culture, and their communities. As demonstrated in the above quotation, Adelaine struggles with the idea that sharing her truth will provide the grounds for Jimmy to pathologize and ultimately reject her, rather than bringing justice to her perpetrator.

Yet, while Adelaine's silence can be interpreted in relation to Jimmy, it should also be read in a larger socio-political context. Cindy Holmes and Sarah Hunt argue that silence about sexual abuse in Indigenous communities cannot simply be attributed to shame and fear. It should also be connected to racist and patriarchal attitudes toward Indigenous peoples, women, and queer and non-binary folk most particularly, as well as concerns about what sharing such knowledge will perpetuate: "While the literature [on violence in Indigenous communities] names shame, fear, silence and hiding violence, it does not widely address the context of racialized state interventions and pervasive racist-sexist stereotypes about Indigenous peoples that produce this silence and shame."[111] Thus, while on one hand, Adelaine's untold truth distances her from those who love her and care for her, on the other hand, speaking that truth represents the potential for another kind of distance, one shaped by others' perspective on her pain, including Jimmy's, but also her family's and the settler state's. Within this limited framework, Adelaine's choice, then, is not to speak her truth but to forget it – or, more precisely, to repress it: to keep it from signifying in the physical world.

It is important to make plain here that forgiveness is never presented as an option in this short story. There are zero instances of the word in its twenty pages, yet forgiveness remains germane to Robinson's story in its very lack. Unlike Millicent, who battles with an ideologically driven demand to forgive a sexual predator and the physical and emotional unwillingness to do so, Adelaine carries only resentment and hatred, which find their way out in acts of violence committed against other youth or are dampened by the use of alcohol and drugs. That forgiveness is not directly presented as one of Adelaine's options in "Queen of the North" can, in part, be attributed to the fact that she is the direct survivor of sexual abuse, whereas Millicent is a witness, an interlocuter, albeit a devastatingly close one. Indeed, part of Millicent's struggle in *The Rain Ascends* is to decide whether or not she can forgive on behalf of survivors, which she ultimately concludes she cannot. For Adelaine, however, the fact of that violence on her own body makes it impossible to consider forgiveness as an option, particularly given that her truth, which remains unsignified, represents the semiotic context to render it legible.

In this sense, non-forgiveness, or resentment, is a means of self-protection and self-interest. Glen Coulthard articulates Indigenous unforgiveness as sovereign expressions of care, for Indigenous peoples, communities, and land. He writes "Indigenous peoples' individual and collective resentment – expressed as an angry and vigilant unwillingness to forgive – ought to be seen as an affective indication that we care deeply about ourselves, about our land and cultural communities, and about the rights and obligations we hold as first peoples."[112] Martha Minow makes a similar argument when she suggests, in *Between Vengeance and Forgiveness,* that "through vengeance, we express our basic self-respect."[113] The lack of forgiveness in "Queen of the North," then, while an indication of the upshot of structural racism and colonialism, can also be read as an articulation of care: a refusal to show mercy, not only to an abusive uncle, but, more expansively, to the settler colonial system that (re)produces sexual violence via the dehumanization of Indigenous peoples.

If we are querying forgiveness in "Queen of the North," we need to ask first, forgiveness for whom? TRC Commissioner Murray Sinclair convincingly argues that many survivors don't see forgiveness as possible because it extends beyond individual bodies into the structures of Canadian nation making and maintenance. For many, he suggests, forgiveness is not something that can be applied to a system or a structure: "Many people say they can never forgive anybody. We've heard elders say you can't forgive an institution that doesn't have a soul or a spirit."[114] Similarly, the lack of forgiveness in "Queen of the North" can be read as a response to a system in which forgiveness is incomprehensible because the trauma cannot be contained within a single actor.

Indeed, the scope of abuse and trauma is essential to understanding unforgiveness in "Queen of the North." Although Adelaine's uncle Josh is her abuser, a fact that cannot be erased or excused, he is also the victim of sexual abuse at the hands of Father Archibald, a priest at a residential school. Adelaine discovers this fact after suffering abuse from Josh for a number of years. The evidence comes to her in the form of "a picture of a priest with his hand on a little boy's shoulder." The little boy, Adelaine's mother tells her, is her uncle. The inscription on the back of the photo reads, "Dear Joshua ... How are you? I miss you terribly. Please write. Your friend in Christ, Archibald."[115] That Archibald abused Josh is made apparent to Adelaine when she learns that she can fend off her uncle's advances by mentioning Archibald's name when he enters the room. What Robinson points to, by connecting Adelaine's trauma to the legacy of residential schools in this photograph, is the fallacy by which family violence is assumed by non-Indigenous peoples to be a product of "deficient" communities, rather than a specific condition and product of residential schools and settler colonialism.

The fact of state violence and its effects on Indigenous families is well known and documented. In 1996, the Royal Commission on Aboriginal Peoples (RCAP) illustrated that family violence in Indigenous communities is directly linked to racist interventions by the settler state, including residential schools. Situating family violence historically, RCAP states,

> First, Aboriginal family violence is distinct in that it has invaded whole communities and cannot be considered a problem of a particular couple or an individual household. Second, the failure in family functioning can be traced in many cases to interventions of the state deliberately introduced to disrupt or displace the Aboriginal family. Third, violence within Aboriginal communities is fostered and sustained by a racist social environment that promulgates demeaning stereotypes of Aboriginal women and men and seeks to diminish their value as human beings and their right to be treated with dignity.[116]

The extent of residential school abuse, as outlined by RCAP, and unpacked in detail in the work of Holmes and Hunt, is baked right into Robinson's story. After inspecting the photograph of Josh and Father Archibald, Adelaine immediately recalls "that famous priest who got eleven years in jail. He'd molested twenty-three boys while they were in residential school."[117] Although the number of charges differs slightly, the reference to the eleven years in jail connects the priest that Adelaine recalls here to Arthur Plint, who in 1995 was pronounced a "sexual terrorist" by BC Supreme Court Justice Douglas Hogarth.[118] Plint was a supervisor at Alberni Indian Residential School, which was stationed on Vancouver Island, about fifteen-hundred kilometres south of Kitamaat, and run by the United Church, from 1947 to 1968. Charges against Plint arose following a 1992 study conducted by the Nuu-chah-nulth Tribal Council, which found that 130 people had suffered some form of abuse at residential schools in the area.[119] In 1995, Plint pled guilty to eighteen charges against him, which included victims from ages six to thirteen. Almost three decades after he had left his position at Alberni

Indian Residential School, he was sentenced to eleven years in prison at the age of seventy-seven.[120]

With references to Plint and the residential school system woven into the heart of her short story, then, what Robinson establishes in "Queen of the North" are the multiple and complex layers and valences through which family abuse, nested within the settler colonial system, must be accounted for. While Josh's actions cannot be excused, the church and the state also hold direct responsibility for the abuse of Indigenous children, which echoes out beyond the walls and timelines of the residential school system itself into the homes of Indigenous youth. It points outward, to ongoing structures of settler colonialism, where analysis of violence in Indigenous communities must be directed.

By refusing to attend to the structural contexts of sexual abuse, the settler state continues to put vulnerable communities at risk. Holmes and Hunt argue that, "rather than making visible intersections of ongoing state neglect, racism, sexism, homophobia, and other expressions of colonialism in contributing to overwhelming realities of physical and sexual violence, public discourse naturalizes violence within Indigenous families and blames Indigenous peoples."[121] Changing the conversation about violence in Indigenous families, as Holmes and Hunt argue we must do, means reading outward, toward the *longue durée* of settler colonialism, as a means of interpreting and intervening in it. Read contextually, Adelaine's discovery of her uncle's abuse rightly brings her no closer to forgiveness, because it highlights the impacts of intergenerational trauma and the ways in which violence, as it originated in residential schools, replicates and repeats itself in an ongoing loop – which Robinson signifies by beginning "Queen of the North" at the same place the story ends: with the return of Josh's fishing boat. We see signification of this loop elsewhere in the story as well. As mentioned above, after she discovers the photo of Josh and Father Archibald, Adelaine also learns that mentioning Archibald's name when Josh attempts to rape her will drive him away.[122] In order to draw a more explicit connection between his abuse and her own, and thus interrupt the ongoing cycle of violence as it impacts her and her community, Adelaine pastes a photo of Josh's face onto the picture of Father Archibald, and her own face onto the face of the boy. She then places that montage, along with a blood clot from her period, into a hat box and "tie[s] it up with a bright red ribbon." With the photo montage, she includes a card that reads "it was yours so I killed it."[123]

Adelaine's gift (she actually refers to it as a "present" in the subsequent paragraph) adds new complexity and depth to my reflections on reciprocity in Chapter 4. Here, what is being "returned" to the perpetrator via the gift are the conditions and pain of his actions as they are being (re)inflicted on a new subject. In creating the photo montage, Adelaine makes explicit the ways in which her uncle's actions are, in fact, uncanny re-articulations of his own abuse, and thus a reawakening of the past in the present moment. The "return" of the gift in this moment is, thus, not the return of *hau*, but the return of the repressed – the articulation of the colonial violence that, as Holmes and Hunt argue, is wilfully disavowed in colonialist readings of Indigenous family violence. In Adelaine's montage, however, the origins of that violence – residential schools – are writ large in an image that folds past and present, subject and object, perpetrator and survivor.

As detailed above, forgiveness is most often understood as the consequence of placing oneself in the position of the other.[124] Worthington writes, "The victim is presumed most likely to forgive if he or she can accurately identify the perspective and especially the emotions felt by the offender and respond with sympathy, compassion or love to those emotions."[125] Even decision-based forgiveness, which is defined as the survivor "letting go of resentment and bitterness" for their own benefit (rather than the perpetrator's), requires an intimate engagement with the subjective space of the transgressor in that the survivor is asked to see "the other as having acted in a way as human beings do."[126] Millicent demonstrates the psychological limits of this type of engagement in *The Rain Ascends* when she is compelled, via the narrative of sublime forgiveness, to take up the "I" of someone for whom forgiveness is a vehicle of violence.

But what does one do with forgiveness when there is no definitive subject to attribute it to? As Sinclair has indicated, forgiving the concept of the church (let alone the abstract ideology of settler colonialism) does not make sense within the frameworks by which many survivors of residential schools understand that concept. Presuming that forgiveness is possible means presupposing that a community has the capacity and epistemological framework for processing it, and that the community has the time or desire to commit to scaffolding that framework for a perpetrating group that has demonstrated, time and time again, that it only has its own interests at heart. The photograph that Adelaine discovers and interacts with links the abuse her uncle committed to a much larger and entangled web of structural violence, in which settler colonialism and residential schools are the prime movers. Josh is a piece of the problem, of course, but the production of his identity must be read within the larger cycles of violence perpetuated by residential schools and settler colonialism. In this sense, forgiveness is untenable because the crime is in excess to the subject. For Adelaine to forgive Josh, against whom she harbours a righteous and self-protecting resentment, would be to overlook the larger system to which his actions are attached.

Further, to forgive Father Archibald, or, for that matter, Arthur Plint, would be to disregard a residential school system that actively dehumanized Indigenous children and facilitated sexual predation. Even to forgive residential schools, if it is possible to forgive an ideological state apparatus (and Sinclair suggests it is not), is to gloss over the violence of settler colonialism, which continually parses Indigeneity through deficit models and thereby justifies the necessity of apartheid schooling and labour camp education. This is all to say that while "Queen of the North" takes up similar themes to *The Rain Ascends,* forgiveness is not on the table in Robinson's story, because forgiveness, in the labyrinth of residential schools, and intergenerational trauma, is a ghost of a word when inserted into the syntax of settler colonialism. To borrow from Billy-Ray Belcourt, "all that is left is the signified. / people die that way."[127]

Without truth, forgiveness is a weapon of the powerful. The distinction between the forgiveness represented by Tutu and that represented by Kogawa is philosophically subtle and demands close attention. Arguably, both these authors see the potential for healing in the concept of forgiveness. Yet, while Tutu sees forgiveness as an imperative, the only means of building a shared future, Kogawa ultimately concludes that, as imperative, forgiveness is a cudgel and shield: a shield to those in power, who would inflict harm beneath its shelter, and a cudgel to those who attempt to reconcile the ontology of forgiveness with an unforgiveable act. For Robinson, however, the structures of violence that provide for the abuse of children and restrict survivors' ability to speak their truths leave "forgiveness" without a signifier – that is, nothing will render it material within the narratives of residential schools and settler colonialism.

Held together, the detail explored by these writers – Wagamese, Tutu, Kogawa, and Robinson – brings much-needed attention to the concept of forgiveness as it manifests in the TRC of Canada. It is much needed because this TRC marginalizes that discourse while foregrounding apology and reconciliation. Skipping over the discourse of forgiveness (by which I do not mean asking for or bestowing it, but critically engaging with it) disavows the ways in which forgiveness saturates the genealogy of the TRC, leaving it to operate covertly, often insidiously. All four of the approaches I have investigated here are invested in the power of living beyond legacies of abuse and historical injustice. The essential difference, of course, is that while Tutu insists that forgiveness is categorical, that it must be offered "without limit," Wagamese, Kogawa, and Robinson all insist that a limit is necessary, and they illustrate how the demand to forgive undermines the labour and violence that can be inflicted beneath the insistence of that rubric.

Conclusion

In the ways that they confront the forgiveness imperative, exposing the intensity with which that imperative clings to individuals and the harm it inflicts in the process, *Medicine Walk, The Rain Ascends,* and "Queen of the North" offer necessary windows into the religious and political ideologies that, left unchecked, will go on to haunt the TRC of Canada. Indeed, *The Rain Ascends* provides provocative insight into the tone and tenor of reconciliation in Canada before the TRC even commenced, and thus into the structure of feeling into which that TRC was launched and continues to unfold. Similarly, "Queen of the North" presents us with a residential school scenario in which the implications of violence that spread out from those schools foreclose the possibility of forgiveness inasmuch as they narrow the scope of what can be seen as forgivable. Unless we are able to map the ongoing consequences of residential schools onto instances of violence in Indigenous families, and thus disrupt the deficit narrative that continues to frame Indigenous-settler relations in Canada, forgiveness will continue to be syntactically indecipherable. Truth, and the ongoing struggle to make it heard, is the only way forgiveness will be legible in the context of the TRC of Canada. To quote and paraphrase Barkaskas and Hunt: truth before reconciliation. Truth before forgiveness.

Unlike apology, then, which is framed as a noble *decision* of the perpetrator, forgiveness, in the context of the TRC, is often not conceived as a choice, but as a *requirement* of survivors. Quite obviously, the expectation of forgiveness that finds its impetus in a Christian tradition of suffering is based in severely imbalanced power dynamics, which leaves the onus of responsibility (and the pain that accompanies it) on the most vulnerable. While this imbalance/suffering is often justified (and oftentimes glorified) by reconciliation leaders such as Tutu and forgiveness scholars like Govier, the model assumes as a foundation at least a minimal ethical responsibility from the perpetrator, which justifies suffering as a means to an end – be that end reconciliation or nation-state sovereignty. In *The Rain Ascends,* of course, unending faith in the humanity of the perpetrator is debunked, proven to be not only the cause of more stress and harm for the survivor, but also a space in which the perpetrator can, aided and abetted by forgiveness, commit further violence and harm. This warning should hit particularly close to home in the contexts of the TRC of Canada given that, although Prime Minister Justin Trudeau has asked for forgiveness, the state itself has made no serious moves to address the fundamental issues of settler colonialism that undergird residential schools and the ongoing discrepancies between settler and Indigenous communities. With these issues off the table, pursuing forgiveness risks inflicting further damage on survivors and their families.

Left unaddressed, without due care to its settler colonial implications, and without detailed feedback from community, the default for forgiveness is not a choice but a demand. Survivors are expected to take up this demand and suffer through it, ostensibly for their own benefit. Indeed, because of the nature of TRCs, and because of the deep and complex ways in which forgiveness has been folded into that system, forgiveness is part of the model that Canada and Indigenous peoples have inherited. Ignoring forgiveness or striking it from the agenda risks generating an unattended space in which it is tacitly proliferated as something that is natural, inevitable, and universal. *Medicine Walk, The Rain Ascends,* and "Queen of the North" provide spaces in which to challenge and think critically about (un)forgiveness as it echoes out of the TRC and Canada's own short history of reconciliation – not to dismiss it or to convince survivors of its banality, but to engage with it carefully and critically, placing in the forefront, always, truth and the right to refuse.

Conclusion

"Shallow Reconciliation" and the Indigenous Future Imaginary

> When it comes to reconciliation and working with Indigenous leadership, there has been over 150 years of disappointment in British Columbia ... I'm not the first person to stand before you and disappoint Indigenous people.
>
> – JOHN HORGAN, PREMIER OF BRITISH COLUMBIA[1]

> I heard a sound like an echo turned inside out.
>
> – CHERIE DIMALINE, *THE MARROW THIEVES*[2]

On the penultimate page of her 2017 dystopian novel *The Marrow Thieves,* Métis author and editor Cherie Dimaline evokes the sound of an echo as a means to capture the electricity that emanates from the reunification of two residential school survivors. The scene is significant for a number of reasons, not least because it contains the only instance of the word "reconciliation" in a novel in which one of the primary plot points is the return of residential schools in an apocalyptic future. This particular passage is also significant, however, because of the aural imagery that Dimaline builds around the word, like whispers of scaffolding that direct and inflect readers' understanding of survivor experiences.

Before they were forced into residential schools by Recruiters – Dimaline's dystopian articulation of the Indian agent – the two men in this scene, Miigwans (Miig) and Isaac, were a happily married couple. Flashbacks throughout the novel make clear the love and commitment that the two shared, which makes the scene of their reunion that much more moving. While establishing their love for one another, however, Dimaline also makes clear that before they are reunited both men understand the other to be dead – killed in the residential schools that stole them away from one another. As a means to memorialize Isaac, Miig even wears an amulet that he believes holds his husband's remains around his neck. He refers to this amulet as his heart, gesturing to the embodied grief and melancholia that still permeate Isaac's loss.

The representation of sound that Dimaline builds around this single instance of the word "reconciliation," conjugated in the below quoted passage as a present participle, is guttural and provocative. It speaks to the intensity of being reunited with a loved one who is presumed lost; a family member who is actively being grieved and is now, for all intents and purposes, returned from the dead:

> [Isaac] slowed to a walk now, the welcoming party and the newcomers falling in behind. He slowed all his movements, as if focusing his eyes and *reconciling* what they saw took motion from his muscles. *I heard a sound like an echo turned inside out*, and then Miig, who had been standing still, trying to see, to understand, under the blue smoke of moonlight, finally took a step forward. [emphasis added][3]

"*Like an echo turned inside out*." As an activation site for close reading, this phrase offers a poetic moment of reflection from which to contemplate reconciliation as it resonates out of the TRC and into what Jason Edward Lewis terms the "Indigenous future imaginary."[4] The echo that Dimaline describes here is not a reconciliation of words, nor of policies; nor is it a reconciliation of settlers and Indigenous peoples. What is at stake in this single instance of the word is a reconciliation of capital "T" Truths: of knowing as certain the genocide inflicted by residential schools while at the same time being held in the gaze of a loved one who was forced into those schools. It is a reconciliation built on love and care and grief. It is a reconciliation founded in ontological dissonance perpetuated under settler colonialism. But, perhaps most importantly, the echo with which Dimaline ends her novel is a reconciliation of survivors. Outside the colonial gaze, away from the multifarious meanings that have been layered on the word in the wake of the TRC, reconciliation as a future for Indigenous peoples is imagined as a reflection of the love with which they will rebuild in the wake of the settler apocalypse.

As it is in our present times, reconciliation in Dimaline's future imaginary is fraught and often dangerous territory. Indeed, outside of Indigenous relations, as represented in Miig and Isaac's reunion, the processes of reconciliation in *The Marrow Thieves* are most often represented as not only futile, but as a visceral threat to the lives of the Indigenous characters. The action in *The Marrow Thieves* is told primarily through Francis (known as French). His "coming-to story" is a cautionary tale against reconciliatory processes and the hope for improved Indigenous-settler relations.[5] Right at the beginning of the novel, just when he is on the cusp of meeting Miig and the other Indigenous characters that will form his new family, we learn that French lost his father to settlers when, "in a last-ditch effort to talk to the Governors in the capital," he, and members of the Indigenous council, are disappeared.[6] The word "disappeared" is the most appropriate choice here, as it reflects the disappearances in Latin America; disappearances that led to that foundational TRC in Chile. Like those individuals, French's father and his comrades are simply gone after this meeting, leaving no word for their friends or families.

Closer to the end of the novel, French learns that it was Miig that led French's father and the others to the capital. At this point, Miig shares with French what he knows about that fateful day, explicitly connecting the dots between reconciliatory negotiations and the loss of Indigenous diplomats:

> They [the Indigenous diplomats] had this crazy notion that there was goodness left, that someone, somewhere, would see just how insane this whole school thing was. That they could dialogue. That they could explain the system had to die and a new one be built in its place. Like that wasn't scarier to those still in the system than all the dreamlessness and desert wastelands in the world.[7]

In a reconciliation reading of *The Marrow Thieves,* this is one of the most important passages in the entire novel. I say this because it most explicitly outlines the hegemony of capitalism and settler colonialism and the futility of state-centred reconciliation within it. What Dimaline makes clear here, is that settler colonialism is not simply a way of being that settlers struggle to find an escape hatch from. Rather, more devastatingly, it is a structure that those same people do not want to escape – even as it is a harbinger of the apocalypse. The settler disavowal that Dimaline foregrounds here, in the

Marxist sense of the word, is the very function of ideology: to obscure the alienation inflicted by the capitalist/colonialist systems beneath a perpetually deferred promise of a fulfilled self: "they do this, as Marx puts it, "without being aware of it."[8]

It is against this ideological backdrop that Dimaline sets up her critique of what she identifies elsewhere as "shallow reconciliation." In an interview with Trevor Corkum of *49th Shelf*, she defines shallow reconciliation as settlers expressing remorse and guilt while at the same time refusing to acknowledge that "the Western way of thinking about our world is a broken theory, that Indigenous Traditional Knowledge is vital to any forward movement."[9] Shallow reconciliation is an apology or reparation that never moves beyond the cosmetic. It does nothing to address, for instance, the racism and white supremacy that allows white settlers to go free for the murder of Indigenous youth; shallow reconciliation does not consider the return of land as a viable form of restitution. Shallow reconciliation is sixty-seven long-term drinking water advisories for Indigenous communities across Canada; shallow reconciliation is the gap between "nation-to-nation" dialogues and the continued development of colonial state energy infrastructure. Shallow reconciliation is an echo of settler colonialism filtered through the theatre of regret. For Dimaline, without addressing the structures through which we understand Indigenous-settler relations, the events of racism and settler colonialism will continue to make themselves known, both in the present as well as in our shared futures.

Returning to *The Marrow Thieves*, the disappearance of the Indigenous diplomats helps to clarify that shallow reconciliation, read here as dialogue between Indigenous peoples and settlers, is a complete non-starter given that that system remains premised on saving and restructuring the Western world; in fact, it is not just a non-starter, it is the beginning of the path toward a new genocide. French's father and the others go to the capital with the hope that they can convince settlers to see that the colonial system is broken. But life without that framework is, for those settlers, more frightening than the apocalypse itself. What is required for Indigenous healing in *The Marrow Thieves* then, is not dialogue, or recognition, or any other articulation of liberalism, but radical dissent and the collapse of the existing system. Glen Coulthard articulates that change this way: "without such a massive transformation in the political economy of contemporary settler-colonialism, any efforts to rebuild [Indigenous] nations will remain parasitic on capitalism, and thus on the perpetual exploitation of our lands and labour."[10]

The Marrow Thieves provides a provocative site through which to critique shallow reconciliation. It also affords us, as Daniel Heath Justice puts it, the opportunity to "imagine otherwise"[11] – beyond the performance of regret and the Indigenous-settler dialogues that *The Marrow Thieves* critiques.

Before turning to *The Marrow Thieves* in depth, however, I would like to examine some of the fallout from reconciliation in the years following the release of *Honouring the Truth, Reconciling for the Future: Summary of the Final Report of the Truth and Reconciliation Commission of Canada,* and the conflicting meaning that has been inscribed on reconciliation as it echoes out of Canada and its settler colonial contexts.[12] Locating the TRC of Canada one final time, within the tension between the global and the local, provides further critical ground through which to interpret the echo that resonates throughout *The Marrow Thieves,* and to read reconciliation from the Indigenous future imaginary.

Reconciliation: The Global and the Local

As I hope I have demonstrated in this book, "reconciliation" is a troubling word. And Canada has its own specific troubles. Writing on the prevalence of reparations politics that emerged out of the Cold War, Roy Brooks explains that "we have clearly entered what can be called the 'Age of Apology.'"[13] In the Canadian context in particular, Brooks may well have chosen the most apt phrase for this country's current epoch. As Mitch Miyagawa has pointed out (with reference to the numerous apologies offered in the country since 2006), Canada is indeed a sorry state.[14] Still, the seemingly perpetual repetitions of this age's core vernacular (acknowledgment, apology, redress, forgiveness, and reconciliation – the concepts from which I have structured the chapters of this book) may have been repeated so much as to evacuate those words of the meaning inscribed on them during previous TRCs.[15]

In a 2016 tweet, Anishinaabe author and comedian Ryan McMahon perhaps most succinctly summed up the naïveté with which the word "reconciliation" has been inflected in Canada: "The Reconciliation Industry that is building in Canada looks more like a basic life skills program. 'Be nice to each other. Don't be racist.'"[16] In *Dancing on Our Turtle's Back,* Leanne Betasamosake Simpson provides another biting critique of Canadian reconciliation politics, this time pointing to the mechanics of Canadian regret: "In the eyes of liberalism," she writes, "the historical 'wrong' has now been 'righted' and further transformation is not needed, since the historic situation has been remedied."[17] McMahon and Simpson leave us with a number of important questions about the theatre of regret as it unfolds in the settler state: Does reconciliation, as it was articulated out of South America and South Africa, still hold meaning in Canada? Are settler Canadians able to hear what the word once meant in other political contexts? Is structural change in Canada possible through reconciliation? What kind of reconciliation legacy will emanate out of this country? And what will this legacy mean for future applications of the TRC model?

I follow from thinkers such as McMahon and Simpson when I argue that reconciliation, stripped of its political resonance as it reverberates through settler state machinery, is at risk of becoming a floating signifier: a sign without a referent.[18] Sadly, however, this is not where we began. The original call for reconciliation came directly from residential school survivors and their families in the form of the Indian Residential Schools Settlement Agreement (IRSSA), ratified in May 2006. Billed as "a holistic and comprehensive response to the Indian residential school legacy,"[19] the IRSSA included the Common Experience Payment (CEP), the Independent Assessment Process (IAP), the aforementioned Truth and Reconciliation Commission (TRC), Health and Healing Services for survivors and their families, and $20 million for the Commemoration Fund for national and community commemorative projects.[20] As a community-driven initiative, reconciliation held the potential for social justice and a new way of conceiving Indigenous-settler relations.

Yet, at the time I am writing this conclusion, "reconciliation" echoes most loudly not in the mouths of survivors or their families, but from the pulpits and chambers of settler politicians as what Tom Clark, Ravi de Costa, and Sarah Maddison identify as a "regulatory ideal" – as opposed to an appeal for truth and structural change.[21] State-centred reconciliation in Canada, as McMahon points out, is all too often a discourse of "being nice" with little to no mention of structural violence, land rights, or Indigenous self-determination and sovereignty.

While it has been mobilized to address historical injustice and political transition in places such as Chile and South Africa, the success of reconciliation and the TRC model on an international level is contingent on its local adoption and adaptation. Throughout this book, I have argued against the TRC as a template. Chile and South Africa each developed and refined a truth and reconciliation process out of political circumstances that differ radically in both form and content from one another and from the TRC of

Canada. Rendering a one-to-one application out of these practices is fraught at best and dangerous at worst.

Of course, there are benefits to adopting an internationally recognized conflict resolution model. Ratifying a TRC brings with it a certain political heft and the potential to illuminate violences that have been relegated to the substratum of national politics. That said, the translation of an international model into local contexts also risks eliding key issues specific to the injured parties: in Canada's case, issues related to land and sovereignty. The tension between the global and the local thus necessitates an ever-vigilant approach to the TRC model and the implementation of reconciliation. In order to be a tool levied against power, reconciliation must be a localized process informed by the specific communities and territories it claims to redress.

Unfortunately, however, it is not clear that this is what is happening in Canada, a country which, at least from the top down, maintains a very colonial reconciliation practice dependent largely on national diplomacy anchored in the salt water thesis. Indeed, despite the work of survivors, as well as Murray Sinclair and his commissioners, many Canadians still believe that the TRC of Canada is a government instrument rather than a judicially determined survivor initiative. Reframing reconciliation and objecting to its translation into state vernacular is thus a necessary part of the work ahead.

The TRC has been explicit in how this reframing should take place. From its own emphasis on local practices, *Honouring the Truth, Reconciling for the Future* gestures to two separate and distinct forms of reconciliation: state-centred reconciliation and Indigenous-centred reconciliation. Both must be held as equally possible futures for the TRC and, as such, both must be taken seriously. The two definitions of reconciliation are not mutually exclusive, but they do exist on a continuum, with plenty of room for movement between them. The difference between the two far ends of the continuum, however, should be self-explanatory: one belongs to the settler colonial state, while the other is collectively maintained and stewarded by Indigenous peoples. The TRC itself emphasizes this distinction and cautions against falling into a state-centred demarcation of reconciliation:

> What is clear to this Commission is that Aboriginal peoples and the Crown have very different and conflicting views on what reconciliation is and how it is best achieved. The Government of Canada appears to believe that reconciliation entails Aboriginal peoples' acceptance of the reality and validity of Crown sovereignty and parliamentary supremacy, in order to allow the government to get on with business. Aboriginal people, on the other hand,

see reconciliation as an opportunity to affirm their own sovereignty and return to the "partnership" ambitions they held after Confederation.[22]

On the whole, land, sovereignty, and self-determination are the issues that will define the future of reconciliation in Canada. In state-centred reconciliation, or what I am calling here, borrowing from Dimaline, "shallow reconciliation," the colonial government maintains its authority over land and continues with the business of colonial nation making, including, of course, the right to name (and preclude) its territories and citizens; on the other path, however, Indigenous peoples reclaim power and control over their own lands, cultures, and identities, and the state is no longer the envelope in which rights, territory, and belonging are contained or guaranteed.

Despite warnings from the TRC, however, since the release of its final report we've seen Canada moving toward state-centred reconciliation, evoking the term "reconciliation" as a means to assert sovereignty and control over Indigenous territories. In British Columbia, for instance, Premier John Horgan demonstrated that "reconciliation" had indeed become a floating signifier in government vernacular. On December 12, 2017, Horgan announced that his government would be proceeding with the Site C project, a hydroelectric dam on the Peace River in northeastern British Columbia. The traditional territories of seven First Nations cover the Peace region and two Treaty 8 First Nations had already initiated legal claims against Horgan's predecessors. Indigenous resistance to the project was and is strong, thoughtful, and sovereign. The area to be flooded has been inhabited by the aforementioned Indigenous peoples for over ten thousand years, and the land continues to be used for medicines, hunting, trapping, and ceremony.[23] These territories are not only historically important; they also continue to be used and lived on, drawing out a long chain of continuity that readily establishes Indigenous sovereignty, particularly when interpreted in the light of the *Tsilhqot' in v. British Columbia* decision:[24] "We're still here," Chief Roland Willson of the West Moberly First Nation told reporters, "we're still using the valley."[25]

In 2016, Amnesty International released a report asserting that the Site C project threatens the human rights of Indigenous peoples.[26] According to that report, "any advantages claimed for Site C have to be considered in light of the otherwise avoidable harm that would be done to the cultures, livelihoods, health, and safety of Indigenous peoples."[27] Because Site C represents an ongoing articulation of settler colonialism, particularly *terra nullius* (the erasure of Indigenous presence from Indigenous land), the very definition of reconciliation is also at stake here. Chief Lynette Tsakoza of the Prophet River First Nation writes that, "the damage to the Peace River is not yet irreversible. Stopping Site C is a perfect opportunity to demonstrate to all Canadians that the government takes reconciliation seriously."[28]

It is difficult to assert that Horgan takes reconciliation seriously, however. Or, if he does, that the gravity has any impact on his politics. To be fair, Horgan has been vocal about his party's support for Indigenous peoples. He was the first premier to publicly acknowledge that the province of British Columbia is on unceded territory, and the province was the first to pass the United Nations Declaration on the Rights of Indigenous Peoples (UNDRIP).[29] That said, in his Site C press release, Horgan leaves the idea of unceded territory to the political past and positions "progress" as an inevitability – an inevitability that has worked, and will continue to work, at the expense of Indigenous peoples: "When it comes to reconciliation and working with Indigenous leadership," Horgan told the press in 2017, "there has been over 150 years of disappointment in British Columbia ... I'm not the first person to stand before you and disappoint Indigenous people."[30] In this statement, the premier positions reconciliation as a victim of the inexorable growth of settler colonial state infrastructure. By connecting his government's failure to 150 years of settler colonialism, Horgan makes explicit in a few sentences what Indigenous scholars have been saying about state-centred reconciliation since the onset of the discourse: that it is a "pacifying discourse" operating to "absolve the ... government's responsibility to transform the colonial relationship between Canada and Indigenous nations."[31]

Horgan's Site C decision is just one example illustrating how Canada's definition of reconciliation has broken almost entirely from the TRC genealogy. In Canada, the party that wields the knife also wants to administer the bandage. This is new terrain for TRCs, and it should be regarded with steadfast suspicion. For one thing, shallow reconciliation presents a serious challenge to reconciliation historians and theorists because, as a template, TRCs are not well-equipped to contend with Indigenous sovereignty – they are, in fact, anti-sovereignty initiatives aimed at deconstructing borders (both emotional and physical) and foregrounding common ground between disparate groups and across party lines. That TRCs run *counter* to sovereignty is one of the reasons we do not see their rise as an international movement until the end of the Cold War, when *realpolitik* measures began to relax.

It is imperative, therefore, that we first acknowledge that the reconciliation inherited by Canada and Indigenous peoples from its predecessors is ill-equipped to facilitate movement toward Indigenous-centred, or deep, reconciliation. It is also imperative that we insist on a reconciliation that centres Indigenous perspectives and creates space for Indigenous voices by quieting settler colonial attempts to define the work – an act which only furthers, discursively, the legacies of *terra nullius*.[32]

From this perspective, transitional justice, with its roots in the International Military Tribunal at Nuremberg, is just another distraction for the local contexts of this TRC and Indigenous-centred applications of reconciliation.[33] As I have argued in Chapter 1, one of the primary differences that separates the TRC of Canada from its predecessors in Chile and South Africa is the fact that there has been no concrete change in government from the period of the genocide (in Canada's case, the time when residential schools were in operation) to the period of the apology. Conservative and Liberal parties have taken turns holding power from Confederation in 1867 to the present day. Both have offered separate apologies to residential school surviours at different periods, and both have carried on with colonial nation building despite this acknowledgment of and apology for past actions. In both Chile and South Africa, reconciliation was a handmaiden to massive political change: the overthrow of the totalitarian rule of Pinochet and of the apartheid politics of the National Party, respectively. In Canada, however, reconciliation seems to mean politics as usual.

While there is perhaps some argument to be made about "transition" and the ways in which white settler Canadians have shifted their perspectives on Indigenous peoples since the TRC, we cannot ignore the fact that the colonial policies and power structures that undergirded historical Canada remain, at their root, the same today as they were when the residential school system began. Indeed, "there are more First Nations kids in child welfare today than at the height of residential schools."[34] The policies might not be quite as explicitly racist now, or they may be performed in ways that obscure their colonial intents, but it is no less the case that Canada's government continues to operate so as to dispossess Indigenous peoples of their lands and resources, in part via control over the definition of "Indian," as determined in the *Indian Act*. Reconciliation in Canada is not transitional justice; it is, at best, as Ravi de Costa defines it, a "discursive lever," which is to say it is a rhetorical tool for fine-tuning the status quo for its appearance in the theatre of regret.[35]

Again, pursuing a transitional justice model in Canada distracts from Indigenous sovereignty and self-determination. If not treated as a unique, independent commission, the TRC of Canada will have been simply procedural, intent more on reproducing the genealogy of the TRC than serving local communities. Anishinaabe Elder, writer, and residential school survivor Fred Kelly argues, "We must ... insist that the Aboriginal peoples have meaningful participation in the design, administration, and evaluation of the reconciliation process so that it is based on their local culture and language."[36] This may seem a rather obvious point to make, but Kelly demonstrates deep insight here by insisting on the importance of Indigenous involvement in the ongoing definition of reconciliation. Part of what makes the TRC process so powerful, but also so potentially dangerous, is the political and ideological baggage it carries with it as a transnational project. In fact, the excitement and perceived success of a TRC can be enough to override common sense, leading to unwieldy situations in which, for instance, perpetrators are allowed to enforce their own sentences.[37]

If reconciliation is going to succeed in Canada, the history of settler colonialism must be leveraged – that is, it must be mobilized as a wedge to crack open Canada's tightly sealed racist past – and simultaneously undone in order to generate a reconciliation that directly serves Indigenous sovereignty and land rights. In other words, once its use value as a transnational politic has been cashed, which it arguably has been as I write this, reconciliation must be taken out of the arms of history and put into the hands of the community, to be shaped into an instrument that not only addresses the past but also, significantly, alters the material present and futures of Indigenous peoples. As it stands, reconciliation is at serious risk of being entirely recuperated into the Canadian state as yet another fallacious example of our benevolence, tolerance, and accountability.

Honouring the Truth makes explicit the way in which reconciliation in Canada must move forward, by putting the concept in the hands of Indigenous peoples. But it is also clear that the path it recommends will be difficult, if not impossible, to traverse under the obdurate influence of settler colonialism. This is, of course, because certitude in the superiority of Western ways of knowing continues to guide the actions and politics of the Canadian state and its citizens. But it is also because the legacy of reconciliation fits too easily into the engine of settler colonialism, adding fuel to a fire that has always justified its actions by promising – spuriously – to improve the lives of Indigenous peoples, whether through the "gift of civilization," the saving grace of faith, or the grand utility of progress. Packaged by the state as a "solution" for Indigenous peoples, reconciliation is only another recipe for colonial snake oil. Indeed, while shallow reconciliation might appear, on the surface, to be a much gentler approach to settler colonialism than say the

Indian Act or the *White Paper*, without structural change behind it, it is still settler colonialism: it bolsters nationalism, legitimates dispossession, promotes assimilation, and reimagines politics from a universalistic notion of perpetual peace that flattens difference and presupposes Western metaphysics.

In order to overturn shallow reconciliation then, we must be willing to re-imagine what reconciliation is and whom it serves. We must be willing to unravel the genealogy of the TRC and look toward the future of Indigenous-settler relations in Canada, asking "Reconciliation for whom? Reconciliation of what?"

In what follows, I return to *The Marrow Thieves* to provide a tentative reading of shallow reconciliation, looking more closely at the image of "the echo turned inside out." In projecting reconciliation into a dystopic future, I argue, Dimaline generates a critical space through which to consider the fallout of reconciliation as impacted by scarcity economics and the colonial politics that are (re)enacted through them. Or, in other words, as a future projection of Canada's present-day reconciliation politics, *The Marrow Thieves* offers an instrument through which to hear those politics as what Gayatri Spivak identifies as "the *a-venir* of a history not written," that is the forthcoming of a past in the future tense, an echo.[38]

Ultimately, what the future imaginary provides are the hermeneutics that make visible the colonial ideologies of shallow reconciliation. Doing so clears the epistemological space necessary to imagine reconciliation otherwise and to project Indigenous worlds into futures where settler colonialism is not guaranteed.

Reconciliation and the Indigenous Future Imaginary

To begin, however, what can speculative fiction (sf) such as *The Marrow Thieves* tell us about reconciliation? For one, reconciliation itself, although the prefix hints at a past – a non-existent past in which Indigenous peoples and settlers enjoyed an equal playing field – is about imagining the future: a future where relations between disparate parties are renewed, or, as stated in Schedule 'N' of the TRC mandate, where "the events of the past [are] behind us."[39] Shallow reconciliation, however, is less of a future than an inexorable continuation of the colonial present. Indeed, Indigenous sf scholar Dallas Hunt points out that the future imagined in Canada's reconciliation politics always already begins from the continued existence of settler colonialism and the ongoing survival of whiteness. Within the frameworks of what Hunt identifies as "the hermeneutics of reconciliation," settlers perceive Indigenous peoples as being willing to "grant their claims to land, and even their Indigeneity" to them.[40] This is a failing, not of Indigenous peoples, who are excluded from how the nation state imagines futurity, but of settler imaginations, which are unable to conceive of worlds beyond the ever-receding horizon of settler colonial ideology.[41] If reconciliation is a discourse of the future then, in the hands of the settler state, it is an echo of the same old colonial politics, which centre whiteness, perpetuate *terra nullius*, and reinforce the status quo.

Against settler narratives of Indigenous erasure, the Indigenous future imaginary looks beyond the hermeneutics of reconciliation to imagine worlds in which settler futurity is not guaranteed and where reconciliation is configured around the downfall of settler colonialism – as, for instance, in Nalo Hopkinson's *Brown Girl in the Ring*. According to Hunt, reconfiguring reconciliation as an Indigenous futurity does not "require the literal death of people who currently inhabit the position of settler, but the total transformation of existing relations ... between Indigenous peoples and settlers toward something as yet unimagined that would ensure the thriving of Indigenous lands and lives."[42] In other words, Indigenous reconciliation requires the creative labour of what Daniel Justice calls "imagining otherwise," the act of articulating futures that centre Indigenous relationality and "consider the radical possibilities of Indigenous futurities, broadly conceived."[43]

For Hunt, as with a number of the theorists that engage Indigenous futurisms, Indigenous sf creates flourishing Indigenous presence in the face of deleterious settler ideologies – including reconciliation – and centres Indigenous law, culture, politics, protocols, and tradition in the process.[44] According to Justice, the stories told in Indigenous sf "carry the past forward. They give [Indigenous peoples] a future, even if it's only an imagined one." Justice goes on to demonstrate exactly why imagining otherwise is important for Indigenous peoples: "without that imagined possibility, it's all too easy to believe that we don't belong here, and that's a road to a very frightening place indeed."[45] For both Hunt and Justice, Indigenous sf holds the power of manifesting possible futures and therefore generating Indigenous hope in the present, particularly in the face of hegemonic colonial politics and policies.

There is a rich tradition of scholarship to draw from in a study of Indigenous sf and a number of authors, aside from Hunt and Justice, have inflected my reading of *The Marrow Thieves*. The non-linear relationships between past, present, and future, as represented by these thinkers, are particularly instructive in unpacking Dimaline's novel. Grace Dillon, who coined the phrase "Indigenous futurisms," argues that when taken up by Indigenous authors, sf has the "capacity to envision Native futures, Indigenous hopes, and dreams recovered by rethinking the past in a new framework."[46] In Dillon's sense of the genre, sf is a means of amplifying Indigenous ways of being while revitalizing Indigenous storytelling via new genres and media (including virtual and augmented realities, video games, video, and film). As she puts it, "Indigenous Futurisms offer new ways of reading our own ancient natures" and, as such, they can empower new generations of Indigenous storytellers to share their stories and worldviews.[47] Kristina Baudemann agrees, adding to Dillon's analysis that Indigenous futurisms also provide the means to reframe colonialism and, through that reframing, enact resurgence: "by revisiting different aspects of colonization in their Indigenous futurisms ... North American Indigenous artists turn the causes for trauma into building blocks for stories about Indigenous futures."[48]

The future also provides a productive space from which to critique the past while throwing into relief present-day colonial violence. Indigenous critics such as Lou Cornum and Lindsay Nixon illustrate the potential of Indigenous futurisms to interrogate what it means to be Indigenous in a settler colonial present and to push back against the claustrophobic hegemony of the settler state. Cornum argues that sf resonates so deeply with many Indigenous authors because it provides the opportunity to "revers[e] the telescope's gaze and to reassess who is exploring whom."[49] They go on to elaborate that there is a deep critical component to Indigenous sf, which calls into question who has the privilege of writing about the future.[50] Tied to this privilege is a critique of technology and sf's historical relationship with resource extraction: "Extractive and exploitative endeavours are just one mark of the settler death drive, which Indigenous futurism seeks to overcome by imagining different ways of relating to notions of progress and civilization."[51]

Similarly, for Nixon, Indigenous futurisms illustrate the contemporary and ongoing apocalypse of settler colonialism, as well as Indigenous resistance to what they call "the dystopic now":

> The future imaginary and its catalogue of science fictive imageries affords Indigenous artists a creative space to respond to the dystopian now ... Indigenous artists have no problem portraying possible undesirable futures wherein colonial capitalist greed has resulted in the subjugation of life within all creation, because these narratives are evocative of our known

> realities ... we are living in a dystopian settler-occupied oligarchy fueled by resource extraction and environmental contamination, completely alternative to our traditional ways of being and knowing.[52]

For Cornum and Nixon, Indigenous futurisms offer the opportunity to critique the ongoing violences of settler colonialism while providing Indigenous authors, artists, and critics a platform to imagine resistance, resurgence, and the possibility of alternative realities through the past and the present. Or, as Erica Violet Lee puts it in "Reconciling in the Apocalypse," "in knowing the histories of our relations and of this land, we find the knowledge to recreate all that our worlds would've been, if not for the interruption of colonization."[53]

Lee captures the Indigenous future imaginary in how she entreats us to think Indigenous futures beyond, around, and through the rupture of colonialism. For Jason Edward Lewis, speculative fiction provides unique opportunities for Indigenous peoples to claim future spaces by calling back to the past and building worlds independent of settler colonialism. According to Lewis, who works across fiction, theory, programming, and new media studies, the Indigenous future imaginary provides opportunities for Indigenous peoples "to centre our practice in the cultural discourse and practices that frame it, and create a distinct future where we are not dependent on the gatekeepers to open the gates – not required, even, to storm those gates, or go around them. It has allowed us to create a distinct future in which we strike out on our own, into new territory."[54]

As a theoretical ground, Lewis defines the Indigenous future imaginary in relation to Charles Taylor's social imaginary. It is here that his thought diverges somewhat from Dillon's, insofar as Lewis attempts to articulate the future as an unfinished social construction, rather than a genre:

> One can think of the future imaginary as a distinct part of the current "social imaginary," described by Charles Taylor as "the way ordinary people 'imagine' their social surroundings ... not expressed in theoretical terms, but carried in images, stories, and legends." It forms the popular vocabulary that we use to describe what we see when we see the future.[55]

Working from Taylor, Lewis argues that the future is brought into being through a collective imagining articulated out of the past and present. What the future becomes then is, at least in part, a reflection of what we imagine it to be. In Lewis's conception, our current future imaginary was primary formulated in the 1950s and '60s, by authors such as Jules Verne and H.G. Welles:

"then we had popular culture renditions of it – *Star Wars, Blade Runner,* and *Alien* – in the '70s and the '80s, but we haven't seen anything new since then; we've just seen iterations of the same visions."[56] These iterative re-imaginings of future states, built out of discourses of power and dystopia that centre male whiteness, have deeply informed the ways in which the public understands the future as such. Because of the weight they hold in the zeitgeist, these imaginaries have thus also coded the ways in which our shared futures continue to be manifested and played out in the larger colonial project.

As is further evident from the examples Lewis cites, Indigenous peoples have traditionally not been included in the future imaginary. Settler colonialism works at the expense of Indigenous futures, relegating Indigenous peoples to the past via the myth of the dead or dying Indian, and by positioning modernity and Indigeneity as mutually exclusive terms.[57] However, and this is at the core of Lewis's methodology as a researcher and developer, by bringing Indigenous peoples together to imagine futures outside of manifest destiny and *terra nullius* there lies the potential not just to imagine otherwise, but to manifest Indigenous future states. Lewis's conception of Indigenous sf is thus premised less on dismantling settler colonialism than it is on making space for Indigenous futures as extensions of traditional relationships to land, language, culture, law, and politics. Indigenous peoples "are now turning towards claiming territory in the future imaginary," Lewis writes, "or better yet, creating our own.[58] Via the future imaginary, Indigenous authors and artists are undoing the colonial storytelling that has, for too long, centred whiteness on the horizon. In doing so they are also projecting Indigenous peoples and ideas into the future to claim that space for the Indigenous peoples of yesterday, today, and tomorrow.

The auditory figuration of the echo, I argue, provides an evocative figuration through which to further consider the Indigenous future imaginary. In how it bends past and future, and, in the process, "hybridiz[es] the present,"[59] the future imaginary illustrates Indigenous futurity not as a linear projection but as a folded chronology, existing, as Mark Rifkin puts it, "beyond settler time."[60] That is to say, in the Indigenous future imaginary the echo of the past is in front of the future; it leads and defines those contexts, rather than providing a backdrop for present-day decisions.

Dennis Runnels, a Nez Percé linguist, helps to clarify this point, illustrating how time is differently spatialized within Indigenous worldviews:

> Europeans believe in progress. You say you leave the past behind, you see the future before you and you move on into the future. In our

> understanding that's a fallacy. The past in not behind! The past is right before us, right under us. We stand on the bones of our ancestors, on the dead bodies of plants and animals that went before. Even the buildings we see right in front of us are from the past. Everything we see is from the past. It's right there in front of us.[61]

Here, Runnels illustrates the ways in which the past always already echoes into the present and inflects the future. Understood not as a linear model, then, but as a "flat circle" the Indigenous future imaginary attunes us to the past and present as much as it does to speculative futures, providing for unique insight into a wide spectrum of chronologies.[62] Elizabeth Lapensée also reflects on this idea in her definition of Indigenous futurisms:

> Indigenous Futurisms recognizes space–time as simultaneously past, present, and future, and therefore futurism is as much about the future as it is about right now. In my work, it means telling alternate histories, dreaming about liquid technology, imagining a future where unceded territories are taken back.[63]

Turing to *The Marrow Thieves,* then, to read Dimaline's work as an echo of reconciliation, is to say that it reflects back at us, from the Indigenous future imaginary, a history of settler colonialism, including shallow reconciliation. In this sense, the return of residential schools in *The Marrow Thieves* is just as much about the precarity of our contemporary TRC moment, articulated out of the theatre of regret, as it is about a future dystopia brought on by resource scarcity. *The Marrow Thieves* makes the guts of our present moment – steeped as it is in the age of apology – audible in ways that are unavailable when heard only through the technologies of our dystopic now. Turned inside out, that is inflected through the Indigenous future imaginary, Dimaline casts light on state-centred reconciliation as deferred colonial violence and makes space for Indigenous futurities by laying waste to colonial systems.

The Marrow Thieves: Reading Reconciliation through the Future Tense

Set in the near future, sometime after 2050, Dimaline's novel describes a world that, due to climate change brought on by industrial capitalism, has become nearly uninhabitable.[64] In this future, the polar ice caps have melted and the global population is being driven south in pursuit of land and potable water. The clamour for resources in the wake of this apocalypse amplifies present-day settler colonialism as nation-states, now with renewed vigour, violently uproot Indigenous peoples from their lands in order to make space for the wealthy and the white. Miig recounts the onset of the apocalypse to French and the other members of the small group that are moving north in search of a home amongst Indigenous kin: "half the population was lost in the disaster and from the disease that spread from too many corpses and not enough graves."[65]

Settler greed, amplified by the lack of resources, is at the centre of *The Marrow Thieves'* plot, and Dimaline exploits that greed in order to illustrate the existential threat that scarcity economics represents for Indigenous peoples, past, present, and future. However, she does not stop at natural resources, at least the ones we typically think can be extracted. The twist that she offers here, turning resource extraction inward to Indigenous bodies, plays a large role in the success of the book, not only because of the creativity of the trope, but because of the deep socio-political resonances it connotes. That twist is this: among all of the environmental changes that have occurred in Dimaline's novel, settlers have also lost the ability to dream. French identifies this loss, with reference to Albert Camus's titular novel, as the plague: "That's what they were calling the dreamlessness when it started, a plague of madness."[66] Madness because, without dreams – without the promise of settler futurity – there is no lifeline for settlers to anchor a sense of self. The plague in *The Marrow Thieves* therefore not only represents the demise of settler futurity, it is also an indication of the decline of settler colonialism.

While it is never directly explained in the novel, there are many possible interpretations for Dimaline's choice to disconnect settlers from dreams and the unconscious, one of them being that the dream of progress (that ever-burning engine of colonialism) has died with the apocalypse, and with it settlers' ability to imagine or project a future. Fredric Jameson also postulates a theory we might draw from in unpacking Dimaline's trope: in *Postmodernism, or, The Cultural Logic of Late Capitalism,* he argues that late capitalism itself will lead to the death of dreams, inasmuch as capitalism's most consistent logic is the materialization of desire, a perennial unearthing that pushes the limits of the psychic apparatus to such a degree that the unconscious "finally rise[s] dripping and convulsive into the light of day."[67] In other words, for Jameson capitalism renders Freud's psychic mechanism inside out, giving the unconscious free reign as a monstrous externality. Applying this theory to *The Marrow*

Thieves, then, is to see the upshot of late capitalism, not only in the unavoidable (yet disavowed) destruction of the natural environment, but also in the erosion of the psychic apparatus that fuels that destruction.

The reasons for the plague in *The Marrow Thieves,* however, are ultimately of little consequence. Its outcome is where Dimaline most wants to draw our attention. Indeed, settlers losing their dreams doesn't mean that capitalism and colonialism (which are inextricably intertwined in *The Marrow Thieves*) suddenly grind to a halt. Rather, true to the history of settler colonialism, it means that efforts are redoubled to find fuel for the machine. When non-Indigenous people discover that Indigenous peoples have maintained their connection to dreams while the rest of humanity has lost it, there is a renewed push to commoditize Indigenous cultures and bodies. As Miig tells French and the rest of the group, "they [white settlers] are motivated by the need to be able to survive. And they see that solution in us."[68]

With renewed obsession in Indigenous culture, settlers soon discover that dreams can be extracted from Indigenous bone marrow and they work toward producing a vaccine for dreamlessness. Miig, passing these stories on to the younger generation, describes these events bluntly, using language that connects the extraction of dreams to the removal of water and bitumen, amongst other things, from traditional territories: "they found a way to siphon the dreams right out of our bones."[69] This is the resource extraction not of the settler future imaginary, but rather of the energy that makes settler futures possible. With the very continuation of settler existence in question, Indigenous dreams are the lifeblood through which settler futurity can be projected and restructured. As such, the stakes of *The Marrow Thieves* are much more than a future tense (for settlers or for Indigenous peoples); they are the ability to imagine a future, which is demonstrated in the novel as fundamental to a people's survival.

While it may appear far-fetched at first glance, or a product simply of the speculative, historical context helps to illustrate that settlers have, in fact, been syphoning off of Indigenous peoples for a very long time. The extractive violence that Dimaline formulates in *The Marrow Thieves* recapitulates what Adam Gaudry identifies as the "New Age" consumption of Indigeneity, a growing appropriation movement with deep historical roots that promises "spiritual fulfillment and authentic community" to white settlers reeling from the alienation inflicted by modernity and late capitalism.[70] For Gaudry, the New Agers' appropriation of Indigeneity is politically manifested in the contemporary creation of "Métis" individuals and "Métis" communities with no connection to the historically continuous and still living Métis peoples. In appropriating identity to facilitate their own political survival, Gaudry argues, New Agers "undermin[e]the work done by [Métis] ancestors, elders, and contemporary leaders in allowing [them] to survive decades of genocidal policies."[71] In sum, Gaudry identifies an expropriation of Indigenous identity that fuels the engine of settler colonialism via settlers' "continuing usurpation of indigenous space."[72] Or, in other words, echoing Patrick Wolfe's formulation for settler colonialism, Gaudry reminds us that it is not just resources taken from the land that fuel settler colonialism: it is Indigenous identity itself.

The consumption of Indigeneity that Gaudry outlines is reflected and amplified through the future imaginary in *The Marrow Thieves,* which features a Métis protagonist (French). When settlers discover that Indigenous peoples have retained the ability to dream, they renew the New Age obsession with Indigenous peoples. Dimaline uses New Age explicitly here, writing that "at first people turned to Indigenous people the way the New Agers had, all reverence and curiosity ... and then they changed on us, like the New Agers, looking for ways they could take what we had and administer it themselves."[73] The past and the present echo loudly in the future here, with settlers finding new appetite for Indigenous identity, positioned in the novel as the stuff that will save them and their futures.

The New Agers of *The Marrow Thieves* quickly determine that dreams, and thus white settler salvation, can be extracted from Indigenous bone marrow and administered without the need for actual living beings. Indigenous peoples, literally boiled down into a readily consumable, essentialist representation (dreams, bone marrow), become "little more than a crop" in the apocalypse and Indigenous bodies become entirely subject to the will and desires of the colonial sovereign.[74] In this sense, Dimaline not only mirrors the extraction already taking place in the settler colonial system (as demonstrated by Gaudry with the usurpation of Indigenous identity, but also evident in the resource extraction taking place in traditional territories across Canada), she also amplifies the material and ontological violence of settler appropriation/expropriation as it connects specifically to Indigenous bodies.

It should come as no surprise that capitalist production plays a key role in Dimaline's extraction narrative. Once Indigenous dreams are transformed into a commodity, the next step, in order to meet settler demand for the vaccine, is establishing the means to most efficiently bring those dreams to market. In the internal monologue French has about the development of this dystopic means of production, he speculates on the twisted research questions that must have informed the capitalist process behind dream extraction: "How could they best appropriate the uncanny ability we had to dream? How could they make ceremony better, more efficient, more economical?"[75] The answers to these questions are, of course, Fordism and market capitalism. Dimaline's settlers need to build factories to extract and distribute those dreams; they need staff, and procedures that will facilitate those processes; they need warehouses to contain Indigenous peoples and the "product" they extract from them.

It is precisely at this point in *The Marrow Thieves* that residential schools re-enter the conversation. If, as Wolfe suggests, settler colonialism is fueled by usurpation of Indigeneity, infrastructure must be in place to facilitate those processes.[76] Dimaline draws our attention to how that infrastructure functions, but it is also critiqued by the TRC. *Honouring the Truth* readily establishes that residential schools met precisely the purpose Wolfe names, extracting children from their families, and language and culture from children, thus clearing the space for settlers to project their belonging onto the land. Identifying these schools as primary contributors to Canada's cultural genocide, the authors of *Honouring the Truth* argue that

> The Canadian government pursued this policy of cultural genocide because it wished to divest itself of its legal and financial obligations to Aboriginal people and gain control over their land and resources. If every Aboriginal person had been "absorbed into the body politic," there would be no reserves, no Treaties, and no Aboriginal rights.[77]

In Dimaline's apocalypse, the idea of being "absorbed in to the body politic" is rendered material through consumption of Indigenous bone marrow. This gruesome metaphor for assimilation does not simply relieve settlers of accountability in the novel, however, it provides for the continued existence of the settler state. Dimaline tracks the idea even further by linking Indigenous bodies, as product, to colonial-capitalist infrastructure. In this move, we see that the gap between the metaphor and the real is actually much, much smaller than we might have initially imagined. Settlers are able to bring Indigeneity to market so quickly and so efficiently because the means of production – residential schools – are already in place; they are just lying dormant, barely beneath the surface of a colonial ideology that stretches, unbroken, through past, present, and future.

In the interview with Trevor Corkum that I quote from in the opening section of this conclusion Dimaline discusses the possibilities which the world of *The Marrow Thieves* opened up to her as a novelist and cultural critic:

> The best part about this book is that, being in the future, I could and do talk about anything and everything: refuting the Bering Strait theory, global warming, residential schools and the danger of shallow reconciliation efforts, commodification of culture.[78]

Here, Dimaline identifies the fertile space of the Indigenous future imaginary, particularly the opportunity it provides to critique the settler establishment – including capitalism and reconciliation. While the TRC is not directly mentioned in *The Marrow Thieves,* this interview helps to illustrate the ways in which that commission, and its outputs, which were published two years before the novel, inflected its writing and, in turn, provide for intertextual analysis, which I initiated, via French's father, at the beginning of this chapter.

It is toward intertextuality, between *The Marrow Thieves* and the TRC, that I want to continue to push my reading here. Indeed, inasmuch as *The Marrow Thieves* is about the return of residential schools – the very thing that the TRC attempts to redress – it is difficult *not* to read (failed) reconciliation between the lines of the novel. Which is to say, if settlers in the text feel that they have the latitude to rebuild these schools, then the contemporary TRC process, at least as it has been projected into the future of Dimaline's novel, never succeeded in reaching the core of the problem. The schools "return" in *The Marrow Thieves* because, in an ideological sense, they never left. Indeed, Dimaline establishes, early on, that the new residential schools are echoes of the past: "they were based on the old residential school system they used to try to break our people to begin with."[79]

There are further indicators that allow us to read reconciliation into *The Marrow Thieves.* For instance, in the pre-apocalypse flashbacks offered by the main characters, primarily Miig, we have some indication that there has been a transition period, between the first and second comings of the schools, during which Indigenous-settler relations appeared to improve. For instance, describing his own coming-to story, Miig tells French and the rest of the group about the goodwill settlers showed to Indigenous peoples before the threat of climate change became real. Isaac, who made his living as a poet before settlers began harvesting bone marrow, is a central figure in these stories, acting as a vector through which to establish the climate of shallow reconciliation. According to Miig, Isaac was at the centre of what he calls the Indigenous literature "renaissance" predating the apocalypse.[80] Given that he felt valued by the settler literary community during this time, Miig argues, Isaac was inclined to ignore early rumours about the new residential schools, and he continued writing and sharing his work at public readings. However, the trust that Isaac puts in an ostensibly "reconciled" settler public is, in Miig's retelling, ultimately what contributes to his husband's capture and removal to the schools. Miig concludes that it was his husband's belief that Indigenous-settler relations took place on an equal playing field that blinded him to the actual power dynamics at play and the fact that, given the choice of preserving settler futurity or maintaining Indigenous humanity, settlers would readily, "forget the art in the Indian and instead see only the commodity."[81]

Here, adroitly gesturing toward the Indigenous literary renaissance that Canada was enjoying at the time she was writing *The Marrow Thieves*, Dimaline nimbly draws attention to an era of "reconciliatory" relations in *The Marrow Thieves* while highlighting the fragility of that moment as it exists within the broader context of climate change and resource scarcity. Thrilled that his work is being taken up by a larger audience, Isaac, at least in Miig's interpretation of the events, fails to see the fact that Indigenous-settler relations are "healthy" only at a surface level. Beneath that surface an expansive, and no less insidious, network of settler colonialism still flourishes. When Miig speaks to the commodification of Indigeneity, then, he is referring, specifically, to how readily Indigenous peoples are dehumanized in a colonial system that privileges the continuation of that system above all else. When scarcity threatens settler cutures, Indigenous art only functions inasmuch as it serves to perpetuate that failing machinery.

While not entirely visible, shallow reconciliation sets a subtle backdrop for the Indigenous literary renaissance flashback that Miig describes in *The Marrow Thieves*. In "Reading for Reconciliation: Indigenous Literatures in a Post-TRC Canada," Aubrey Jean Hanson argues that the TRC has had a distinguishable impact on Indigenous literatures, particularly in their use in educational settings. According to Hanson, the shift toward Indigenous literature can be traced to Carolyn Bennett, Minister for Indigenous and Northern Affairs. Shortly after the TRC's *Calls to Action* were released in 2015, Bennett suggested in a CBC interview that there should be an "Indigenous book club month" to help "eliminate the ignorance that we all had because it [residential school history] wasn't taught in schools."[82] Hanson demonstrates that Bennett's remarks facilitated larger conversations on Indigenous literatures in Canada and contributed to a national turn toward Indigenous literature in the country's educational contexts.[83]

There are a number of layers to unpack in Bennett's "book club." While, at face value, the Indigenous literature "renaissance" that she helped to initiate appears to illustrate an improvement in the Canadian socio-political environment, a shift which can be linked directly to reconciliation and the TRC, Hanson very carefully points out that "reading for reconciliation" is often at odds with the discourses of resurgence emerging in Indigenous communities. Hanson's concern is that, without the proper tools and resources in place, "reading for reconciliation" risks perpetuating a discourse that ignores the political contexts of Indigenous writing, particularly how much of this literature positions "Indigenous communities as sites of power and regeneration."[84] Instead of asserting sovereignty, then, reading for reconciliation draws focus toward the dissimulation of difference between settlers and Indigenous peoples and perpetuates the logics of Canadian multiculturalism, which have always been antithetical to Indigenous sovereignty.[85] In other words, reconciliation facilitates the status quo without addressing the deeper structural concerns that inform Indigenous politics and aesthetics. It is not so much that settlers forget the art and see only the commodity in Indigenous literature for Hanson, but rather that the art is read against the grain of Indigenous politics, which obscures the sovereignty, resistance, and resurgence implicit to those texts.

We see "reading for reconciliation" mirrored in *The Marrow Thieves* in the Indigenous literary renaissance experienced by Isaac. While, on the one hand, settler audiences are drawn to the poet's work and what he represents as an Indigenous author, on the other hand, there is no structural difference, held within the *longue durée* of settler colonialism, evoked in the relationship between settlers and Indigenous authors/texts. What is always already at stake in Isaac's experience then is the extraction of words and ideas that ultimately serve settler interests. In this sense, the subsequent extraction of Indigenous dreams is only an amplification of what is already happening in the settler consumption of Indigenous literature. This is, of course, no fault of Isaac's, rather it is the inevitable upshot of a system in which the consumption of Indigenous poems and stories is aligned specifically with assimilation – at the expense of difference.

Isaac's story is one window into the climate of reconciliation that Dimaline is working out of and through. With her conceptualization of shallow reconciliation in mind, we can further investigate the "return" of residential schools in *The Marrow Thieves*, particularly with an ear toward hearing that echo as it resonates against our contemporary moment. Indeed, there are a number of questions that beg our attention in the return of these schools in the future: what provides for their regrowth? Why did they lay dormant for so long? And how and why are they able to return so readily?

Again, Miig, as one of the primary storytellers in the group (the other being Minerva, whom I will turn to in the next section), provides the most direct insight into residential schools and their return.

Miig is one of the few individuals to escape from the new residential schools with their lives and, as such, he provides a unique perspective on their functionality and intent. In the below passage, he describes the return of residential schools as they are called out of Canada's colonial "history" and once again put into the service of the settler state:

> Soon [after discovering that dreams could be extracted from the marrow of Indigenous peoples], they needed too many bodies, and they turned to history to show them how to best keep us warehoused, how to best position the culling. That's when the new residential schools started growing up from the dirt like poisonous brick mushrooms.
>
> We go to the schools and they leach the dreams from where our ancestors hid them, in the honeycombs of slushy marrow buried in our bones. And us? Well, we join our ancestors, hoping we left enough dreams behind for the next generation to stumble across.[86]

Here, Dimaline makes legible the continuity of settler control over Indigenous lives and lands even as it extends out of reconciliation and into the future imaginary. Residential schools, the colonial technology used to regulate and discipline Indigenous bodies in the nineteenth and twentieth centuries, have not been not erased from the settler colonial timeline in *The Marrow Thieves*. If the world that French and Miig occupy is to be read as an extension of our own, and there is every indication that it should, from the callback to the original schools to the evocation of New Age appropriation, then the TRC of Dimaline's future has indeed failed, as stated in "Schedule 'N,'" to "put the events of the past behind us."[87] Rather, that past, made material in the figure of the residential school, has simply been buried beneath a thin stratum of earth: waiting for the moment when that technologies can once again be mobilized to serve the futurity of the settler state.

To take this argument further, *The Marrow Thieves* warns of an uncanny upshot of shallow reconciliation, by which I mean, with reference to Sigmund Freud, that the new residential schools represent the return of the repressed. For Freud, repression is comparable "to ordering an undesirable guest out of [the] drawing room."[88] He writes that "the essence of repression lies simply in turning something away, and keeping it at a safe distance, from the conscious."[89] Kept out of view, away from the conscious mind, the repressed event or object is given free rein to "proliferate in the dark," until the moment it is released.[90] The repressed's inevitable return, then, is, for Freud, the very definition of the uncanny: given that it "is in reality nothing new or alien, but something which is familiar and old-established in the mind and which has become alienated from it only through the process of repression."[91]

While reading Freud with Indigenous literature is always fraught, the return of the repressed maps readily onto *The Marrow Thieves* and the idea of shallow reconciliation. I feel comfortable applying Freudian theory here, where I would not as a means to interpret the actions of Indigenous characters, because what Dimaline is describing is very much a critique of the settler imagination and a psychic apparatus intent on the erasure of Indigenous humanity. As such, Freud's work helps to illustrate what Dimaline herself helps to make explicit: the through line of colonial ideology as rendered through the disavowal afforded by reconciliation.

Further, I argue that Dimaline is grappling with her own, unique, representation of settler repression, for which Freud's ideas only provide a jumping-off point. Indeed, in Dimaline's formulation, residential school technology is never removed from the colonial psychic apparatus. Rather, as an "unwanted guest" (defined as such in the theatre of regret), it is simply buried beneath a thin stratum of reconciliation, where it is left to fester and proliferate. The "return" of the schools in the novel is thus settler colonial technology rendered as Frankenstein's monster: an uncanny articulation of what the original schools attempted to accomplish, which is, simply put, the removal of Indigeneity from Indigenous bodies. Or, to use Miig's vernacular, what echoes back to us in *The Marrow Thieves* is what he identifies as "the second coming" of the settler colonial genocide.[92]

We can tease out the implications of Dimaline's use of the uncanny further via close reading of Miig's description of the schools. In Miig's characterization, the school's return is likened to the image of "poisonous brick mushrooms." This simile helps to further elaborate the connection that Dimaline is tracing between settler colonialism, the future imaginary, and the return of residential schools, insofar as it demonstrates the mechanics of the settler colonial echo as it stretches across past, present, and future.

Unpacking Miig's use of mushrooms in the above description requires some knowledge of fungi and their rhizomatic structures, which helps to clarify the mechanics of settler repression as Dimaline is articulating them. "Poisonous brick mushrooms" obviously alludes to the toxic (re)growth of residential school structures, built out of the genocidal materials of settler colonialism that form an (unbroken) baseline for Indigenous-settler relations in the novel. However, the use of "mushrooms" itself provides for deeper insight into the ways in which Dimaline positions the rebirth of the schools. While mushrooms themselves are easily removed from a landscape's topography, fungi are sustained by a large network of mycelium, which can lay dormant underground for a number of seasons, even as the vegetation above the soil is eradicated. According to Gilles Deluze and Félix Guattari, who made mushrooms a popular philosophical trope in late 1980s, the network of a mycelium or rhizome "has no beginning or end; it is always in the middle, between things, interbeing, intermezzo."[93] In this sense, while it is possible to address a node or growth in the network, focusing on the single instance (or event, in Wolfe's formulation) ignores the immensity of the "underground" system that nurtures and supports it.

Following Dimaline's mushroom simile through, then, and elaborating on her articulation of "shallow reconciliation," state-centred initiatives that attempt to redress residential schools alone may indeed result in temporary changes in the state's visible landscape. However, without attending to the racism and white supremacy that provides for these schools, which often remain buried (however shallowly) in a reconciliatory culture, the root of the problem will always remain dormant, waiting just below the surface for the conditions necessary for new, or even accelerated, growth. In *The Marrow Thieves*, then, the changing environment, scant resources, and settler illness, encourage residential schools to rise undeterred out of the earth to be mobilized, once again, toward the survival of the settler state. In this sense, "poisonous brick mushrooms" not only describes the genocidal content of residential schools, as they erupt in the future imaginary of *The Marrow Thieves*, the simile also draws our attention to the immense structure of settler colonialism that continues to support these systems even as shallow reconciliation redresses what is most visible.

In this sense, "shallow reconciliation" is defined across Dimaline's work, from the *49th Shelf* interview to *The Marrow Thieves*, as a political system that simply does not dig deep enough. Shallow reconciliation is surface work; it does not attend to the labyrinthine structures of racism, Indigenous dehumanization, and white supremacy that support and enable violent technologies, such as the residential school, to exist. Left to fester just below the surface, these structures survive to rebirth the very same systems that settler society, in the wake of the TRC, for instance, once gleefully proclaimed to be dead.

Again, the echo is an instructive figuration here. Drawing on passages similar to the one I quote from above, Megan E. Cannella also argues that

The Marrow Thieves folds time and space to critique the colonial present. Cannella writes that, "while Dimaline's novel is set in the future, the violence that its protagonists are trying to escape and survive is a callback to a long history of violent eradication attempts levied against the Indigenous communities of North America."[94] There is something to be made here of the "callback" that Cannella evokes in this essay, a callback which, I argue, appears to be tremendously at odds with reconciliation as it is being framed by the settler state in Canada. While Schedule "N" of the TRC mandate suggests that we can "put the events of the past behind us," *The Marrow Thieves* demonstrates that the genocide of Indigenous peoples is not simply a historical event. It does not simply call back. It echoes forward. Indeed, as a product of structural violence, residential school technologies are supertemporal: resonating across the past, present, and future. Putting the "events of the past behind us" not only misdiagnoses how residential schools function in settler ideology, it relaxes those who oppose those schools against the inevitability of their return. To be attuned to the past in this formulation, *The Marrow Thieves* suggests, is to practise futurity as vigilance against disavowal.

With the supertemporal in mind, I would like to draw a tentative conclusion about the *The Marrow Thieves* as a critique of shallow reconciliation. We hear the "echo" of residential schools in this novel, I argue, not because these schools are part of Canada's past, but because the past is not over. Residential schools are indelibly written across our present and our futures as a nation. Earlier in this conclusion, I drew on Runnels and Lapensée to illustrate the Indigenous future imaginary as a "flat circle." These thinkers very materially illustrate that, in many Indigenous perspectives on time, "the past is right before us." This is not a fanciful claim about the metaphysics of time; it is a very material argument about the ways in which history manifests itself in the present and future, as an echo striking the surface of the forthcoming. *The Marrow Thieves* makes that argument in no less material terms: in this novel, residential schools are part of our past, certainly, but they loom just as large in our futures.

The Marrow Thieves opens up a space for readers to imagine reconciliation otherwise: that is, not as a holistic healing measure, as mainstream discourse would have it, but as a radical reconfiguration of Indigenous-settler relations. Read from the future imaginary, Dimaline provides a window through which to view the fallout of a reconciliation that is unable to address the structural violence, including racism and white supremacy, that dehumanizes Indigenous peoples and gives rise to instruments of genocide.

The consequence of this shallow reconciliation, Dimaline suggests, is the inevitable return of an ideology buried, but not deep enough: a future replete with the echo of history, rendered all the more monstrous as a result of its repression.

Language and Incommensurability in *The Marrow Thieves*

I don't want to end this book, or my analysis of *The Marrow Thieves*, by foregrounding settler colonialism. While Dimaline's work highlights the cycles of violence implicit to that system, and the inability of shallow reconciliation to redress them, it is primarily a novel about Indigenous hope and resurgence. In Lewis's sense of the idea, *The Marrow Thieves* works toward the creation of an Indigenous future imaginary – by which I mean a future projected outside of relentless restructuring of settler colonialism. Like Hopkinson's *Brown Girl in the Ring*, Dimaline's novel throws into relief the colonial metaphysics of dystopia and holds up the settler apocalypse as an opportunity for Indigenous peoples to flourish: "we have the knowledge," an Indigenous friend of French's father assures him, even as they are scrambling to survive Recruiters and ward off the genocide of the new residential schools, "when we heal our land we are healed also."[95] Amidst all despair, there is a deep sense of hope in these moments. If the settler colonial state is destroyed in the apocalypse, that same apocalypse represents possibility for Indigenous peoples, particularly when the land can be reclaimed and healed.

For these reasons, and others, which I elaborate on below, I want to end this book by calling back to an earlier echo in Dimaline's text, an echo that reverberates through one of the novel's most important characters, Minerva, whom I mention only briefly above.[96] Ultimately, it is through her connection to her land, her language (Cree), and the history of her people that Minerva finds the potential for breaking the cycle of residential schools. She does so by centering Indigenous voices and drawing them across past, present, and future.[97]

The figuration of the echo continues to be a useful analytic tool here. However, at this point, I will be looking at how it can be mobilized against the colonial machine to make space for Indigenous futures. Using the figure of the echo herself, Leanne Betasamosake Simpson argues that Indigenous languages "echo the sounds of our ancestors, the sounds of the land, and (o) debwewin, the sound of our hearts."[98] For Simpson, language and stories are given new life as they travel through Indigenous bodies, tracing out intimate connections to time and place as they reawaken old words and old worlds. In this sense, she suggests, Indigenous bodies "become houses of ancient sound" in which past, present, and future intermingle, generating the strength and sustenance that facilitate resurgence while drawing families and community closer together.[99] Storytellers and language speakers have a vital role in the community, as their bodies are the echo chambers through which the ongoing presence of ancestors and the land resonate. This in itself is, according to Simpson, a future-oriented practice, given that, through their connections to the past, storytellers and language speakers "create the social space where ... new and imagined worlds can exist, even if only for seconds or moments."[100]

Simpson's work with the echo is easily read into *The Marrow Thieves*. As a Cree elder, language speaker, and knowledge keeper, Minerva is a house of ancient sound. She carries within her a deep knowledge of her language and culture, and she plays an essential role in educating the younger members of the group.[101] Early on, Dimaline establishes the importance of Minerva's contributions, particularly with language, even while French maligns her and what he sees as the "women's work" of homesteading. In conversation with Rose, a young Indigenous woman his own age, French proclaims, "I hate when it's my turn for Homesteaders. It's so useless." Rose's reply is contemptuous given the connection to her heritage she is afforded through the Elder: "Stuck with Minerva? Huh, you have no idea."[102] When French presses her on this point, he is shocked to learn that Rose has been learning Cree from Minerva, a connection that he appears to value more than the hunting lessons he is receiving from Miig, as demonstrated in the small temper tantrum he throws in reaction to Rose's pronouncement.

Frustrated with French's performances of masculinity (an ongoing issue with this character), Rose leaves only one of Minerva's words with him, "nishin," despite his demand that he deserves to know more. When she leaves, he holds this small piece of language like the precious object it is, much as Miig holds what he believes to be Isaac's remains. French's relationship to Minerva's teachings in this early scene helps to demonstrate the profound connection that he and the other Indigenous characters find in Indigenous languages amidst the rubble of the apocalypse: "I turned the word over in my throat like a stone; a prayer I couldn't add breath to, a world I wasn't willing to release. It made my lungs feel heavy, my heart grow light, until the juxtaposition of the two phased into sleep."[103] In French's reflections on "nishin," in this scene, language functions as a teleporter might in a science fiction novel, folding time and space in the circle it draws to bind the past with the future. Through a single word, the echo of an Indigenous history resonates through French's body, providing a glimpse into another world and another way of being. Here, French shows himself to be both entranced by and alienated from that power and Minerva is established as the connecting tissue that holds the potential for him, and his makeshift family, to imagine otherwise, toward an Indigenous past and through it into an Indigenous future imaginary.

The transportive effect that French finds in this small word is consistent with the power that Simpson locates in her own language, as she experiences it out of the present-day apocalypse of settler colonialism.[104] In "Bubbling Like a Beating Heart: Reflections on Nishnaabeg Poetic and Narrative Consciousness," Simpson reflects on the potential of Indigenous languages to connect Indigenous peoples to the land, history, tradition, and to one another. While French finds that the word "nishin" transports him to another place and time, Simpson is moved by the word "Otonabee," which refers to the Otonabee River, an anglicized version of "Odenabi," "the river that beats like a heart."[105] For Simpson, "Otonabee" is a site of cultural connection that links her to a powerful source of decolonization. She writes,

> When I hear or read the word "Otonabee," I think "Odenabe" and I am immediately connected to both a physical place within my territory and a space where my culture communicates a multi-layered and nuanced meaning that is largely unseen and unrecognized by non-Indigenous peoples. I am pulled into a Nishnaabeg presence, a decolonized and decolonizing space where my cultural understandings flourish.[106]

Here, Simpson beautifully demonstrates the power of language to carry within it intimate truths of place, power, and relationship. "Otonabee," in her conception, is more than an anglicized Anishinaabemowin word mobilized by settlers to map a river. It is a portal into another, decolonial, state of being. For Simpson, Indigenous land and history "echo" in the bodies of the Indigenous peoples who take words like "Otonabee" into their mouths because those words are inextricably tied to the land and to tradition. These echoes fold time and place: empowering individuals through a chain of relationship that each individual word holds and signifies. For French, "nishin" evokes this power of teleportation, which is so much more than an sf trope here. In a dystopic reality in which he has been abstracted from his family and home, the word connects him to the breath, lives, and lands of his ancestors. It is an echo *turned inside out,* or what Simpson identifies elsewhere as "a flourishment of the Indigenous inside," awakened through his breath and body and rendered, externally, into the possibility of a new world.[107]

What we see in this early scene with Minerva is a small glimpse into what she represents, as an articulation of the future imaginary. By the end of the novel, through language and the echo, Minerva also comes to represent the most significant possibility for decolonization within the crumbling hegemony of the settler apocalypse. It is through her that French and his community are afforded the opportunity to imagine otherwise and rebuild their own, Indigenous-centred reconciliation with the land and one another.

Minerva, a name also given to the Roman goddess of war, is hardly a symbol of reconciliation as we know it from the TRC geneology. As a Cree-speaking – and Cree-dreaming – Elder, Minerva's Indigeneity, or, more specifically, her connection to her language and her ancestors, is ultimately incommensurable with the residential school technology used to drain the life and the dreams from Indigenous bodies. These systems, it turns out, are unable to process the complexity of Indigenous subjectivity when it is rendered through the intricate webs of relationality that form those subjects: relations to land, and to language, to ancestors, and to the long chain of Indigenous presence on the territories now occupied by settlers. As such, Minerva represents the destruction of residential school technology and those who maintain it:

> She sang. She sang with volume and pitch and *a heartbreaking wail that echoed through her relatives' bones,* rattling them in the ground under the school itself. Wave after wave, changing her heartbeat to drum, morphing her singular voice to many, pulling every dream from her own marrow and into her songs. And there were words: words in the language that the conductor couldn't process, words that Cardinals couldn't bear, words the wires couldn't transfer. [emphasis added][108]

In this passage, Minerva connects to what Simpson identifies as "decolonized spaces of resurgence."[109] She takes the echo of her ancestors, cradled deep within the marrow of her bones, and turns it directly into the machinery of the new residential schools. As a "house of ancient sound," Minerva's voice and her body overflow with the ongoing histories of Indigenous presence. The immensity of that presence, what it holds in terms of time, space, and community, is more than the extractive colonial system can contain, and as a result, "the system fail[s], fail[s] all the way through."[110] In other words, what settlers assume to be a vaccine in *The Marrow Thieves* – dreams,

Indigenous essence, marrow – is ultimately their poison. Rendered through the echoes of her ancestry, Minerva's Indigeneity cannot be processed, transferred, or even withstood by those technologies or the agents that control them.

What is at stake in the echo that Minerva taps into in this scene, is clearly not reconciliation. Rather, it is that which cannot be reconciled: the incommensurable. By tapping into the echo, which in Minerva's case means her language, culture, and community, the Elder holds the power to explode the extractive technology of the new residential schools, reaching deep within the system to penetrate the guts of the machine. She does so, insofar as the embodied presence inscribed in her language (which, as Simpson points out, is "largely unseen and unrecognized by non-Indigenous peoples")[111] is in excess to a system designed to consume only what it can assimilate – that is, what can be rendered legible in, and beneficial to, a settler colonial framework. Incommensurability, that which refuses or resists reconciliation, is thus key to how Dimaline formulates Minerva's resistance and, from that resistance, the possibility of an Indigenous future imaginary that literally explodes from within the heart of the settler apocalypse.

In sum, incommensurability is a wrench in the gears of settler colonialism. Dimaline's work is not the only Indigenous writing to grapple with this idea. Building on the work of Franz Fanon and Albert Memmi, Eve Tuck and K. Wayne Yang argue that

> incommensurability is an acknowledgement that decolonization will require a change in the order of the world ... This is not to say that Indigenous peoples or Black and brown peoples take positions of dominance over white settlers; the goal is not for everyone to merely swap spots on the settler-colonial triad, to take another turn on the merry-go-round. The goal is to break the relentless structuring of [settler colonialism] – a break and not a compromise.[112]

For Tuck and Yang, because it has no common comparison or measure, the incommensurable is that which cannot, and should not, be assimilated, incorporated, or reconciled into the operation of settler politics or ideologies – and therefore remains distinct, self-determined, and sovereign. In this sense, while it suggests the radical disruption of the settler machine, the incommensurable is not simply a turn toward anarchy – it represents the implementation of, and adherence to, Indigenous ways of knowing held in the wake of the settler apocalypse. In Tuck and Yang's words, "Native futures, the lives to be lived once the settler nation is gone – these are the unwritten possibilities made possible by an ethic of incommensurability."[113]

Indeed, the incommensurable, as it is framed by scholars such as Tuck and Yang, is about creation and resurgence, as much as it is about destruction. Jodi Byrd and Michael Rothberg compliment this point, suggesting that "incommensurability signals the presence of a power differential ... [but it can also] lay the groundwork for the destabilization of that very differential."[114] For Byrd and Rothberg, incommensurability is directly connected to the problem of translation, or, more specifically, to the problem of settler reception. They argue that incommensurability demonstrates settler unwillingness, or inability, to recognize the other as such. Taking their cue from Gayatri Spivak's work on the subaltern, Byrd and Rothberg suggest that the incommensurable, as it unfolds out of the relationship between the elite and the oppressed, or between settlers and Indigenous peoples, is that which cannot be heard by the group holding power, even as it is articulated within or against a colonial structure. It is in this non-recognition that the power and potential of incommensurability lies.

In opposition to the incommensurable, reconciliation is attentive only to what it can absorb in the framework it provides and subsists on. Dale Turner draws our attention toward the assimilative ethic of reconciliation in his analysis of *R v. Van der Peet,* the 1996 decision by the Canadian Supreme Court that ostensibly made room for Indigenous forms of evidence in Canadian courts of law. While many at the time saw *R v. Van der Peet* as a progressive shift toward a more equitable juridical system, Turner argues that, despite the gesture toward Indigenous knowledge in that decision, the Canadian courts continued to dictate the terms by which that evidence was understood, which rendered the translation of that knowledge, from Indigenous to Canadian contexts, partial at best, and assimilative at worst.[115]

Following Turner, Byrd and Rothberg argue that *R v. Van der Peet* simultaneously acknowledges Indigeneity while disavowing it, often in the same sentence. For instance, the decision reads that "the court must take into account the perspective of the aboriginal peoples, *but that perspective must be framed in terms cognizable to the Canadian legal and constitutional structure*" [emphasis by Turner].[116] Turner's emphasis here makes the paradox of this claim clear: Indigenous knowledge – and Indigenous ways of knowing – is only recognizable in the Canadian legal structure when they have been reconciled in such a way as to be legible within that structure. What is incommensurable, then, is the meaning that cannot be translated: what Byrd and Rothberg, drawing from Jean-François Lyotard, call *differend.* This differend, reconciliation notwithstanding, remains unrecognizable within the Canadian structure.[117] In the words of Byrd and Rothberg, it "marks the place of a form of difference yet to be acknowledged."[118]

Leveraged toward decolonization, then, that remainder, that differend, is the hard kernel through which resistance can be formulated, from the inside out. As that which refuses recognition, the incommensurable is the sand in the gears of the machinery that builds, and rebuilds, settler colonialism. In this sense, the incommensurable is antithetical to reconciliation insofar as it does not ask, "what will a shared Indigenous future look like?" Rather, it demands to know why that question is even necessary. Tuck and Yang, thinking toward the Indigenous future imaginary, put the difference between reconciliation and incommensurability this way:

> Reconciliation is about rescuing settler normalcy, about rescuing a settler future. Reconciliation is concerned with questions of what will decolonization look like? What will happen after abolition? What will be the consequences of decolonization for the settler? Incommensurability acknowledges that these questions need not, and perhaps cannot, be answered in order for decolonization to exist as a framework.[119]

The sound of "an echo turned inside out," I argue, is also the sound of the incommensurable. Not quite a difference that is *yet* to be acknowledged, but a difference, within the strictures of settler colonialism, that *refuses* to be acknowledged. It is the sound of decolonization as radical discord. In this sense, Minerva represents the incommensurable insofar as her sovereign Cree self cannot be incorporated into colonial machinery that runs specifically for the purpose of guaranteeing settler futurity. In a system that literally feeds off of the essence of Indigeneity (dreams, marrow), Minerva holds up the power of her community, her history, her land, and her ancestors, all that she carries in her language and her stories, in her voice and her body. It is through the web of these connections, the depth of which French glimpses in the word "nishin," that she accesses a temporality and geography with so great a scope that she is able to explode colonial infrastructure from the bowels: settler colonial technology "torn down by the words of a dreaming old lady."[120]

Thus, we have here two instructive echoes in *The Marrow Thieves:* the first is the echo that I unpacked at the beginning of this chapter, articulated through the figuration of the new residential schools, which represents the ongoing cycles of settler colonialism and the prophecy of their return as it is articulated through the structures of shallow reconciliation. This is the echo of colonialism, which iterates itself *ad nauseam* in order to rescue settler futures.

Minerva's echo, however, figured as the incommensurable, represents a potential end to that ongoing cycle of violence. When Minerva brings down the residential school system in *The Marrow Thieves*, her echo resonates with sovereignty and self-determination. This echo is connected, deeply and powerfully, with Minerva's voice, her culture, and her language because, in Simpson's sense of Indigenous languages, it bends time and space, carrying with it the full weight of land, language, culture, and community – not just in the present, or even the future, but in the enduring continuity of Indigenous presence across time and space.

The Indigenous echo, as incommensurable, thus represents a space that does not simply make Indigeneity more legible, or less feared, within the settler colonial paradigm (the aim of shallow and state-centred reconciliation). It also dismantles the materiality of the colonial structures that seek to recuperate the TRC by rendering those reconciliations as endpoints for Indigenous-settler relations. In other words, Minerva's echo (re)centres Indigenous voices from the inside out, disrupting the guarantee of settler futurity.

For Dimaline, turning the echo inside out, by which I mean, here, disrupting the relentless restructuring of settler colonialism, is an antidote to shallow reconciliation. In returning voice to survivors and their families through her own echo, Minerva provides French, Miig, and their kin the opportunity to finally, and passionately, (re)imagine an Indigenous future. Indeed, based on her intervention, French commits the final words of *The Marrow Thieves* to the possibility afforded to Indigenous peoples in the wake of the apocalypse and Minerva's radical disruption: "I understood just what we would do for each other, just what we would do for the ebb and pull of the dream, the bigger dream that held us all. Anything. Everything."[121] This is the Indigenous future imaginary: the space to imagine breath, relationality, and even worlds, without the incessant weight of a bloated and decaying colonial structure.

"Like an Echo Turned Inside Out"

I began this book with a quotation from Jacques Derrida, who in 2001 wrote: "No one would decently dare to object to the imperative of reconciliation."[122] Novels such as *The Marrow Thieves*, written in the wake of the TRC of

Canada, put the lie to this statement. Yet, while Indigenous literature and critical theory is helping to shift the conversation toward objection, reconciliation is still far too entangled with notions of what it means to be good – a good neighbour, a good citizen, a good leftist – to be disparaged in certain company. In this sense, to elaborate on Derrida's remarks, questioning reconciliation, particularly if you are Indigenous or a person of colour, is still a risk. But we, as scholars, activists, and community members, must indeed dare to continue to object. As allies, for whom contesting reconciliation does not draw the hate and threats to personal well-being that it does for Indigenous people, taking up some of this labour and bearing witness to Indigenous peoples' criticisms is a necessary act of solidarity. If reconciliation continues to be made commensurable, that is, a complement to how Canada understands itself, it will become another tool of empire.

Of particular concern if we refuse to object, is what shallow reconciliation might produce in a colonial future, a fear narrativized by Dimaline in *The Marrow Thieves*. For what is the reappearance of residential schools in that novel but the return of settler hatred and greed after they were buried – momentarily – beneath the appearance of improved relations. In *The Marrow Thieves,* once the demand for resources outweighs the global capital accumulated through reconciliation, residential schools, or something like them, have the potential to return – as the repressed always does – even stronger and more monstrous than before. This is to say that shallow reconciliation, or state-centred reconciliation, in its failure to address the structural issues endemic to its local contexts, does not attend to the ways in which residential schools are symptomatic of the larger disease of settler colonialism. In this sense, we must be prepared to read language that insists we "put the events of the past behind us," as the TRC's Schedule "N" would have it, as disavowal, rather than an indication of healing or even "moving on."

If we are willing to admit that reconciliation is failing, how do we turn it inside out? This book has focused on reconciliation stories: the stories that various nation states tell us; the stories Indigenous writers, Elders, survivors, and community members share; the stories that have formed the bedrock of Canadian identity; and the stories that theorists and analysts tell one another in attempts to make sense of it all. But the story of reconciliation is, of course, only one short paragraph, an epigram really, in the long chapter that makes up Indigenous-settler relations. Derrida foresaw reconciliation as an instrument of power. Dimaline fictionalizes that power and amplifies its monstrosity. If we want to interrupt shallow reconciliation, we must hold power to account and hold reconciliation up to both history *and* the future.

That all said, in the face of settler colonialism and the much, much longer story of Indigenous presence on the lands now known as Canada, the story of reconciliation may sound absurd. In many ways, it is – particularly when read out of the political history that defines it in the contexts of political transition. But that doesn't mean we should abandon it. To do so would be to further ignore the voices of thousands of Indian Residential School survivors and their families. It would mean erasing the detailed and extensive work of the TRC and its commissioners, and it would mean giving in to the idea that settler colonialism always determines the meaning of shared space – that Indigenous peoples cannot define reconciliation in a way that serves their own needs and ideologies. I don't believe this is true nor do I believe that we have to concede to governmental interpretations and definitions. The TRC itself entreats us to take up *Indigenous-centred* reconciliation, to reject state-centred narratives and to imagine otherwise. In this sense, reconciliation must remain in conversation for as long as Indigenous peoples and allies can make it uncomfortable – incommensurable – within the narrative of the Canadian state. As Pam Palmater puts it, "if it feels good, it's not reconciliation."[123] We are all responsible for how this story will unfold – and responsible to the ways in which it implicates us and authorizes us to remember in certain ways and forget in others.

In this book I have attempted to identify fissures in some of the state's reconciliation narratives and illustrate how they displace and distort the ongoing history of settler colonialism. I have tried to interrupt the momentum behind the international TRC process by illustrating how uncomfortably Canada and its history with Indigenous peoples fit within that mould. In doing so, I hope I have generated some space to think and speak outside of its moral structures and imperatives. If reconciliation is possible, it can be so only if held in balance with truth: the truth of residential schools of course, but also the truth of settler colonialism, the truth of racism and white supremacy, the truth of the ongoing violence committed against Indigenous peoples as a foundation of Canadian state diplomacy. Much of this truth is incommensurable with how Canadians understand themselves and will be met with resistance, but reconciliation without truth will only ever be shallow.

Being accountable to reconciliation looks like Indigenous peoples *and* allied settlers continuing to hold up the incommensurable and therefore pushing against the violent banality of reconciliation as it is performed on the proscenium of the theatre of regret.

Notes

Introduction

1 Stan McKay, "Expanding the Dialogue on Truth and Reconciliation – In a Good Way," in *From Truth to Reconciliation: Transforming the Legacy of Residential Schools,* ed. Marlene Brant Castellano, Linda Archibald, and Mike DeGagné (Ottawa: Aboriginal Healing Foundation, 2008), 105. This collection of essays is available for download from the AHF site: http://www.ahf.ca/downloads/from-truth-to-reconciliation-transforming-the-legacy-of-residential-schools.pdf.

2 Jacques Derrida, *On Cosmopolitanism and Forgiveness,* trans. Mark Dooley and Michael Hughes (New York: Routledge, 2001), 50.

3 I am borrowing here from Patrick Wolfe, who, in his foundational essay on settler colonialism, argued that "invasion is a structure, not an event." See Patrick Wolfe, "Settler Colonialism and the Elimination of the Native," *Journal of Genocide Research* 8, 4 (2006): 388.

4 Michael Turner, "Witnesses: Art and Canada's Indian Residential Schools," *Canadian Art,* November 22, 2013, https://canadianart.ca/reviews/witnesses-belkin/.

5 My reflections on witnessing and my analysis of Rebecca Belmore's *Apparitions* are based on ideas originally developed in a previous essay. See David Gaertner, "'Aboriginal Principles of Witnessing' and the Truth and Reconciliation Commission of Canada," in *Arts of Engagement: Taking Aesthetic Action in and beyond the Truth and Reconciliation Commission,* ed. Dylan Robinson and Keith Martin (Waterloo, ON: Wilfrid Laurier University Press, 2016), 135–55. Reprinted with permission from the publisher.

6 The Indian Residential Schools Settlement Agreement is a 2006 agreement between the Canadian government and Indigenous peoples in Canada to redress the damage inflicted by Indian Residential Schools. It includes the TRC. Citing irreconcilable

differences with the other two commissioners, Harry Laforme, the original chair of the Commission, resigned from his position less than a year into the five-year TRC mandate. Murray Sinclair, who would eventually see the TRC through, was appointed soon after. I provide more details on this change in leadership in Chapter 1.

7 I am thinking most specifically here of Ronald Niezen's book *Truth and Indignation: Canada's Truth and Reconciliation Commission on Indian Residential Schools,* Pamela Rose Toulouse's *Truth and Reconciliation in Canadian Schools,* and the collection of essays edited by Dylan Robinson and Keavy Martin, *Arts of Engagement: Taking Aesthetic Action in and beyond the Truth and Reconciliation Commission of Canada.*

8 Patricia M. Barkaskas and Sarah Hunt, "Truth before Reconciliation: Reframing/Resisting/Refusing Reconciliation" (lecture, Simon Fraser University Institute for the Humanities, Vancouver, BC, March 10, 2017).

9 Shoshana Felman and Dori Laub, *Testimony: Crises of Witnessing in Literature, Psychoanalysis, and History* (New York: Routledge, 1992), 204.

10 I am very grateful to Elder Larry Grant for sharing his knowledge of Coast Salish witnessing ceremonies with me. Many thanks also to those who have shared their knowledge of those ceremonies in their research and community practices at the University of British Columbia, particularly my students.

11 M. Teresa Carlson, Keith Thor Carlson, Brian Thom, and Albert "Sonny" McHalsie, "Spoken Literature," in *You Are Asked to Witness: The Stó:lõ in Canada's Pacific Coast History,* ed. Keith Thor Carlson (Chilliwack, BC: Stó:lõ Heritage Trust, 1996), 184–85.

12 Ibid., 184.

13 Ibid.

14 Ibid.

15 "Witness Ceremony Conducted by Elder Larry Grant," *NationTalk,* July 28, 2009, http://nationtalk.ca/story/witness-ceremony-conducted-by-elder-larry-grant.

16 Jordan Wilson, "Gathered Together: Listening to Musqueam Lived Experiences," *Biography* 39, 3 (2016): 482.

17 "Witness Blanket Weaves Residential School Memories Together," CBC News, December 14, 2015, www.cbc.ca/news/canada/manitoba/witness-blanket-cmhr-winnipeg-1.3363889.

18 Ibid.

19 Shari Narine, "Witness Blanket Will Tell Story of Indian Residential Schools," *Windspeaker,* September 1, 2013, https://ammsa.com/publications/windspeaker/witness-blanket-will-tell-story-indian-residential-schools.

20 Frieda Esau Klippenstein, review of "Witness Blanket," by Cary Newman (Master Carver), exhibit at the Canadian Museum for Human Rights, December 2015 to June 2016, *Manitoba History* 80 (2016): 51.

21 Shari Narine, "Honorary Witnesses Promise to Spread the Word," *Windspeaker,* August 1, 2012, www.ammsa.com/publications/windspeaker/honorary-witnesses-promise-spread-word-trc-event.

22 Shelagh Rogers, "Shelagh Rogers Her Journey from Her Head to Her Heart as Hon. Witness," *Indigenous Corporate Training Inc.* (blog), September 17, 2013, www.ictinc.ca/blog/shelagh-rogers-journey-head-heart-honorary-witness-trc.

23 Narine, "Honorary Witnesses."

24 Judy Iseke, "Indigenous Digital Storytelling in Video: Witnessing with Alma Desjarlais," *Equity and Excellence in Education* 44, 3 (2011): 323.

25 Ibid., 311.

26 Ibid.

27 Ibid., 312.

28 Sarah Hunt, "Researching within Relations of Violence: Witnessing as Methodology," in *Indigenous Research: Theories, Practices, and Relationships,* ed. Deborah McGregor, Jean-Paul Restoule, and Rochelle Johnston (Toronto: Canadian Scholars Press, 2018), 284.

29 As Barbara Johnson asks, "Is the witness the one who *sees,* the one who *undergoes,* or the one who *propagates,* the accident to which he bears witness?" *Défigurations du langage poétique* (Paris: Flammarion, 1979), 169–70. Cited and translated by Shoshana Felman in Felman and Laub, *Testimony,* 23.

30 Hunt, "Researching within Relations of Violence," 9.

31 Ibid., 12.

32 Derrida, *On Cosmopolitanism and Forgiveness,* 50.

33 Rebecca Belmore, artist statement in *Witnesses: Art and Canada's Indian Residential Schools* (Vancouver: Morris and Helen Belkin Art Gallery, 2013), 35. Images from the exhibit can be viewed at https://e-artexte.ca/id/eprint/29265/.

34 Geoffrey Carr, "Bearing Witness: A Brief History of the Indian Residential Schools in Canada," in *Witnesses,* 11.

35 David Garneau, "Imaginary Spaces of Conciliation and Reconciliation: Art, Curation and Healing," in Robinson and Martin, *Arts of Engagement,* 21–23.

36 Gaertner, "'Aboriginal Principles of Witnessing,'" 135–55. I am also thinking here of Audra Simpson's articulation of refusal in *Mohawk Interruptus: Political Life Across the Borders of Settler States* (Durham, NC: Duke University Press, 2014).

37 bell hooks, *Yearning* (Boston, MA: South End Press, 1990), 52

38 Rachel Flowers, "Refusal to Forgive: Indigenous Women's Love and Rage," *Decolonization: Indigeneity, Education and Society* 4, 2 (2015): 32–49.

Chapter 1: The Theatre of Regret

1 Antjie Krog, *Country of My Skull* (London: Jonathan Cape, 1994), 50.

2 Leanne Betasamosake Simpson, "Plight," in *This Accident of Being Lost* (Toronto: House of Anansi Press, 2017), 6.

3 Edward Said, "Resistance, Opposition and Representation," in *The Postcolonial Studies Reader,* ed. Bill Ashcroft, Gareth Griffiths, and Helen Tiffin, 2nd ed. (New York: Routledge, 2006), 95.

4 Gearoid Millar, "Truth and Reconciliation Commissions," in *The Oxford International Encyclopedia of Peace,* ed. Nigel Young, online ed. (Oxford: Oxford University Press, 2010), www.oxfordreference.com/view/10.1093/acref/9780195334685.001.0001/acref-9780195334685-e-719?rskey=sUAKvJ&result=4. Millar's article was published in 2010. Since it was released, commissions have been approved in Brazil, Nepal, the Philippines, Sri Lanka, and Tunisia.

5 Kevin Avruch and Beatriz Vejarano, "Truth and Reconciliation Commissions: A Review Essay and Annotated Bibliography," *Social Justice: Anthropology, Peace, and Human Rights* 2, 1–2 (2001): 43.

6 I am drawing here on Stuart Hall, who argues that race, as a floating signifier, is dependent on context and thus can be appropriated to reproduce dominant power relations. Stuart Hall, *Race, the Floating Signifier*, dir. Sut Jhally (Media Education Foundation, 1997).

7 Walter Cronkite, "Listening in on the Nuremberg Trials," on *All Things Considered*, hosted by Michele Norris, radio program, February 20, 2006, www.npr.org/templates/story/story.php?storyId=5225486.

8 "Second Day: Wednesday, November 21, 1945," in *Trial of the Major War Criminals before the International Military Tribunal*, vol. 2 (Nuremberg: International Military Tribunal, 1947), 99, www.loc.gov/rr/frd/Military_Law/pdf/NT_Vol-II.pdf.

9 Norbert Ehrenfreund, *The Nuremberg Legacy: How the Nazi War Crimes Trials Changed the Course of History* (New York: Palgrave Macmillan, 2007), 54.

10 UN General Assembly, Resolution 95 (I), Affirmation of the Principles of International Law Recognized by the Charter of the Nürnberg Tribunal, A/RES/95(I) (December 11, 1946), https://legal.un.org/avl/ha/ga_95-I/ga_95-I.html.

11 Ehrenfreund, *The Nuremberg Legacy*, 123.

12 Ibid.

13 Desmond Tutu, *No Future without Forgiveness* (New York: Doubleday, 1999), 20.

14 Giorgio Agamben, *Homo Sacer: Sovereign Power and Bare Life*, trans. Daniel Heller-Roazen (Stanford, CA: Stanford University Press, 1998), 19.

15 Hannah Arendt, *Eichmann and the Holocaust* (London: Penguin Books, 2005), 113.

16 The American Anthropological Association made plain the cultural bias implicit in human rights in 1947. In an open letter the association asked, "How can the proposed Declaration be applicable to all human beings and not be a statement of rights conceived only in terms of values prevalent in the countries of Western Europe and America?" See Johannes Morsink, *The Universal Declaration of Human Rights* (Philadelphia: University of Pennsylvania Press, 2000), iv.

17 Also known as the General Treaty for the Renunciation of War or the World Peace Act, the Kellogg-Briand Pact was signed on August 27, 1928, by the United States, France, the United Kingdom, Italy, Japan, Weimar Germany, and a number of other countries. The pact renounced aggressive war and prohibited the use of war as an instrument of national policy except in matters of self-defence.

18 William O. Douglas, *An Almanac of Liberty* (Garden City, NY: Doubleday, 1954), 96.

19 Jacques Derrida, "Force of Law: The 'Mystical Foundations of Authority,'" in *Acts of Religion*, ed. Gil Anidjar (New York: Routledge, 2001), 295.

20 Ehrenfreund, *The Nuremberg Legacy*, 52.

21 Ibid., 106.

22 Cherie Booth, "Prospects and Issues for the International Criminal Court: Lessons from Rwanda and Yugoslavia," in *From Nuremberg to The Hague: The Future of International Criminal Justice*, ed. Phillipe Sands (Cambridge: Cambridge University Press, 2003), 157–59.

23 Tutu, *No Future without Forgiveness*, 8.

24 Truth and Reconciliation Commission (TRC) of Canada, *Truth and Reconciliation Commission of Canada: Calls to Action* (Winnipeg: TRC, 2015), http://trc.ca/assets/pdf/Calls_to_Action_English2.pdf. See Calls to Action 28, 57, 69, 70, 92.

25 Here, I am drawing from Jacques Derrida: "a force that justifies itself or is justified in applying itself, even if this justification may be judged from elsewhere to be unjust or unjustifiable." See "Force of Law: The 'Mystical Foundations of Authority,'" in *Acts of Religion,* ed. Gil Anidjar (New York: Routledge, 2001), 233.

26 Nathan Stormer, "Recursivity: A Working Paper on Rhetoric and Mnesis," *Quarterly Journal of Speech* 99, 1 (2013): 28.

27 Of course, many individuals and groups have pushed back against the universal definition of Nuremberg principles as human rights. For instance, see American Anthropological Association, "Statement on Human Rights," *American Anthropologist* 49, 4 (1947): 539–43.

28 Judith Butler, *Excitable Speech: A Politics of the Performative* (New York: Routledge, 1997), 15.

29 Ibid., 51.

30 Priscilla B. Hayner, "Fifteen Truth Commissions – 1974 to 1994: A Comparative Study," *Human Rights Quarterly* 16, 4 (1994): 611.

31 Ibid.

32 The 1974 Commission is not to be confused with Uganda's second inquiry in 1986 (which has received much more attention, academic and otherwise). The full mandate for the 1974 commission has been published by the United States Institute of Peace and can be found on the United States Institute of Peace website.

33 Richard H. Ullman, "Human Rights and Economic Power: The United States versus Idi Amin," *Foreign Affairs* 56, 3 (April 1978): 529–43.

34 P.G. Okoth, "The Military in Transition to Democracy in Uganda," in *Uganda: Landmarks in Rebuilding a Nation,* ed. Petter J. Langseth, J. Katorobo, E. Brett, and J. Munene, 2nd ed. (Kampala, Uganda: Fountain Publishers, 1997), 258.

35 Hayner, "Fifteen Truth Commissions," 611.

36 Ibid.

37 Ullman, "Human Rights and Economic Power," 529–43.

38 Hayner, "Fifteen Truth Commissions," 611.

39 Ibid.

40 Ibid., 613.

41 Ibid.

42 Elazar Barkan, *The Guilt of Nations* (Baltimore: Johns Hopkins University Press, 2001), xii.

43 "Independence in a Divided Country," *New Vision,* October 12, 2009, www.newvision.co.ug/new_vision/news/1234672/independence-divided-country.

44 Barkan, *The Guilt of Nations,* 318.

45 See the report from the law firm White and Case, *Latin American Truth Commissions: Confronting the Past,* ed. Jonathan C. Hamilton, July 29, 2014, www.whitecase.com/sites/whitecase/files/files/download/publications/ProBono-Report-Latin-America-Truth-Commissions.pdf for a more detailed account of these foundational commissions.

46 Aryeh Neier, "An Overview of the Issue and Human Rights Watch Policy," *Human Rights Watch* 4 (December 1989): 2, quoted in Hayner, "Fifteen Truth Commissions," 614–15.
47 Anita Ferrara, *Assessing the Long-Term Impact of Truth Commissions: The Chilean Truth and Reconciliation Commission in Historical Perspective* (New York: Routledge, 2104), 139.
48 Tutu, *No Future without Forgiveness*, 27–29.
49 Hayner, "Fifteen Truth Commissions," 623.
50 Although the setting within the play is ambiguous, making its content applicable to any number of war-torn communities, Dorfman himself was clear on its location: "I wrote *Death and the Maiden* for Chile." This comment by Dorfman was delivered at a public event and cited by James Weaver and Jeanne Colleran in "Whose Memory? Whose Justice? Personal and Political Trauma in Ariel Dorfman's *Death and the Maiden*," *Performance Research* 16, 1 (2011): 34.
51 Ariel Dorfman, *Death and the Maiden* (New York: Penguin, 1994), 39.
52 Ibid., 38.
53 Weaver and Colleran, "Whose Memory? Whose Justice?," 24.
54 Naomi Roht-Arriaza, *The Pinochet Effect: Transitional Justice in the Age of Human Rights* (Philadelphia: University of Pennsylvania, 2005), viii.
55 Ibid.
56 Hayner, "Fifteen Truth Commissions," 613–15.
57 Matt James, "Uncomfortable Comparisons: The Canadian Truth and Reconciliation Commission in International Context," *Les ateliers de l'éthique* 5, 2 (2010): 27, doi.org/10.7202/1044312ar.
58 Roht-Arriaza, *The Pinochet Effect*, ix.
59 Ibid., 71.
60 Paige Arthur, "How 'Transitions' Reshaped Human Rights: A Conceptual History of Transitional Justice," *Human Rights Quarterly* 31, 2 (2009): 324.
61 Hayner, "Fifteen Truth Commissions," 331.
62 Ibid., 622.
63 Catherine Cole, *Performing South Africa's Truth Commission: Stages of Transition* (Bloomington: Indiana University Press, 2009), xii.
64 Audrey R. Chapman and Hugo van der Merwe, *Truth and Reconciliation in South Africa: Did the TRC Deliver?*, ed. Audrey R. Chapman and Hugo van der Merwe (Philadelphia: University of Pennsylvania Press, 2008), vii.
65 Cole, *Performing South Africa's Truth Commission*, x.
66 Marvin Frankel and Ellen Saideman, *Out of the Shadows of the Night: The Struggle for International Human Rights* (New York: Delacorte Press, 1989), 103–4.
67 Tutu, *No Future without Forgiveness*, 19.
68 Ibid., 20.
69 Tutu sees Chile's commission as having failed in these regards: "General Pinochet and his officers and government forgave themselves, they alone knew what precisely they had done" (*No Future without Forgiveness*, 27).
70 Martha Minow, *Between Vengeance and Forgiveness: Facing History after Genocide and Mass Violence* (Boston, MA: Beacon Press, 1998), 91.

71 Tutu, *No Future without Forgiveness,* 156.

72 Everett L. Worthington Jr., *Forgiveness and Reconciliation: Theory and Application* (New York: Routledge, 2006), 55–59.

73 Ibid., 21.

74 Tutu, *No Future without Forgiveness,* 35.

75 Blaise Pascal, *Pascal's Pensées,* trans. W.F. Trotter (New York: E.P. Dutton, 1958), 73.

76 Tutu, *No Future without Forgiveness,* 10.

77 "Home," Reconciliation Australia (website), accessed January 2, 2012, www.reconciliation.org.au/. The website has since been updated.

78 Ibid. The mission of Reconciliation Australia has since been changed to "promot[ing] and facilitat[ing] reconciliation by building relationships, respect and trust between the wider Australian community and Aboriginal and Torres Strait Islander peoples."

79 Damien Short, "Reconciliation, Assimilation, and the Indigenous Peoples of Australia," *International Political Science Review* 24, 4 (2003): 491.

80 The Stolen Generations are the children of Australian Aboriginal and Torres Strait Islander descent who were removed from their families by the Australian government.

81 Reconciliation Australia, *The State of Reconciliation in Australia: Our History, Our Story, Our Future* (report), February 2016, http://iaha.com.au/wp-content/uploads/2016/02/The-State-of-Reconciliation-report_FULL_WR.pdf.

82 Ibid.

83 "Reconciliation Walk," Monument Australia (website), accessed March 18, 2015, http://monumentaustralia.org.au/themes/culture/indigenous/display/23459-reconciliation-walk.

84 Tony Davis, "Marching for a Fresh Beginning," *Sydney Morning Herald,* May 28, 2010, www.smh.com.au/national/marching-for-a-fresh-beginning-20100527-whuu.html.

85 Damien Short, *Reconciliation and Colonial Power: Indigenous Rights in Australia* (Aldershot, UK: Ashgate Publishing Limited, 2008), 7.

86 Ibid., 117.

87 "National Apology," National Museum Australia (website), accessed March 15, 2015, www.nma.gov.au/defining-moments/resources/national-apology.

88 Rosanne Kennedy, "An Australian Archive of Feelings: The Sorry Books Campaign and the Pedagogy of Compassion," *Australian Feminist Studies* 26, 69 (2011): 257.

89 Damien Short, "When Sorry Isn't Good Enough: Official Remembrance and Reconciliation in Australia," *Memory Studies* 5, 3 (2012): 302.

90 Jeff Corntassel, "Who's Sorry Now? Government Apologies, Truth Commissions, and Indigenous Self-Determination in Australia, Canada, Guatemala, and Peru," *Human Rights Review* 9, 4 (2008): 478.

91 Eve Tuck, "Suspending Damage: A Letter to Communities," *Harvard Education Review* 79, 3 (2009): 411.

92 Ibid.

93 Short, *Reconciliation and Colonial Power,* 17.

94 Reconciliation Australia, *The State of Reconciliation in Australia,* 8.

95 Ibid., 14.

96 Ibid.

97 *Mabo v. Queensland* (No. 2), decided on June 3, 1992, was a landmark case in the Australian High Court that dismissed the doctrine of *terra nullius*, recognizing Native title in Australia for the first time.

98 Garth Nettheim, "Judicial Revolution or Cautious Correction? Mabo v Queensland," *University of New South Wales Law Journal* 16, 1 (1993): 1–2.

99 Short, "Indigenous Peoples of Australia," 502.

100 John Borrows, "Practical Reconciliation, Practical Re-Colonization," *Land, Rights, Laws: Issues of Native Title* 2, 27 (2004): 2.

101 Aboriginal and Torres Strait Islander Social Justice Commissioner, *Social Justice Report 2001* (Sydney, AU: Human Rights and Equal Opportunity Commission, 2001), 28, www.humanrights.gov.au/sites/default/files/content/social_justice/sj_report/sjreport02/Social_Justice_Report02.pdf.

102 Larissa Behrendt, "Blood from a Stone," *Arena*, August 2, 2002, https://arena.org.au/blood-from-a-stone/.

103 Indeed, by apologizing for residential schools, the Canadian government abstracted the violence of those schools from settler colonialism and its ongoing systems of violence. See Chelsea Vowel, "Fool Me Once: Colonialism Denial Finds a Happy Home in Canadian Media," *âpihtawikosisân* (blog), September 23, 2013, https://apihtawikosisan.com/2013/09/fool-me-once-colonialism-denial-finds-a-happy-home-in-canadian-media/.

104 Erin Hanson, "The Residential School System," Indigenous Foundations (website), accessed April 20, 2016, http://indigenousfoundations.arts.ubc.ca/the_residential_school_system/.

105 J.R. Miller, *Shingwauk's Vision: A History of Native Residential Schools* (Toronto: University of Toronto Press, 1996), 41, 75–76.

106 Duncan Campbell Scott, "Indian Affairs, 1867–1912," in *Canada and Its Provinces: A History of the Canadian People and Their Institutions by One Hundred Associates and General Editors*, vol. 7, *The Dominion: Political Evolution Part 2*, ed. Adam Shortt and Arthur G. Doughty (Toronto: The Publishers Association of Canada, printed by Edinburgh University Press, 1914), 622–23.

107 Ian Mosby, "Administering Colonial Science: Nutrition Research and Human Biomedical Experimentation in Aboriginal Communities and Residential Schools, 1942–1952," *Histoire sociale/Social history* 46, 91 (2013): 146–47.

108 Miller, *Shingwauk's Vision*, 176.

109 Ibid., 251, 320.

110 Ibid., 328–29, 331, 335, 357, 439.

111 Ibid., 251–53.

112 Ibid., 311. See also chapter two of *Shingwauk's Vision*.

113 Fred Kelly, "Confessions of a Born Again Pagan," in *From Truth to Reconciliation: Transforming the Legacy of Residential Schools*, ed. Marlene Brant Castellano, Linda Archibald, and Mike DeGagné (Ottawa: Aboriginal Healing Foundation, 2008), 16.

114 The CEP and IAP are payment models for survivors. Under the CEP, survivors who attended recognized residential schools were eligible to receive $10,000 and an additional $3,000 for each year they attended a residential school. Under the IAP,

survivors could apply for up to $250,000 for serious sexual, physical, or mental abuse. Proof of this abuse had to be demonstrated, generating what many saw as a "pay-for-pain" model of restitution (see "Pay for Pain, Indians Say," *Washington Times*, August 12, 2001, www.washingtontimes.com/news/2001/aug/12/20010812-024814-7852r/).

115 "Chairman Quits Troubled Residential-School Commission," CBC News, October 20, 2008, www.cbc.ca/news/canada/chairman-quits-troubled-residential-school-commission-1.704043.

116 Ibid.

117 "Will Truth Bring Reconciliation? Justice Murray Sinclair Says Not without Education," CBC Radio, December 6, 2015, www.cbc.ca/radio/unreserved/taking-the-first-steps-on-the-road-to-reconciliation-1.3347611/will-truth-bring-reconciliation-justice-murray-sinclair-says-not-without-education-1.3348070.

118 Ronald Niezen, *Truth and Indignation: Canada's Truth and Reconciliation Commission on Indian Residential Schools* (Toronto: University of Toronto Press, 2013), 5.

119 See Hayner, "Fifteen Truth Commissions."

120 James, "Uncomfortable Comparisons," 24.

121 Glen Coulthard, *Red Skin, White Masks* (Minneapolis: University of Minnesota Press, 2014), 108.

122 Short, *Reconciliation and Colonial Power*, 86.

123 Matt James, "Wrestling with the Past: Apologies, Quasi-Apologies, and Non-Apologies in Canada," in *The Age of Apology: Facing Up to the Past*, ed. Mark Gibney, Rhoda E. Howard-Hassman, Jean-Marc Coicaud, and Nicholas Steiner (Philadelphia: University of Pennsylvania Press, 2009), 137.

124 Ibid., 139.

125 Ibid., 146.

126 Ibid., 148.

127 Dan Levin, "Canada Offers $85 Million to Victims of Its 'Gay Purge,' as Trudeau Apologizes," *New York Times*, November 28, 2017, www.nytimes.com/2017/11/28/world/canada/canada-apology-gay-purge-compensation.html.

128 Catherine McIntyre, "Read Justin Trudeau's Apology to Residential School Survivors in Newfoundland," *Maclean's*, November 24, 2017, www.macleans.ca/news/canada/read-justin-trudeaus-apology-to-residential-school-survivors-in-newfoundland/.

129 Canada, Parliament, *House of Commons Debates (Hansard)*, 39th Parl., 2nd Sess., Vol. 142, No. 110 (June 11, 2008) at 1525 (Right Hon. Stephen Harper).

130 Sarah Maddison and Laura J. Shepherd, "Peacebuilding and the Postcolonial Politics of Transitional Justice," *Peacebuilding* 2, 3 (2014): 255.

131 Canadian Press, "Ski Resort a Step Closer after High Court Ruling in Grizzly Bear Spirit Case," *APTN National News*, November 2, 2017, http://aptnnews.ca/2017/11/02/ski-resort-a-step-closer-after-high-court-ruling-in-grizzly-bear-spirit-case/.

132 *Ktunaxa Nation v. British Columbia*, 2017 SCC 54 at para 10, [2017] 2 S.C.R. 386.

133 TRC of Canada, *Honouring the Truth, Reconciling for the Future: Summary of the Final Report of the Truth and Reconciliation Commission of Canada* (Winnipeg: TRC, 2015), 206, http://nctr.ca/assets/reports/Final%20Reports/Executive_Summary_English_Web.pdf, quoted in Val Napoleon and Hadley Friedland, "An Inside Job:

Engaging with Indigenous Legal Traditions through Stories," *McGill Law Journal* 61, 4 (2016): 729.

134 Sarah Hunt points out that *terra nullius* is founded in the disavowal and erasure of Indigenous legal traditions within the system of settler colonialism: "For Indigenous peoples, the myth of the 'discovery' of Canada upon which the legitimacy of the nation itself depends, serves to continually erode our self-determination and legitimacy as peoples capable of formulating law. Our dehumanization is inherent in how the nation itself comes into being." See Cindy Holmes, Sarah Hunt, and Amy Piedalue, "Violence, Colonialism, and Space: Towards a Decolonizing Dialogue," *ACME: An International E-Journal for Critical Geographies* 14, 2 (2015): 554.

135 Napoleon and Friedland, "An Inside Job," 727.

136 Heidi Kiiwetinepinesiik Stark, "Respect, Responsibility, and Renewal: The Foundations of Anishinaabe Treaty Making with the United States and Canada," *American Indian Culture and Research Journal* 34, 2 (2010): 148.

137 Napoleon and Friedland, "An Inside Job," 754.

138 Katie Glaskin, "Innovation and Ancestral Revelation: The Case of Dreams," *Journal of the Royal Anthropological Institute* 11, 2 (2009): 297–314.

139 Napoleon and Friedland, "An Inside Job," 738.

140 Daniel Heath Justice, *Why Indigenous Literatures Matter* (Waterloo, ON: Wilfrid Laurier University Press, 2017), 32.

141 Ibid., 67.

142 Napoleon and Friedland, "An Inside Job," 750.

143 The "internal viewpoint" approach is similar to what Janice Acoose and others, including Daniel Justice, call literary sovereignty: "Exercising sovereignty, we must name/define our own literatures and take control of the Indigenous-literary territory." Janice Acoose, "Deconstructing Five Generations of White Christian Colonial Rule," in *Residential Schools: The Stolen Years,* ed. Linda Jaine, 2nd ed. (Saskatoon, SK: University Extension Press, 1995), 46–47.

144 Napoleon and Friedland, "An Inside Job," 744.

145 Stark, "Respect, Responsibility, and Renewal," 157.

146 Ibid.

147 John Milloy, *The Plains Cree: Trade, Diplomacy and War, 1790 to 1870* (Winnipeg: University of Manitoba Press, 1988), xiv.

148 Kiera Ladner, *Indigenous Governance: Questioning the Status and the Possibilities for Reconciliation with Canada's Commitment to Aboriginal and Treaty Rights* (West Vancouver: National Centre for First Nations Governance, 2006), 2, http://fngovernance.org/ncfng_research/kiera_ladner.pdf.

149 Stark, "Respect, Responsibility, and Renewal," 152.

150 Ibid.

151 Ibid., 156.

152 Daniel Heath Justice, "'Go Away, Water!': Kinship Criticism and the Decolonization Imperative," in *Reasoning Together: The Native Critics Collection,* ed. Craig Womack (Norman: University of Oklahoma Press, 2008), 150.

153 Ibid., 163.

154 Ibid., 150.

155 Tutu, *No Future without Forgiveness,* 113.
156 Robert A. Williams Jr., *Linking Arms Together: American Indian Treaty Visions of Law and Peace, 1600–1800* (New York: Routledge, 1999), 83–84, quoted in Stark, "Respect, Responsibility, and Renewal," 147.
157 Simpson, "Plight," 5.
158 Ibid., 5.
159 Ibid., 6.
160 Billy-Ray Belcourt, "Colonialism: A Love Story," in *This Wound Is a World* (Calgary: Frontenac House, 2017), 27.
161 See, for instance, Richard Wagamese, "Returning to Harmony," in *Response, Responsibility and Renewal: Canada's Truth and Reconciliation Journey,* ed. Gregory Younging, Jonathan Dewar, and Mike DeGagné (Ottawa: Aboriginal Healing Foundation, 2009), 146.
162 Belcourt, "Epilogue," in *This Wound Is a World,* 59.
163 Ibid., 58.
164 Belcourt, "If I Have a Body, Let It Be a Book of Sad Poems," in *This Wound Is a World,* 22.
165 Michaela Driver, "The Stressed Subject: Lack, Empowerment and Liberation," *Organization* 21, 1 (2014): 93.
166 Ibid.
167 Mohammed Abu-Nimer, introduction to *Reconciliation, Justice and Coexistence: Theory and Practice,* ed. Mohammed Abu-Nimer (Lanham, MD: Lexington Books, 2001), 3.
168 Donald W. Shriver Jr., "Truths for Reconciliation: An American Perspective," Commons Learning Portal, National Park Service (website), updated April 4, 2017, https://mylearning.nps.gov/library-resources/truths-for-reconciliation-an-american-perspective/.
169 David Garneau, "Imaginary Spaces of Conciliation and Reconciliation: Art, Curation and Healing," in *Arts of Engagement: Taking Aesthetic Action in and Beyond the Truth and Reconciliation Commission of Canada,* ed. Dylan Robinson and Keavy Martin (Waterloo, ON: Wilfrid Laurier University Press, 2015), 33.
170 Ibid.
171 Billy-Ray Belcourt, "Fatal Naming Rituals," *Hazlitt,* July 19, 2018, https://hazlitt.net/feature/fatal-naming-rituals.
172 Ibid.
173 Dimitri Nasrallah, "Leanne Betasamosake Simpson Redefines What It Means to Be Indigenous in the 21st Century," *Quill & Quire,* May 2017, https://quillandquire.com/authors/leanne-betasamosake-simpson-redefines-what-it-means-to-be-indigenous-in-the-21st-century/.
174 "Appendix 1: Schedule 'N': Mandate for the Truth and Reconciliation Commission," in Castellano et al., *From Truth to Reconciliation,* 413.

Chapter 2: Listen to the Bones

1 Joshua Whitehead, "you tell me you love me between two & three a.m," in *Full-Metal Indigiqueer* (Vancouver: Talonbooks, 2017), 79.

2 Louise Bernice Halfe, "Dedication to the Seventh Generation," in *Burning in this Midnight Dream* (Regina, SK: Coteau, 2016), 1.
3 Whitehead, "you tell me you love me," in *Full-Metal Indigiqueer,* 79.
4 Cindy Holmes and Sarah Hunt, "Everyday Decolonization: Living a Decolonizing Queer Politics," *Journal of Lesbian Studies* 19, 2 (2015): 159.
5 Anna Lauren Hoffmann, "Data, Technology, and Gender: Thinking about (and from) Trans Lives," in *Spaces for the Future: A Companion to Philosophy of Technology,* ed. Joseph C. Pitt and Ashley Shew (New York: Routledge, 2018), 11.
6 Ibid.
7 Whitehead, "to my mister going to bed," in *Full-Metal Indigiqueer,* 76.
8 Holmes and Hunt, 159.
9 Holmes and Hunt, "Everyday Decolonization," 159.
10 Whitehead, "the hive," in *Full-Metal Indigiqueer,* 110.
11 Gerald Vizenor, "Aesthetics of Survivance," in *Survivance: Narratives of Native Presence* (Lincoln: University of Nebraska Press, 2008), 1.
12 Michelle Raheja, *Reservation Reelism: Redfacing, Visual Sovereignty, and Representations of Native Americans in Film* (Lincoln: University of Nebraska Press, 2010), 153.
13 Whitehead, "re(z)erving paradise," *Full-Metal Indigiqueer,* 50.
14 Whitehead, "what I learned in pre-cal math," *Full-Metal Indigiqueer,* 41.
15 Whitehead, "to my mister going to bed," 76.
16 Whitehead, "slay bells reign in suburbia," *Full-Metal Indigiqueer,* 47.
17 Ibid., 48.
18 For more on the "dead Indian," see Thomas King, "Dead Indians: Too Heavy to Lift," *Hazlitt,* November 30, 2012, https://hazlitt.net/feature/dead-indians-too-heavy-lift.
19 Whitehead, "slay bells reign in suburbia," 48.
20 Ibid.
21 Nicholas Tavuchis, *Mea Culpa: A Sociology of Apology and Reconciliation* (Stanford, CA: Stanford University Press, 1991).
22 Ibid., 20.
23 I speak more to this particular euphemism in Chapter 4.
24 Leonard Monkman, "Genocide against Indigenous Peoples recognized by Canadian Museum for Human Rights," CBC News. May 17, 2019. https://www.cbc.ca/news/indigenous/cmhr-colonialism-genocide-indigenous-peoples-1.5141078.
25 John Paul Tasker, "It Is 'Its Own Thing': Andrew Scheer Disagrees with Indigenous Inquiry's Genocide Finding," CBC News, June 10, 2019, www.cbc.ca/news/politics/scheer-mmiwg-genocide-1.5169000. For more on the salt water thesis, see Chapter 5.
26 Joanna Quinn, *The Politics of Acknowledgement: Truth Commissions in Uganda and Haiti* (Vancouver: UBC Press, 2010), 3.
27 Sigmund Freud, "Repression" (1915), in *The Complete Psychological Works of Sigmund Freud,* ed. James Strachey, vol. 14 (New York: W.W. Norton & Company, 1976), 2977.
28 Quinn, *Politics of Acknowledgement,* 33.
29 Gerhard Werle, "Without Truth, No Reconciliation," *Law and Politics in Africa, Asia and Latin America* 29, 1 (1996): 58–72.

30 *Azanian Peoples Organization (AZAPO) and Others v. President of the Republic of South Africa and Others,* 1996 (4) SA 671 (CC), para 17.
31 Desmond Tutu, *No Future without Forgiveness* (New York: Doubleday, 1999), 143.
32 Ronald Niezen, *Truth and Indignation: Canada's Truth and Reconciliation Commission on Indian Residential Schools* (Toronto: University of Toronto Press, 2013), 5.
33 "Appendix 1: Schedule 'N': Mandate for the Truth and Reconciliation Commission," in *From Truth to Reconciliation: Transforming the Legacy of Residential Schools,* ed. Marlene Brant Castellano, Linda Archibald, and Mike DeGagné (Ottawa: Aboriginal Healing Foundation, 2008), 414. The entire clause states that the Commission shall not name names in their events, activities, public statements, report or recommendations, or make use of personal information or of statements made which identify a person, without the express consent of that individual, unless that information and/or the identity of the person so identified has already been established through legal proceedings, by admission, or by public disclosure by that individual. Other information that could be used to identify individuals shall be anonymized to the extent possible.
34 Niezen, *Truth and Indignation,* 3.
35 Matt James, "Uncomfortable Comparisons: The Canadian Truth and Reconciliation Commission in International Context," *Les ateliers de l'éthique* 5, 2 (2010): 32.
36 Ada Pecos Melton, "Indigenous Justice Systems and Tribal Society," in *Justice as Healing: Indigenous Ways,* ed. Wanda D. McCaslin (St. Paul, MN: Living Justice Press, 2005), 108.
37 Konstantin Petoukhov, "An Evaluation of Canada's Truth and Reconciliation Commission (TRC) through the Lens of Restorative Justice and the Theory of Recognition" (master's thesis, University of Manitoba, 2011), 100.
38 *Canadian Charter of Rights and Freedoms,* s 10, Part 1 of the *Constitution Act, 1982,* being Schedule "B" to the *Canada Act 1982* (UK), c 11.
39 For more on this, see Assembly of First Nations, *Breaking the Silence: An Interpretive Study of Residential School Impact and Healing as Illustrated by the Stories of First Nations Individuals* (Ottawa: Assembly of First Nations, 1994).
40 Randy Fred, "Introduction," in Celia Haig-Brown, *Resistance and Renewal: Surviving the Indian Residential School* (Vancouver: Arsenal Pulp Press, 1988), 25.
41 Ibid., 21.
42 Frances Widdowson, "The Political Economy of 'Truth and Reconciliation': Neotribal Rentierism and the Creation of the Victim/Perpetrator Dichotomy" (paper presented at the annual meeting of the Canadian Political Science Association, Ryerson University, Toronto, ON, May 30–June 1, 2017), 1, https://cpsa-acsp.ca/documents/conference/2017/Widdowson.pdf.
43 Ibid.
44 See Mark Francis, "The 'Civilizing' of Indigenous People in Nineteenth-Century Canada," *Journal of World History* 9, 1 (Spring 1998): 51–87.
45 The final report of the TRC clearly repudiates the argument that Indian Residential Schools were sufficiently educational in nature: "The educational goals of the schools were limited and confused, and usually reflected a low regard for the intellectual capabilities of Aboriginal people. For the students, education and technical training

too often gave way to the drudgery of doing the chores necessary to make the schools self-sustaining. Child neglect was institutionalized, and the lack of supervision created situations where students were prey to sexual and physical abusers." TRC of Canada, *Honouring the Truth, Reconciling for the Future: Summary of the Final Report of the Truth and Reconciliation Commission of Canada* (Winnipeg: TRC, 2015), 3–4, http://nctr.ca/assets/reports/Final%20Reports/Executive_Summary_English_Web.pdf.

46 Ken Coates, "Second Thoughts about Residential Schools," *The Dorchester Review* 4, 2 (Autumn/Winter 2014): 27.

47 Ibid., 29.

48 Crystal Fraser and Ian Mosby, "Setting Canadian History Right? A Response to Ken Coates' 'Second Thoughts about Residential Schools,'" ActiveHistory.ca (blog), April 7, 2015, http://activehistory.ca/papers/paper-20/.

49 It is important to point out that Tavuchis identifies himself as the perpetrator in his use of "we" here (*Mea Culpa,* 22).

50 Georg Wilhelm Friedrich Hegel, *Phenomenology of Spirit,* trans. A.V. Miller (Oxford: Oxford University Press, 1977), 111.

51 Glen Coulthard, *Red Skin, White Masks* (Minneapolis: University of Minnesota Press, 2014), 28.

52 Frantz Fanon, as quoted by Coulthard in *Red Skin, White Masks* (Minneapolis: University of Minnesota Press, 2014), 40.

53 Coulthard, *Red Skin, White Masks,* 40.

54 Eve Tuck, "Suspending Damage: A Letter to Communities," *Harvard Education Review* 79, 3 (2009): 412.

55 Ibid.

56 bell hooks, "Choosing the Margin as a Space of Radical Openness," *Framework: The Journal of Cinema and Media* 36 (1989): 23.

57 Dallas Hunt, "'In Search of Our Better Selves': Totem Transfer Narratives and Indigenous Futurities," *American Indian Culture and Research Journal* 42, 1 (2018): 84.

58 Tuck, "Suspending Damages," 415.

59 Ibid., 416.

60 Louise Bernice Halfe, *Blue Marrow* (Regina, SK: Coteau, 2004), 15. Unless otherwise indicated, all citations from *Blue Marrow* are from the Coteau edition.

61 Portions of this section have been adapted from my introduction to *Sôhkêyihta: The Poetry of Sky Dancer Louise Bernice Halfe,* ed. David Gaertner (Waterloo, ON: Wilfrid Laurier University Press, 2018). Reprinted with permission from the publisher.

62 Halfe, *Blue Marrow,* 17.

63 Ibid., 34.

64 Louise Bernice Halfe, "The Residential School Bus," in *Residential Schools: The Stolen Years,* ed. Linda Jaine, 2nd ed. (Saskatoon, SK: University Extension Press, 1995), 93.

65 Janice Acoose, "Deconstructing Five Generations of White Christian Colonial Rule," in Jaine, *Residential Schools,* 6.

66 Shoshana Felman and Dori Laub, *Testimony: Crises of Witnessing in Literature, Psychoanalysis, and History* (New York: Routledge, 1992), 57.

67 Ibid., 91.

68 Cindy Holmes and Sarah Hunt, *Indigenous Communities and Family Violence: Changing the Conversation* (Prince George, BC: National Collaborating Centre for Aboriginal Health, 2017), 5, https://issuu.com/nccah-ccnsa/docs/rpt-familyviolence-holmes-hunt-en.

69 Ibid., 52.

70 Margo Greenwood, Sarah de Leeuw, Nicole Marie Lindsay, and Charlotte Reading, *Determinants of Indigenous Peoples' Health in Canada: Beyond the Social* (Toronto: Canadian Scholars Press, 2015), xii, quoted in Holmes and Hunt, *Indigenous Communities and Family Violence,* 9.

71 I am thinking specifically of the opening sentence of the TRC mandate here: "There is an emerging and compelling desire *to put the events of the past behind* us so that we can work towards a stronger and healthier future" [emphasis added]. "Appendix 1: Schedule 'N,'" 413.

72 Holmes and Hunt, *Indigenous Communities and Family Violence,* 10.

73 Halfe, *Blue Marrow,* 7.

74 Ibid., 69.

75 Elizabeth Cook-Lynn, "Why I Can't Read Wallace Stegner," in *Why I Can't Read Wallace Stegner and Other Essays* (Madison: University of Wisconsin Press, 1996), 7.

76 Warren Cariou, "Haunted Prairie: Aboriginal 'Ghosts' and the Spectre of Settlement," *University of Toronto Quarterly* 75, (2006): 730.

77 Halfe, *Blue Marrow,* 69.

78 Roland Chrisjohn and Sherri Young, *The Circle Game: Shadows and Substance in the Indian Residential School Experience in Canada* (Penticton, BC: Theytus Books, 1997), 20, http://data2.archives.ca/rcap/pdf/rcap-32.pdf.

79 Ibid., 17.

80 Ibid., 2.

81 Ibid., 8.

82 Ibid., 6.

83 Ibid., 15.

84 Laura Ann Cranmer, "Exploring Voice and Silence in the Poetry of Beth Cuthand, Louise Halfe and Marlene Nourbese Philip," in *(Ad)dressing Our Words: Aboriginal Perspectives on Aboriginal Literatures,* ed. Armand Ruffo (Penticton, BC: Theytus, 1990), 127.

85 Louise Bernice Halfe, "Crying for Voice," in *Bear Bones and Feathers* (Regina, SK: Coteau Books, 1994), 6.

86 Ibid.

87 Ibid.

88 Halfe, *Blue Marrow,* 94.

89 Ian Mosby, "Administering Colonial Science: Nutrition Research and Human Biomedical Experimentation in Aboriginal Communities and Residential Schools, 1942–1952," *Histoire sociale/Social history* 46, 91 (2013): 147.

90 Halfe, "My Ledders," in *Bear Bones and Feathers,* 104. For more on rez english, see Jeanette C. Armstrong, "Land Speaking" in *Speaking for the Generations: Native Writers on Writing.* ed. Simon J Ortiz (Tuscon: University of Arizona Press, 1998), 192.

91 Halfe, *Blue Marrow,* 54 [emphasis in the original].
92 Ibid.
93 Méira Cook, "Bone Memory: Transcribing Voice in Louise Bernice Halfe's Blue Marrow," *Canadian Literature* 166 (2000): 98.
94 Ibid., 33.
95 "Louise Bernice Halfe: Returning," reading at the Words Aloud 4 Spoken Word Festival in Durham, Ontario, November 2007, video, 5:36, March 25, 2009, featuring reading of "Returning," www.youtube.com/watch?v=m6IAaDv4zLE.
96 Halfe, "Der Poop," in *Bear Bones and Feathers,* 102.
97 "Louise Bernice Halfe: Dear Pope," reading at the Words Aloud 4 Spoken Word Festival in Durham, Ontario, November 2007, video, 2:01, March 24, 2009, featuring reading of "Der Poop," https://www.youtube.com/watch?v=B-9SA6DpwJA.
98 Cariou, "Haunted Prairie," 731.
99 Halfe, *Blue Marrow,* 3, 19.
100 Ibid., 20.
101 Ibid., 18.
102 Ibid., 101.
103 Ibid., 8.
104 Samantha Nock, "Being a Witness: The Importance of Protecting Indigenous Women's Stories," *Rabble.ca* (blog), September 5, 2014, http://rabble.ca/blogs/bloggers/samantha-nock/2014/09/being-witness-importance-protecting-indigenous-womens-stories.
105 Niigaanwewidam James Sinclair, "The Power of Dirty Waters: Indigenous Poetics," in *Indigenous Poetics in Canada,* ed. Neal McLeod (Waterloo, ON: Wilfrid Laurier University Press, 2014), 208.
106 Méira Cook, "Bone Memory: Transcribing Voice in Louise Bernice Halfe's Blue Marrow," *Canadian Literature* 166 (2000): 93.
107 Shelley Stigter, "The Dialectics and Dialogics of Code-Switching in the Poetry of Gregory Scofield and Louise Halfe," *American Indian Quarterly* 30, 1/2 (2006): 57.
108 Cook, "Bone Memory," 93.
109 Stigter, "Code-Switching," 57.
110 Mary Lou Fox, sidebar, in *Response, Responsibility and Renewal: Canada's Truth and Reconciliation Journey,* ed. Gregory Younging, Jonathan Dewar, and Mike DeGagné (Ottawa: Aboriginal Healing Foundation, 2009), 253. This collection of essays is available for download from the AHF site: http://www.ahf.ca/downloads/trc2.pdf.
111 Leanne Betasamosake Simpson, *Dancing on Our Turtle's Back* (Winnipeg: ARP Publishing, 2011), 49.
112 Halfe, *Blue Marrow,* 109.
113 Leanne Betasamosake Simpson, "Gdi-nweninaa: Our Sound, Our Voice," in *Learn, Teach, Challenge: Approaching Indigenous Literatures,* ed. Deanna Reder and Linda M. Morra (Waterloo, ON: Wilfrid Laurier University Press, 2016), 289.

Chapter 3: To Acknowledge, but Not to Accept

1 Thomas King, *Green Grass, Running Water* (Toronto: Harper Perennial, 1993), 430.
2 Ibid.

3 Roy L. Brooks, "The Age of Apology," in *When Sorry Isn't Enough: The Controversy over Apologies and Reparations for Human Justice,* ed. Roy L. Brooks (New York: New York University Press, 1999), 3.

4 Elazar Barkan, *The Guilt of Nations* (Baltimore: Johns Hopkins University Press, 2001), 26.

5 In an interview with Peter Gzowski, Thomas King notes that Coyote's apology is also a nod to the apology Salman Rushdie offered to the Muslim people for *The Satanic Verses* after Ayatollah Ruhollah Khomeini of Iran issued a fatwa ordering Muslims to kill Rushdie. Rushdie's apology was rejected. Peter Gzowski, "Peter Gzowski Interviews Thomas King on *Green Grass, Running Water,*" *Canadian Literature* 161/162 (1999): 73.

6 Nicholas Tavuchis, *Mea Culpa: A Sociology of Apology and Reconciliation* (Stanford, CA: Stanford University Press, 1991), 19.

7 Ibid., 69.

8 Aaron Lazare, *On Apology* (New York: Oxford University Press, 2004), 7.

9 See Jonathan R. Cohen, "Advising Clients to Apologize," *Southern California Law Review* 72 (1999): 1009–69; and Peter Rehm and Denise Beatty, "Legal Consequences of Apologizing," *Journal of Dispute Resolution* 1 (1996): 115–40.

10 Lazare, *On Apology,* 7.

11 Ibid.; also Rachel Gotbaum, "Practice of Hospital Apologies is Gaining Ground," on *All Things Considered,* hosted by Michele Norris, radio program, October 6, 2007, www.npr.org/templates/story/story.php?storyId=15073418.

12 Kevin Sack, "Doctors Say 'I'm Sorry' before 'See You in Court,'" *New York Times,* May 18, 2008, www.nytimes.com/2008/05/18/us/18apology.html.

13 Notably, however, the United States has yet to offer an apology to Indigenous peoples.

14 Robert Smith, "Apology to First Nations Peoples," Remembering the Children (website), accessed June 29, 2019, www.rememberingthechildren.ca/partners/documents/ApologiesfromChurches.pdf.

15 "The Apologies," United Church of Canada (website), accessed November 7, 2019, www.united-church.ca/social-action/justice-initiatives/apologies.

16 Susan Alter, *Apologizing for Serious Wrongdoings: Social, Psychological and Legal Considerations* (Ottawa: Law Commission of Canada, 1999), 34.

17 British Columbia, Office of the Ombudsman, *The Power of Apology: Removing Legal Barriers,* by Howard Kushner, special report no. 27 (Victoria: Office of the Ombudsman, Province of British Columbia, 2006), 16.

18 This second apology, delivered by the Right Reverend Bill Phipps, moderator of the United Church of Canada, came in response to the Canadian government's Statement of Reconciliation, discussed in this chapter, and was directed more specifically to survivors of residential schools. This response was titled "To Former Students of United Church Indian Residential Schools, and to Their Families and Communities." See "Apologies (1986, 1998), Response (1988), Crest Update (2012)," United Church of Canada (website), accessed November 7, 2019, www.united-church.ca/sites/default/files/resources/apologies-response-crest.pdf.

19 Omar El Akkad, "Ottawa Rolls Out String of Apologies," *Globe and Mail,* May 14, 2008, www.theglobeandmail.com/news/national/ottawa-rolls-out-string-of-apologies/article672343/.

20 Roland Chrisjohn and Tanya Wasacase, "Half Truths and Whole Lies," in *Response, Responsibility and Renewal: Canada's Truth and Reconciliation Journey,* ed. Gregory Younging, Jonathan Dewar, and Mike DeGagné (Ottawa: Aboriginal Healing Foundation, 2009), 219.
21 Louise Bernice Halfe, *Blue Marrow* (Regina, SK: Coteau, 2004), 90.
22 Erin Anderssen, "Natives Finally Get Ottawa's Apology: 'Deeply Sorry' for Residential Schools," *Globe and Mail,* January 7, 1998.
23 "Canadian Government's Apology to Aboriginal People," *ABC Newslink,* January 8, 1998.
24 Matt James, "Wrestling with the Past: Apologies, Quasi-Apologies, and Non-Apologies in Canada," in *The Age of Apology: Facing Up to the Past,* ed. Mark Gibney, Rhoda E. Howard-Hassman, Jean-Marc Coicaud, and Nicholas Steiner (Philadelphia: University of Pennsylvania Press, 2009), 141.
25 Quoted in Wendy Cox, "Government Paper Warns of Risks of Apologizing for Residential Schools," *Canadian Press Newswire,* July 26, 1998, ProQuest (359517973). At the time of writing, I have submitted a Freedom of Information request to the Government of Canada for the report Cox discusses ("Residential Schools Discussion Paper") but they claim to have no record of it.
26 Paulette Regan, "An Apology Feast in Hazelton: Indian Residential Schools, Reconciliation, and Making Space for Indigenous Legal Traditions," in *Indigenous Legal Traditions,* ed. Law Commission of Canada (Vancouver: UBC Press, 2007), 46.
27 Jane Stewart, "Statement of Reconciliation for Damage Done to Aboriginal Populations in Canada," Crown-Indigenous Relations and Northern Affairs Canada (website), last modified September 15, 2010, www.rcaanc-cirnac.gc.ca/eng/1100100015725/1571590271585.
28 Ibid.
29 Michael R. Marrus, "Official Apologies and the Quest for Historical Justice," *Journal of Human Rights* 6, 1 (2007): 94.
30 I recognize that by attributing the apology solely to Stewart here – namely, by using the pronoun "she" – I am eliding the many government voices behind the Statement of Reconciliation, and thus the multiple "irresponsible" agents involved. What should be noted, however, is the way in which government apology, which represents a legion of voices, both past and present, is almost always framed through a single agent. As such, the actor who delivers the apology – i.e., the Minister of Northern Development and Indian Affairs (as opposed to the prime minister) – becomes an essential element of how the apology is received and interpreted.
31 Janet Bavelas, *An Analysis of Formal Apologies by Canadian Churches to First Nations,* Occasional Paper No. 1 (Victoria, BC: University of Victoria Centre for Studies in Religion and Society, 2004), 9, http://web.uvic.ca/psyc/bavelas/2004ChurchApol.pdf.
32 Ibid., 12.
33 Mitch Miyagawa, "A Sorry State," *Walrus,* December 12, 2009, https://thewalrus.ca/a-sorry-state/.
34 Carrie Barr and Jackie Gillberry, "'Sorry ... I'm Canadian': An Analysis of When Canadians Use the Word 'Sorry,'" *Strathy Undergraduate Working Papers on Canadian English* 8 (2010): 37.

35 Meredith Rossner and Mythily Meher, "Emotions in Ritual Theories," in *Handbook of the Sociology of Emotions,* ed. Jan E. Stets and Jonathan H. Turner, vol. 2 (New York: Springer, 2014), 205.
36 Marie Clements, *Burning Vision* (Burnaby, BC: Talonbooks, 2003), 95–96.
37 Rita Wong, "Decolonizasian: Reading Asian and First Nations Relations in Literature," *Canadian Literature* 199 (Winter 2008): 8.
38 Ibid.
39 Clements, *Burning Vision,* 100.
40 Chrisjohn and Wasacase, "Half Truths, Whole Lies," 220.
41 I am referring here to the now defunct PMO page, preserved in the Government of Canada digital archive: "Prime Minister Harper Offers Full Apology on Behalf of Canadians for the Indian Residential Schools System," Government of Canada (website), last modified June 11, 2008, www.canada.ca/en/news/archive/2008/06/prime-minister-harper-offers-full-apology-behalf-canadians-indian-residential-schools-system.html.
42 Canada, Parliament, *House of Commons Debates (Hansard),* 39th Parl., 2nd Sess., Vol. 142, No. 110 (June 11, 2008) at 1525 (Right Hon. Stephen Harper).
43 Fred Kelly, "Confession of a Born Again Pagan," in *From Truth to Reconciliation: Transforming the Legacy of Residential Schools,* ed. Marlene Brant Castellano, Linda Archibald, and Mike DeGagné (Ottawa: Aboriginal Healing Foundation, 2008), 22.
44 See David Gaertner, "Translating Reconciliation," in *Translation Effects: The Shaping of Modern Canadian Culture,* ed. Louise von Flotow, Sherry Simon, and Kathy Mezei (Montréal/Kingston: McGill-Queen's University Press, 2014), 454.
45 Frederic Baraga and John D. Nichols, *A Dictionary of the Ojibway Language* (St. Paul: Minnesota Historical Society Press, 1992), 85.
46 Canada, Parliament, *House of Commons Debates (Hansard),* 39th Parl., 2nd Sess., Vol. 142, No. 110 (June 11, 2008) at 1520 (Right Hon. Stephen Harper).
47 Canada, Parliament, *House of Commons Debates (Hansard),* 39th Parl, 2nd Sess, Vol 142, No 110 (June 11, 2008) at 1525 (Right Hon. Stephen Harper).
48 Marc L. Bergman and Gabriele Kasper, "Perception and Performance in Native and Nonnative Apology," in *Interlanguage Pragmatics,* ed. Gabriele Kasper and Shoshana Blum-Kulka (Oxford: Oxford University Press, 1993), 82.
49 James V. Scott, "The Importance of Apology in Healing and Reconciliation" (presentation, Truth Telling and Reconciliation Conference, University of Calgary, June 14–17, 2007).
50 Alter, *Apologizing for Serious Wrongdoings,* 34.
51 Dugald Christie, "Gratuitous Apologies: A Discussion Paper on Apology Legislation," *University of British Columbia Law Review* 402 (2007): 763.
52 Tavuchis, *Mea Culpa,* 5.
53 Kushner, *The Power of Apology,* 15.
54 Roland Chrisjohn and Sherri Young, *The Circle Game: Shadows and Substance in the Indian Residential School Experience in Canada* (Penticton, BC: Theytus Books, 1997), 3, http://data2.archives.ca/rcap/pdf/rcap-32.pdf.
55 J.L. Austin, *How to Do Things with Words* (Cambridge, MA: Harvard University Press, 1962), 79.
56 Ibid., 160.

57 Ibid., 80.
58 Ibid., 5.
59 Clements, *Burning Vision,* 29.
60 Miyagawa, "A Sorry State."
61 The decision to use these measures should not be credited to Harper alone, however. The "Full Apology" was an exceptionally complicated event that depended on far more than the Conservatives for its realization. Former NDP leader Jack Layton played a significant role in making the apology happen, and Liberal MP Gary Merasty introduced a motion in the House of Commons calling on MPs to apologize, which the Conservatives passed. The 2006 apology for the Chinese head tax also provided precedent and added to the pressure for a residential school apology (see Bill Curry, "Mounting Sense of Urgency Was Apology's Catalyst," *Globe and Mail,* June 13, 2018, www.theglobeandmail.com/news/national/mounting-sense-of-urgency-was-apologys-catalyst/article674297/). That being said, for the sake of clarity, I will refer to the statement as the "Harper apology" and compare it to the "Stewart apology."
62 Phil Fontaine, "Phil Fontaine's Shocking Testimony of Sexual Abuse," interview by Barbara Frum, *The Journal,* CBC, television program, October 30, 1990, www.cbc.ca/archives/entry/phil-fontaines-shocking-testimony-of-sexual-abuse.
63 Austin, *How to Do Things with Words,* 161.
64 Tavuchis, *Mea Culpa,* 95.
65 Drew Hayden Taylor, "Cry Me a River, White Boy," in Younging et al., *Response, Responsibility and Renewal,* 102.
66 *Apology Act,* SBC 2006, c 19, s 2.
67 *Evidence Act,* SS 2006, c E-11.2, div 4, s 23.1.
68 *Evidence Act,* RSA 2000, c A-18, s 26.1.
69 *Apology Act,* SM 2007, c 25, s 2.1. For more on this bill, see Leandro Zylberman, "Apology Legislation: Should It Be Safe to Apologize in Manitoba? An Assessment of Bill 202," in "Underneath the Golden Boy," ed. Bryan Schwartz and Heather Bell Guest, special issue, *Manitoba Law Review* UTGB 6 (2009): 175, http://themanitobalawjournal.com/wp-content/uploads/articles/UTGB_6/Apology-Legislation.pdf.
70 *Apology Act,* RS 2008, c 34, s 3.
71 *Apology Act,* SNL 2009, c A-10.1, s 3.
72 Leslie MacLeod, *A Time for Apologies: The Legal and Ethical Implications of Apologies in Civil Cases,* Cornwall Public Inquiry Research Paper (Phase 2), April 12, 2008, xvi, www.attorneygeneral.jus.gov.on.ca/inquiries/cornwall/en/report/research_papers/Phase_2_RP/3_Macleod_Apologies.pdf. To be clear, the Yukon Act failed at second reading, but it was being considered during the first part of 2008.
73 *Apology Act,* SO 2009, c 3, s 2.
74 Russell J. Getz, "Policy Paper on Apology Legislation" (paper, Uniform Law Conference of Canada, Charlottetown, PEI, September 9–13, 2007), www.ulcc.ca/en/home/119-josetta-1-en-gb/uniform-actsa/apology-act-presentation-dexcuses/1128-policy-paper-on-apology-legislation.
75 Ibid.
76 See, for instance, Gene Marks, "3 Reasons Why Apologizing Hurts Your Business," *Entrepreneur,* March 2, 2015, www.entrepreneur.com/article/243353, which presents

quite a convincing (if not disheartening) argument against apology in the business sector. Marks's cynical perspective on the human condition translates smoothly to government: "The minute that you admit fault, whether it's justified or not, a client will see an opening to profit. This is just human nature."

77 Getz, "Policy Paper on Apology Legislation."

78 Ibid.

79 Christie, "Gratuitous Apologies," 761.

80 Ibid., 763.

81 Ibid., 767.

82 David Ljunggren, "Every G20 Nation Wants to be Canada, Insists PM," *Reuters,* September 25, 2009, www.reuters.com/article/columns-us-g20-canada-advantages/every-g20-nation-wants-to-be-canada-insists-pm-idUSTRE58P05Z20090926.

83 Glen T. Morris, "International Law and Politics: Toward a Right to Self-Determination for Indigenous Peoples," in *The State of Native America: Genocide, Colonization, and Resistance,* ed. M. Annette Jaimes (Boston, MA: South End Press, 1992), 74.

84 Stephen Hui, "Shawn Atleo Criticizes Stephen Harper over 'No History of Colonialism' Remark," *Georgia Straight,* October 2, 2009, www.straight.com/blogra/shawn-atleo-criticizes-stephen-harper-over-no-history-colonialism-remark.

85 Clements, *Burning Vision,* 100.

86 Carl D. Schneider, "What It Means to Be Sorry: The Power of Apology in Mediation," *Conflict Mediation Quarterly* 17, 3 (2000): 265.

87 Tavuchis, *Mea Culpa,* 17.

88 Jacques Derrida, *Cosmopolitanism and Forgiveness,* trans. Mark Dooley and Michael Hughes (New York: Routledge, 2001), 59.

89 Albert Speer, *Inside the Third Reich: Memoirs,* trans. Richard Winston and Clara Winston (New York: Simon and Schuster, 1970), 113.

90 Tavuchis, *Mea Culpa,* 21.

91 See John Fund, "The Big Liar," *National Review,* February 15, 2016, https://www.nationalreview.com/magazine/2016/02/15/big-liar/.

92 Ibid.

93 Frances Widdowson, "The Political Economy of 'Truth and Reconciliation': Neotribal Rentierism and the Creation of the Victim/Perpetrator Dichotomy" (paper, Annual Meeting of the Canadian Political Science Association, Ryerson University, Toronto, ON, May 30–June 1, 2017), 5, https://cpsa-acsp.ca/documents/conference/2017/Widdowson.pdf.

94 Rex Murphy, "Natives Need to Tone Down the Anger," *National Post,* January 12, 2013, https://nationalpost.com/opinion/rex-murphy-natives-need-to-tone-down-the-anger.

95 Robert Jago, "Why Is Senator Lynn Beyak Publishing Racist Letters on Her Website?," *Walrus,* January 3, 2018, https://thewalrus.ca/why-is-senator-lynn-beyak-publishing-racist-letters-on-her-website/.

96 Emma Prestwich, "Murray Sinclair Responds to People Who Want Indigenous People to Get Over Residential Schools," *Huffington Post,* March 30, 2017, https://www.huffingtonpost.ca/2017/03/30/murray-sinclair-residential-schools_n_15708156.html.

97 Quoted in Marrus, "Official Apologies," 40.

98 James, "Wrestling with the Past," 139.

Chapter 4: Redress as a Gift

1 Rauna Kuokkanen, "The Logic of the Gift: Reclaiming Indigenous Peoples' Philosophies," in *Re-Ethnicizing the Minds? Cultural Revival in Contemporary Thought,* ed. Thorsten Botz-Bornstein and Jürgen Hengelbrock (Amsterdam: Rodopi, 2006), 268.

2 Grace L. Dillon, "Indigenous Scientific Literacies in Nalo Hopkinson's Ceremonial Worlds," *Journal of the Fantastic in the Arts* 18, 1 (2007): 24.

3 Ibid.

4 Nalo Hopkinson, *Brown Girl in the Ring* (Toronto: Sister Vision Press, 1992), 11.

5 I am reminded here of Glen Coulthard's article "For Our Nations to Live, Capitalism Must Die," *Unsettling America: Decolonization in Theory & Practice* (blog), November 3, 2013, https://unsettlingamerica.wordpress.com/2013/11/05/for-our-nations-to-live-capitalism-must-die/.

6 Hopkinson, *Brown Girl in the Ring,* 11. The headlines appear in the novel, in this order, as a sort of public art installation documenting the settler apocalypse.

7 Gordon Collier, "Spaceship Creole: Nalo Hopkinson, Canadian-Caribbean Fabulist Fiction, and Linguistic/Cultural Syncretism," in "A Pepper Pot of Cultures: Aspects of Creolization in the Caribbean," ed. Gordon Collier and Ulrich Fleischmann, special issue, *Matatu: Journal for African Culture and Society* 27/28, 1 (2003): 444.

8 Dillon, "Indigenous Scientific Literacies," 31.

9 David T. McNab, *No Place for Fairness: Indigenous Land Rights and Policy in the Bear Island Case and Beyond* (Montréal/Kingston: McGill-Queen's University Press, 2009), 39–42.

10 Ibid., 54.

11 Ibid.

12 Ibid., 6.

13 Dallas Hunt, "'In Search of Our Better Selves': Totem Transfer Narratives and Indigenous Futurities," *American Indian Culture and Research Journal* 42, 1 (2018): 84.

14 Roy Miki, *Redress: Inside the Japanese Canadian Call for Justice* (Vancouver: Raincoast Books, 2004), 322.

15 Guy Beauregard, "After Redress: A Conversation with Roy Miki," *Canadian Literature* 201 (Summer 2009): 73.

16 Rauna Kuokkanen, *Reshaping the University: Responsibility, Indigenous Epistemes, and the Logic of the Gift* (Vancouver: UBC Press, 2007), 85.

17 Quoted in Jennifer Lind, *Sorry States: Apologies in International Politics* (Ithaca: Cornell University Press, 2008), 101.

18 David Art, *The Politics of the Nazi Past in Germany and Austria* (Cambridge: Cambridge University Press, 2006), 49.

19 Daniel Philpott, *Just and Unjust Peace: An Ethic of Political Reconciliation* (New York: Oxford University Press, 2012), 182.

20 Franz Peter Plenker, "Über Wiedergutmachung," *Forum Psychoanal* 18 (2002): 350.

21 Ibid.

22 Desmond Tutu, *No Future without Forgiveness* (New York: Doubleday, 1999), 20.

23 Ibid., 61.

24 Daniel Levy and Natan Sznaider, "Forgive and Not Forget: Reconciliation between Forgiveness and Resentment," in *Taking Wrongs Seriously: Apologies and Reconciliation,* ed. Elazar Barkan and Alexander Karn (Palo Alto, CA: Stanford University Press, 2006), 92.
25 Nicholas Balabkins, *West German Reparations to Israel* (New Brunswick, NJ: Rutgers University Press, 1971), 127. They are alluding to the prayer "If I forget thee, Jerusalem, let my right-hand wither ..." that is recited during a marriage ceremony, for instance.
26 Kuokkanen, *Reshaping the University,* 85.
27 Ibid., 87.
28 Ibid., 90.
29 Balabkins, *West German Reparations to Israel,* 150.
30 Ibid., 190.
31 Elazar Barkan, *The Guilt of Nations* (Baltimore: Johns Hopkins University Press, 2001), 12.
32 Pierre Bourdieu, "Selections from *The Logic of Practice,*" in *The Logic of the Gift: Toward an Ethic of Generosity,* ed. Alan D. Schrift (New York: Routledge, 1997), 217.
33 Balabkins, *West German Reparations to Israel,* 85.
34 Bourdieu, "Selections from *The Logic of Practice,*" 191.
35 Kuokkanen, *Reshaping the University,* 36.
36 Miki, *Redress,* 234. Ukrainian Canadians were the first group to be interned under the *War Measures Act.* An apology for this "crime against humanity" is still outstanding.
37 I am drawing here from Giorgio Agamben, who writes, "The sovereign, having the legal power to suspend the validity of the law, legally places himself outside of the law." *Homo Sacer: Sovereign Power and Bare Life,* trans. Daniel Heller-Roazen (Stanford, CA: Stanford University Press, 1998), 15. That said, we do not need Agamben to appreciate how Canada and Canadians dehumanized racialized Canadians during this period. For a more specific analysis of white supremacy in Canada, particularly in British Columbia, please see Peter Ward, *White Canada Forever: Popular Attitudes and Public Policy toward Orientals in British Columbia* (Montreal/Kingston: McGill-Queen's University Press, 1978).
38 Patrick Wolfe, "Settler Colonialism and the Elimination of the Native" *Journal of Genocide Research* 8, 4 (2006): 387.
39 Ann Gomer Sunahara, *The Politics of Racism: The Uprooting of Japanese Canadians during the Second World War* (Toronto: Lorimer, 1981), 109–11.
40 P. Whitney Lackenbauer, "Vanishing Indian, Vanishing Military: Military Training and Aboriginal Lands in Twentieth Century Canada" (PhD diss., University of Calgary, 2003), 225.
41 Ibid., 243.
42 Ann Gomer Sunahara, 56.
43 Ian Mackenzie Papers, MG27111B5, vol. 24, PAC. Quoted in Gomer, 56.
44 Ibid.
45 Miki, *Redress,* 18–19.
46 Ibid., 51.

47 Ibid., 9.
48 Ibid., 325.
49 Ibid.
50 Ibid., 234.
51 On moves to innocence, see Eve Tuck and K. Wayne Yang, "Decolonization Is Not a Metaphor," *Decolonization: Indigeneity, Education and Society* 1, 1 (2012): 9–24.
52 Ibid., 233.
53 Ibid., 324.
54 Ibid., 325.
55 Patricia E. Roy, *The Triumph of Citizenship: The Japanese and Chinese in Canada, 1941–67* (Vancouver: UBC Press, 2007), 239.
56 Ibid., 132.
57 Miki, *Redress,* 324.
58 Priscilla B. Hayner, *Unspeakable Truths: Transitional Justice and the Challenge of Truth Commissions,* 2nd ed. (New York: Routledge, 2011), 211.
59 Jennifer Matsunaga, "Two Faces of Transitional Justice: Theorizing the Incommensurability of Transitional Justice and Decolonization in Canada," *Decolonization: Indigeneity, Education and Society* 5, 1 (2016): 28.
60 "Appendix 1: Schedule 'N': Mandate for the Truth and Reconciliation Commission," in *From Truth to Reconciliation: Transforming the Legacy of Residential Schools,* ed. Marlene Brant Castellano, Linda Archibald, and Mike DeGagné (Ottawa: Aboriginal Healing Foundation, 2008), 411.
61 Glen Coulthard, *Red Skin, White Masks* (Minneapolis: University of Minnesota Press, 2014), 135.
62 Jeffery Simpson, "The Latest Instalment of Victim Politics, Canadian-Style," *Globe and Mail,* June 23, 2006, www.theglobeandmail.com/opinion/the-latest-instalment-of-victim-politics-canadian-style/article1104922/.
63 Kevin Loring, *Where the Blood Mixes* (Vancouver: Talonbooks, 2009), 95.
64 Ibid., 24.
65 Aboriginal Healing Foundation, *The Indian Residential Schools Settlement Agreement's Common Experience Payment and Healing: A Qualitative Study Exploring Impacts on Recipients* (Ottawa: Aboriginal Healing Foundation, 2010), ix. This study is available for download from the AHF site: http://www.ahf.ca/downloads/cep-2010-healing.pdf.
66 Gloria Galloway, "Ottawa Starts Compensating Residential School Survivors over Rejected Claims," *Globe and Mail,* March 3, 2017, https://www.theglobeandmail.com/news/politics/ottawa-starts-compensating-residential-school-survivors-over-unfairly-rejected-claims/article34196586/.
67 Legal Services of British Columbia, *Indian Residential Schools Settlement: The Common Experience Payment and the Independent Assessment Process* (fact sheet), August 2013, http://www.llbc.leg.bc.ca/public/pubdocs/bcdocs2014/541693/indian-residential-schools-settlement-eng.pdf.
68 "Pay for Pain, Indians Say," *Washington Times,* August 12, 2001, www.washingtontimes.com/news/2001/aug/12/20010812-024814-7852r/.
69 Loring, *Where the Blood Mixes,* 24.

70 Ibid., 26.

71 Christine Fiddler, "Long Wait for IAP Claimants Seeking Compensation for Residential School," *Saskatchewan Sage*, March 27, 2012, http://ammsa.com/publications/saskatchewan-sage/long-wait-iap-claimants-seeking-compensation-residential-school.

72 Aboriginal Healing Foundation, *Indian Residential Schools Settlement Agreement*, 36.

73 Assembly of First Nations, Annual Report 2012–2013, June 2013, 85, https://www.afn.ca/wp-content/uploads/Annual%20Reports/2013%20AFN%20Annual%20Report%20EN%20USB.pdf.

74 Ronald Niezen, *Truth and Indignation: Canada's Truth and Reconciliation Commission on Indian Residential Schools* (Toronto: University of Toronto Press, 2013), 47.

75 Ibid.

76 Loring, *Where the Blood Mixes*, 56.

77 Louise Bernice Halfe, *Blue Marrow* (Regina, SK: Coteau, 2004), 90.

78 Loring, *Where the Blood Mixes*, 58–59.

79 Ibid., 24.

80 Marcel Mauss, *The Gift: Forms and Functions of Exchange in Archaic Societies*, trans. Ian Cunnison (New York: W.W. Norton, 1967), 1.

81 Shoshana Felman and Dori Laub, *Testimony: Crises of Witnessing in Literature, Psychoanalysis, and History* (New York: Routledge, 1992), 2.

82 Loring, *Where the Blood Mixes*, 26.

83 Shari Narine, "Day Scholars and Excluded Schools Spark Reconciliation Debate," *Windspeaker*, January 1, 2011, https://ammsa.com/publications/windspeaker/day-scholars-and-excluded-schools-spark-reconciliation-debate.

84 See Barker et al., "Intergenerational Trauma: The Relationship between Residential Schools and the Child Welfare System among Young People Who Use Drugs in Vancouver, Canada," *Journal of Adolescent Health* 65, 2 (2019): 248–54.

85 Loring, *Where the Blood Mixes*, 25.

86 Ibid., 48.

87 Michael Ignatieff, "Afterword: Reflections on Coexistence," in *Imagine Coexistence: Restoring Humanity after Violent Ethnic Conflict*, ed. Antonia Chayes and Martha Minow (San Francisco: Jossey-Bass, 2003), 331.

88 Ignatieff wrote the introduction to Jillian Edelstein's *Truth and Lies: Stories from the Truth and Reconciliation Commission in South Africa* and the afterword to *Imagine Coexistence: Restoring Humanity after Violent Ethnic Conflict*, edited by Antonia Chayes and Martha Minow. Probably his most widely read piece on the TRC of Canada is an op-ed written for the *National Post*, entitled "Setting the Record Straight" (June 22, 2007). In that piece, Ignatieff condemns Canada for the residential school system, but the word "colonization" is never used in the article.

89 According to Ignatieff, groups are able to coexist "not because they like or understand each other very well but because cooperation rewards each group sufficiently for individuals to believe that continued coexistence is worthwhile" (Ignatieff, "Afterword," 329). While I agree that the idealist rhetoric of coexistence often disavows the structural inequities that reconciliation must address, in a settler state the "institutional guarantee" that Ignatieff balances his argument on is too deeply

embedded in capitalist/colonial ideology for this claim to be a viable counter position to the idealism he wishes to critique.

90 Bourdieu, "Selections from *The Logic of Practice*," 199.
91 Loring, *Where the Blood Mixes*, 95.
92 Ibid., 88.
93 Bruce Granville Miller, "Bringing Culture In: Community Responses to Apology, Reconciliation and Reparations," *American Indian Culture and Research Journal* 30, 4 (2006): 9.
94 Ibid., 6.
95 Maggie Hodgson, "Reconciliation: A Spiritual Process," in Castellano et al., *From Truth to Reconciliation*, 375.
96 Dara Kelly and Patrick Kelly, "An Ethic of Reciprocity: Illuminating the Stó:lö Gift Economy," in *Indigenous Spiritualities at Work: Transforming the Spirit of Enterprise*, ed. Chellie Spiller and Rachel Wolfgramm (Charlotte, NC: Information Age Publishing, 2015), 191.
97 Mauss, *The Gift*, 5.
98 Kuokkanen, *Reshaping the University*, 30.
99 Rauna Kuokkanen, "The Gift as a Worldview in Indigenous Thought," in "*Il Dono*/The Gift: A Feminist Analysis," ed. G. Vaughan, special issue, *Athanor* 8 (2004): 81.
100 Ibid., 82.
101 Ibid., 90.
102 Kuokkanen, "The Logic of the Gift," 258.
103 Kelly and Kelly, "An Ethic of Reciprocity," 191.
104 Ibid., 198.
105 Ibid., 199.
106 "The History of the Potlatch Collection," U'mista Cultural Centre (website), accessed November 21, 2019, https://www.umista.ca/pages/collection-history.
107 Kelly and Kelly, "An Ethic of Reciprocity," 200.
108 Rachel Flowers, "Refusal to Forgive: Indigenous Women's Love and Rage," *Decolonization: Indigeneity, Education and Society* 4, 2 (2015): 40.
109 Kuokkanen, *Reshaping the University*, 45.
110 Kelly and Kelly, "An Ethic of Reciprocity," 202.
111 Ibid., 203.
112 Ibid., 204.
113 Ibid., 203.
114 Louise Bernice Halfe, *Blue Marrow* (Regina, SK: Coteau, 2004), 90.

Chapter 5: An Exercise in Forgiveness

1 Rachel Flowers, "Refusal to Forgive: Indigenous Women's Love and Rage," *Decolonization: Indigeneity, Education and Society* 4, 2 (2015): 47.
2 Joy Kogawa, *The Rain Ascends* (Toronto: Penguin Canada, 2003), 182.
3 Richard Wagamese, *Medicine Walk* (Toronto: McClelland and Stewart, 2014), 243.
4 Richard Wagamese, "Returning to Harmony," in *Response, Responsibility and Renewal: Canada's Truth and Reconciliation Journey*, ed. Gregory Younging,

Jonathan Dewar, and Mike DeGagné (Ottawa: Aboriginal Healing Foundation, 2009), 146.

5 Ibid., 144.

6 Trudy Govier, *Forgiveness and Revenge* (Abingdon, UK: Routledge, 2002), 97.

7 Richard Wagamese, "Truth and Reconciliation," in *One Story, One Song* (Toronto: Douglas and McIntyre, 2011), 188.

8 Richard Wagamese, "Returning to Harmony," 144.

9 Glen Coulthard, *Red Skin, White Masks* (Minneapolis: University of Minnesota Press, 2014), 111.

10 This is the title of Tutu's 1997 book, *No Future without Forgiveness.*

11 Everett L. Worthington Jr., *Forgiveness and Reconciliation: Theory and Application* (New York: Routledge, 2006), 84.

12 Jacques Derrida, *Cosmopolitanism and Forgiveness,* trans. Mark Dooley and Michael Hughes (New York: Routledge, 2001), 31.

13 On moves to innocence, see Eve Tuck and K. Wayne Yang, "Decolonization Is Not a Metaphor," *Decolonization: Indigeneity, Education and Society* 1, 1 (2012): 1–40.

14 Wagamese, *Medicine Walk,* 60.

15 Ibid., 16.

16 Ibid., 49.

17 Ibid., 48.

18 Ibid., 152.

19 Ibid., 169.

20 Ibid., 167.

21 Ibid., 169.

22 Ibid.

23 Martha Minow, *Between Vengeance and Forgiveness: Facing History after Genocide and Mass Violence* (Boston, MA: Beacon Press, 1998), 17.

24 Coulthard, *Red Skin, White Masks,* 115.

25 Flowers, "Refusal to Forgive," 42.

26 Jacques Derrida, *Aporias,* trans. Thomas Dutoit (Stanford, CA: Stanford University Press, 2000), 8.

27 Wagamese, *Medicine Walk,* 243.

28 Govier, *Forgiveness and Revenge,* 110.

29 Tutu opened and closed his commission with a prayer that evoked God and asked "that the end may bring about that reconciliation and love for our neighbour which our Lord himself commanded." Desmond Tutu, *No Future without Forgiveness* (New York: Doubleday, 1999), 113. For more on mercy as salvation, see Michael Jerryson, Mark Juergensmeyer, and Margo Kitts, eds., *The Oxford Handbook of Religion and Violence* (Oxford: Oxford University Press, 2013), 544.

30 Desmond Tutu, *No Future without Forgiveness,* 156.

31 Ibid., 273.

32 Ibid., 118.

33 Ibid., 156.

34 Douglas White, *Forgiveness and Suffering: A Study of Christian Belief* (Cambridge: Cambridge University Press, 1913), 77.

35 Richard Long, "Forgiven: The Summit June 11–13, 2010," National House of Prayer (website), January 18, 2010, http://nhop.ca/forgiven-the-summit-june-11-122010/.
36 "Native Residential School Forgiveness Granted," CBC News, June 12, 2010, www.cbc.ca/news/canada/native-residential-school-forgiveness-granted-1.956939.
37 Ibid.
38 Deborah Gyapong, "Aboriginal Leaders Offer Forgiveness to Harper Government," *ChristianWeek,* June 18, 2010, www.christianweek.org/aboriginal-leaders-offer-forgiveness-to-harper-government/.
39 Nancy Macdonald, "Sen. Murray Sinclair on Truth and Reconciliation's Progress," *Maclean's,* June 1, 2016, www.macleans.ca/news/canada/sen-murray-sinclair-on-the-progress-of-truth-and-reconciliation/.
40 Susana Mas, "Truth and Reconciliation Chair Says Final Report Marks Start of 'New Era,'" CBC News, December 15, 2015, www.cbc.ca/news/politics/truth-and-reconciliation-final-report-ottawa-event-1.3365921.
41 Mark Kennedy, "Archbishop Urges Penance for Mistreatment of Aboriginal Children at Residential Schools," *Ottawa Citizen,* May 27, 2015, http://www.bishop-accountability.org/news2015/05_06/2015_05_26_Kennedy_ArchbishopUrges.htm.
42 Ibid.
43 Wolfgang Palaver, "Mimetic Theories of Religion and Violence," in Jerryson, Juergensmeyer, and Kitts, *Oxford Handbook of Religion and Violence,* 546.
44 Lewis B. Smedes, *Forgive and Forget: Healing the Hurts We Don't Deserve* (New York: Harper and Row, 1984), 47.
45 We can see the beginnings of this manifestation in the TRC of Canada mandate (Schedule "N"), which in its first sentence identifies "an emerging and compelling desire to put the events of the past behind us." See "Appendix 1: Schedule 'N': Mandate for the Truth and Reconciliation Commission," in *From Truth to Reconciliation: Transforming the Legacy of Residential Schools,* ed. Marlene Brant Castellano, Linda Archibald, and Mike DeGagné (Ottawa: Aboriginal Healing Foundation, 2008), 413.
46 See for instance, conservative pundit Rex Murphy's editorial in the *National Post,* in which he proclaims that Indigenous protests are "a rude dismissal of Canada's generosity." Murphy's fundamental claim in this piece is that "the Canadian present is a vastly different place from the Canadian past" and Indigenous peoples need to move on from history. Rex Murphy, "A Rude Dismissal of Canada's Generosity," *National Post,* October 19, 2013, http://news.nationalpost.com/full-comment/rex-murphy-a-rude-dismissal-of-canadas-generosity.
47 The quotations in this chapter are taken from the Penguin edition.
48 The only internment novel to precede *Obasan* is John Okada's *No-No Boy* (Seattle: University of Washington Press, 1978). *No-No Boy* focuses on the Japanese American experience of internment.
49 Guy Beauregard, "After *Obasan:* Kogawa Criticism and Its Futures," *Studies in Canadian Literature* 26, 2 (2001): 5.
50 Mason Harris, "Joy Kogawa (1935–)," in *Canadian Writers and Their Works: Fiction Series,* ed. Robert Lecker, Jack David, and Ellen Quigley, vol. 11 (Toronto: ECW Press, 1996), 147.
51 Arnold E. Davidson, "A Daughter's Dilemma," review of *The Rain Ascends,* by Joy Kogawa, *Canadian Literature* 154 (1997): 148–50.

52 Ibid.
53 See, for instance, Elder Fred Kelly's autobiographical piece "Confessions of a Born Again Pagan," in Castellano et al., *From Truth to Reconciliation*, 13–41. In this deeply moving essay, Kelly describes his abuse at the hands of priests in residential schools.
54 Benjamin Lefebvre, "In Search of Someday: Trauma and Repetition in Joy Kogawa's Fiction," *Journal of Canadian Studies* 44, 3 (Fall 2010): 156.
55 Kogawa, *The Rain Ascends*, 192, quoted in Lefebvre, "In Search of Someday," 156.
56 Shoshana Felman and Dori Laub, *Testimony: Crises of Witnessing in Literature, Psychoanalysis, and History* (New York: Routledge, 1992), 91.
57 Ibid., xviii.
58 Ronald Niezen, *Truth and Indignation: Canada's Truth and Reconciliation Commission on Indian Residential Schools* (Toronto: University of Toronto Press, 2013), 3.
59 Felman and Laub, *Testimony*, xx.
60 Kogawa, *The Rain Ascends*, 121.
61 Ibid., 1.
62 Ibid., 163.
63 Ibid., 47, 53.
64 See Chapter 4 of this book, or Roy Miki, *Redress: Inside the Japanese Canadian Call for Justice* (Vancouver: Raincoast Books, 2004), 50.
65 Kogawa, *The Rain Ascends*, 53.
66 Ibid., 74.
67 Joy Kogawa, *Obasan* (Markham, ON: Penguin Canada, 2017), 65.
68 Joy Kogawa, *Itsuka* (Toronto: Viking Press, 1992), 25.
69 Ibid., 26.
70 Felman and Laub, 163.
71 Cherry Clayton, "Interview with Joy Kogawa 'Kawaiso' (A Word Used to Comfort Children)," *Canadian Ethnic Studies* 34, 2 (2002): 114.
72 Ann Gomer Sunahara, *The Politics of Racism: The Uprooting of Japanese Canadians during the Second World War* (Toronto: Lorimer, 1981), 1.
73 Donald Goellnicht, "Minority History as Metafiction: Joy Kogawa's *Obasan*," *Tulsa Studies in Women's Literature* 8, 2 (1989): 296.
74 Cindy Holmes and Sarah Hunt, *Indigenous Communities and Family Violence: Changing the Conversation* (Prince George, BC: National Collaborating Centre for Aboriginal Health, 2017), 7, https://issuu.com/nccah-ccnsa/docs/rpt-familyviolence-holmes-hunt-en.
75 Cindy Holmes, Sarah Hunt, and Amy Piedalue, "Violence, Colonialism and Space: Towards a Decolonizing Dialogue." *ACME: An International Journal for Critical Geographies* 14, 2 (2015), 550.
76 TRC of Canada, *Honouring the Truth, Reconciling for the Future: Summary of the Final Report of the Truth and Reconciliation Commission of Canada* (Winnipeg: TRC, 2015), 105, http://nctr.ca/assets/reports/Final%20Reports/Executive_Summary_English_Web.pdf.
77 Kogawa, *The Rain Ascends*, 65.
78 Tutu, *No Future without Forgiveness*, 27–30.
79 Priscilla B. Hayner, "Fifteen Truth Commissions – 1974 to 1994: A Comparative Study," *Human Rights Quarterly* 16, 4 (1994): 605.

80 Kogawa, *The Rain Ascends,* 16.
81 Worthington, *Forgiveness and Reconciliation,* 75.
82 Davidson, "A Daughter's Dilemma," 139.
83 Antjie Krog, *Country of My Skull* (London: Jonathan Cape, 1994), 169.
84 Tutu, *No Future without Forgiveness,* 286.
85 Krog, *Country of My Skull,* 65. Krog describes more symptoms on 222.
86 Kogawa, *The Rain Ascends,* 56.
87 Ibid., 163.
88 Ibid., 182.
89 Ibid., 200.
90 Worthington, *Forgiveness and Reconciliation,* 79.
91 Cynthia Cohen, "Engaging with the Arts to Promote Coexistence," in *Imagine Coexistence: Restoring Humanity after Violent Ethnic Conflict,* ed. Antonia Chayes and Martha Minow (San Francisco: Jossey-Bass, 2003), 274.
92 Worthington, *Forgiveness and Reconciliation,* 24.
93 Ibid., 102.
94 John A. Macdonald, Canada's first prime minister, is famously quoted as stating that "the great aim of our legislation has been to do away with the tribal system and assimilate the Indian people in all respects with the other inhabitants of the Dominion as speedily as they are fit for the change." Canada, Parliament, Sessional Paper No. 20b, 6th Parl., 1st Sess., Vol. 16 (January 3, 1887), 37 (Hon. John A. Macdonald).
95 Kogawa, *The Rain Ascends,* 184.
96 Ibid., 179.
97 Susan Lazaruk, "77-Year Old Pedophile Sentenced to 11 Years," *Windspeaker,* June 1, 1995, https://ammsa.com/publications/windspeaker/77-year-old-pedophile-sentenced-11-years.
98 TRC of Canada, *Honouring the Truth,* 107.
99 Ibid., 105.
100 Ibid.
101 Ibid.
102 Ibid., 107.
103 Ibid.
104 Ibid.
105 *The Canadian Encyclopedia,* s.v. "Eden Robinson," by Jules Lewis, accessed November 9, 2017, https://www.thecanadianencyclopedia.ca/en/article/eden-robinson/.
106 Patricia M. Barkaskas and Sarah Hunt, "Truth before Reconciliation: Reframing/Resisting/Refusing Reconciliation" (lecture, Simon Fraser University, Vancouver, BC, March 10, 2017), https://www.sfu.ca/humanities-institute/public-events/archive/2016–17/tbeforer.html.
107 Marlene Brant Castellano, "A Holistic Approach to Reconciliation: Insights from Research of the Aboriginal Healing Foundation," in Castellano et al., *From Truth to Reconciliation,* 398.
108 Vladimir Nabokov, *Lectures on Literature,* ed. Fredson Bowers (New York: Harcourt, 1980), 6.
109 For a more detailed analysis of naming in Robinson see Nancy Van Styvendale, "Naming as Performative Re-Membering in Eden Robinson's 'Queen of the North,'"

in "A Canadian Post/national," ed. David Stouck and Jordan Stouck, special issue, *Journal of Commonwealth and Postcolonial Studies* 9, 1 (Spring 2002): 93–104.

110 Eden Robinson, "Queen of the North," in *Traplines* (New York: Metropolitan Books, 1996), 200.

111 Holmes and Hunt, *Indigenous Communities and Family Violence*, 29.

112 Coulthard, *Red Skin, White Masks*, 126.

113 Minow, *Between Vengeance and Forgiveness*, 10.

114 Canadian Press, "Residential School Survivors Find It Hard to Forgive," CTV News, February 21, 2010, https://www.ctvnews.ca/residential-school-survivors-find-it-hard-to-forgive-1.485516.

115 Robinson, "Queen of the North," 212.

116 Canada, Royal Commission on Aboriginal Peoples, *Report of the Royal Commission on Aboriginal Peoples*, vol. 3, *Gathering Strength* (Ottawa: Canada Communication Group, 1996), 52, http://data2.archives.ca/e/e448/e011188230-03.pdf.

117 Robinson, "Queen of the North," 212.

118 Lazaruk, "77-Year Old Pedophile Sentenced to 11 Years."

119 Nuu-chah-nulth Tribal Council, *Residential Schools: The Nuu-chah-nulth Experience; Report of the Nuu-chah-nulth Tribal Council Indian Residential Schools Study, 1992–1994* (Port Alberni, BC: Nuu-chah-nulth Tribal Council, 1996).

120 Lazaruk, "77-Year Old Pedophile Sentenced to 11 Years."

121 Holmes and Hunt, *Indigenous Communities and Family Violence*, 5.

122 Robinson, "Queen of the North," 212.

123 Ibid., 213.

124 As Worthington writes in his own extensive study of forgiveness, "Almost every major theory of promoting forgiveness in the clinic has targeted empathy as a key player" (*Forgiveness and Reconciliation*, 102).

125 Worthington, *Forgiveness and Reconciliation*, 74. Worthington defines decisional forgiveness against hollow forgiveness, in which the subject forgives only as a result of societal pressure, and emotional forgiveness, in which the subject experiences a psychological change in their relation to the perpetrator.

126 Ibid., 75.

127 Billy-Ray Belcourt, "Gay Incantations," in *This Wound Is a World* (Calgary: Frontenac House, 2017), 11.

Conclusion

1 Quoted in Rob Shaw, "NDP Government Decides to Continue Construction on Site C Dam," *Vancouver Sun*, December 12, 2017, http://vancouversun.com/news/politics/ndp-government-decides-to-continue-construction-on-site-c-dam.

2 Cherie Dimaline, *The Marrow Thieves* (Toronto: Dancing Cat Books, 2017), 230–31.

3 Ibid.

4 Jason Lewis, "A Brief (Media) History of the Future Imaginary," *Public* 27, 54 (2016): 45.

5 Dimaline uses the phrase "coming-to story" to describe the post-apocalyptic story arcs of each character before they came together as a group. See, for instance, "Wab's coming-to story." Dimaline, *The Marrow Thieves*, 80.

6 Dimaline, *The Marrow Thieves*, 7.
7 Dimaline, *The Marrow Thieves*, 141.
8 Karl Marx, *Capital*, trans. Ben Fowkes (New York: Vintage, 1977), 166–67.
9 Trevor Corkum and Cherie Dimaline, "The Chat with 2017 Governor General's Award Winner Cherie Dimaline," *49th Shelf*, November 27, 2017, https://49thshelf.com/Blog/2017/11/282/The-Chat-with-2017-Governor-General-s-Award-winner-Cherie-Dimaline.
10 Glen Coulthard, "For Our Nations to Live, Capitalism Must Die," *Rabble.ca*, November 6, 2013, https://rabble.ca/news/2013/11/our-nations-to-live-capitalism-must-die.
11 Daniel Heath Justice, *Why Indigenous Literatures Matter* (Waterloo: Wilfrid Laurier University Press, 2018), 143.
12 TRC of Canada, *Honouring the Truth, Reconciling for the Future: Summary of the Final Report of the Truth and Reconciliation Commission of Canada* (Winnipeg: TRC, 2015).
13 Roy L. Brooks, "The Age of Apology," in *When Sorry Isn't Enough: The Controversy over Apologies and Reparations for Human Justice*, ed. Roy L. Brooks (New York: New York University Press, 1999), 3.
14 Mitch Miyagawa, "A Sorry State," *Walrus*, December 12, 2009, https://thewalrus.ca/a-sorry-state/.
15 Experts refer to this phenomenon as "semantic satiation:" the "loss of meaning of a word following its massed evocation." J.P. Das, *Verbal Conditioning and Behaviour* (Oxford: Pergamon, 1969), 92.
16 Ryan McMahon (@RMComedy), Twitter, March 16, 2016, 9:35 a.m., https://twitter.com/RMComedy/status/710142395422216192?ref_src=twsrc%5Etfw.
17 Leanne Betasamosake Simpson, *Dancing on Our Turtle's Back* (Winnipeg: ARP Publishing, 2011), 22.
18 As in Chapter 1, I draw on Stuart Hall who argues that race, as a floating signifier, is dependent on context and thus can be appropriated to reproduce dominant power relations. Stuart Hall, *Race, the Floating Signifier*, dir. Sut Jhally (Media Education Foundation, 1997).
19 "Appendix 1: Schedule 'N': Mandate for the Truth and Reconciliation Commission," in Castellano et al., *From Truth to Reconciliation*, 413.
20 Fred Kelly, "Confessions of a Born Again Pagan," in *From Truth to Reconciliation: Transforming the Legacy of Residential Schools*, ed. Marlene Brant Castellano, Linda Archibald, and Mike DeGagné (Ottawa: Aboriginal Healing Foundation, 2008), 26.
21 Tom Clark, Ravi de Costa, and Sarah Maddison, "Non-Indigenous People and the Limits of Settler Colonial Reconciliation," in *The Limits of Settler Colonial Reconciliation: Non-Indigenous People and the Responsibility to Engage*, ed. Tom Clark, Ravi de Costa, and Sarah Maddison (Singapore: Springer, 2016), 2.
22 TRC of Canada, *Honouring the Truth, Reconciling for the Future: Summary of the Final Report of the Truth and Reconciliation Commission of Canada* (Winnipeg: TRC, 2015), 187, http://nctr.ca/assets/reports/Final%20Reports/Executive_Summary_English_Web.pdf.
23 Amnesty International, "The Point of No Return: The Human Rights of Indigenous Peoples in Canada Threatened by the Site C Dam," 2016, 5, www.amnesty.ca/sites/amnesty/files/Canada%20Site%20C%20Report.pdf.

24 *Tsilhqot' in v. British Columbia* established that, "the Crown is *always* required to obtain Indigenous consent prior to an incursion of Aboriginal title" [emphasis in original]. Rachel Gutman, "The Stories We Tell: Site-C, Treaty 8, and the Duty to Consult and Accommodate," *Appeal* 23 (2018): 11.

25 Zoë Ducklow, "Site C Threatens Treaty Rights, Way of Life, Say Some First Nations," *The Tyee,* April 26, 2017, https://thetyee.ca/News/2017/04/26/Site-C-Threatens-First-Nations-Rights/.

26 Amnesty International, "The Point of No Return," 3–18.

27 Ibid., 16.

28 Chief Lynette Tsakoza quoted in Amnesty International, "The Point of No Return," 16.

29 Justine Hunter, "Horgan's Acknowledgment of Unceded Indigenous Territory a Milestone for B.C.," *Globe and Mail,* October 22, 2017, www.theglobeandmail.com/news/british-columbia/horgans-acknowledgment-of-bcs-unceded-territory-part-of-a-path-forward/article36686705/. Legislative Assembly, *Bill 41 – 2019: Declaration on the Rights of Indigenous Peoples Act* (2019), https://www.leg.bc.ca/parliamentary-business/legislation-debates-proceedings/41st-parliament/4th-session/bills/first-reading/gov41-1.

30 Rob Shaw, "NDP Government Decides to Continue Construction on Site C Dam," *Vancouver Sun,* December 12, 2017, http://vancouversun.com/news/politics/ndp-government-decides-to-continue-construction-on-site-c-dam.

31 Glen Coulthard, *Red Skin, White Masks* (Minneapolis: University of Minnesota Press, 2014), 127.

32 Warren Cariou discusses the contemporary implications of *terra nullius,* namely the ongoing erasure of Indigenous peoples from settler points of view, in "Edgework: Indigenous Poetics as Re-placement," in *Indigenous Poetics in Canada,* ed. Neal McLeod (Waterloo: Wilfrid Laurier University Press, 2014), 35–36.

33 James Rowan, "War Crimes Tribunals, Crimes against Humanity and Transitional Justice," *International Encyclopedia of the Social and Behavioral Sciences,* 2nd ed. (Oxford: Elsevier, 2015), 382–88.

34 Cindy Blackstock quoted in Ashifa Kassam, "Ratio of Indigenous Children in Canada Welfare System Is 'Humanitarian Crisis,'" *Guardian,* November 4, 2017, www.theguardian.com/world/2017/nov/04/indigenous-children-canada-welfare-system-humanitarian-crisis.

35 Ravi de Costa, "Discursive Institutions in Non-Transitional Societies: The Truth and Reconciliation Commission of Canada," *International Political Science Review* 38, 2 (2017): 185.

36 Kelly, "Confessions of a Born Again Pagan," 22–23, also quoted in TRC of Canada, *Honouring the Truth,* 195.

37 Roland Chrisjohn makes this exact point about the TRC of Canada: "In general, the perpetrators of a crime do not get to enforce their own sentence, unless, of course, the survivors are Indigenous people and the perpetrators are anyone else." Roland Chrisjohn and Tanya Wasacase, "Half Truths, Whole Lies," in *Response, Responsibility and Renewal: Canada's Truth and Reconciliation Journey,* ed. Gregory Younging, Jonathan Dewar, and Mike DeGagné (Ottawa: Aboriginal Healing Foundation, 2009), 225.

38 Gayatri Chakravorty Spivak, "Echo," *New Literary History* 24, 1 (1993): 25.
39 "Appendix 1: Schedule 'N': Mandate for the Truth and Reconciliation Commission," in Castellano et al., *From Truth to Reconciliation,* 413.
40 Dallas Hunt, "'In Search of Our Better Selves': Totem Transfer Narratives and Indigenous Futurities," *American Indian Culture and Research Journal* 42, 1 (2018): 74.
41 Lewis, "Brief," 36–37.
42 Ibid., 86.
43 D. Hunt, 78.
44 Ibid., 79–80.
45 Daniel Heath Justice, *Why Indigenous Literatures Matter* (Waterloo, ON: Wilfrid Laurier University Press, 2017), 155–56.
46 Grace L. Dillon, "Imagining Indigenous Futurisms," in *Walking the Clouds: An Anthology of Indigenous Science Fiction,* ed. Grace L. Dillon (Tucson: University of Arizona Press, 2012), 2.
47 Ibid.
48 Kristina Baudemann, "Indigenous Futurisms in North American Indigenous Art: The Transforming Visions of Ryan Singer, Daniel McCoy, Topaz Jones, Marla Allison, and Debra Yepa-Pappan," *Extrapolation* 57, 1–2 (2016): 127.
49 Lou Cornum, "The Space NDN's Starmap," in *Read, Listen, Tell: Indigenous Stories from Turtle Island,* ed. Sophia McCall, Deanna Reder, David Gaertner, and Gabrielle L'Hirondelle Hill (Waterloo, ON: Wilfrid Laurier University Press, 2017), 365.
50 Ibid.
51 Ibid., 366.
52 Lindsey Nixon, "sâkihito-maskihkiy acâhkosiwikamikohk," *GUTS,* May 20, 2016, http://gutsmagazine.ca/visual-cultures/.
53 Erica Violet Lee, "Reconciling in the Apocalypse," Canadian Centre for Policy Alternatives, March 1, 2016, https://www.policyalternatives.ca/publications/monitor/reconciling-apocalypse.
54 Lewis, "Brief," 45.
55 Ibid., 37.
56 Jason Lewis in conversation with Rebecca Smyth, "Jason Edward Lewis: The Indigenous Future Imaginary," *Luma Quarterly* 3, 1 (2016), https://lumaquarterly.com/issues/2015/003-winter/jason-edward-lewis/.
57 Thomas King, *The Inconvenient Indian: A Curious Account of Native People in North America* (Toronto: Doubleday Canada, 2012), 53.
58 Lewis, "Brief," 37.
59 Ibid., 41.
60 Mark Rifkin, *Beyond Settler Time: Temporal Sovereignty and Indigenous Self-Determination* (Durham: Duke University Press, 2017).
61 Quoted in Hartmut Lutz, "Canadian Multicultural Literatures: Ethnic Minorities and 'AlterNatives,'" in *The Canadian Alternative,* ed. Klaus Martens (Würzburg: Königshausen and Neumann, 2003), 46.
62 Oglála Lakȟóta performance artist Kite makes reference to Indigenous time as a "flat circle," in conversation with Nicole Kelly Westman, "Concrete Constructs of Linearity,"

LUMA Quarterly 2, 8 (2017), lumaquarterly.com/issues/volume-two/008-spring/concrete-constructs-of-linearity.

63 Elizabeth Lapensée, "Strange Horizons – Decolonizing Science Fiction and Imagining Futures: An Indigenous Futurisms Roundtable by Rebecca Roanhorse, Elizabeth LaPensee, Johnnie Jae, and Darcie Little Badger." *Strange Horizons*, January 30, 2017, http://strangehorizons.com/non-fiction/articles/decolonizing-science-fiction-and-imagining-futures-an-indigenous-futurisms-roundtable/.

64 Dimaline never offers an exact date for her dystopia. She does, however, provide dates on a character's health card, issued 04/11/2049. Dimaline, *The Marrow Thieves*, 176.

65 Dimaline, *The Marrow Thieves*, 26.

66 Dimaline, *The Marrow Thieves*, 53.

67 Fredric Jameson, *Postmodernism, or, The Cultural Logic of Late Capitalism* (Durham: Duke University Press, 1991), 67.

68 Dimaline, *The Marrow Thieves*, 54.

69 Ibid., 89.

70 Adam Gaudry, "Communing with the Dead: The 'New Métis,' Métis Identity Appropriation, and the Displacement of Living Métis Culture," *American Indian Quarterly* 42, 2 (Spring 2018): 173.

71 Ibid., 185.

72 Patrick Wolfe, *Settler Colonialism and the Transformation of Anthropology: The Politics and Poetics of an Ethnographic Event* (London and Washington: Cassell, 1999), 3.

73 Dimaline, *The Marrow Thieves*, 88.

74 Ibid., 26.

75 Ibid., 88.

76 Wolfe, *Settler Colonialism*, 3.

77 TRC of Canada, *Honouring the Truth, Reconciling for the Future*, 3.

78 Dimaline, "The Chat with," n.p.

79 Dimaline, *The Marrow Thieves*, 5.

80 Ibid., 101.

81 Ibid., 102.

82 Carolyn Bennett quoted in Aubrey Jean Hanson, "Reading for Reconciliation? Indigenous Literatures in a Post-TRC Canada," *ESC: English Studies in Canada* 43, 2–3 (June/September 2017): 71.

83 Hanson, 71–72.

84 Ibid., 74

85 Jenny Burman, "Multicultural Feeling, Feminist Rage, Indigenous Refusal" *Cultural Studies – Critical Methodologies* 16, 4 (2016): 362.

86 Ibid., 89–90.

87 I am once again drawing from Schedule 'N' of the TRC which establishes the commission as a means to "put the events of the past behind us." "Appendix 1: Schedule 'N': Mandate for the Truth and Reconciliation Commission," in Castellano et al., *From Truth to Reconciliation*, 413.

88 Sigmund Freud, "Repression," in *The Complete Psychological Works of Sigmund Freud*, ed. James Strachey, vol. 14 (New York: W.W. Norton, 1976), 2983.

89 Ibid., 2978.
90 Ibid., 2980.
91 Sigmund Freud, "The Uncanny," in *The Monster Theory Reader*, ed. Jeffrey Andrew Weinstock (Minneapolis: University of Minnesota Press, 2020), 74.
92 Ibid., 87.
93 Gilles Deluze and Félix Guattari, *A Thousand Plateaus: Capitalism and Schizophrenia*, trans. Brian Massumi (Minneapolis: University of Minnesota Press, 1987), 25.
94 Megan E. Cannella, "Dreams in a Time of Dystopic Colonialism: Cherie Dimaline's The Marrow Thieves and Louise Erdrich's Future Home of the Living God," in *Displaced: Literature of Indigeneity, Migration, and Trauma* (New York: Routledge, 2020), 111.
95 Dimaline, *The Marrow Thieves*, 193.
96 I want to thank Karlene Harvey for drawing my attention to this second echo in *The Marrow Thieves* and for the insight she has shared with me on Minerva. Check out her artwork at www.karleneharvey.com.
97 Simpson, *Dancing on Our Turtle's Back*, 110.
98 Leanne Betasamosake Simpson, "'Bubbling Like a Beating Heart': Reflections on Nishnaabeg Poetic and Narrative Consciousness," in *Indigenous Poetics in Canada*, ed. Neal McLeod (Waterloo, ON: Wilfred Laurier University Press, 2014), 110.
99 Neal McLeod, quoted in Simpson, ibid.
100 Ibid.
101 Dimaline, *The Marrow Thieves*, 37–38.
102 Ibid., 38.
103 Ibid., 39.
104 Nayuka Gorrie has said, "Colonisation was our apocalypse, and we are already living in a dystopian future, so we are ahead of the game." Quoted in Tyson Yunkaporta, "I'm Part of the World's Oldest Living Culture, but Could I Kill a Zombie with a Boomerang?," *The Guardian*, September 26, 2017, www.theguardian.com/artanddesign/2017/sep/27/im-part-of-the-worlds-oldest-living-culture-but-could-i-kill-a-zombie-with-a-boomerang.
105 Simpson, *Dancing on Our Turtle's Back*, 107.
106 Ibid., 108.
107 Simpson, *Dancing on Our Turtle's Back*, 16.
108 Dimaline, *The Marrow Thieves*, 172.
109 Simpson, "Bubbling," 116.
110 Dimaline, *The Marrow Thieves*, 173.
111 Simpson, "Bubbling," 108.
112 Eve Tuck and K. Wayne Yang, "Decolonization Is Not a Metaphor," *Decolonization: Indigeneity, Education and Society* 1, 1 (2012): 31.
113 Ibid., 36.
114 Jodi A. Byrd and Michael Rothberg, "Between Subalternity and Indigeneity," *Interventions* 13, 1 (2011): 8.
115 Dale Turner, *This Is Not a Peace Pipe* (Toronto: University of Toronto Press, 2006), 95.
116 Turner quoted in Byrd and Rothberg, 6.
117 Jean-François Lyotard, *The Differend: Phrases in Dispute* (Minneapolis: University of Minnesota Press, 1989), quoted in Byrd and Rothberg, Between Subalternity and Indigeneity, 7.

118 Ibid.

119 Tuck and Yang, "Decolonization Is Not a Metaphor," 35.

120 Dimaline, *The Marrow Thieves*, 173.

121 Ibid., 231.

122 Jacques Derrida, *On Cosmopolitanism and Forgiveness*, trans. Mark Dooley and Michael Hughes (New York: Routledge, 2001), 50.

123 Pam Palmater, "Truth and Reconciliation in Canada: If It Feels Good, It's Not Reconciliation." The 2018 Woodrow Lloyd Lecture, University of Regina, February 15, 2018.

Selected Bibliography

Beyond the citations, the core of the ideas represented in this text have been informed by a select number of thinkers and authors – most notably in the field of Indigenous studies. I offer this selected bibliography as a means to further hold up that work while proffering a shared critical foundation for future research in reconciliation studies, Indigenous literatures, and Canadian literature.

Acoose, Janice. "Deconstructing Five Generations of White Christian Colonial Rule." In *Residential Schools: The Stolen Years,* edited by Linda Jaine, 2nd ed., 3–13. Saskatoon, SK: University Extension Press, 1995.

Armstrong, Jeanette C. "Land Speaking." In *Speaking for the Generations: Native Writers on Writing,* edited by Simon J. Ortiz, 175–94. Tucson: University of Arizona Press, 1998.

Assembly of First Nations. *Breaking the Silence: An Interpretive Study of Residential School Impact and Healing as Illustrated by the Stories of First Nations Individuals.* Ottawa: Assembly of First Nations, 1994.

Barkaskas, Patricia M., and Sarah Hunt. "Truth before Reconciliation: Reframing/Resisting/Refusing Reconciliation." Lecture given at the Simon Fraser University Institute for the Humanities, Vancouver, BC, March 10, 2017.

Beauregard, Guy. "After *Obasan:* Kogawa Criticism and Its Futures." *Studies in Canadian Literature* 26, 2 (2001): 5–22.

Behrendt, Larissa. "Blood from a Stone." *Arena,* August 2, 2002. https://arena.org.au/blood-from-a-stone/.

Belcourt, Billy-Ray. "Fatal Naming Rituals." *Hazlitt,* July 19, 2018. https://hazlitt.net/feature/fatal-naming-rituals.

–. *This Wound Is a World.* Calgary: Frontenac House, 2017.

Belmore, Rebecca. Artist Statement. In *Witnesses: Art and Canada's Indian Residential Schools*. Vancouver: Morris and Helen Belkin Art Gallery, 2013. Exhibition catalogue.

Borrows, John. "Practical Reconciliation, Practical Re-Colonization." *Land, Rights, Laws: Issues of Native Title* 2, 27 (2004): 1–12.

Byrd, Jodi A. *Transit of Empire: Indigenous Critiques of Colonialism*. Minneapolis: University of Minnesota Press, 2011.

Cariou, Warren. "Haunted Prairie: Aboriginal 'Ghosts' and the Spectre of Settlement." *University of Toronto Quarterly* 75 (2006): 727–34.

–. "Edgework: Indigenous Poetics as Re-placement." In *Indigenous Poetics in Canada*, edited by Neal McLeod, 31–38. Waterloo, ON: Wilfrid Laurier University Press, 2014.

Carlson, M. Teresa, Keith Thor Carlson, Brian Thom, and Albert "Sonny" McHalsie. "Spoken Literature." In *You Are Asked to Witness: The Stó:lõ in Canada's Pacific Coast History*, edited by Keith Thor Carlson, 181–89. Chilliwack, BC: Stó:lõ Heritage Trust, 1996.

Chrisjohn, Roland, and Tanya Wasacase. "Half Truths, Whole Lies." In *Response, Responsibility and Renewal: Canada's Truth and Reconciliation Journey*, edited by Gregory Younging, Jonathan Dewar, and Mike DeGagné, 217–32. Ottawa: Aboriginal Healing Foundation, 2009.

Chrisjohn, Roland, and Sherri Young. *The Circle Game: Shadows and Substance in the Indian Residential School Experience in Canada*. Penticton, BC: Theytus Books, 1997. http://data2.archives.ca/rcap/pdf/rcap-32.pdf.

Clements, Marie. *Burning Vision*. Burnaby, BC: Talonbooks, 2003.

Cook-Lynn, Elizabeth. *Why I Can't Read Wallace Stegner and Other Essays*. Madison: University of Wisconsin Press, 1996.

Corntassel, Jeff. "Toward Sustainable Self-Determination: Rethinking the Contemporary Indigenous-Rights Discourse." *Alternatives* 33 (2008): 105–32.

–. "Who's Sorry Now? Government Apologies, Truth Commissions, and Indigenous Self-Determination in Australia, Canada, Guatemala, and Peru." *Human Rights Review* 9, 4 (2008): 465–89.

Cornum, Lou. "The Space NDN's Starmap." In *Read, Listen, Tell: Indigenous Stories from Turtle Island*, edited by Sophia McCall, Deanna Reder, David Gaertner, and Gabrielle L'Hirondelle Hill, 364–72. Waterloo, ON: Wilfrid Laurier University Press, 2017.

Coulthard, Glen. "For Our Nations to Live, Capitalism Must Die." *Unsettling America: Decolonization in Theory & Practice* (blog), November 3, 2013. https://unsettlingamerica.wordpress.com/2013/11/05/for-our-nations-to-live-capitalism-must-die/.

–. *Red Skin, White Masks*. Minneapolis: University of Minnesota Press, 2014.

de Costa, Ravi. "Discursive Institutions in Non-Transitional Societies: The Truth and Reconciliation Commission of Canada." *International Political Science Review* 38, 2 (2017): 185–99.

Dillon, Grace L. "Imagining Indigenous Futurisms." In *Walking the Clouds: An Anthology of Indigenous Science Fiction*, edited by Grace L. Dillon, 1–14. Tucson: University of Arizona Press, 2012.

–. "Indigenous Scientific Literacies in Nalo Hopkinson's Ceremonial Worlds." *Journal of the Fantastic in the Arts* 18, 1 (2007): 23–41.

Dimaline, Cherie. "The Chat with 2017 Governor General's Award Winner Cherie Dimaline." Interview by Trevor Corkum, *49th Shelf* (blog), November 27, 2017. https://49thshelf.com/Blog/2017/11/282/The-Chat-with-2017-Governor-General-s-Award-winner-Cherie-Dimaline.

–. *The Marrow Thieves*. Toronto: Dancing Cat Books, 2017.

Fabris, Michael. "Enacting Indigenous Jurisdiction(s) in the Settler Colonial Cityscape." Paper presented as part of panel discussion entitled "The Everyday Violence of Law: Indigenous Peoples, Violence, Resistance," with Sarah Hunt, Patricia Barkaskas, and Natalie Clark at the International Meeting on Law and Society, Mexico City, June 23, 2017.

Flowers, Rachel. "Refusal to Forgive: Indigenous Women's Love and Rage." *Decolonization: Indigeneity, Education and Society* 4, 2 (2015): 32–49.

Fraser, Crystal, and Ian Mosby. "Setting Canadian History Right? A Response to Ken Coates' 'Second Thoughts about Residential Schools.'" ActiveHistory.ca (blog), April 7, 2015. http://activehistory.ca/papers/paper-20/.

Fred, Randy. "Introduction." In *Resistance and Renewal: Surviving the Indian Residential School,* by Celia Haig-Brown, 25–26. Vancouver: Arsenal Pulp Press, 1988.

Garneau, David. "Imaginary Spaces of Conciliation and Reconciliation: Art, Curation and Healing." In *Arts of Engagement: Taking Aesthetic Action in and beyond the Truth and Reconciliation Commission of Canada,* edited by Dylan Robinson and Keavy Martin, 21–42. Waterloo, ON: Wilfrid Laurier University Press, 2015.

Greenwood, Margo, Sarah de Leeuw, Nicole Marie Lindsay, and Charlotte Reading, *Determinants of Indigenous Peoples' Health in Canada: Beyond the Social.* Toronto: Canadian Scholars Press, 2015.

Halfe, Louise Bernice. *Bear Bones and Feathers,* edited by Patrick Lane. Regina, SK: Coteau Books, 1994.

–. *Blue Marrow*. Regina, SK: Coteau, 2004.

–. *Burning in this Midnight Dream*. Regina, SK: Coteau, 2016.

–. "The Residential School Bus." In *Residential Schools: The Stolen Years,* edited by Linda Jaine, 2nd ed., 92–98. Saskatoon, SK: University Extension Press, 1995.

Hanson, Aubrey Jean. "Reading for Reconciliation? Indigenous Literatures in a Post-TRC Canada." *ESC: English Studies in Canada* 43, 2–3 (June/September 2017): 69–90.

Holmes, Cindy, and Sarah Hunt. "Everyday Decolonization: Living a Decolonizing Queer Politics." *Journal of Lesbian Studies* 19, 2 (2015): 154–72.

–. *Indigenous Communities and Family Violence: Changing the Conversation*. Prince George, BC: National Collaborating Centre for Aboriginal Health, 2017. https://issuu.com/nccah-ccnsa/docs/rpt-familyviolence-holmes-hunt-en.

Holmes, Cindy, Sarah Hunt, and Amy Piedalue. "Violence, Colonialism, and Space: Towards a Decolonizing Dialogue." *ACME: An International Journal for Critical Geographies* 14, 2 (2015): 540–70.

Hopkinson, Nalo. *Brown Girl in the Ring*. Toronto: Sister Vision Press, 1992.

Hunt, Dallas. "'In Search of Our Better Selves': Totem Transfer Narratives and Indigenous Futurities." *American Indian Culture and Research Journal* 42, 1 (2018): 71–90.

Hunt, Sarah. "Researching within Relations of Violence: Witnessing as Methodology." In *Indigenous Research: Theories, Practices, and Relationships*, edited by Deborah McGregor, Jean-Paul Restoule, and Rochelle Johnston, 282–95. Toronto: Canadian Scholars Press, 2018.

Iseke, Judy. "Indigenous Digital Storytelling in Video: Witnessing with Alma Desjarlais." *Equity and Excellence in Education* 44, 3 (2011): 311–29.

Justice, Daniel Heath. "'Go Away, Water!': Kinship Criticism and the Decolonization Imperative." In *Reasoning Together: The Native Critics Collection*, edited by Craig Womack, 147–68. Norman: University of Oklahoma Press, 2008.

–. *Why Indigenous Literatures Matter*. Waterloo, ON: Wilfrid Laurier University Press, 2017.

Kelly, Dara, and Patrick Kelly. "Illuminating the Stó:lö Gift Economy." In *Indigenous Spiritualities at Work: Transforming the Spirit of Enterprise*, edited by Chellie Spiller and Rachel Wolfgramm, 191–208. Charlotte, NC: Information Age Publishing, 2015.

King, Thomas. *The Inconvenient Indian: A Curious Account of Native People in North America*. Minneapolis: University of Minnesota Press, 2013.

–. *Green Grass, Running Water*. Toronto: Harper Perennial, 1993.

Kino-nda-niimi Collective, ed. *The Winter We Danced: Voices from the Past, the Future, and the Idle No More Movement*. Winnipeg: ARP Books, 2014.

Kogawa, Joy. *Obasan*. Toronto: Lester and Orpen Dennys, 1994.

–. *Itsuka*. New York: Viking, 1992.

–. *The Rain Ascends*. Toronto: Knopf Canada, 1995.

Kovach, Margaret. "Situating Self, Culture, and Purpose in Indigenous Inquiry. In *Learn, Teach, Challenge: Approaching Indigenous Literatures*, edited by Deanna Reder and Lina M. Morra, 95–106. Waterloo, ON: Wilfrid Laurier University Press, 2016.

Kuokkanen, Rauna. "The Gift as a Worldview in Indigenous Thought." In "Il Dono/ The Gift: A Feminist Analysis," edited by G. Vaughan. Special issue. *Athanor* 8 (2004): 81–95.

–. "The Logic of the Gift: Reclaiming Indigenous Peoples Philosophies." In *Re-Ethnicizing the Minds? Cultural Revival in Contemporary Thought*, edited by Thorsten Botz-Bornstein and Jürgen Hengelbrock, 251–74. Amsterdam: Rodopi, 2006.

–. *Reshaping the University: Responsibility, Indigenous Epistemes, and the Logic of the Gift*. Vancouver: UBC Press, 2007.

Ladner, Kiera. *Indigenous Governance: Questioning the Status and the Possibilities for Reconciliation with Canada's Commitment to Aboriginal and Treaty Rights*. West Vancouver, BC: National Centre for First Nations Governance, 2006. http://fngovernance.org/ncfng_research/kiera_ladner.pdf.

Lee, Erica Violet. "Reconciling in the Apocalypse." *Canadian Centre for Policy Alternatives*, March 1, 2016, www.policyalternatives.ca/publications/monitor/reconciling-apocalypse.

Lefebvre, Benjamin. "In Search of Someday: Trauma and Repetition in Joy Kogawa's Fiction." *Journal of Canadian Studies* 44, 3 (Fall 2010): 154–203.

Lewis, Jason. "A Brief (Media) History of the Future Imaginary." *Public* 27, 54 (2016): 36–49.

Lightfoot, Sheryl. *Global Indigenous Politics: A Subtle Revolution*. London: Routledge, 2016.

Loring, Kevin. *Where the Blood Mixes*. Vancouver: Talonbooks, 2009.

Matsunaga, Jennifer. "Two Faces of Transitional Justice: Theorizing the Incommensurability of Transitional Justice and Decolonization in Canada." *Decolonization: Indigeneity, Education and Society* 5, 1 (2016): 24–44.

McCall, Sophie. *First Person Plural: Aboriginal Storytelling and the Ethics of Collaborative Authorship*. Vancouver: UBC Press, 2011.

Miki, Roy. *Redress: Inside the Japanese Canadian Call for Justice*. Richmond: Raincoast Books, 2004.

Miyagawa, Mitch. "A Sorry State." *Walrus*, December 12, 2009, https://thewalrus.ca/a-sorry-state/.

Napoleon, Val, and Hadley Friedland. "An Inside Job: Engaging with Indigenous Legal Traditions through Stories." *McGill Law Journal* 61, 4 (2016): 725–54.

Nixon, Lindsay. "sâkihito-maskihkiy acâhkosiwikamikohk." *GUTS*, May 20, 2016, http://gutsmagazine.ca/visual-cultures/.

Nock, Samantha. "Being a Witness: The Importance of Protecting Indigenous Women's Stories." *Rabble.ca* (blog), September 5, 2014. http://rabble.ca/blogs/bloggers/samantha-nock/2014/09/being-witness-importance-protecting-indigenous-womens-stories.

Raheja, Michelle. *Reservation Reelism: Redfacing, Visual Sovereignty, and Representations of Native Americans in Film*. Lincoln: University of Nebraska Press, 2010.

Regan, Paulette. "*Unsettling the Settler Within: Indian Residential Schools, Truth Telling, and Reconciliation in Canada*. Vancouver: UBC Press, 2010.

Robinson, Dylan, and Keavy Martin, eds. *Arts of Engagement: Taking Aesthetic Action in and beyond the Truth and Reconciliation Commission of Canada*. Waterloo, ON: Wilfrid Laurier University Press, 2016.

Robinson, Eden. *Traplines*. New York: Metropolitan Books, 1996.

Rogers, Shelagh. "Shelagh Rogers Her Journey from Her Head to Her Heart as Hon. Witness." *Indigenous Corporate Training Inc.* (blog). September 17, 2013. https://www.ictinc.ca/blog/shelagh-rogers-journey-head-heart-honorary-witness-trc.

Short, Damien. *Reconciliation and Colonial Power: Indigenous Rights in Australia*. Aldershot, UK: Ashgate Publishing Limited, 2008.

Simpson, Audra. *Mohawk Interruptus: Political Life across the Borders of Settler States*. Durham, NC: Duke University Press, 2014.

Simpson, Leanne Betasamosake. *Dancing on Our Turtle's Back*. Winnipeg: ARP Publishing, 2011.

–. "Gdi-nweninaa: Our Sound, Our Voice." In *Learn, Teach, Challenge: Approaching Indigenous Literatures*, edited by Deanna Reder and Linda M. Morra, 289–300. Waterloo, ON: Wilfrid Laurier University Press, 2016.

–. *This Accident of Being Lost*. Toronto: House of Anansi Press, 2017.

–. "'Bubbling Like a Beating Heart': Reflections on Nishnaabeg Poetic and Narrative Consciousness." In *Indigenous Poetics in Canada,* edited by Neal McLeod. 107–20. Waterloo: Wilfred Laurier University Press, 2014.

Sinclair, Niigaanwewidam James. "The Power of Dirty Waters: Indigenous Poetics." In *Indigenous Poetics in Canada,* edited by Neal McLeod, 203–16. Waterloo, ON: Wilfrid Laurier University Press, 2014.

Smith, Linda Tuhiwai. *Decolonizing Methodologies: Research and Indigenous Peoples.* London/New York: Zed Books, 1999.

Stark, Heidi Kiiwetinepinesiik. "Respect, Responsibility, and Renewal: The Foundations of Anishinaabe Treaty Making with the United States and Canada." *American Indian Culture and Research Journal* 34, 2 (2010): 145–64.

Sunhara, Ann Gomer. *The Politics of Racism: The Uprooting of Japanese Canadians during the Second World War.* Toronto: Lorimer, 1981.

Taylor, Drew Hayden. "Cry Me a River, White Boy." In *Response, Responsibility and Renewal: Canada's Truth and Reconciliation Journey,* edited by Gregory Younging, Jonathan Dewar, and Mike DeGagné, 99–108. Ottawa: Aboriginal Healing Foundation, 2009.

Tomiak, Julie-Ann. "Indigenous Self-Determination, Neoliberalization, and the Right to the City: Rescaling Aboriginal Governance in Ottawa and Winnipeg." PhD dissertation, Carleton University, 2011. www.collectionscanada.gc.ca/obj/thesescanada/vol2/002/NR83226.PDF.

Truth and Reconciliation Commission of Canada. *The Final Report of the Truth and Reconciliation Commission of Canada.* Vol. 1, *Summary.* Toronto: James Lorimer, 2015.

–. *Honouring the Truth, Reconciling for the Future: Summary of the Final Report of the Truth and Reconciliation Commission of Canada.* Winnipeg: Truth and Reconciliation Commission of Canada, 2015. http://nctr.ca/assets/reports/Final%20 Reports/Executive_Summary_English_Web.pdf.

–. *Truth and Reconciliation Commission of Canada: Calls to Action.* Winnipeg: Truth and Reconciliation Commission of Canada, 2015. http://nctr.ca/assets/reports/Calls_to_Action_English2.pdf.

Tuck, Eve. "Suspending Damage: A Letter to Communities." *Harvard Education Review* 79, 3 (2009): 409–27.

Tuck, Eve, and K. Wayne Yang. "Decolonization Is Not a Metaphor." *Decolonization: Indigeneity, Education and Society* 1, 1 (2012): 1–40.

Vizenor, Gerald. "Aesthetics of Survivance." In *Survivance: Narratives of Native Presence,* edited by Gerald Vizenor. Lincoln: University of Nebraska Press, 2008.

Vowel, Chelsea. "Fool Me Once: Colonialism Denial Finds a Happy Home in Canadian Media." *âpihtawikosisân* (blog), September 23, 2013. https://apihtawikosisan.com/2013/09/fool-me-once-colonialism-denial-finds-a-happy-home-in-canadian-media/.

–. *Indigenous Writes: A Guide to First Nations, Métis and Inuit Issues in Canada.* Winnipeg: Highwater Press, 2016.

Wagamese, Richard. *Medicine Walk.* Toronto: McClelland and Stewart, 2014.

–. *One Story, One Song.* Toronto: Douglas and McIntyre, 2011.

–. "Returning to Harmony." In *Response, Responsibility and Renewal: Canada's Truth and Reconciliation Journey,* edited by Gregory Younging, Jonathan Dewar, and Mike DeGagné, 139–48. Ottawa: Aboriginal Healing Foundation, 2009.

Whitehead, Joshua. *Full-Metal Indigiqueer*. Vancouver: Talonbooks, 2017.

Wilson, Jordan. "Gathered Together: Listening to Musqueam Lived Experiences." *Biography* 39, 3 (2016): 469–94.

"Witness Ceremony Conducted by Elder Larry Grant." *NationTalk,* July 28, 2009, http://nationtalk.ca/story/witness-ceremony-conducted-by-elder-larry-grant.

Wong, Rita. "Decolonizasian: Reading Asian and First Nations Relations in Literature." *Canadian Literature* 199 (Winter 2008): 180–232.

Index

Although they have different names, for ease of reference all commissions are listed here as Truth and Reconciliation Commissions. The full and correct name of each commission is also included in the original language with reference to the populated entry.